GHOST TOWNS

Colorado Style

VOLUME THREE
SOUTHERN REGION

KENNETH JESSEN

J. V. Publications L.L.C.

2212 Flora Ct.
Loveland, Colorado 80537

Ghost Towns, Colorado Style
Volume Three - Southern Region
Copyright © 2001 by Kenneth Jessen

Published by J. V. Publications, 2212 Flora Ct., Loveland, CO 80537

First Edition

1 2 3 4 5 6 7 8 9

Library of Congress Catalog Card Number: 98-66536
ISBN 0-9611662-4-x (pbk.)

Printed in the United States of America

Book designed and produced by LaVonne Ewing. Illustrations by Julia McMillan, Benjamin Jessen and Kenneth Jessen. Maps drawn by Kenneth Jessen. Contemporary photography by Kenneth Jessen and Sonje Jessen. Photographic processing and printing by Gerards; digital imaging by Superior One Hour Photo.

To my wonderful family,
Sonje, Todd, April, Andrew, Chris, Ben and Dusty

Window at San Acacio. *(drawing by Julia McMillan)*

Acknowledgements

Thanks goes to LaVonne Ewing for her cover and book design. Many thanks to the patient staff at the Denver Public Library. In addition, thanks go to my editors Sandy Perlic, Mary Edelmaier, Carolyn Acheson and Susan Hoskinson. For fine illustrations, I also would like to thank Julia McMillan and Benjamin Jessen. Larry Hartsell provided valuable information on Copperfield, and Alexa Watson, Bureau of Land Management, located a number of towns including Titusville, Current Creek, Bare Hills City, Clinton, Blackburn, Murnane and Meserole. Additional information on the coal mining towns near Trinidad was provided by Al Vigil.

About The Author

This is Kenneth Jessen's twelfth book; other works include *Railroads of Northern Colorado, Thompson Valley Tales, Eccentric Colorado, Colorado Gunsmoke, Bizarre Colorado, Estes Park - A Quick History, Georgetown - A Quick History, An Ear in His Pocket* and *Ghost Towns, Colorado Style Volumes One and Two.* Ken is the author of more than 600 published articles plus several booklets. His column on Colorado ghost towns is featured in the *Loveland Reporter-Herald.* Jessen has made several on-screen appearances on "Colorado GetAways" (KCNC Channel 4). The author is a life member of the Colorado Railroad Museum, a longtime member of the Rocky Mountain Railroad Club, a member of the Colorado Historical Society and one of the founders of the Western Outlaw-Lawman History Association. He also belongs to the San Luis Valley Historical Society and the Summit Historical Society. He owns and operates J. V. Publications L.L.C.

Jessen spent 33 years as an engineer with Hewlett-Packard. Now retired, he continues to work part-time as a system design engineer and technical writer.

Sonje Jessen was a major contributor to this book and acted as editorial consultant. She also was instrumental in locating and photographing many of the ghost towns on various field trips.

The Jessens live in Loveland, Colorado.

THE AREAS OF

GHOST TOWNS
Colorado Style

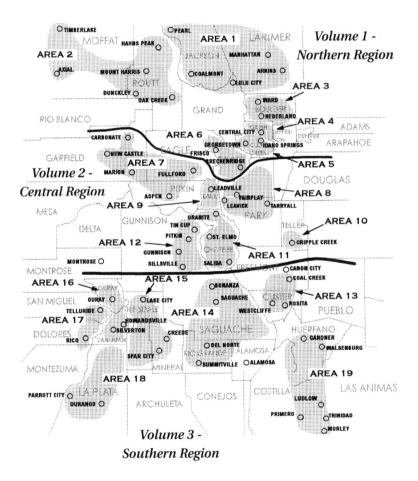

Volume 1 -
Northern Region

Volume 2 -
Central Region

Volume 3 -
Southern Region

THE THREE VOLUMES OF

GHOST TOWNS
Colorado Style

Volume One - Northern Region
ISBN: 0-9611662-8-2

Includes the following counties:
Boulder, Clear Creek, Gilpin, Grand, Jackson, Larimer,
Moffat, Routt and Summit

Volume Two - Central Region
ISBN: 0-9611662-9-0

Includes the following counties:
Chaffee, Eagle, Garfield, Gunnison, Lake, Park, Pitkin and Teller

Volume Three - Southern Region
ISBN: 0-9611662-4-x

Includes the following counties:
Conejos, Costilla, Custer, Dolores, Fremont, Hinsdale,
Huerfano, Las Animas, La Plata, Mineral, Montezuma,
Ouray, Rio Grande, Saguache, San Juan and San Miguel

VOLUME THREE - SOUTHERN REGION

Table of Contents

Bibliography *(see references at the end of each town story)*

Organization Of This Book

This three-volume series is broken into areas, an area being similar to a chapter. In most cases, an area is a group of adjacent counties having similar historical development. Within an area, there may be a few ghost town sites or many. Most sites can be visited in one or two days. Depending on available space, historic and contemporary photographs provide a perspective of how a given town once appeared and how it looks today.

An overall map plus a table of contents is presented at the beginning of each area. Each area has an introduction with short stories about people and events that shaped the area's history. After the introduction, the story of each town is presented in alphabetical order. Where little information exists on a group of towns, they may be combined into one story.

Each town history begins with a summary of its general location, accessibility and any historic structures still standing. Within the text are facts on how the town was named, when it was founded, and if it had its own post office. The text also may include the peak population, an estimate of the number of structures, and a general description of the businesses and schools. For a town that has vanished, a chronology of its disappearance may be included, based on the observations of other historians. For towns that are difficult to locate, maps are included to guide the adventurous. Many town sites are on private property, and this is noted in the text.

For some readers, it is important to know the sources for the information on that particular town. Endnotes present this material for each story.

Research For This Project

Every possible reliable source of information that added to knowledge about a particular town was consulted. Some sources, where the research was not performed well, were intentionally ignored: other sources were used to distill the history of a particular site. In some cases, newspaper articles and court records were consulted. Postal records form the backbone for much of the material. To provide some insight as to what remains, nearly all of the many town sites included in this work were visited. These field trips provided additional detail to the U.S. Geological Survey topographic maps. In some cases, Trails West maps, U.S. Forest Service maps and the *Colorado Atlas & Gazetteer* were consulted to verify road locations and numbers.

INTRODUCTION

This series is presented in three volumes and concentrates on towns and mining camps in the Colorado mountains. The first volume covers the northern region, the second volume covers the central region and this volume covers the southern region of the state. Although emphasis is placed on towns that are completely or partially abandoned, other towns important to understanding the region's history also are included.

What's A Ghost Town?

Just the mention of a ghost town piques the interest of many people. It is one of the most romantic historical topics Colorado offers. This series of books attempts to answer the question of why once thriving communities, some with substantial business districts, were abandoned and fell to ruin? Many have disappeared leaving hardly a trace. Based on mining activity, some towns went through cycles of being abandoned, occupied, then abandoned. There are more than 600 ghost town sites in the Colorado mountains alone, not to mention hundreds of sites on the plains. Most of the towns in the Colorado mountains were associated with the mining industry, but there are also abandoned agricultural settlements that did not survive because of lack of water, transportation or competition from nearby towns.

The term "ghost town" is applied liberally in this work to describe any town, mining camp or even a collection of shanties that at some point in time were completely or partially abandoned. All sites covered had names, but this does not imply that other clusters of shacks, homes or cabins were not as important. The use of the word "town" is misleading since many places did not have the characteristics of a town, such a post office, stores, hotels, schools, churches or a government. Again applying a liberal definition, a ghost town also could be a town that is a ghost of its former self. Some ghost towns could better be referred to as camps since they were never anything more than a collection of cabins and tents scattered near a mine. Despite arguments over definitions, there are unique and interesting stories behind each location.

Many towns and camps were never officially surveyed or registered, much less incorporated. "New" ghost towns have been found during recent years in some of the more remote areas of the state. Real estate developers have been around for a long time, and there are sites that were surveyed, promoted, given names and even presented on maps although not a single structure was ever built. In many cases, a group of cabins high on a mountainside will remain anonymous. Some smaller, less significant camp will appear in this and other ghost town books only because of it had a name.

Changes in the mountain economy, especially after World War II, drastically altered the fate of many abandoned towns. Breckenridge, Frisco and Keystone in Summit County are filled with new buildings and are fully occupied. They hardly seem like former ghost towns, but at one time they were nearly abandoned and are included in this work. The old cabins at Gold Hill, White Pine and Platoro have been purchased, restored and now meet the demand for mountain property. In 1999, a developer purchased Turret near Salida and subdivided this fine example of a ghost town. New mountain homes will spring up amid Turret's abandoned buildings. This work deals with traditional ghost towns as well as those rejuvenated by changes in the economy.

Most mining towns and camps were directly associated with the recovery of gold and silver. Other towns were based on mining coal, uranium, copper, iron, molybdenum, gypsum and other minerals. Some towns acted as supply points to the mining towns, and transportation was the primary industry. A number of mill towns processed ore. There are also many abandoned towns once supported by agriculture.

Within these three volumes, more than 600 towns are covered, but this only scratches the surface of what is yet to be explored. Many sites are not located on detailed maps, and for others, the location is unknown. Complicating the issue are towns that went through several name changes.

The mental picture of a ghost town is a group of ramshackled, abandoned cabins set in a deep, forested valley high in the mountains where the only noise is the wind. There are certainly picturesque places like this, but few traces remain of most ghost towns. Some were destroyed by fire and never rebuilt, others were located in an avalanche track and eventually leveled, while still others fell victim to vandals. Coal mining companies, like Colorado Fuel & Iron, razed the buildings in their mining towns. Most buildings were made of wood, which is biodegradable. After a century or more of high winds and heavy snows, the majority of structures have disappeared. Large trees grew in the middle of many an old cabin, and the forest swallowed others from view. In several cases, buildings from one town were moved to form a new town. Even heavy two-story log buildings were skidded to other sites.

At the rate Colorado's ghost town structures are vanishing, little physical evidence will be left for the next generation. Relative to the thousands of structures that once existed, very little is done today toward preserving what few remain. The emphasis of modern society is on progress, not preservation.

On the positive side, where once destructive mining practices stripped the land void of vegetation, the natural healing process is restoring the land. Mine tailing piles are being contoured to conform to the terrain. In some cases, toxic water draining from abandoned tunnels has been channeled to treatment plants. Trees, clear-cut more than a century ago, have now grown back. After the passage of another century, much of Colorado will again look like it did prior to the arrival of industrial civilization.

A simplification of early Colorado demographic history goes something like this: gold or silver was discovered, thousands of prospectors poured into the area, towns were established and gained instant population. When the ore was exhausted, the population moved on and abandoned the town as quickly as it was built. These same people went on to found another town near the latest discovery. If a new strike was made near a once-abandoned town, it would be repopulated and possibly expanded. Sometimes the abandonment of a town was related to the ability to process the ore. If a new smelting process was introduced, the once-abandoned site would again flourish. Colorado society during the 1860s through the 1880s was very mobile, and the majority of people were willing to pick up and move on, leaving their homes behind.

Surprising reversals of fortune included the town of Nevadaville, at one time larger than Denver. Today, Nevadaville is almost a ghost town, and only a small fraction of its original buildings remain. It is a challenge to find any remains of Parkville, located in Summit County. At one time, Parkville was the county seat and the largest town in the region. Another county seat was Parrott City, and little remains of this settlement. Despite its importance, the site no longer appears on maps. Little is left of the Garfield County seat of Carbonate, located on a high plateau north of Glenwood Springs. Oro City, forerunner to Leadville, supported a population of 10,000, yet hardly a stick of wood remains at the site. Dayton was the Lake County seat until the ore was exhausted, and it was abandoned. Dayton was discovered by tourists wanting a peaceful place to relax and was reborn as Twin Lakes. Other towns, such as Ruedi, Montgomery, old Dillon, Sopris, Dora City, are below reservoirs. Victims of avalanches, Masontown, Tomichi and Woodstock, were never rebuilt.

Unusual names are pervasive among Colorado's ghost towns, such as Sky City and Spook City, west of the San Luis Valley, or Royal Flush, northeast of Hahns Peak. West of Boulder was a camp named Puzzler, and not far away in Gilpin County, Wideawake was named by alert miners. Mosquito got its name when the flattened remains of that insect were found on the blank line where the founders were to fill in its name. Orient was located in the northeast corner of the San Luis Valley, and Bachelor City once sat in a meadow above Creede. The remains of Pieplant are located northeast of Taylor Reservoir. Stringtown, a partially abandoned town located south of Leadville, still shows up on some contemporary maps.

It is my sincere hope that you will find these books entertaining and informative.

Kenneth Jessen
2212 Flora Court
Loveland, CO 80537

AREA THIRTEEN 13

Fremont and Custer Counties

continued

AREA 13: Custer and Fremont Counties

Selected Towns

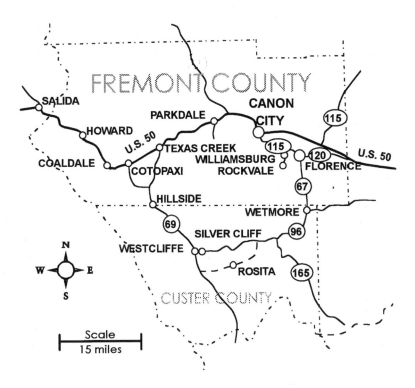

Introduction to Custer and Fremont Counties

All of Area 13 was once Fremont County. In 1877, Custer County was carved out of a portion of Fremont County in response to the mining activity in the Wet Mountain Valley. From then on, the two counties developed differently. At first, Fremont County was dominated by part of the north-south trade route between the Denver area and New Mexico. Agriculture played a major role. Railroads also gave Fremont County a boost when the Denver & Rio Grande built its primary transcontinental route from Cañon City through the Royal Gorge. To a lesser degree, the Atchison, Topeka & Santa Fe also played a role in the development of the area's transportation.

Coal was discovered early in Fremont County's history, but it took time to develop. During the latter part of the 1800s, coal mining grew to become a major industry with a number of towns established south of Cañon City. Other industries, such as cement and oil, also played a role in the county's development. Today, tourism, agriculture and the state penitentiary dominate the region's economy.

Custer County was, at first, ranch country. After the discovery of precious metals, its economy shifted to mining. Silver Cliff quickly grew to become the state's third largest town. After the ore deposits were exhausted, many of the mining towns were abandoned and, ranching sustained its economy. Today, tourism and mountain property development play a key role in the county's economy.

The Cotopaxi Cattle War

One of the more unusual events in this area's history was a "war" of sorts. There was little violence in either Fremont or Custer counties during their development. When violence did erupt, it was not over gold or silver, but cattle. This particular story centers on several leading characters. College-educated L. Edwin Watkins was once a schoolteacher and turned to ranching in 1877. A good-looking man, his business was to supply beef to the mining camps, tie cutters and railroad workers. So much blood covered his slaughter ground that the gulch was named Bloody Gulch, and the mountain near the gulch became Bloody Mountain. Watkins surrounded himself with hired hands and joined in with another rancher named Ernest Christenson to promote the beef industry.

Opposing Watkins was another rancher, Ira Mulock. He had three sons living with him on his homestead and a brother nearby on another homestead. Mulock was certain Watkins was a cattle rustler. Mulock also was sure that some cattle with his "IM" brand had been stolen and the brand changed by Watkins.

The third character in this story was Henry Thomas, more commonly known as "Gold Tom." He had a placer claim and got his nickname because he carried gold dust and gold nuggets with him. Gold Tom named his claim Cotopaxi for the Andean volcano. The settlement that grew along the Arkansas River near his claim became known by the same name.

Possibly to deflect any rumors that he was a rustler, Watkins openly suspected a man named Richard McCoy. To prove this, Watkins hired Gold Tom to gather evidence. The stocky, six-foot McCoy had four sons and two daughters living on his homestead in Sand Gulch between Cotopaxi and Texas Creek.

The cattle rustling continued, and a man named Fisher drifted into the area presenting himself as a horse trader. He made friends with one of the local cowboys, and the two men went to the Watkins ranch, presumably to look for a lost cow. A stockade with gun ports first caught their attention. Watkins was friendly at first. When the cow couldn't be located, Watkins offered one of his own cows as a replacement. Upon examining the cow, the two men pointed out that its brand looked like it had been altered. Watkins suddenly became furious and threatened the men.

Soon after this encounter with Watkins, Fisher's body was found in the mountains. He had been shot to death, and his real identity as a cattle detective became known. As for the cowboy, he was never seen again.

In April 1883, Fisher's death prompted the local cattlemen's association to send two seventeen-year-olds out to spy on the operations at the Watkins ranch by posing as out-of-work cowboys. They reported back that there was cattle rustling taking place and that the cattle had their brands altered, just as Mulock had suspected. They also discovered sixty stolen horses hidden in a secret pasture. On July 14, 1883, an article appeared in the local newspaper announcing that forty head of cattle belonging to Mulock had been stolen and their brands changed. Now that some information had been made public, it was time for action.

The Watkins ranch was visited by members of the cattlemen's association. They were greeted by Watkins holding a rifle. He refused to let them by to examine any of the cattle, and their only choice was to retreat. The cattlemen soon returned as a group of twenty heavily armed men. The group included the three Mulock boys. Watkins and his hired hands were outnumbered and could only watch as the cattlemen cut out forty head they believed belonged to Mulock. Watkins immediately rode to Salida and filed charges against the cattlemen's association for theft.

Later, the sheriff arrested the party of twenty cattlemen, but Watkins also was arrested for rustling and held on a $4,000 bond. The general feeling was to arrest both sides and let the courts sort out the matter. While in custody and trying to raise bond money, Watkins was taken by force and lynched by a group of vigilantes. The deputy guarding him was powerless to do anything. No one was ever convicted of this crime. In 1888, one of Watkins' accomplices turned state's evidence admitting that upwards to 3,000 cattle had been stolen by Watkins and his associates.

Rosemae Wells Campbell, in her book, *From Trappers to Tourists,* points out that there are conflicting stories as to how Gold Tom met his end. The story with the most credibility begins with George Meyers and one of the McCoys. The two men were intent upon harassing Gold Tom. They doused him with a bucket of water, and in another incident, they sicked a dog on him. They bragged about "getting" Gold Tom, and they carried revolvers to prove their point.

Fed up, Gold Tom came to Cotopaxi June 6, 1884, heavily armed with enough firepower and ammunition to wage a small war. After he tied up his horse, he spotted Meyers sitting outside a building. Gold Tom drew one of his Colt revolvers and fired. The bullet missed and ricocheted. This gave Meyers just enough time to dive through the nearest door. Meyers, however, found himself boxed in with no escape route. Cornered, he turned and fired back at Gold Tom, killing him on the spot.

The court determined that Meyers had acted in self-defense, and he was released. Fortune hunters later dug up the land around Gold Tom's cabin looking for nuggets.

Pioneer Joseph Lamb

At the tender age of twenty-three, Joseph Milton Lamb traveled by oxcart caravan to Denver and joined other "'59ers" at Cherry Creek and the South Platte River. (Lamb family members believe Joseph Lamb arrived in Denver in 1857, well ahead of the gold rush.) He and a small group of men were among the first gold seekers to arrive at California Gulch, south of the future city of Leadville. Lamb learned how to pan for gold and located claims that yielded good returns. After about 2 years, the gold was exhausted on his claims and he moved on. For a while, Lamb ran

Custer County pioneer Joseph Milton Lamb settled along Texas Creek in 1871. He constructed the first permanent cabin in the area. *(Courtesy of John Lamb)*

pack trains from Cañon City to Leadville through land controlled by the Ute Indians.

In 1862, he joined Nat Rich. The two were hired to drive fifty head of Texas steers from Cañon City to Leadville to satisfy the demand for fresh beef. Their route took them to a creek where the steers were bedded down. During the night, the howl of a mountain lion stampeded the herd, and it took 2 days to round up the steers. For this reason, the men named the stream Texas Creek. Lamb liked the country, and he returned in 1871 to homestead.

In 1863, Lamb made quite a name for himself when he

joined a posse to hunt down Colorado's worst serial killers, the Espinosas. They had murdered at least thirty-three people and had killed all who could identify them until an incident near Fairplay. One man was lucky enough to escape with his life. Based on the description given by this man, a posse was formed in Fairplay. The posse knew they were gaining on the killers by examining each successive camp. Finally, they found a fire that was still smoldering. They knew that if they traveled all night, they would overtake the Espinosas.

The following morning, the posse saw two horses in an open meadow in what was later named Espinosa Gulch north of Garden Park. As they waited, one of the Espinosas came out in the open to take the hobble off one of the horses. Lamb recognized the man and shot him through the chest. He reloaded and waited. The second Espinosa appeared. Lamb lifted his rifle and took careful aim. As he was ready to pull the trigger, one of the posse members stopped him, thinking that the man in the distance was a fellow posse member. Espinosa saw Lamb and fled to the San Luis Valley where later he was gunned down by Tom Tobin.

The posse members examined the man Lamb shot. The bullet cut the fourth rib on each side of his chest. As they were

While removing ties from the Grape Creek line, Joseph Lamb purchased the Denver & Rio Grande section house located at Blackburn and moved it to his homestead. *(Courtesy of John Lamb)*

ready to leave, a shot was fired from the top of a cliff. The bullet went through the rim of Lamb's hat, just missing his skull and cutting through his undershirt. The posse couldn't sleep that night and abandoned the chase.

In 1864, Lamb became a member of the Colorado Volunteers to fight the Indians who were making raids on farms south of Denver. This placed Lamb under the command of Colonel John Chivington. On November 29, 1864, Lamb witnessed the worst day in Colorado history, the Sand Creek Massacre. Innocent, unarmed Indians from several tribes, who had been promised protection by the U.S. Government, were slaughtered and mutilated at the hands of the Colorado Volunteers. Lamb did not approve of these actions, and later he said that the soldiers were out of control.

Lamb continued his freighting operation from Cañon City to Leadville until his marriage in 1871. At the time, the area belonged to the Ute Indians. Ute Chief Colorow told Lamb he could not construct a permanent structure. Lamb was forced to live in a teepee with his new bride, but he pleaded with Colorow to allow him to construct a cabin. He reminded Colorow that he had warned the chief of an Arapaho raiding party coming up the Arkansas River valley. Colorow finally gave Lamb permission to build a cabin on Texas Creek, the first in this part of Colorado. It wasn't long before the Ute Indians agreed by treaty to move to the western part of the state.

At his new Texas Creek homestead, he found himself on one of the major supply routes into the upper Arkansas River region. He sold all the produce he could raise to the passing traffic.

As the network of railroads penetrated into the mountains, wagon and stagecoach traffic dwindled along the road. By 1885, Lamb was so poor he was forced to sell his farm and move to Hillside. He filed on 160 acres and constructed a new home. By this time, he and his wife were raising eight children. After building a four-room house, disaster struck, and the house burned to the ground. Lamb and his wife had to start all over again and build another home. The family of ten lived in a 16-foot by 36-foot

As shown in this 1908 photograph, the Blackburn section house was moved to the Lamb homestead in Sand Gulch. *(Courtesy of John Lamb)*

log cabin for 7 years. After failing to make payments, the mortgage company foreclosed. One of his daughters filed on a homestead adjoining the farm so that he at least had a place to camp. During this time, Lamb got a contract to haul ties from the abandoned Denver & Rio Grande line in Grape Creek to the Bull-Domingo Mine north of Silver Cliff. He purchased the section house located at Blackburn and moved it to the new homestead.

Despite all of the hardships, Joseph Lamb prevailed. He died at the age of eight-three at his son's Sand Gulch homestead. Many of his descendants still live in Colorado.

Frank R. Lamb, *The Pioneer Story of Joseph Milton Lamb*, Master Printers, Cañon City, Colorado, (no date), pp. 2-7.

Interview with John Lamb, Littleton, Colorado, June 5, 2000, with his editorial comments included in this manuscript.

Rosemae Wells Campbell, *From Trappers to Tourists: Fremont County 1830-1950*, Century One Press, Colorado Springs, Colorado, 1972, pp. 187-189, 191-197.

BARE HILLS CITY

- *Fremont County, City Creek drainage*
- *No access to site; private property*
- *Town had a post office; remaining structures unknown*

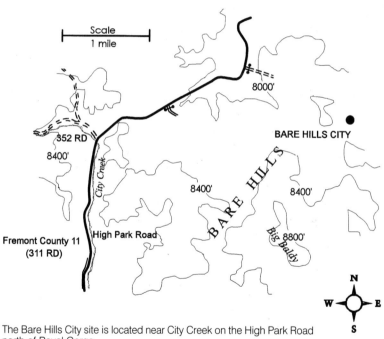

The Bare Hills City site is located near City Creek on the High Park Road north of Royal Gorge.

A t a point 3 miles west of Marigold City, an incredible 1,200 lots were laid out to establish Bare Hills City. A school district was set up in August 1896 for the few families living near Bare Hills City. The district was annulled in 1901 without having constructed a schoolhouse.

A post office opened in Bare Hills City in 1896 under the name "Barehills." It remained open until 1901. There were fourteen mining companies listed as operating in the area, but the economy was based on ranching.

Bare Hills City was located south of a tributary of High Creek on the northeast side of 9,002-foot Big Baldy. The closest road to the site is Fremont County 11 (311 RD). The site sits on private property, and it is not known if any trace of this town remains. There are two roads that head over to the town site, however, both are private and posted no trespassing.

KENNETH JESSEN

Post Office Department Reports of Site Locations 1837-1950, National Archives and Records Administration, Washington, D.C., 1986.

Rosemae Wells Campbell, *From Trappers to Tourists: Fremont County 1830-1950,* Century One Press, Colorado Springs, Colorado, 1972, pp. 177-178.

William H. Bauer, James L. Ozment and John H. Willard, *Colorado Post Offices,* Colorado Railroad Museum, Golden, Colorado, 1990, p. 16.

BENT'S PICKET POST, EL CUERVO, HARDSCRABBLE PLAZA and SAN BUENAVENTURA

Early Fremont County Settlements

- *Fremont County, various drainages*
- *No access to most sites; private property*
- *None of the settlements had post offices; no structures remain*

William Bent was most likely responsible for Fremont County's first settlement. It took the form of a simple picket trading post. Its exact location has been debated, however, one likely place is on the north bank of the Arkansas River near the mouth of Hardscrabble Creek. Not only was Bent's Picket Post an early settlement, Bent also is credited with operating the first commercial business in the future state of Colorado.

In 1830, French trappers from Taos, New Mexico, established a trading post on a bluff near the confluence of Mineral and Adobe creeks. The idea was to trade with the Ute Indians along their trail from the plains into the Wet Mountains. Since crows had been spotted flying overhead, it was named El Cuervo, Spanish for raven or crow. Americans knew the place as the Crow's Nest.

El Cuervo was more of a place of business than it was a town. Maurice LeDuc (also spelled LeDoux) settled across one of the creeks from El Cuervo. He cultivated the land and trapped. He also built a cabin and a jacal of vertical logs set into the ground in a circular pattern to act as a crude fortress.

In her book, *From Trappers to Tourists*, author Rosemae

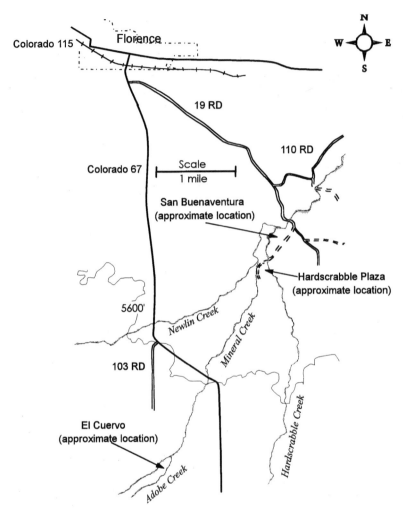

Approximate locations are shown for these early Colorado settlements based on the research of Rosemae Wells Campbell for her book, *From Trappers to Tourists: Fremont County 1830-1950.*

Wells Campbell speculates that El Cuervo could have supported a distillery operated by Matt Kincade. For a time, the United States placed a ban on transporting whiskey into the area. This produced a ready market for locally made distillates. A large cistern discovered many years after El Cuervo was abandoned, led to this conclusion.

Near the confluence of Adobe and Newlin creeks, San Buenaventura was established in 1843 by Charles Beaubien, a naturalized Mexican citizen. To encourage development in the northern portion of what was then Mexico, its governor gave land grants to prominent citizens who had the wealth to settle the area. Beaubien received such a grant and brought several Taos farmers and their families to settle the area. San Buenaventura soon was abandoned, however, because Santa Anna cut off trade into the area as a result of the growing conflict with the United States.

In 1844, George Simpson moved into the now-deserted San Buenaventura, and he, Joe Doyle and Alec Barclay constructed a trading post just south of the site. It was located about one and one-quarter miles above the confluence of Hardscrabble and Newlin creeks. For defense against Indian raids, a high adobe wall was constructed around the post. The place was called Plaza del Rio Penasco Amarillo or Hardscrabble Plaza. Simpson planted apple seeds from Missouri and invited seventy others to join him.

Mild winters favored this agricultural community. Campbell speculated it also could have been a haven for desperadoes illegally bringing whiskey into the area. Indians received whiskey and corn in exchange for robes and skins. These trade items were taken to Taos and Santa Fe to purchase more whiskey.

George Simpson and his common-law wife, Isabel, had a daughter in 1844. She was the first child not of either Hispanic or Indian blood born in Colorado. The birth prompted a celebration where curious Indians came to view the white child. Not much later, Simpson, Isabel and their child traveled to Taos. The child was baptized and the couple properly married.

Remote Hardscrabble Plaza was not without its violence. Tom Whittlesey believed that his mistress was having an affair with a man named LaFontaine. Tom dismembered his mistress before killing LaFontaine. This gave Whittlesey the dubious title of "Tomas el Matador." He managed to escape and was never seen again.

A dozen or so adobe rooms were constructed within the plaza, and hired hands constructed their own dwellings near the creek. In 1846, the trading routes changed, and Simpson left the plaza. Lancaster P. Lupton opened a store at the plaza, and the following year, Simpson returned to raise corn. Hostile raids by Ute Indians forced the abandonment of Hardscrabble Plaza.

In 1852, Spanish-speaking families tried to settle around the plaza, but they met with the same resistance from the Ute Indians. El Cuervo also was occupied for a brief period until hostile Utes killed the occupants and burned its buildings.

Some gold seekers may have used some of the rooms at Hardscrabble Plaza in 1859. George Simpson returned to determine if the place could be repopulated. Soon, it was abandoned for good, and no recognizable foundations or structures remain today. A sign located along Colorado 67 north of the Custer County line provides motorists with a brief history of the area.

Rosemae Wells Campbell, *From Trappers to Tourists: Fremont County 1830-1950*, Century One Press, Colorado Springs, Colorado, 1972, pp. 7-8, 10, 14-19, 25, 65.

BLACKBURN and CLINTON

Remote Ghost Towns

- *Custer County, Grape Creek and Dead Mule Gulch drainages*
- *Accessible on foot and by graded dirt road*
- *Both towns had post offices; no structures remain*

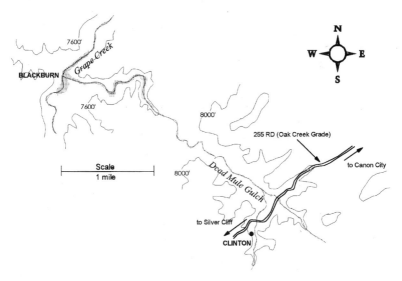

Blackburn was a station along the Denver & Rio Grande, and Clinton was a stage stop along the Oak Creek Grade between the Westcliffe-Silver Cliff area and Cañon City.

Blackburn was a station along the Denver & Rio Grande's narrow gauge branch to Westcliffe along Grape Creek. The station was located where Dead Mule Gulch enters Grape Creek. Structures included a section house. It gained its own post office in 1881, coincident with the arrival of the railroad. The post office closed in 1889 after a devastating flood washed out the railroad, and it was not economical to repair. For photographs of the Blackburn section house, see "Pioneer Joseph Lamb" in the introduction to Area 13. Nothing remains at the site, and the only access road near the site is marked private.

Clinton was a stage stop on the Oak Creek Grade between the Westcliffe-Silver Cliff area and Cañon City. Its specific location was where the Oak Creek Grade crosses Dead Mule Gulch. A wagon road led from Clinton west to Blackburn. Clinton had a general merchandise store and sawmill. Presumably, there were a few homes at the site. A post office opened in 1879 and lasted until 1881 when railroad service was established and stagecoach travel declined. Located on private property are stones marking the corner of a foundation, and several hundred feet beyond is a stone wall.

George A. Crofutt, *Crofutt's Grip-Sack Guide of Colorado*, 1885 Edition, Johnson Books, Boulder, Colorado, reprint 1981, p. 81.

Joanne West Dodds, *Custer County: Rosita, Silver Cliff and Westcliffe*, Focal Plain, (publisher's city and state not given), 1994, p. 19.

Post Office Department Reports of Site Locations 1837-1950, National Archives and Records Administration, Washington, D.C., 1986.

William H. Bauer, James L. Ozment and John H. Willard, *Colorado Post Offices,* Colorado Railroad Museum, Golden, Colorado, 1990, pp. 21, 34.

BROOKSIDE

Founded on Land Homesteaded by Sylvester Davis

- *Fremont County, Arkansas River drainage*
- *Accessible via paved road; occupied site*
- *Town had a post office; several structures remain*

Brookside is an occupied town site, and a few of the company-constructed cottages remain standing. These old stone buildings sit on the edge of the town site. *(Kenneth Jessen 109A10)*

Brookside still has a few residents, but like so many other Fremont County coal-mining towns, it is only a fraction of its original size. Located on the south side of the Arkansas River, it is a close suburb of Cañon City.

In 1873, Sylvester Davis settled near some springs. Because of these springs, the area was called Springfield. A coal seam was found near Springfield, and mining began on a small scale. The Atchison, Topeka & Santa Fe needed coal to fuel its steam locomotives and purchased the coal deposit, including most of the land around the mine. Because of a small brook that ran though the property, the railroad named it the Brookside Mine. The town that formed near the mine was called Brookside and was founded in 1888. Next to Brookside, Sylvester Davis platted the town of Springfield. When Brookside was incorporated in 1913, its boundaries included Springfield.

A half-acre of land was overlooked when the railroad did its survey. The Atchison, Topeka & Santa Fe had a strict policy of no saloons, however, privately owned saloons, gambling houses and dance halls were constructed on the half acre. It was dubbed Hell's Half Acre, and its most famous watering hole was the Fremont Saloon offering free lunches and five-cent beers. Aiding the business in Hell's Half Acre was a temperance movement in Cañon City that closed its saloons.

In 1910 during the filming of several Westerns, notable cowboy actor Tom Mix frequented the Fremont Saloon with local rancher Woody Higgins. They took turns shooting a lemon off the top of a glass at one end of the bar. The poorer shot had to buy drinks that evening. The damage done to the saloon was more than offset by increased patronage.

The Brookside Mine was operated by the Cañon City Coal Company. (Since the Atchison, Topeka & Santa Fe owned the coal deposit and adjacent land, the coal company was probably a subsidiary of the railroad.) The company built cottages and a home for the supervisor. The company also built its own company store in competition with the privately owned store run by Joe Vezzetti.

The mine superintendent's son, Jim Tingley Jr., made life miserable for the Italian miners. They could not afford to retaliate because of the position Jim's father held. One Sunday afternoon, young Jim Jr. pestered and insulted the Italian miners at a Hell's

Half Acre saloon. He spit into a glass of beer held by Joe Gedda, and Gedda had to be restrained from beating young Tingley to a pulp. A week later, Gedda was dancing with his married sister when young Tingley entered with a pair of revolvers. Tingley fired at Gedda's feet yelling "Dance, Dago, dance." To this, Gedda quickly grabbed one of the revolvers and twisted it around in Tingley's hand. With the barrel now pointing at Tingley, the gun discharged, killing the supervisor's son. Gedda escaped during the confusion and was never seen again. He later wrote his family from Australia.

After the funeral for Jim Tingley Jr., the father used his position to fire every Italian miner at Brookside. The company officials transferred the superintendent to another mine far from Brookside.

A one-room schoolhouse was built at the edge of town. Later it was replaced with a two-story structure. The new schoolhouse was of frame construction and quite tall and narrow. Because the building swayed in the wind, school had to be dismissed on gusty days. Guy wires were tied to the building in an attempt to stabilize the structure. It was replaced in 1921 by a brick schoolhouse.

During the 1913-1914 strike, the Brookside Mine was closed. It was not possible to reopen the mine at the end of the strike because it had filled with water. The mine was sold in 1933 to Charles Vezzetti and his business partners. They opened a new coal seam to avoid the water, and the mine continued to operate for years to come.

Brookside faded away to less than a dozen structures. All traces of Hell's Half Acre have disappeared. ***For a map showing the location of Brookside, see "Wolf Park."***

Antoinette V. Cresto, *King Coal: Coal Mining in Fremont County*, self-published, 1980, pp. 30-35.

Rosemae Wells Campbell, *From Trappers to Tourists: Fremont County 1830-1950*, Century One Press, Colorado Springs, Colorado, 1972, pp. 107-108.

William H. Bauer, James L. Ozment and John H. Willard, *Colorado Post Offices*, Colorado Railroad Museum, Golden, Colorado, 1990, p. 24.

CHANDLER

Once a Town of 600

- *Fremont County, Chandler Creek drainage*
- *Accessible via graded dirt roads*
- *Town had a post office; no structures remain*

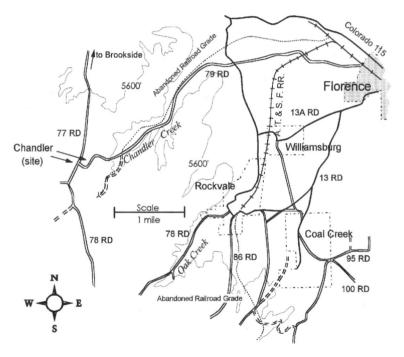

Chandler was located in an open, arid plain up Chandler Creek west of Williamsburg and south of Brookside. Foundations can be seen on either side of 77 RD.

Cement foundations spread out over an arid plain mark the Chandler site at the intersection of 77 RD and 79 RD. It was once the home of 600 people. Even some of the shrubs that once stood by its houses have been removed. On a small rise overlooking the town site was the Chandler Mine.

A. C. Chandler homesteaded west of Williamsburg along Chandler Creek during the mid-1800s. After coal was discovered near the Chandler homestead, the Western Fuel Company opened the Chandler Mine. A company town was constructed near the mine in 1890, the same year Chandler got its post office. The Western Fuel Company owned the entire eleven-block town site and constructed neat company cottages complete with landscaping and lawns. Only those working for the company were allowed to build in Chandler. Other structures included a company store, boardinghouse and one saloon. A one-room schoolhouse was built to accommodate fifty to sixty children. Fire destroyed the original schoolhouse, and it was replaced by a two-room schoolhouse with an auditorium.

Noted Denver photographer L.C. McClure took this view of Chandler sometime between 1900 and 1920. Note the long, neat rows of company cottages. *(Denver Public Library MCC-3615)*

All that remains of Chandler today are concrete foundations. *(Kenneth Jessen 125C2)*

The Chandler Mine was purchased by the Victor-American Fuel Company, owners of other mines and mining towns in Colorado. The Chandler Mine grew into a maze of 36 miles of tunnels. Loaded mine cars were pulled out of the mine by mules, and 100 of these animals lived in an underground stable, never seeing the light of day. At its peak, 350 men toiled underground.

During the 1903-1904 coal miners' strike, the Victor-American Coal Company hired 100 scabs to keep the mine open. A repeat of the same thing happened during the 1913-1914 coal miners' strike.

The coal reserves were exhausted by 1942, and the mine was closed. The post office closed the same year. The Atchison, Topeka & Santa Fe pulled the last train of loaded coal cars out of town and soon removed the tracks. Chandler's structures were sold in place either to be razed or dismantled. The site can be reached via graded dirt roads.

Antoinette V. Cresto, *King Coal: Coal Mining in Fremont County*, self-published, 1980, pp. 36-37.

Rosemae Wells Campbell, *From Trappers to Tourists: Fremont County 1830-1950*, Century One Press, Colorado Springs, Colorado, 1972, pp. 109-111.

William H. Bauer, James L. Ozment and John H. Willard, *Colorado Post Offices*, Colorado Railroad Museum, Golden, Colorado, 1990, p. 32.

COAL CREEK

Platted by Henry Teller and His Brother

- *Fremont County, Coal Creek drainage*
- *Accessible via paved road; occupied site*
- *Town has a post office; original structures remain*

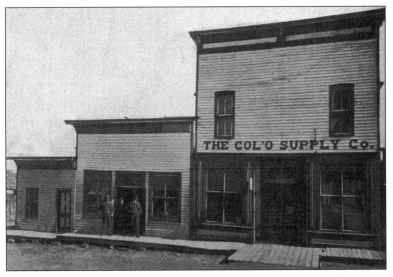

Typical of most Colorado Fuel & Iron towns, Coal Creek had a Colorado Supply Company store. This photograph was taken around 1901 or 1902. Note the other independent stores to the left. *(Kenneth Jessen collection CP116)*

Jesse Frazer was a "'59er" who arrived in Colorado with the gold-seekers. Instead of prospecting, however, he settled 10 miles south of Cañon City to homestead. He planted apple trees, and along with Benjamin Rockafellow, established an apple industry.

A year later, Frazer discovered a small coal seam on his property, and he and several others filed a claim. They dug the coal by hand and hauled it by wagon to area farmers. Some of the coal was sold in Cañon City. Although the mine closed in 1863, it represented a modest beginning for what became a major Fremont County industry.

Henry Teller, well-known Central City lawyer and politician, along with his brother, Willard, platted the town of Coal Creek near the deposit discovered by Jesse Frazer. The town grew quickly, and a post office opened in 1873. The name of the town and its post office changed to Coalcreek in 1894 and back to Coal Creek in 1964.

Railroad service, to what became the Coal Creek Mine, was provided by the Denver & Rio Grande from its line into Cañon City. The railroad used much of the coal as fuel for its locomotives. The Denver & Rio Grande maintained a small depot in Coal Creek.

Coal Creek grew to a town of 5,000, a fact hard to believe based on what remains of the town today. It supported the second-largest school district in Fremont County, only exceeded by Cañon City. In 1883, the town got its own newspaper, the weekly *Coal Creek Enterprise.* The town site was expanded to accommodate its growing population and was incorporated in 1889.

The town had several drug stores, two hotels, several grocery stores and sixteen saloons. Other businesses included a "notions" store, several millinery shops, hardware store, macaroni factory and several livery stables. After the purchase of the mine by Colorado Fuel & Iron, a Colorado Supply Company store was completed.

As the school district grew, the original one-room schoolhouse yielded to a large, two-story structure. When the town's population began to fall, the second story was removed. Still later, this building was abandoned, and the school district consolidated with the Florence district.

Coal Creek was the site of Fremont County's worst fire in June 1907. It began in the roof of Alf Salmon's bottling works, and before it could be contained, the fire consumed almost all of the town's buildings. Losses exceeded over 100 structures, and most of Coal Creek's residents were left homeless. The town was never rebuilt, although attempts were made to plat a new town. Eventually, the coal deposit was exhausted, the mine closed and the tracks of the Denver & Rio Grande removed.

Coal Creek is located about 2 miles southwest of Florence along a paved road. It is not an abandoned town and has a few occupied homes.

For a map showing Coal Creek's location, see "Chandler."

Today, Coal Creek is an occupied town. The Masonic Lodge dates to 1887.
(Kenneth Jessen 108C8)

Antoinette V. Cresto, *King Coal: Coal Mining in Fremont County*, self-published, 1980, pp. 10-13.

Rosemae Wells Campbell, *From Trappers to Tourists: Fremont County 1830-1950*, Century One Press, Colorado Springs, Colorado, 1972, pp. 98-99.

William H. Bauer, James L. Ozment and John H. Willard, *Colorado Post Offices*, Colorado Railroad Museum, Golden, Colorado, 1990, p. 35.

COALDALE, BARNES CITY and VALLIE

- *Fremont County, Arkansas River and Hayden Creek drainages*
- *Accessible via paved and graded dirt roads; Coaldale is an occupied site*
- *Towns had post offices; some structures remain*

Near the confluence of Hayden Creek and the Arkansas River a settlement started based on a charcoal industry built by the Harps brothers. Along with seven charcoal kilns, the brothers also constructed a brick store that acted as the nucle-

One of the coke or charcoal ovens at Coaldale. It sits along the Hayden Creek Road. *(Kenneth Jessen 124D6)*

us for this small settlement. Wood cutters were paid by the cord for cutting and hauling wood to the kilns. The charcoal produced was required by the smelters for the reduction of oxides to purify metallic ore. There was a ready market for this product in towns such as Salida, Leadville and Cañon City.

The town took the name of Hayden Creek and got its own post office in 1878. In 1880, the name was changed to Palmer. This name lasted 7 years when the name changed again to Hendricks for a local rancher.

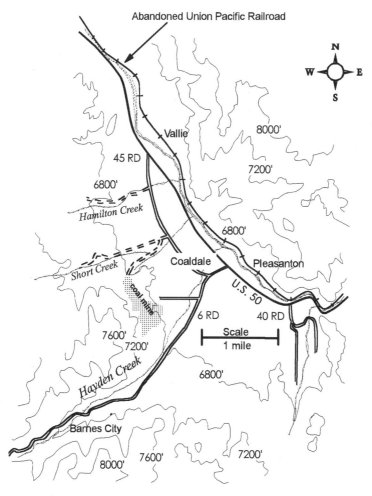

Coaldale is located just off of U.S. 50 between Cañon City and Salida. Vallie sits on the north side of the Arkansas River; Barnes City is located up Hayden Creek.

Beside the railroad, Hayden Creek was where the road over Hayden Pass from the San Luis Valley met the Arkansas River road between Cañon City and Salida.

Coal was discovered in the area, and the economy of Hayden Creek switched from ranching to mining. In 1891, the town and the post office changed their names to Coaldale, reflecting the new industry. A large gypsum mine also was opened by the Portland Cement Company near the town.

Coaldale was never abandoned and is an occupied town today. The remains of one of the charcoal kilns sits alongside the Hayden Creek road.

Barnes City was located southwest of Coaldale along Hayden Creek. Although there may have been other reasons for its existence, it became a popular resort complete with a dance hall. Fine food was served, and its owners specialized in summer picnics.

Barnes City got its start from the often-used practice of salting. A couple of promoters purchased high-grade ore from a Cripple Creek mine and spread the ore along Hayden Creek to be "discovered." When assayed, the ore was rich in gold. A syndicate was formed under the direction of the promoters. To make it look legitimate, a tunnel was dug, and then investors were informed that unfortunately nothing of any value was discovered. The resort was constructed from the money derived from this scheme.

At one time, there were as many as 300 homes in Barnes City. The town became a ghost after the resort declined in popularity. Many of the houses were moved while others became summer homes. The site is where 6 RD crosses Hayden Creek. A few rock foundations can be seen on either side of the road, but no structures remain.

Vallie was located 2 miles west of Coaldale along the Arkansas River on the north bank. A man named Wasson homesteaded here and constructed a two-story log home. Lack of water forced Wasson to abandon his homestead. When the Denver & Rio Grande reached this spot, Vallie was established for its workers and their families. A section house and depot were constructed. Nothing remains at the site today.

Rosemae Wells Campbell, *From Trappers to Tourists: Fremont County 1830-1950*, Century One Press, Colorado Springs, Colorado, 1972, pp. 207-211, 213.

William H. Bauer, James L. Ozment and John H. Willard, *Colorado Post Offices*, Colorado Railroad Museum, Golden, Colorado, 1990, pp. 35, 70, 110.

COLFAX

German Colonization

- *Custer County, South Colony Creek drainage*
- *Accessible via graded dirt road*
- *Town had a post office; no structures remain*

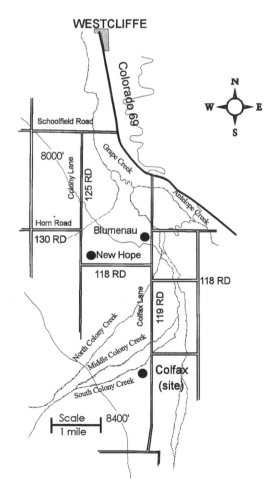

The Colfax site is south of Westcliffe on Colfax Lane immediately south of South Colony Creek.

Carl Wulsten devised a plan to allow poor German immigrants to move West and start a new life. He petitioned Congress to modify the existing Homestead Act to include colonies. Such a law was passed in 1869 to allow members of a colony to work the land for 5 years on a communal basis and obtain title to a plot of land within the colony.

Wulsten formed his colony in Chicago and sent a committee to what was then part of Fremont County. The spot selected was in the Wet Mountain Valley 15 miles south of Westcliffe and just south of South Colony Creek. The creek flowed out of the Sangre de Cristo Mountains, thus providing a reliable water supply. Wulsten petitioned Congress for 40,000 acres of undeveloped land for his colony.

In February 1870, members of what was called the Colfax Agricultural and Industrial Colonization Company of Fremont County left Chicago. The colonists organized into two companies of Colorado militia to allow them to receive arms and other help in reaching their destination. At the end of the railroad tracks at Fort Wallace, Kansas, the colonists received 100 ambulances and enough horses for the journey. Tents were supplied as well.

Various figures have been given regarding the colony's size, but the 1870 census places the number at 230. To qualify as a member, the individual had to be between 21 and 45 years old and in good health. There were a few older members with specialized skills.

The town of Colfax was established and named for Vice-President Schuyler Colfax. The colonists hoped that Colfax could aid in awarding a land grant. The colony never received such a grant. Its members were technically squatters on public land.

After the town of Colfax was laid out into lots, a drawing was held to determine who got which lot. Homes were built quickly to protect the members against the high mountain valley weather. The town hall had a bell suspended on a rope tied between two trees. A store and blacksmith shop were constructed, but the doctor's office was in a tent.

A post office opened in 1870. It remained open until 1879, long after the colony had disbanded and left Colfax. No doubt it served the area ranchers during its latter years. The post office eventually was moved to Blumenau.

In December 1870, a pre-dawn explosion destroyed the colony store and all the provisions for the remainder of the winter. By spring, the hardships proved too great and the colony disbanded. A few remained in the Wet Mountain Valley and established their own homesteads. Others moved to Cañon City, Pueblo or Denver, and some probably returned to Chicago.

The Colfax site can be reached by traveling south on 125 RD and passing over North, Middle and South Colony creeks. Nothing remains at the site from the colony.

Wetmore

Joanne West Dodds, *Custer County: Rosita, Silver Cliff and Westcliffe*, Focal Plain, 1994, pp. 26-28.
Muriel Sibell Wolle, *Stampede to Timberline*, Sage Books, Chicago, 1949, pp. 274-275.
William H. Bauer, James L. Ozment and John H. Willard, *Colorado Post Offices*, Colorado Railroad Museum, Golden, Colorado, 1990, 36.

CONCRETE
Established on a Firm Foundation

- *Fremont County, Arkansas River drainage*
- *No access; private property*
- *Town had a post office; no structures remain*

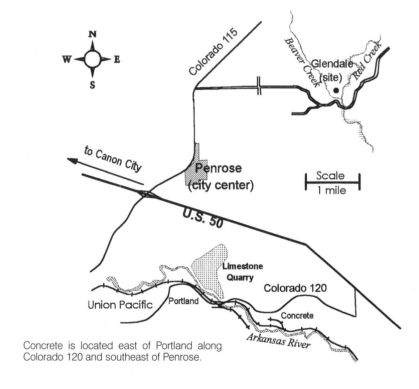

Concrete is located east of Portland along Colorado 120 and southeast of Penrose.

Vast deposits of limestone were discovered along the Arkansas River during the 1880s. In 1898, Denver contractors Geddis and Seerie began to manufacture cement equal to some of the best-imported product at the time.

46

The remains of the town of Concrete sit about a mile east of Portland near the tracks of the Denver & Rio Grande (now the Union Pacific). The location was ideal for the U.S. Portland Company to open a plant. Founded in 1905, Concrete was constructed for the workers and got its own post office three years later.

The town of Portland was established by a rival company, the Colorado Portland Cement Company. Both companies were bought out by the Ideal Cement Company. To consolidate operations, the town of Concrete was abandoned in favor of using Portland.

The Concrete site sits on private property and is fenced. Many foundations, covering a wide area between Colorado 120 and the river, can be seen.

The site where Concrete was located is littered with foundations stretching from Colorado 120 to the Arkansas River. *(Kenneth Jessen 125C3)*

Rosemae Wells Campbell, *From Trappers to Tourists: Fremont County 1830-1950*, Century One Press, Colorado Springs, Colorado, 1972, pp. 65-66.

William H. Bauer, James L. Ozment and John H. Willard, *Colorado Post Offices*, Colorado Railroad Museum, Golden, Colorado, 1990, p. 36.

CURRENT CREEK and MICANITE

- *Fremont County, Current Creek and Mack Gulch drainages*
- *Accessible via graded dirt roads*
- *One town had a post office; remaining structures unknown*

These old buildings are all that is left of Current Creek. *(Sonje Jessen SJ133)*

Current Creek was along the first wagon road constructed west from Cañon City. The road followed an old Indian trail. The community of Current Creek was founded in 1868, and its economy was based on ranching. A school district was organized in 1871 for educating children from the fifty or so families living in the area. During the 1880s, O. P. Allen operated a general store at Current Creek.

48

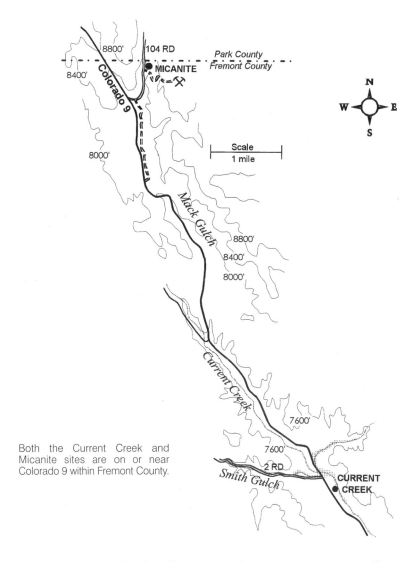

Both the Current Creek and Micanite sites are on or near Colorado 9 within Fremont County.

The town gained sufficient population to merit a post office in 1870. As an indication of just how sparsely populated the area was, in the application for the post office, the line for the number of inhabitants was left blank. The line that followed asked for the number of families within 2 miles. The answer was "two at present." The next question on the application asked for the number of families one-half the distance to the nearest post office and to that, this line was filled in with "six one way, three the other." The post office operated until 1894 when its name was simplified to Current. It closed in 1901. George Crofutt listed Current Creek's population at fifty in his 1885 grip-sack guide.

The Fremont County Cattle Growers Protective Association was formed in Current Creek in 1897 to rid the area of cattle rustlers. The town, however, didn't last long. Nearby Guffey, located in Park County, began to take over as the region's business center.

The town of Current Creek was located just south of where Smith Gulch joins Current Creek. Several old cabins sit on the site today on the east side of Colorado 9, but they are located on private property.

Located north of Current Creek on the Fremont County line was the small mining camp of Micanite. It got its own post office in 1904, and it remained open until 1925. The site is on the east side of 104 RD a short distance from its intersection with Colorado 9 and is marked by a crude loading ramp. Above the ramp is the foundation of a building. A four-wheel drive road leads up to the mica mine. Unfortunately, little is known about this camp.

George A. Crofutt, *Crofutt's Grip-Sack Guide of Colorado*, 1885 Edition, Johnson Books, Boulder, Colorado, reprint 1981, p. 85.

Post Office Department Reports of Site Locations 1837-1950, National Archives and Records Administration, Washington, D. C., 1986.

Rosemae Wells Campbell, *From Trappers to Tourists: Fremont County 1830-1950*, Century One Press, Colorado Springs, Colorado, 1972, p. 117.

William H. Bauer, James L. Ozment and John H. Willard, *Colorado Post Offices*, Colorado Railroad Museum, Golden, Colorado, 1990, pp. 41, 98.

CUSTER CITY

Named for Famous General

- *Custer County, Tyndall Gulch drainage*
- *Site on private property; no public access*
- *Town did not have a post office; no structures remain*

This is Custer City. Note that this building advertises the "Custer Mining & Realty Co." and the "First Colorado Shaft." Hardly noticeable to the immediate right and in the background is the statue of General Custer. *(Denver Public Library x-7586)*

According to Joanne West Dodds in her booklet, *Custer County: Rosita, Silver Cliff and Westcliffe*, three attempts were made to establish a town at this site. The first attempt was in 1877, but lack of an adequate water supply caused its failure. In 1892, there was a public sale of lots by the Custer Camp Town Site Company with one third of the purchase price down, the next third in

30 days and the final payment at the end of 60 days. For those spending $50 or more, a free wagon ride to the site was included. In this dry, hilly country relatively near Querida, this second attempt at forming a town also met in failure.

In 1902, a 50-acre town site was laid out, and contracts were let to construct thirty-two buildings. Unlike the other attempts, a water supply was developed, and underground water mains were installed into the rocky soil. Fire hydrants protruded up along Custer City's grid of empty streets. Although historical accounts mention the construction of a sixteen-room hotel and a billiard parlor, the only structure to appear in a photograph was the office of the Custer Mining & Realty Company. It was more of a shack than a permanent building. Near this office was the First Colorado Mine. No ore was ever shipped from this mine. Custer City, such as it was, didn't have electricity or telephone service. To promote the sale of lots, J. W. Adsmond walked 42 miles from Custer City to Pueblo to claim that Pueblo was within walking distance.

Custer County was carved out of Fremont County in 1877 in response to the mining activity in

This bronze statue of General George Armstrong Custer was erected as part of the grand opening of Custer City. It was unveiled on June 10, 1902. All that remains today is part of the base. *(Denver Public Library x-7585)*

the Wet Mountain Valley. This was only a year after General
George Armstrong Custer was defeated and lost his life at the
Battle of the Little Bighorn. Custer City is the only Colorado town
to be named for this man.

On June 10, 1902, the grand opening of Custer City was
held. The event centered on the unveiling of a statue of General
Custer, complete with sword in hand. The statue was mounted on
a stone base and placed in a small fenced park in the center of
what was to become Custer City. Custer's widow was invited to
attend and unveil the statue, but could not come. A delegation
from Denver, headed by Governor James Orman and former
Governor Alva Adams, did arrive. The governor was accompanied
by his staff dressed in both Confederate and Union Civil War uniforms. A young lady from nearby Querida pulled the cord to
unveil the statue.

Custer City was about the sale of lots and mining stock
rather than the founding of a legitimate town. Few structures
were ever constructed at the site. Custer City never had enough
residents to file for a post office.

The Custer City site is located on a hillside a half-mile west
of the main road through Querida, 329 RD. It is on private property being developed for mountain vacation homes. Access to the
site may be blocked by a locked gate. Although moved from its
original location, part of the base of the statue sits in a meadow by
the access road. No structures remain, and permission should be
obtained to visit the site. ***For a map showing the location of
Custer City, see "Rosita."***

Joanne West Dodds, *Custer County: Rosita, Silver Cliff and Westcliffe,* Focal Plain, 1994, p. 15.
Robert L. Brown, *Ghost Towns of the Colorado Rockies*, Caxton Printers, Caldwell, Idaho, 1977,
pp. 115-118.

DAWSON CITY and TITUSVILLE

Obscure Towns

- *Fremont County, Grape Creek and Titusville Gulch drainages*
- *Access to Dawson City is a demanding four-wheel drive road*
- *Titusville had a post office; no structures remain*

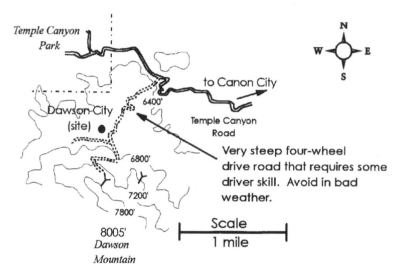

The four-wheel drive road to the Dawson City site is steep and narrow. It requires good tires and some driver skill. There is little evidence of Dawson City.

Dawson City started as a cluster of tents located southwest of Cañon City above the Temple Canyon Road. It was platted in June 1899 by the Greenhorn Mining Company based on an ore deposit on Dawson Mountain. Tents and a frame boardinghouse provided shelter for some; others may have commuted from Cañon City.

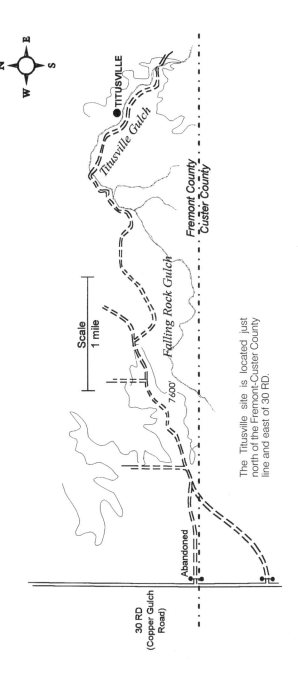

N E S W

TITUSVILLE

Titusville Gulch

Fremont County
Custer County

Falling Rock Gulch

Scale
1 mile

7600'

Abandoned

30 RD
(Copper Gulch
Road)

The Titusville site is located just
north of the Fremont-Custer County
line and east of 30 RD.

Little activity was reported from Dawson City. The Joker Mining and Milling Company, however, gave George Dalton a contract to extend its 500-foot tunnel in 1901. Assays showed that the gold and copper found in the ore would yield $69 a ton, a marginal proposition given the site's remote location. Little came from the mines at Dawson City, and the site was soon abandoned.

Today, access to the site is a steep, four-wheel drive road that requires good tires and some driver skill. The road starts at a strange stone monument along the Temple Canyon Road. Evidence at the site is scant with a piece of pipe, some cut timber, rusting tin cans, broken bottles, but little else. The access roads to the mines can be seen from the Temple Canyon Road on the north slope of Dawson Mountain.

Titusville was a town of 160 people and was located just north of the Custer-Fremont county line in Titusville Gulch, which empties into Falling Rock Gulch. It served as a stage stop on the road between Cañon City and the mining towns in the Wet Mountain Valley. After the Denver & Rio Grande completed its narrow gauge line from the Arkansas River up Grape Creek in 1881, traffic through Titusville dropped dramatically. Ironically, this was the same year the town got its post office with mail delivered from the railroad station at Blackburn. The town dwindled, and the post office closed 2 years later.

Using aerial photographs taken in 1937 by the U.S. Forest Service, two to three structures appear at the site. It is not known if any of these structures still survive. Contemporary mountain property development restricts access to the site. The road from the southwest is posted "no trespassing" as well as the road from the northwest. The road leading directly east from 30 RD has been abandoned and is fenced off.

Post Office Department Reports of Site Locations 1837-1950, National Archives and Records Administration, Washington, D.C., 1986.

Rosemae Wells Campbell, *From Trappers to Tourists: Fremont County 1830-1950,* Century One Press, Colorado Springs, Colorado, 1972, pp. 127-128, 141.

William H. Bauer, James L. Ozment and John H. Willard, *Colorado Post Offices,* Colorado Railroad Museum, Golden, Colorado, 1990, p. 141.

DORA CITY
Below the Waters of DeWeese Reservoir

- *Custer County, Grape Creek drainage*
- *Not accessible; site under the DeWeese Reservoir*
- *Town had a post office; no structures remain*

The Dora City site is under DeWeese Reservoir north of Westcliffe. The settlement dates to 1879, and some details about it are covered in an article in the *Colorado Daily Chieftain*. To encourage settlement, town lots were given away to anyone who would build. A correspondent for the *Denver Daily Tribune* reported that at sunrise on June 2, 1879, the settlement consisted of two frame houses and one tent, but before sunset, there were six houses nearing completion. Dora City's economy was based on nearby mines and the Chamber's smelting furnace. By 1880, the population reached 100, and the town had two stores, a restaurant, two lumber yards, plus several other businesses. It got its own post office in 1879, and in 1883, the name of the town and the post office was changed to Grove. The post office remained open for another five years.

The town probably was abandoned around 1888 when the post office closed. Prior to construction of DeWeese Reservoir in 1903, what buildings remained were removed to clear the site.

For a map showing the location of Dora City, see "Ula."

Don and Jean Griswold, *Colorado's Century of "Cities,"* self-published, 1958, p. 200.

George A. Crofutt, *Crofutt's Grip-Sack Guide of Colorado*, 1885 Edition, Johnson Books, Boulder, Colorado, reprint 1981, p. 88.

Joanne West Dodds, *Custer County: Rosita, Silver Cliff and Westcliffe,* Focal Plain, 1994, pp. 19, 22.

Post Office Department Reports of Site Locations 1837-1950, National Archives and Records Administration, Washington, D.C., 1986.

William H. Bauer, James L. Ozment and John H. Willard, *Colorado Post Offices*, Colorado Railroad Museum, Golden, Colorado, 1990, pp. 46, 64.

GALENA, ILSE, YORKVILLE and SILVER PARK

- *Custer and Fremont Counties, Oak Creek drainage*
- *Accessible via graded dirt roads*
- *Towns had post offices; no structures remain*

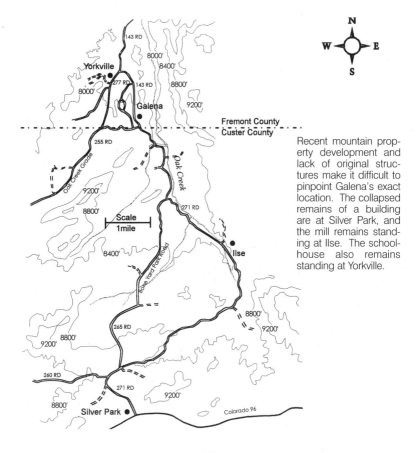

Recent mountain property development and lack of original structures make it difficult to pinpoint Galena's exact location. The collapsed remains of a building are at Silver Park, and the mill remains standing at Ilse. The schoolhouse also remains standing at Yorkville.

Galena was located about a half mile north of the Fremont County line on the stage route (143 RD) between Rosita and Cañon City. The town started in 1877 and had several stores and a post office. The post office, however, closed the following June 1878. As the population of Galena grew, the post office reopened in 1879 and remained until the town was abandoned in 1885. Other businesses included an assay office and hotel. The town was a stage stop between Rosita and Cañon City, and its economy was supported by the nearby Star Mine. When historian Muriel Sibell Wolle visited the site in the 1940s, she noted that the only remaining structure at Galena was a large, two-story house. The site is void of structures, and recent mountain property development limits access.

Frank Andracich, a Dutch immigrant, was plowing his land in Custer County. His plow struck a strip of ground that did not yield and would not turn over. He had intended to plant a potato crop. What Andracich struck was a 27-foot wide vein of crystallized lead. As the extent of the deposit was determined, 150 mining

This restored schoolhouse at Yorkville is one of the few structures that dates back to the town's beginnings. *(Kenneth Jessen 125A8)*

claims were filed. Only a few had ore in paying quantities. One miner allegedly commented that it was a terrible big deposit, and the name "Terrible" was applied to the mine.

In 1878, a few homes were constructed on the Andracich ranch next to the deposit. The town of Ilse formed. Although it had three saloons, it was never very large. In 1884, it got a post office, which operated intermittently until 1929. There was also a general store at Ilse as well as a hotel and boardinghouse. Much of the town was destroyed by a fire in 1887, which started in the second story of the post office. The town was never rebuilt, and the mine closed the following year.

At first, the ore was dug out of the ground and shipped directly to a Pueblo smelter. Later, a concentration mill was built at Ilse powered by water from nearby Oak Creek. The Terrible Mine became the largest producer. The Grant Smelter in Denver took over operations, and the mill was enlarged. It employed about 100 men.

Frank Andracich tried to find the mother lode near his ranch, but all of his attempts met with failure. The deposit apparently was an isolated pocket. After he ran out of money, he borrowed from others. When he couldn't borrow any more money, he ran out on his creditors and went to Idaho. It was in Idaho that he struck it rich in silver mining, became a millionaire and began tracing his old creditors. He returned to Colorado to pay off his debts, five-fold according to some accounts.

Mining ended in 1888, and today the mill and a large water-filled open pit mine are all that remain. Ilse can be reached by taking 271 RD north from Colorado 96 about halfway between McKenzie Junction and Silver Cliff. The route follows 271 RD to the right at its intersection with 265 RD. Continuing on 271 RD, Ilse is about a mile north of Willow Creek.

Little is known about Yorkville. The schoolhouse that served Yorkville sits along 277 RD just south of its intersection with 143 RD. Despite sparse information about Yorkville, it did get a post office in 1875. The post office remained in operation until 1881.

At one time, the town had a few houses. No structures remain at the site today; however, the home of George Griffin was moved to the reconstructed town of Buckskin Joe near the Royal Gorge. It acts as the miner's supply store in this re-creation of a Colorado mining town.

Silver Park got a post office in 1879, but the office closed just 2 years later. A stage station was located at Silver Park along the road into the Wet Mountain Valley. The site is at the intersection of Colorado 96 and 271 RD. The collapsed remains of one building can be seen a short distance from the road. There are several old structures at a nearby ranch that may have been moved from the town site.

This old mill remains standing at Ilse opposite a water-filled open pit mine. *(Kenneth Jessen 108C4)*

Joanne West Dodds, *Custer County: Rosita, Silver Cliff and Westcliffe,* Focal Plain, 1994, p. 22.

Muriel Sibell Wolle, *Stampede to Timberline,* Sage Books, Chicago, 1949, pp. 286-287.

Muriel Sibell Wolle, *Timberline Tailings,* Sage Books, Chicago, Illinois, 1977, pp. 215-216.

Perry Eberhart, *Guide to the Colorado Ghost Towns and Mining Camps,* Sage Books, Chicago, Illinois, 1959, pp. 417, 439.

Robert L. Brown, *Colorado Ghost Towns, Past and Present,* Caxton Printers, Caldwell, Idaho, 1977, pp. 140-143.

Rosemae Wells Campbell, *From Trappers to Tourists: Fremont County 1830-1950,* Century One Press, Colorado Springs, Colorado, 1972, p. 184.

William H. Bauer, James L. Ozment and John H. Willard, *Colorado Post Offices,* Colorado Railroad Museum, Golden, Colorado, 1990, pp. 59, 77, 132, 155.

GLENDALE, HATTON and RED CREEK

- *Fremont County, Beaver and Red Creek drainages*
- *Hatton site can be seen from a graded dirt road*
- *One town had a post office; several structures remain at Hatton*

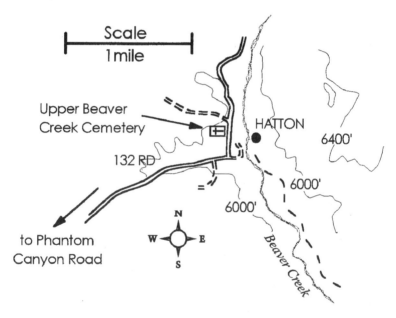

Hatton is located on the east side of Beaver Creek and can be seen from the Colorado State Wildlife area just off of 132 RD.

Glendale was founded in 1868 along Beaver Creek just upstream from its confluence with Red Creek and east of the present-day town of Penrose. This area lacked a business center until John C. McClure constructed the Glendale House for travelers who used the wagon road through the area. The road was improved in 1873 by Robert Spotswood and William McClelland, famous for their stagecoach line.

The two-story Glendale House was constructed of locally quarried pale stone. Large public rooms made the hotel popular for weddings, dances and religious services. The building was made even more attractive by gardens. A barn and corral also were constructed for use by the stagecoach company. As many as 100 passengers passed through Glendale each day. The small town began to fade as rail transportation into the southern part of Colorado replaced stagecoach travel. Glendale never grew sizable enough to merit a post office.

All but the home constructed by John McClure's brother, William, was destroyed by a flood in 1921. Today, the site is on private property and is not accessible to the public. *For a map showing Glendale's location, see "Concrete."*

The Upper Beaver Creek Cemetery served the general area, including the nearby town of Hatton. The cemetery is well maintained. *(Kenneth Jessen 125C5)*

On upper Beaver Creek was the town of Hatton. It got a post office in 1882, and it remained open for 5 years. Area farmers sold their produce in Cañon City and the mining towns. Ranching added to Hatton's economic base. The site is where 132 RD drops down to

The abandoned community of Hatton can be reached only by wading across Beaver Creek. *(Kenneth Jessen 126A18)*

Beaver Creek. The buildings at Hatton can be seen across Beaver Creek on its east bank from the Colorado State Wildlife area just off of 132 RD. There is also a foundation on the west side of the river. The Upper Beaver Creek Cemetery is located farther north along 132 RD.

Red Creek was founded in 1893 based on gold placer deposits. It was located northeast of Hatton in the Salt Canyon drainage. A two-story hotel was constructed, but the settlement never grew large enough to merit a post office. It is not known what access roads exist to the site or what structures might remain.

Rosemae Wells Campbell, *From Trappers to Tourists: Fremont County 1830-1950,* Century One Press, Colorado Springs, Colorado, 1972, pp. 59-61.

William H. Bauer, James L. Ozment and John H. Willard, *Colorado Post Offices,* Colorado Railroad Museum, Golden, Colorado, 1990, p. 69.

GREENWOOD and WETMORE

- *Custer County; Hardscrabble Creek drainage*
- *Accessible via paved roads; occupied towns*
- *One town still has a post office; several structures remain*

This store was the site of a formal portrait of the people of Greenwood. *(Denver Public Library X-9218)*

The community of Greenwood grew around the Greenwood Hotel in 1872, the same year its post office opened. The hotel was a stage stop for traffic between Cañon City and the Wet

Mountain Valley. While meals were served to passengers, fresh horses were hitched to the stagecoach. The town was named for William Greenwood, construction engineer for the Denver & Rio Grande. Greenwood's population apparently fell below what was required to have a post office, and it closed in 1918.

Today the town is not abandoned, although there are several empty old structures.

North of Greenwood is Wetmore, named for mail carrier William H. Wetmore. He delivered mail from Pueblo to Fairplay in South Park and served as a deputy marshal for Lake County. He also surveyed for the government and acted as a correspondent for the Pueblo *Chieftain.* Wetmore got a post office in 1881, and it remains open today.

Wetmore is located at the intersection of Colorado 67 and Colorado 96. This town also is occupied, but like Greenwood, it has several abandoned buildings to add to its character.

Most small Colorado towns had saloons, and Wetmore was no exception. Note the man swinging a bat on the left and the other man leaning into the open window in this 1891 photograph. *(Denver Public Library X-14114)*

Joanne West Dodds, *Custer County: Rosita, Silver Cliff and Westcliffe,* Focal Plain, 1994, pp. 22-24.
William H. Bauer, James L. Ozment and John H. Willard, *Colorado Post Offices,* Colorado Railroad Museum, Golden, Colorado, 1990, pp. 66, 91.

HILLSIDE, COPPERVILLE
and CLEVELAND

- *Custer County, Texas Creek and Copper Gulch drainages*
- *Accessible via paved and graded dirt roads*
- *Hillside has a post office; some structures remain*

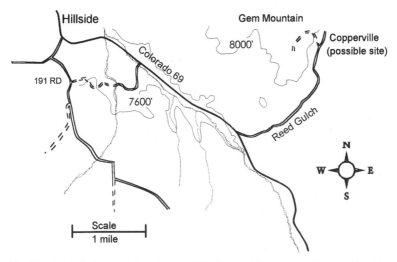

The Cleveland site is located northwest of Hillside, and its exact location could not be determined. The Copperville site is located east of Hillside up Reed Gulch.

The town of Texas Creek, located along U.S. 50, is not to be confused with another town that once had the same name and is located about 10 miles south. The original town of Texas Creek was founded in 1872, and in 1882, its name was simplified to Texas. After two years, the town was renamed Hillside. Postal

Hillside was never a large community, but it remains occupied today. This is the Hillside post office. *(Kenneth Jessen 124D4)*

officials had to contend with two towns in close proximity, both with the name Texas Creek during 1881. Much of Hillside's population left during the 1893 recession when silver prices fell to their lowest value in decades. The population dropped to a dozen and remained as such for many years. The Westcliffe Branch of the Denver & Rio Grande was abandoned in 1938, and Hillside almost became a ghost town.

Today, Hillside is a wide spot in the road with a picturesque frame post office and several homes sitting on the site. The post office serves the surrounding area. Mountain property development is slowly coming into this beautiful, lush part of the Wet

Mountain Valley, and the area's population is increasing. Hillside is located along Colorado 69 between Texas Creek and Westcliffe. Copperville was located somewhere in Reed Gulch near Gem Mountain. It was laid out in 1878 by A. J. Perry, but it never had sufficient population for its own post office. There is little information about the camp, and its exact location could not be determined. At a point 2 miles from Colorado 69 along the Reed Gulch road are foundations near the collapsed remains of a head frame. Around this point are numerous prospect holes, and this is the most likely location for Copperville. Modern mountain property development, however, limits full exploration of the area.

Cleveland, established in 1885, was located northwest of Hillside and was property of the Cleveland Mining Company. According to postal records, Cleveland did not have a post office. Neither Cleveland's size nor its exact location are known.

Wetmore

Don and Jean Griswold, *Colorado's Century of "Cities,"* self-published, 1958, p. 200.

Joanne West Dodds, *Custer County: Rosita, Silver Cliff and Westcliffe,* Focal Plain, 1994, p. 19, 22.

William H. Bauer, James L. Ozment and John H. Willard, *Colorado Post Offices,* Colorado Railroad Museum, Golden, Colorado, 1990, pp. 46, 64.

HOWARD, COPPERFIELD, NESTERVILLE, PLEASANTON, SWISSVALE and WELLSVILLE

- *Fremont County, Arkansas River and Red Gulch drainages*
- *Accessible via paved and graded dirt roads*
- *Some towns had a post office; some original structures remain*

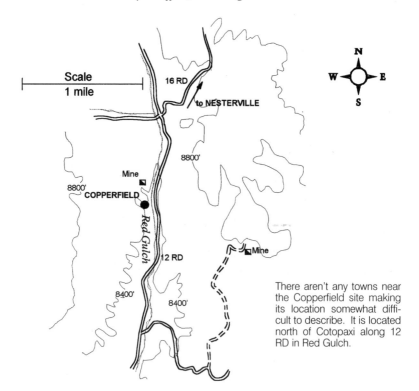

There aren't any towns near the Copperfield site making its location somewhat difficult to describe. It is located north of Cotopaxi along 12 RD in Red Gulch.

Howard is anything but a ghost town, and its history is covered to round out the background of the towns along the Arkansas River.

William Stout and his family were the first settlers in Pleasant Valley. He arrived shortly after the end of the Civil War. More homesteaders followed to ranch and farm on the fertile bottomland. The west end of the valley became known as Howard, named for pioneer John Howard. There was a ready market in the booming mining camps for practically anything grown or raised in the area. Kilns were constructed along the railroad tracks, and cordwood was burned in a reduced oxygen environment to produce charcoal for use in the smelters. This industry lasted until 1904 when the area was depleted of its timber. The ovens were converted to produce coke using nearby coal deposits.

As the tracks of the Denver & Rio Grande approached in 1880, many living in Howard became tie cutters, and the Arkansas River became the means of transporting ties to points along the advancing railroad. In 1882, the post office at Pleasant Valley was moved to Howard, and it remains open to this day.

Laundry is hanging on the clothesline at one of the homes in this early view of Wellsville. The bathhouse can be seen in the distance on the left. *(Denver Public Library X-14042)*

Howard's first church was constructed in 1889. It is located on the north side of the Arkansas River. *(Kenneth Jessen 124D7)*

The people of Howard constructed a schoolhouse, but so many new people arrived coincident with the railroad that it was necessary to build a second schoolhouse.

A branch of the Denver & Rio Grande was constructed in 1903 5.8 miles west to Calcite. This was a Colorado Fuel & Iron quarry town. For more information on Calcite, see *Ghost Towns, Colorado Style, Volume Two*, page 400.

Although little is known about Copperfield, this mining camp got its own post office in 1907. It remained in operation for another 3 years. In 1911, the various mines were merged under the control of the Copperfield Consolidated Copper Company. The company published a prospectus for investors and listed a boardinghouse plus a number of smaller cottages in the town of Copperfield. The town had electricity, mail delivery and a telephone.

Copperfield was located due north of Cotopaxi in Red Gulch on the west side of 12 RD south of the intersection with 16 RD. The site is on the property of Larry Hartsell and consists of the foundation of a single large structure. A mineshaft is located nearby, and on the east side of 12 RD is another mine opening.

Nesterville is located to the northeast of Copperfield on 16 RD. The exact location of the town could not be determined, however, the Nesterville schoolhouse remains standing and is used as a private residence.

Pleasanton began as Pleasant Valley and was established by the railroad at the east end of the valley. It was designed to grow and compete with Howard, but it never evolved much beyond a railroad station. In 1877, it got a post office that was moved to Howard in 1882.

Another small community, which gives the appearance of a modern village, is Swissvale. It is located along U.S. 50 on the south side of the Arkansas River northwest of Howard. A Swiss tie cutter named Max Zeise established a cattle ranch at this location on the north side of the river. It was made a railroad stop from 1880 to 1889, and a section house and siding were built. It never became a town as such.

Immediately west of Swissvale is Wellsville, first settled by George Wells. A small settlement formed in the vicinity of a hot spring, and a post office opened in 1880. A neat-looking resort was constructed at Wellsville with a bathhouse and bathing pool. A small mine, with ore containing both gold and silver, operated in a canyon above the resort. A hotel was built for guests as well as a dance hall. The Fourth of July was a big day in Wellsville with nearly 1,000 people attending the celebration. The post office closed in 1896 as activity at Wellsville faded. Local lore tells of a woman being stabbed to death at Wellsville, and after that, its owner closed the resort.

Today, the mineralized cone of the hot spring can be seen from U.S. 50, but none of the original buildings remain at the site. A sign along U.S. 50 marks Wellsville's location.

Post Office Department Reports of Site Locations 1837-1950, National Archives and Records Administration, Washington, D.C., 1986.

Rosemae Wells Campbell, *From Trappers to Tourists: Fremont County 1830-1950*, Century One Press, Colorado Springs, Colorado, 1972, pp. 213, 215, 222, 224.

William H. Bauer, James L. Ozment and John H. Willard, *Colorado Post Offices,* Colorado Railroad Museum, Golden, Colorado, 1990, pp. 37, 74, 115, 150.

PARKDALE, FINK, ECHO, SPIKEBUCK, TEXAS CREEK and SUNSET CITY

- *Fremont and Custer Counties, Arkansas River, Texas Creek and Cooper Gulch drainages*
- *Access limited to some sites*
- *Some towns had post offices; some structures remain*

The Parkdale post office was an outhouse-sized structure where area residents could pick up their mail. This post office closed in 1970. *(Kenneth Jessen 124D8)*

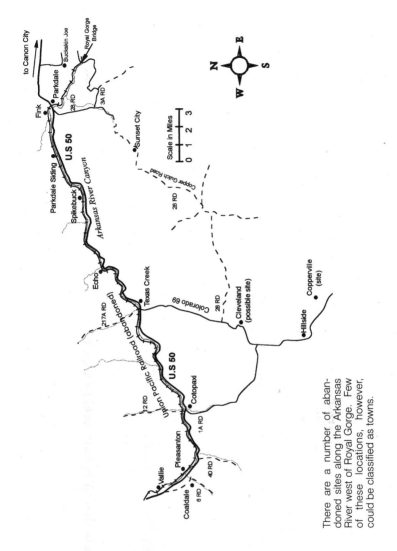

There are a number of abandoned sites along the Arkansas River west of Royal Gorge. Few of these locations, however, could be classified as towns.

Several abandoned buildings remain at Parkdale, including the post office. Even at its prime, the town never grew much beyond fifty people. The wagon road along the Arkansas River crossed at Big Spring Ranch, and the site was known as McCandless Ford for the ranch owner. Because the ford was approximately a dozen miles west of Cañon City, its name became Twelve Mile Ford.

After a bridge was constructed, it was renamed Bridge, then in 1879, it became the community of Parkdale.

Parkdale got its own post office in 1880. It operated intermittently through the 1800s. From 1889 until it was closed in 1970, the Parkdale post office provided steady service.

Near Parkdale is Parkdale Siding. A feldspar plant was constructed near the siding in 1948, and the plant closed the following decade. There are several abandoned homes in a row parallel to the siding. Recent railroad activity involved an excursion line running from Cañon City through the Royal Gorge and a separate quarry operation. Both use Parkdale Siding. The area is posted "no trespassing" limiting exploration.

Near Parkdale was a small place called Fink. A cement plant operated here for a number of years, and one building remains. It could have been a residence or a mine office building. There are also concrete silos and a loading dock at Fink. Access is limited by private property.

Another obscure location was Spikebuck, and as its name implies, it was a railroad town founded by the Denver & Rio Grande. It grew to twenty-five people by 1883 and never became large enough for its own post office. It was home to section hands hired to maintain the track and was listed by the railroad until 1906. The abandoned site is located on the north side of the Arkansas River 6 miles west of Parkdale.

Beyond Spikebuck was another railroad settlement for section hands called Echo. A water tank and home remain standing, but the place is abandoned. Access is limited and the location is on the north side of the Arkansas River.

Where Texas Creek joins the Arkansas River was a place called Ford. It got a post office in 1881, but in 1885, its name was changed to Texas Creek. It was an important junction for the Denver & Rio Grande, and here the line from Westcliffe joined the main east-west line. Today, the remains of the trestle, which took the railroad over Texas Creek, are evident. High on the side of the canyon formed by Texas Creek is a stone wall used to support the

Texas Creek garage. *(Julia McMillan)*

railroad grade. Near Texas Creek is a crumbling row of charcoal ovens, which was once served by a railroad spur. This may have been the town's main industry at one time. Texas Creek got a general store in 1906, and it had a saloon and boardinghouse. The people of Texas Creek constructed a one-room schoolhouse. Today, residents live on both sides of the Arkansas River. The town consists of several homes, the sheriff's office and a general store.

South of Parkdale in Copper Gulch was Sunset City. This mining camp was founded on a placer gold deposit in the streambed. All that remains today are piles of waste rock to mark the site. Few traces of any structures can be found. A new mountain property development is at the edge of the Sunset City site.

Rosemae Wells Campbell, *From Trappers to Tourists: Fremont County 1830-1950*, Century One Press, Colorado Springs, Colorado, 1972, pp. 185, 187.

William H. Bauer, James L. Ozment and John H. Willard, *Colorado Post Offices*, Colorado Railroad Museum, Golden, Colorado, 1990, pp. 56, 111, 140.

PROSPECT HEIGHTS

Platted by Florijan Adamic

- *Fremont County, Forked Gulch drainage*
- *Accessible via paved road; occupied town*
- *Town did not have a post office; structures remain*

Cowboy actor Tom Mix was said to have spent a night or two in the Prospect Heights jail while filming westerns in the area. *(Kenneth Jessen 124D9)*

An informal community developed in 1888 near the Nonac Mine (Cañon spelled backwards). It was immediately south of the town on the south side of the Arkansas River. The mine was purchased by Colorado Fuel & Iron probably in 1896 along with other coal mining towns in the area. They added company-constructed cottages, boardinghouse and company store. School children attended school in Cañon City, and domestic water was purchased from Cañon City. A spur track from the Atchison, Topeka & Santa Fe's main line served the Nonac Mine.

In 1905, Florijan Adamic platted the town of Prospect Heights, which included much of this informal community. At the time, it had 57 residents, but a post office was never established.

This old, abandoned store dates to better days for Prospect Heights, although the community is far from becoming a ghost town. *(Kenneth Jessen 124D10)*

Cañon City voted to eliminate all of its saloons, but in adjacent Prospect Heights saloons were open day and night. The town's saloons enjoyed good patronage, and the railroad delivered loads of whiskey, wine and beer. Ironically, the Atchison, Topeka & Santa Fe did not allow saloons to be constructed on any of its own property.

In 1949, the Nonac Mine closed, and in 1952, C.F.& I. sold its buildings to the Adamic family. This small suburb on the south side of Cañon City remains a nice community with a number of historic structures. One of these buildings is the jail, and according to local legend, one of its "guests" was Western movie star Tom Mix. *See "Wolf Park" for a map showing Prospect Heights.*

Antoinette V. Cresto, *King Coal: Coal Mining in Fremont County*, self-published, 1980, pp. 35-36.

Rosemae Wells Campbell, *From Trappers to Tourists: Fremont County 1830-1950*, Century One Press, Colorado Springs, Colorado, 1972, pp. 111-112.

QUERIDA
And Edmund Chase Bassick's Discovery

- *Custer County, Tyndall Gulch drainage*
- *Accessible via graded dirt road*
- *Town had a post office; one structure remains*

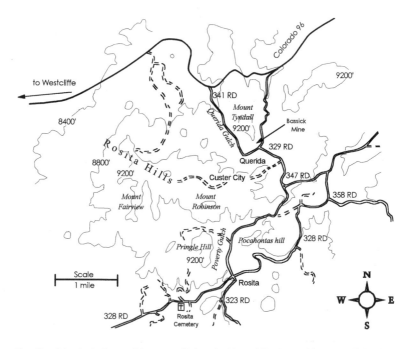

The Querida site is located between Colorado 96 and Rosita and is accessible via a graded dirt road.

Historical writer Joanne West Dodds, in her booklet on Custer County, insists that no one knows just how the Bassick lode was discovered. However, the following story is one that is most repeated.

Edmund Bassick had sailed the seas and prospected around the world. He was said to have made and squandered several fortunes in the process. He lived in Rosita in 1877 and continued prospecting. He earned his living as a miner and worked for the Centennial Mining Company. The mining company had Bassick working on a tunnel in the Rosita area. He and his wife were so poor that credit was denied them just to purchase a packet of pins.

Bassick worked more than 100 prospect holes and had no luck. On his way to work, he passed by an area where John True had found some promising mineralization. Bassick chipped off a sample to have it assayed. This led to the discovery of the Bassick lode.

Muriel Sibell Wolle provides another account of his discovery. Bassick got some sand in his shoe and sat down to take it off. Ants attacked him, and to get even, he decided to demolish the anthill with his pick. This, according to Wolle, was how he discovered the Bassick lode.

The Bassick mill complex sits to the right in this photograph, and the town of Querida is on the left. *(Denver Public Library C-141)*

The Bassick Hotel burned when the town was in its declining years and was never rebuilt. *(Denver Public Library X-13096)*

Bassick lacked money to pay for an assay and had to chop and haul wood to earn enough for the fee. Once he had the money, he had the sample assayed. When the results came back, the sample contained more than 100 ounces of silver per ton. Bassick quit his job, filed a claim and began mining. He named his claim the Maine for his home state, and the first shipment of 10 tons netted him $10,000. He used the money to hire miners to continue working. So great was the output from the Maine that it became one of the few Colorado mines to be self-financing. Bassick found that the deeper the mine, the higher its percentage of gold. At 300 feet, its precious metal output was 70 percent gold and the remainder silver.

The ore deposit in the Maine was in the form of a vertical chimney similar to that found in the Red Mountain area near Silverton. The ore deposit varied from 20 to 80 feet in width within a volcanic vent that had filled with mineralized material. Bassick kept the output from his mine a secret, but it was believed to have generated as much as $200,000 a month with its yearly output well over $1 million.

Edmund Bassick decided he was wealthy enough and could afford to move his family back East. He sold his mine in 1878 to a New York company for $500,000 in cash and one-fifth of the company's stock. The newly formed Bassick Mining Company renamed the mine the Bassick and took over operations. There were many court cases against the mine based on the claims of others. Bassick continued to fight for the mine and died in Denver while involved in one of court cases.

Rosita first served as the area's business center, and most of the miners working at the Bassick Mine lived in Rosita. It was inevitable that a town form close to the mine. A large concentration mill was constructed immediately below the mine, and this provided even more jobs. The town was originally called Bassickville or Bassick City. It was platted in 1880 by the mining company, and lots were leased to those that moved to the town. This was also the year it got a post office under the name "Querida." The origin of the name is unclear, but it means "mistress" or "lover" in Spanish. (It is also spelled Querido in some dictionaries.) By 1881, Querida had a population of 500.

The businesses in Querida sat along one side of its dusty main street with its stores facing the imposing Bassick Mine and Mill complex. A 1907 photograph, taken a year or so after the town was abandoned, shows eighteen false-front stores. There were nearly fifty structures including several stores, boarding-house, two drug stores, two-story hotel and livery stable.

Company officials began to dictate how Querida's citizens should vote and which stores they should patronize. This became a major issue, but Querida was a company town. The company owned the land and the structures. Mill workers and miners formed the Querida Protective Society in their own defense. The local newspaper, the *Querida Drill*, sided with the miners while the editor of the Rosita *Sierra Journal* backed the company. In the spring of 1883, the editors of the two newspapers contemplated settling their differences in a duel.

Mine superintendent C. C. Perkins noticed that in certain areas within the mine ore had been stripped. This form of stealing ore and hiding it in coveralls or lunch pails was called high grading. Miners felt justified in high grading as compensation for long days and low pay. Upon investigation, Perkins found a ton of rich ore in one man's cabin. He had two miners prosecuted and sent to jail. Other miners were fired, and some were told to leave town never to return.

The high grading became so severe that the Pinkerton Detective Agency was hired. The detectives were not known to Querida's residents and went about undercover asking families if they had any rich ore to sell. This sting operation led to the dismissal of more miners.

The Querida Protective Society reacted by sending a letter to the New York owners charging Perkins and his foreman with interfering with their personal freedom. This tactic backfired, and the owners praised Perkins and his foreman. In addition, they both got raises.

Many threats were made by both sides, and it looked like Querida would erupt in violence. Perkins stood his ground and was backed by many. The disgruntled miners finally gave up and many left town.

Querida reached a peak population of 400, but by 1889, it had fallen to just 100. The town's only remaining businesses were the Bassick Mining Company and a general store. The mine and the post office closed in 1906. There was a small resurgence of activity in 1917, and the post office reopened under the name Bassick. In 1920, all mining activity ceased and the town has been abandoned ever since. The Bassick Mine reached a depth of 1,400 feet, and estimates place its output at $20 million.

Today, the foundation of the mill and a large tailing pile sit along the road through the site. One house remains standing in the town itself. From Colorado 96, 341 RD heads south to Querida. The site can also be reached by traveling north on 329 RD from Rosita. Both are graded dirt roads.

Only one house remains standing in Querida today along its dusty, abandoned main street. *(Kenneth Jessen 108C1)*

Don and Jean Griswold, Colorado's Century of "Cities," self-published, 1958, pp. 154-155.

Gayle Turk, Wet Mountain Valley, Little London Press, Colorado Springs, Colorado, 1975, pp. 23-27.

Joanne West Dodds, *Custer County: Rosita, Silver Cliff and Westcliffe*, Focal Plain, 1994, pp. 8-10.

Robert L. Brown, *Jeep Trails to Colorado Ghost Towns*, Caxton Printers, Caldwell, Idaho, 1963, pp. 161-162.

Will Rathbun and Edwin Bathke, "Bassick and His Wonderful Mine," *The Westerners Brand Book*, Vol. XX., Denver, Colorado, 1965, pp. 324-346.

William H. Bauer, James L. Ozment and John H. Willard, *Colorado Post Offices*, Colorado Railroad Museum, Golden, Colorado, 1990, pp. 17, 118.

RADIANT

Used During the Great Depression

- *Fremont County, Newlin Creek drainage*
- *Accessible via a dirt road*
- *Town had a post office; no structures remain*

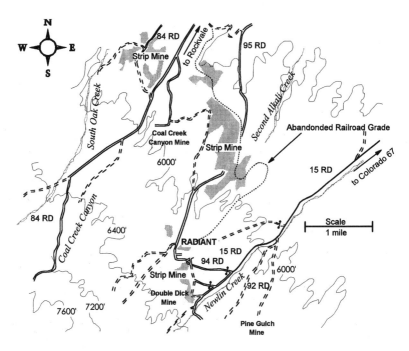

Fremont County 15 RD runs southwest from Colorado 67 south of Florence and passes near the Radiant site. All roads into the site are blocked by gates or fences.

The coal mining town of Radiant was founded 3 miles south of Coal Creek in an area known as the South Field. The Radiant Mine opened in 1903 and dominated the town site, but there were other mines in the area, such as the Double Dick, Pine Gulch and Monarch. The Atchison, Topeka & Santa Fe extended its track from Rockvale south to the Radiant Mine.

At its peak, the mine employed 125 men and reached an output of 800 tons a day. It was owned and operated by the Victor-American Fuel Company. The company built eighty houses in the town. They were illuminated by kerosene lamps and had water piped in from a spring-fed reservoir. The company also constructed a company store, several boardinghouses and school. There was also a saloon.

In 1915, the name was changed to Pyrolite, and in 1926, the name was changed again to Kenwood. The town lasted another 3 years as a coal-mining town, then was abandoned. The Great

The coal mining town of Radiant was located south of Florence. Its name was later changed to Pyrolite, then Kenwood. This photograph by Denver photographer L. C. McClure probably was taken between 1904 and 1915. *(Denver Public Library MCC-3711)*

Depression gripped the United States putting thousands out of work. In 1931, the federal government leased Kenwood for use as a transient camp for the homeless unemployed. Operated by the Federal Emergency Relief Administration, medical care was provided, and a mess hall was set up to feed the several hundred housed in the town. To stay in Kenwood, residents had to either work or attend school. The camp was closed in either 1936 or 1937, and its buildings were razed or removed.

The site is located on private property, and all access roads from 15 RD are blocked by gates or fences. It is not known what remains at the Radiant site.

KENNETH JESSEN

Antoinette V. Cresto, *King Coal: Coal Mining in Fremont County*, self-published, 1980, pp. 37-39.

William H. Bauer, James L. Ozment and John H. Willard, *Colorado Post Offices*, Colorado Railroad Museum, Golden, Colorado, 1990, pp. 82, 117-118.

ROCKVALE

Named by Benjamin Rockafellow

- *Fremont County, Oak Creek drainage*
- *Accessible via paved road; occupied site*
- *Town has a post office; several original structures remain*

This photograph, taken between 1901 and 1902, shows Rockvale during its prime. *(Kenneth Jessen collection CP005)*

Although Rockvale is far from abandoned, it is only a fraction of its original size. The town sits on land originally homesteaded by Colonel William Horace May in 1863. May built his cabin from hand-hewn cottonwood logs, and for defense against Indian attack, gun ports were cut between the logs.

Coal was discovered on the May homestead, and much like other surface deposits in the area, it was mined initially on a small scale. The Cañon City Coal Company was founded in 1880 by

This old fire station is among the historic structures remaining in Rockvale. *(Kenneth Jessen 108C7)*

Benjamin Rockafellow and several other Cañon City businessmen to lease the May deposit. May became a stockholder and director of the company. In 1896, the Cañon City Coal Company was acquired by Colorado Fuel & Iron as part of a program to expand their coal business.

Rockafellow named the town near the mine Rockvale. Residents apparently wanted to call it Rockafellow. Modesty set in, and he used only "Rock" from his name and combined it with "vale" for valley. Other historical accounts relate that the town was named for Rockvale, Maryland. The naming situation became confusing when the post office opened in March 1882. The name "Rockdale" was used, but the following month, it was corrected to Rockvale.

C.F.& I. owned many towns in Colorado, and most were "closed" to privately owned stores. Since Rockvale predated the company's entry, the town had both a company store and privately owned stores for miners to select from. This situation also applied to housing. C.F.& I. wanted all of its employees to live in its neat, well-maintained company cottages. However, private residents were always a part of Rockvale.

May opened a drugstore, and Rockafellow had part-ownership in an emporium. Later, the emporium was acquired by the Colorado Supply Company and made into a company store.

Initially, Rockvale's population reached 100 versus the 500 or so living in the adjacent town of Williamsburg. In 1888, the Cañon City Coal Company platted an addition to Rockvale. Rockvale was incorporated and eventually outgrew Williamsburg.

Its population peaked at 1,500, and by this time, Rockvale had a wide range of businesses including a number of general stores, a couple of livery stables, shoe store, its own barbershops, several candy stores and more than a dozen saloons. The town built a two-story town hall. C.F.& I., besides building company cottages, opened a clubhouse to provide evening recreation as an alternative to drinking at the town's numerous saloons. The company also built an opera house for live performances. The *Paradox* became the town's newspaper.

The Atchison, Topeka & Santa Fe constructed a mining spur south from its main line into Cañon City to serve the Rockvale Mine. The mine's daily output reached 1,200 tons, which required the railroad to run two trains a day. This was the largest coal mine in Fremont County with employment of 300. Later, this spur was extended another 5 miles south to serve mines in the South Field.

Antoinette Cresto in her book, *King Coal*, wrote about Rockvale's ethnic diversity. The immigrants from northern Italy longed for the dancing that was once part of their lives. Although Rockvale had a town hall, the Italians didn't feel welcome. After several fights, the Italians elected to build their own place. A circular enclosure was constructed with walls made of cottonwood logs set vertically into the ground. It was encircled with barbed wire and cedar branches. Water was used to pack down the clay floor. It was known as the Barbed Wire Club.

Many of the ethnic groups loved to play music. The Italians were noted for their mandolins, guitars and accordions while the Slovenians, Czechs and Poles played their organs and violins. Lodges were popular and included the Masonic Lodge, Eastern Star, Foresters of America, Unberto Primo, Western Slovenian Association and the American Federation Union.

As many as 350 elementary-age school children attended the Rockvale School. This required the services of eleven teachers. The original log schoolhouse was replaced by a four-room frame structure. The high-school-age students were taken to Florence, and their tuition was paid for by the Rockvale school district.

Many of the younger children couldn't speak English, and instruction in the English language was the first order of business.

Boys began working in the coal mines as young as age ten to earn money for their families. School was not their primary focus, and boys attended whenever they could. Girls also were absent from school when their mothers needed help. Many children in coal mining towns, such as Rockvale, failed to complete the eighth grade.

After the entry of C.F.& I. in 1896, miners were paid in scrip issued by the company and redeemable at the Colorado Supply Company store. Some of the privately run businesses accepted scrip, but if the store owners demanded cash from the company, the scrip was discounted. The miners could only turn in their scrip for cash if their store account was settled in full. It was a system designed to make a profit for C.F.& I. at the expense of its miners. Every payday, gamblers from Cañon City and Florence came to Rockvale to entice the miners to gamble away what little cash they had.

Rockvale began to decline in 1927 with a coal miners' strike. The strike was produced by a power struggle between the United Mine Workers and the Industrial Workers of the World. Colorado Fuel & Iron warned that if it had to close its mine, it would shut the power off to the large pumps used to keep the underground workings dry. The mine was closed and after C.F.& I. shut off the pumps, the cost of pumping the mine dry was prohibitive.

After the mine closed, a fire destroyed many of the town's buildings. In addition, C.F.& I. sold its company houses, which were either razed or moved. What few houses survive today have been well maintained. Rockvale is southwest of Florence and can be reached by paved road. *For a map showing its location relative to other towns in the area, see "Chandler."*

Antoinette V. Cresto, *King Coal: Coal Mining in Fremont County*, self-published, 1980, pp. 13-20.

Rosemae Wells Campbell, *From Trappers to Tourists: Fremont County 1830-1950*, Century One Press, Colorado Springs, Colorado, 1972, pp. 103-104, 106.

William H. Bauer, James L. Ozment and John H. Willard, *Colorado Post Offices*, Colorado Railroad Museum, Golden, Colorado, 1990, p. 123.

ROSITA

Once Custer County Seat

- *Custer County, Rosita Gulch drainage*
- *Accessible via graded dirt road; occupied site*
- *Town has a post office; several original structures remain*

Rosita had a business district shown in the right-center of this early photograph, however cabins, homes and mining structures were spread out in the valley. *(Denver Public Library X-13226)*

The discovery of silver ore near Rosita started as a hunt for a lost mine. A group of four men, headed by the Smith brothers from Pueblo, went searching for the Doyle Mine in 1863. Joseph Doyle had discovered rich silver ore a few days' ride from his Huerfano County ranch. The assay results showed that the ore was one-half pure silver. Doyle passed away before revealing the mine's location. No claim had been filed. The party of four discovered some low-grade ore containing both gold and silver near the divide separating Grape and Hardscrabble creeks. The Smith Mining District was formed on paper in July 1863, but no development work followed.

Rosita residents pose in front of the post office. The photograph was taken around 1880-1890. *(Denver Public Library X-13219)*

While herding cattle, Daniel Baker discovered an outcropping of galena and showed two other men samples of the ore. They dug a hole to recover more samples. Baker placed the samples in his cabin window.

Richard Irwin, one of Colorado's best-known prospectors, passed through the Wet Mountain Valley in 1870. He picked up several promising samples, and the following December, he returned with Georgetown prospector Jasper Brown. The men just happened to stay with Daniel Baker and noticed the galena specimens in his cabin window. At first, Baker was reluctant to reveal his source, but later he took the two men to the galena outcropping near Rosita Springs. Several claims were staked, but the assay results fell short of ore worth mining. Nothing was nearly as rich as the ore Joseph Doyle had found much earlier.

In 1872, Irwin's prospecting was financed by a Pueblo man,

V. B. Hoyt. The Hardscrabble Mining District was formed, and the first claim placed on file in December 1872. Most of the claims listed Irwin as among the discoverers.

As other prospectors arrived in 1873, the mining camp of Rosita ("small rose" in Spanish) was laid out with thirty-nine lots located around a central plaza. Rosita got a post office the following year. An official plat of the town was filed in 1875 by Boyd and Buell, the same surveyors responsible for early work in Denver, Pueblo and Cañon City.

Of early Rosita, Irwin wrote, "Bill Robinson gave free musical entertainments <sic> nightly on the violin...We lived a happy life of contented luxury...So long as the pitchpipe was convenient and the venison could be had on short notice, we were happy, and borrowed no trouble. Satisfied with our lot in life, we laid off and rested up half the week...On the principle that 'change of employment is rest,' we would all go out and 'shoot the mark' for fun, and then have a dance on the cabin door, turned down on the floor for the occasion." It seemed from Irwin's account of Rosita's early years, no one was in a hurry to start mining.

As for the town, Rosita had a blacksmith shop, the Grand View Hotel, two stores and an assay office by the spring of 1873.

The mines around Rosita were slow to develop, and no ore of any economic value was discovered. The ore was complex, and the area was a long way from a railroad. Wagon roads into the area were primitive. Only ore of the highest grade could be mined for a profit since it had to be packed out for processing. People began to leave Rosita, and one of its stores was forced to close. Several cabins were abandoned.

In the spring of 1874, Colonel Ira James announced plans to build a smelter to convert the area's silver ore into 100-pound silver bricks. Visions of a train of wagons, draped in American flags, hauling piles of pure silver bricks came to the minds of optimistic prospectors in Rosita. The one catch was that the only experience James had was in pigs and corn. He didn't have the slightest idea of how to separate metallic silver from the ore. As for the smelter,

Irwin commented that it would make a better ice cream freezer than a smelter and that Rosita didn't have any need for quantities of ice cream!

What saved Rosita was the discovery of richer veins of ore, and by the fall of 1874, the town quickly grew to 400 structures and supported a population of well over 1,000. The following year, Rosita grew to 1,500. Concentration mills were built to remove as much waste material as possible from the ore, thus making it more economical to ship. In addition to new stores, the town gained three churches. It became among the first Colorado towns to get telephone service. Rosita also had two newspapers, the *Sierra Journal* and the *Rosita Index.* The Rosita Brewing Company kept the saloons well stocked, and the product was in such demand it was shipped as far away as Leadville. The cheese factory was successful until the cows began to graze on wild garlic. This tainted the milk and flavored the cheese, ending this business.

As of 1875, Rosita still lacked a bank, and money from the mines had to be taken to Pueblo, Denver or another larger town. The owner of the rich Pocahontas Mine, Theodore Herr, had to travel to Denver frequently to make deposits. Unfortunately, these deposits attracted the attention of renowned con-artist Walter Stuart, whose real named was Walter Sheridan.

Stuart carefully put on the appearance of a respectable citizen by constructing a nice home in Denver, renting a pew at a prominent Denver church and becoming a bank director. To pull off a swindle in Rosita, he needed a partner. He picked James Boyd to travel to Rosita and pretend to be a man of great wealth. Stuart joined Boyd in Rosita and proposed to its citizens that the town needed a bank. All agreed and a bank was opened.

They hired a group of twenty thugs and placed them under the command of Major Graham, an escapee from the penitentiary in Cañon City. The two men then purchased mining claims near the Pocahontas Mine, including those in dispute. When Herr was on one of his trips to Denver, the gang took control of the mine.

After Herr heard what had happened to his mine, he got an

injunction issued to stop Stuart and Boyd from shipping any ore. Although the details of what followed vary, the gang of thugs, under the direction of Graham, shot up Rosita during a wild spree. An innocent bystander was killed. This precipitated the formation of a vigilante group called the Committee of Safety. The local constable and 100 well-armed citizens marched on the Pocahontas Mine and arrested Graham and one of his henchmen. They were jailed and fined. The bank paid the fines, and the citizens of Rosita began to make the connection between Stuart, Boyd, and the gang of thugs. Other accounts indicate that Graham was killed during a gun battle and his body was tossed into an abandoned mine shaft.

The gang of thugs left town, and Boyd was escorted out of town. The Committee of Safety promised to lynch him if he ever came back to Rosita. In the meantime, Stuart got away with $10,000, leaving behind 80¢ and some worthless bonds. Stuart was later arrested by the Pinkerton Detective Agency in New York City, and he served several years in jail. Later, Stuart returned to Denver to rob the People's Bank of Denver.

To clean up Rosita, the town hired former Denver policeman Jesse Benton. Benton went about disarming and jailing several of Rosita's rougher elements and ordered others to leave town.

In 1934, well after Rosita's decline, the post office was located in this building sitting on a hillside above the town's main street. *(Denver Public Library X-13221)*

This old frame home was once part of the movie set for the making of Saddle the Wind in 1958. *(Kenneth Jessen 074A8)*

Benton was ambushed by Bill Fisher, a Texas gunman hired to kill the new law officer. Although wounded by several of Fisher's bullets, Benton put a round right between the gunman's eyes. Other acts of violence combined with vigilante justice marred Rosita's reputation for years.

In 1876, the quantity of ore shipped from Rosita mines began to drop. This was the beginning of the town's decline. New strikes were made in other areas, such as the Bassick Mine and around Silver Cliff.

A fire swept though Rosita in March 1881. Since the town depended on spring water, there wasn't adequate water to fight the fire. Much of the business district was destroyed, and insurance failed to cover its replacement cost. The town was never rebuilt.

The new boom town of Silver Cliff to the west of Rosita tried to take away the county seat. In a Colorado Supreme Court decision, it was determined that the two-thirds majority vote had not been met by Silver Cliff. This victory for Rosita lasted only until 1886 when Silver Cliff teamed up with Westcliffe to out vote Rosita. A new courthouse was constructed along the road connecting

Silver Cliff and Westcliffe, and the county records were moved. Rosita was soon just another partially abandoned mining camp, but it did retain its post office until 1966.

In 1958, MGM came to Rosita for the filming of *Saddle the Wind* starring John Cassavetes, Robert Taylor and Julie London. Void of buildings along its main street, the movie company moved several structures. New structures made to look old were added. An old two-story home received a new roof and a faded sign indicated it was a rooming house. Weathered false fronts were added to other buildings to create a general store and a saloon.

Only a few of Rosita's original structures remain today, and it is difficult to determine which buildings were modified by the movie company. The town is being redeveloped into mountain property estates, and the once empty lots are being filled with modern homes. The climate is mild, the view is excellent, and the town is accessible nearly all year long.

The Rosita cemetery is the resting place of the controversial Stephen Decature. His life story is covered briefly in *Ghost Towns, Colorado Style, Volume One* beginning on page 423. Carl Wulsten, colonizer of the town of Colfax, is also buried here.

The Rosita Cemetery is located west of the town site and is well worth a visit. It has many old headstones. *(Kenneth Jessen 074A13)*

Gayle Turk, *Wet Mountain Valley*, Little London Press, Colorado Springs, Colorado, 1975, pp. 9-21.

Joanne West Dodds, *Custer County: Rosita, Silver Cliff and Westcliffe*, Focal Plain, 1994, pp. 3-8.

Robert L. Brown, *Jeep Trails to Colorado Ghost Towns*, Caxton Printers, Caldwell, Idaho, 1963, pp. 174-178.

Thomas Noel, Paul Mahoney and Richard Stevens, *Historical Atlas of Colorado*, University of Oklahoma Press, Norman, Oklahoma, 1994, Section 17.

Will Rathbun and Edwin Bathke, "Bassick and His Wonderful Mine," *The Westerners Brand Book*, Vol. XX., Denver, Colorado, 1965, p. 322.

William H. Bauer, James L. Ozment and John H. Willard, *Colorado Post Offices*, Colorado Railroad Museum, Golden, Colorado, 1990, p. 124.

SILVER CLIFF

Became Third-Largest Town in Colorado

- *Custer County, Grape Creek drainage*
- *Accessible via paved road; occupied site*
- *Town has a post office; original structures remain*

The Silver Cliff Town Hall is now used as the town's museum. It is located along Colorado 96. *(Kenneth Jessen 125A11)*

A black-stained cliff near the wagon road between Oak and Grape creeks attracted prospectors ever since rich ore was found near Rosita on the other side of the Wet Mountain Valley. One account credits George S. Hafford as the first to identify the mineral as silver ore in the spring of 1878. He lacked the financial resources to develop his claim and sold it for $25,000 to a Mr. Bailey of Denver. Bailey was said to have extracted $40,000 in silver ore during his first 90 days of ownership.

Another account credits Hafford and two fellow timber workers, R. J. Edwards and Robert Powell, with making the first discovery jointly. Edwards had some of the ore assayed, and the results were encouraging. The assay, however, proved to be in error, and the sample actually contained low-grade ore. The men persisted and heated some other samples producing a melted lump of 75 percent silver. The men promptly staked out several claims.

George Hafford used his wagon to haul supplies to the base of the cliff. The three men worked together at this camp and dug silver directly out of the ground using shovels. The ore was put into sacks and taken to the nearest smelter. They tried to keep their mine a secret, but in this open country the cliff could be seen for miles.

Muriel Sibell Wolle in her book, *Stampede to Timberline*, presents yet another story involving what became the Bull-Domingo Mine 3 miles to the north. According to this story, the Johnny Bull lode was located in 1868, much earlier than the discoveries described thus far. It was discovered by Hunter and Martin. They dug a 10-foot hole and staked out a claim. Discouraged by the results, the men abandoned the claim. In 1878, Daniel L. Rarick of Leadville was grubstaked to prospect in the Wet Mountain Valley and slipped while examining the abandoned Johnny Bull claim. To catch himself, he used his pick. Small pieces of galena clung to the end of the pick. He found a 7-foot vein of solid galena containing silver and staked out the Domingo lode.

When Hunter and Martin heard of this, they tried to resurvey their original Johnny Bull claim to include the Domingo. They took possession of Rarick's claim and began removing ore until an injunction stopped all mining activity.

After Rarick got back the Domingo, the attorneys for the Johnny Bull hunted down the district court judge at his favorite fishing hole. After providing him with some whiskey, they got him to sign a document revoking his former decree. Armed with this document, the Johnny Bull attorneys got the local sheriff to serve Rarick with an order to stop mining.

With most of the Domingo's night shift underground, the Johnny Bull men surrounded the mine. They barricaded the entrance and blocked the ventilation shafts. Using balls of burning waste, they forced the Domingo miners out, and the Johnny Bull men took possession.

Legal battles followed, and both sides settled in 1879. The properties were combined and sold to a New York company. The owners split about a third of a million dollars, and the Bull-Domingo became one of the best producing properties in the area.

The activity around the cliff of silver produced the instant town of Silver Cliff. Primitive dugouts and tents were all over the area south of the cliff. Buildings from partially abandoned towns, such as Rosita, were dismantled and moved to Silver Cliff. The *Rocky Mountain News* reported that in September 1878, only a single cabin existed in Silver Cliff. By the close of November, the new town had 300 houses sheltering 2,000 people. By June 1880, 4,675 called Silver Cliff home, and in 1881, it grew to an astounding 5,040. In this span of 3 years, it became the third-largest town in Colorado exceeded only by Denver and Leadville. Never had a Colorado town grown in population at such a high rate.

Silver Cliff's first business was the Silver Cliff Lunch House, operated by Ed Austin. It consisted of a crude bar and served cold lunches prepared daily in Rosita. Austin started out in Rosita with a combination saloon and lunch house. The operator of one of Silver Cliff's mines suggested that a similar business could be successful in Silver Cliff. The point was driven home when the mine operator produced a chunk of silver ore, telling Austin it could simply be dug out of the ground with a shovel. Austin dismantled a small building in Rosita and moved it to Silver Cliff.

Austin wanted to construct a much larger building to accommodate his growing business. The new building was to be called the Horn Silver Saloon, but the town lacked any sort of organized street system. On September 10, 1878, Ed Austin and Ed Norris used a tape to measure off Cliff and Mill streets to allow construction to start on a post office and Austin's new saloon. The entire street system was surveyed 2 days later.

Austin soon had competition in the form of a saloon opened by Louis Salvich. He cleared $2,000 in ten weeks. (This would be approximately $22,000 converted into today's money.) Salvich was a practical man and washed his bar glasses once a day, independent of the number of customers who had used a particular glass. His bar glasses were clean only for the morning's first customer. After all, water was scarce, and business was good.

By 1880, Silver Cliff had two banks, five hotels, four churches, several mills and even a hospital. Beginning in 1878, the *Silver Cliff*

The Custer County courthouse was constructed between Silver Cliff and Westcliffe after the county seat was moved from Rosita in 1878. This building remained in use as a courthouse until 1928 when a new courthouse was constructed in Westcliffe. *(Denver Public Library X-13581)*

Miner, Silver Cliff Daily Miner, Silver Cliff Daily Prospector, Silver Cliff Weekly Prospector and *Mining Gazette* all went to press, but not a single one survived past 1881. After 1881, seven other newspapers came and went. This was the largest number of individual newspapers ever published in a town of this size in Colorado.

Silver Cliff's street system stretched for nearly 10 miles and residents planted evergreens and flowers to convert what was once a sagebrush-covered flat into a garden. To maintain its street system, Silver Cliff's uniformed officers arrested vagrants and put them to work on a chain gang. Hydrants began to appear after completion of a water works.

Silver Cliff was incorporated in 1879 and held its first election in February. Apparently the outcome was not satisfactory, and a second election was held in April to select its town leaders.

Just to mention a few early businesses, there was Cheap Charlie's Clothing Store, Mint Saloon and Billiard Hall and Elk Horn Corral. The town's first drugstore was opened in a tent and carried only $100 in supplies. Business was so good that its proprietor constructed a permanent building within less than a year and carried over $2,000 in stock. Added to the businesses were churches. The Episcopalians constructed the first church, but the Presbyterians held the town's first church service.

Schoolhouses were built, and classes were started. H. A. McIntyre opened the first bank and moved the interior fixtures from a bank in Rosita to his establishment. Reynolds and DeWalt purchased McIntyre's bank and changed the name to the Merchants and Miners Bank. Eventually, the town got a second bank. The two original hotels in Silver Cliff were followed by eight others. The town had twenty grocery stores and ten dry goods stores by 1881. There were seven meat markets, six barbershops and five hairdressers to keep the town's ladies looking trim. The town supported four flourmills and had two smelters to process the ore.

On the seamy side, Silver Cliff had more than two dozen saloons, five theaters and a number of dance halls. The first dance hall was opened by A. Arbour from Alamosa in 1878. It offered the first dramatic entertainment. The Gem Novelty Theater plus three others were opened by 1880. To draw customers, a 6 p.m. parade was held. A brass band was followed by individuals carrying banners to advertise various establishments. At the end of the parade, the "merchandise" was shown consisting of dance hall girls riding on buckboards.

As covered in the section on Westcliffe, Silver Cliff became the county seat in 1878. It held this title until 1928 when the offices were moved a mile and a half to Westcliffe.

By 1882, the mining boom around Silver Cliff was over. James W. Callaway operated a store at the Bull-Domingo Mine, and in 1883, he traded his Silver Cliff house for a saddle pony, illustrating how far property values fell. The city defaulted on its bonds in 1885, and after a new city council was elected, the bonds were refinanced. People began to leave, and four or five Silver Cliff stores were moved to Westcliffe.

The price of silver declined through the late 1880s, and in 1893, the United States discontinued the silver standard. By this time, silver was trading at about half of its former value. In 1900, only 576 residents remained in Silver Cliff. The population dropped to 250 by 1910, and in the 1940s, only 50 to 75 lived in the town. Its 10 miles of streets are hard to find today and have returned to sagebrush. Some of its historic buildings have been restored and preserved, making a visit worthwhile. Today, Silver Cliff still has a few residents and has never been abandoned.

Gayle Turk, *Wet Mountain Valley*, Little London Press, Colorado Springs, Colorado, 1975, pp. 29-32, 37-38, 58.

Joanne West Dodds, *Custer County: Rosita, Silver Cliff and Westcliffe*, Focal Plain, 1994, pp. 10-14.

Muriel Sibell Wolle, *Stampede to Timberline*, Sage Books, Chicago, 1949, pp. 287-292.

Robert L. Brown, *Ghost Towns of the Colorado Rockies*, Caxton Printers, Caldwell, Idaho, 1977, pp. 323-330.

William H. Bauer, James L. Ozment and John H. Willard, *Colorado Post Offices*, Colorado Railroad Museum, Golden, Colorado, 1990, p. 132.

ULA

First Custer County Seat

- *Custer County, Grape Creek drainage*
- *Accessible via graded dirt road*
- *Town had a post office; no structures remain*

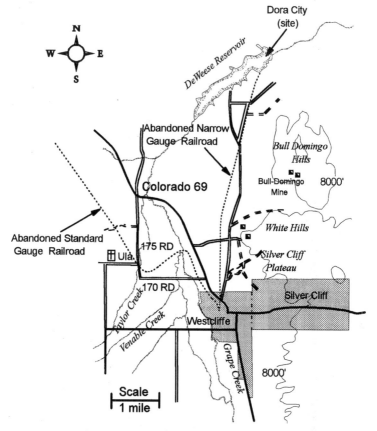

The Ula town site is located at the intersection of 175 RD and 170 RD northwest of Westcliffe. The cemetery is west of the town site.

The origins of Ula date back to the Joseph Davis homestead near the confluence of Taylor and Grape creeks. Joseph's father, Frederick, was also part of this homestead effort. They began by constructing a log cabin, which was replaced by a larger, more comfortable home. The Davis home became the Ula's hotel and general store. This was the nucleus for the town of Ula, founded in 1871. It was one of the oldest Wet Mountain Valley communities.

The Ula post office opened the same year and remained open for the following 20 years. The name, Ula, was a clerical error. The residents petitioned for a post office under the name

The Ula Cemetery is located west of the town site. *(Kenneth Jessen 124D1)*

"Ure" to honor a Ute Indian chief, but when the request came back, it was spelled Ula.

A schoolhouse was built at Ula, and the town established a cemetery in 1872 on donated land. In 1874, a library association began, and in 1876, Heisterberg and Falkenberg built the town's second store. The post office was moved to the new store, and on its second floor, dances were held. The second floor also was used for church services.

Following the creation of Custer County in 1877 from part of Fremont County, Ula was selected as the temporary county seat. After an election a year later, the county seat was moved to Rosita.

Elevating Ula's importance was the arrival of the Denver & Rio Grande in 1910. This new standard gauge railroad replaced the narrow gauge line up Grape Creek and passed by the town.

The Ula site is located northwest of Westcliffe at the intersection of 175 RD and 170 RD (Pines Road). The cemetery is west of the town site along 170 RD. Although there is a ranch close to the town site, it does not appear that any original structures remain.

Joanne West Dodds, *Custer County: Rosita, Silver Cliff and Westcliffe*, Focal Plain, 1994, p. 24.

Muriel Sibell Wolle, *Stampede to Timberline*, Sage Books, Chicago, 1949, pp. 282, 284.

William H. Bauer, James L. Ozment and John H. Willard, *Colorado Post Offices*, Colorado Railroad Museum, Golden, Colorado, 1990, pp. 46, 145.

WESTCLIFFE

Based on Land Development by Railroad

- *Custer County, Grape Creek drainage*
- *Accessible via paved road; occupied site*
- *Town has a post office; original structures remain*

NOTE: The story of Westcliffe is included in this work to round out the area's history. Westcliffe is one of the few older towns in the Wet Mountain Valley to survive.

The Westcliffe schoolhouse, constructed in 1891, is one of several historic structures in the town. *(Kenneth Jessen 108B12)*

Westcliffe was based on both mining and agriculture and eclipsed the older town of Silver Cliff a mile and a half to the east. The story of Westcliffe began with Dr. William A. Bell, then vice president of the Denver & Rio Grande. On land he purchased, Bell and two other investors incorporated the Clifton Company in 1880. It was the general practice of the Denver & Rio Grande to allow private investors to purchase undeveloped land in advance of the railroad's planned route. Bell, being an officer of the railroad, knew the railroad was going to enter the Wet Mountain Valley and acted accordingly. The railroad bypassed Silver Cliff and terminated at the Clifton town site, thus creating a rival town.

The Denver & Rio Grande's narrow gauge main line ran west from Cañon City through the Royal Gorge to Salida. Beginning at a point 1.8 miles west of Cañon City, the branch line into the Wet Mountain Valley was constructed south following Grape Creek. Grading started in 1880, and the next year the railroad was completed.

Taken in the summer of 1983, this old feed and grain store has been restored and painted. It is among several historic structures in Westcliffe. *(Kenneth Jessen 074A7)*

The name Clifton was soon replaced by Westcliffe. Some historical accounts indicate this was Bell's English birthplace. Research by Joanne West Dodds for her booklet on Custer County shows that Bell never lived in such a place. More than likely, the town got its name simply because it was located west of Silver Cliff. As a side note, the "e" at the end of Westcliffe was sometimes omitted, even in its articles of incorporation.

Silver Cliff had grown quickly to become Colorado's third-largest town, but creation of Westcliffe with its railroad spelled the end of Silver Cliff's economic dominance. Some of Silver Cliff's residents raised their homes onto logs and rolled them to the new town. The same year the railroad was completed, Westcliffe got a post office. Growth faltered, and the following year, its post office closed. It wasn't until 1886 that Westcliffe was firmly established, and the post office reopened.

It would be logical to assume that Westcliffe and nearby Silver Cliff would become rivals, but circumstances forced the two communities to work together. Rosita became the Custer County seat in 1878, but the combined population of Silver Cliff and Westcliffe easily eclipsed Rosita. In the 1882 election, Silver Cliff's residents out voted Rosita as the location for the county seat, but the matter ended in court. The ruling was that Silver Cliff failed to get the necessary two-thirds majority. Westcliffe and Silver Cliff conspired to combine their votes, and in the 1886 election, easily out voted Rosita with the necessary majority. Although Rosita was in its declining years, it took a vigilante group to forcibly remove the records. The new courthouse, incidentally, was placed between the two towns. By 1928, much of Silver Cliff was abandoned, and the Custer County seat was moved to Westcliffe where it remains today.

The railroad, that played a key role in Westcliffe's development, was damaged beyond economic repair during an August 1889 cloudburst. Some of the ties were carried for miles down Grape Creek all the way to the Arkansas River. What little rail could be salvaged was removed.

The need for rail service grew with increased production of agricultural products. The Denver & Rio Grande had, in the meantime, converted much of its track to standard gauge. After 11 years, a new branch was constructed to Westcliffe using a route following Texas Creek. This is the only case of a Colorado town getting a second branch of the same railroad using a different route and different gauge. As highways were improved, trucks took over much of the business of hauling agricultural products, and in 1937, the Westcliffe branch was abandoned and removed.

Westcliffe can be reached from several directions over paved roads and is worth visiting. Granted, few of its original businesses remain, but the town is occupied year-round. It offers a motel, gas station, grocery store, café, sporting goods store, bookstore and antique shops.

Rosita

Joanne West Dodds, *Custer County: Rosita, Silver Cliff and Westcliffe*, Focal Plain, 1994, pp. 16-18.

Robert L. Brown, *Colorado Ghost Towns, Past and Present*, Caxton Printers, Caldwell, Idaho, 1977, pp. 295-298.

William H. Bauer, James L. Ozment and John H. Willard, *Colorado Post Offices*, Colorado Railroad Museum, Golden, Colorado, 1990, p. 150.

WILLIAMSBURG

Where the Town Marshal Delivered Water

- *Fremont County, Oak Creek drainage*
- *Accessible via paved road; occupied town*
- *Town had a post office; some original structures remain*

An early view of Williamsburg shows its business district. *(Denver Public Library X-14161)*

Morgan Williams was the first settler at the Williamsburg site. He constructed a brick home, and the town took its name from this pioneer. Just like the town of Coal Creek, Henry and Willard Teller platted Williamsburg. Coal mining centered on the Bear Gulch Mine (also called the Fremont Mine), which began production in 1880. The Denver & Rio Grande extended an existing spur track to the mine in 1881, and by 1882, Williamsburg had grown to forty-four residents. This same year, the town was platted, and under the name "Williamsburgh," it got its own post office. By 1888, the town had grown to 550 and was incorporated.

After the election of a mayor and board of trustees, a stone building was purchased to act as a jail. The town marshal not only had to maintain law and order, but he also had the responsibility of delivering drinking water to every home for a quarter a barrel. The marshal patrolled the streets of Williamsburg from the seat of a tank wagon as he drove to and from the town well. Residents, incidentally, were expected to use water from Oak Creek for washing their clothes.

To finance the town, a poll tax was levied. Failure to pay the tax meant working on a street maintenance gang. Delinquent taxpayers could hire a stand-in, however, to perform their portion of the work.

A one-room schoolhouse was built, and its drinking water was held in a sunken barrel. A single tin dipper hung over the barrel for student use. Some parents objected to this arrangement and provided their children with their own tin cup. As the Williamsburg student population grew, a second room was added to the schoolhouse. The original schoolhouse was replaced in 1921 by a modern brick building.

Located next to Williamsburg was a place called Stringtown. It had its own saloons, store and homes. Stringtown also had a bakery. Charles Vezzetti operated a combination grocery and hardware store in this place. The tracks of the Atchison, Topeka & Santa Fe passed through Stringtown.

During the 1890s, Colorado Fuel & Iron purchased the Bear Gulch Mine and added fifty company houses to Williamsburg. They were rented to its mine workers.

For the 1903-1904 coal miners strike, fifty or so African-American families were brought in as strike breakers. The union lost this strike, and in 1913-1914, the same thing happened again. This time, the miners halted the train carrying the strike breakers and forced the engineer to take the train back to Florence. The Colorado National Guard was called out and provided protection for the scabs.

This strike was over recognition of the United Mine Workers

as a union representing Colorado coal miners. They also wanted a reduction in the workday to 8 hours and higher pay. Miners were paid by the ton, and company representatives weighed the mine cars. Miners often were cheated out of the full weight, and the union wanted supervision over the weighing operation. The miners also didn't want to be constrained to using the company store. The union also lost this strike.

When miners accidentally broke into the previously flooded Ocean Wave Mine, the Bear Gulch Mine also was flooded beyond its pumping capacity. C.F.& I. closed the mine in 1926-1927. The company-constructed houses were sold to either be razed for scrap lumber or moved. Williamsburg declined in size and has been partially abandoned ever since. Its post office closed in 1916. Williamsburg can be reached via a paved road running southeast of Florence.

See "Chandler" for a map showing its location.

Antoinette V. Cresto, *King Coal: Coal Mining in Fremont County*, self-published, 1980, pp. 24-30.

Rosemae Wells Campbell, *From Trappers to Tourists: Fremont County 1830-1950*, Century One Press, Colorado Springs, Colorado, 1972, pp. 99, 101-103.

William H. Bauer, James L. Ozment and John H. Willard, *Colorado Post Offices*, Colorado Railroad Museum, Golden, Colorado, 1990, p. 153.

WOLF PARK

- *Fremont County, Forked Gulch drainage*
- *Accessible via graded dirt road*
- *Town did not have a post office; no structures remain*

Wolf Park was located in a shallow valley 2 miles south of Cañon City. The Cañon Reliance Fuel Company developed the Wolf Park Mine in 1895, and at its peak, the mine employed 150 men. Its output was 450 tons a day. While sinking a new ventilation shaft, two miners drowned after accidentally penetrating an underground lake.

The Atchison, Topeka & Santa Fe laid a spur track to the mine. The coal company constructed thirty houses for the miners. Wolf Park also had a privately owned general store and boardinghouse. School-age children were transported by mule-drawn wagon to a Cañon City school.

The Cañon Reliance Fuel Company closed the mine in 1934 after the coal deposit was depleted. The town was abandoned, and today, the area is being developed for housing. Part of the site was later occupied by a zinc mill, which also was abandoned.

Antoinette V. Cresto, *King Coal: Coal Mining in Fremont County*, self-published, 1980, p. 39.

Rosemae Wells Campbell, *From Trappers to Tourists: Fremont County 1830-1950*, Century One Press, Colorado Springs, Colorado, 1972, p. 112.

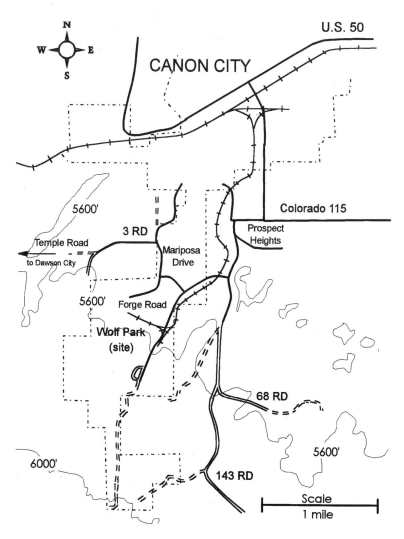

The Wolf Park site is located south of Cañon City, and much of the land is being developed for housing. The site is located along Forge Road.

AREA FOURTEEN

Alamosa, Conejos, Costilla, Rio Grande and Saguache Counties

14

continued

AREA 14: Alamosa, Conejos, Costilla, Rio Grande and Saguache Counties

Selected Towns

Introduction to Alamosa, Conejos, Costilla, Rio Grande and Saguache Counties

Native Americans roamed the vast San Luis Valley for thousands of years. After Mexico gained independence from Spain, the Mexican government encouraged settlement in the undeveloped areas of northern New Mexico and southern Colorado. Generous land grants were given to prominent families to promote settlement. During the late 1840s, Spanish-speaking settlers began to move into the San Luis Valley, and eventually, their settlements extended along the Rio Grande as far north as present-day Del Norte. These Spanish-speaking people established the first permanent towns in Colorado. For the most part, they constructed dwellings with common, single-story walls joined in box-like fashion to form plazas. A plaza, with a common area in the center, was easier to defend than individual homes. In some cases, rather than traditional adobe construction, they used vertical posts placed in the ground as a defensive measure against attack by bands of Native Americans. These early settlers also filed the first recorded water right in 1851 to divert river water into ditches for irrigation.

Non Spanish-speaking settlers came into the San Luis Valley to homestead based on the Homestead Act of 1862. This allowed a settler to construct a home on a 160-acre tract to ranch or farm. After a specified time and a number of improvements, the land became property of the homesteader. Some of the early Spanish-speaking settlers did not understand this act and lost their land.

During the late 1870s, Mormon settlers came into the valley to form agricultural colonies. Some of their towns remain vibrant and successful, while other attempts at settlement failed.

When the Denver & Rio Grande constructed its narrow gauge line over La Veta Pass in 1877 to Garland City, a new era dawned in the San Luis Valley. Its isolation from outside markets was broken. The Denver & Rio Grande pushed on to Alamosa the following year—a town it established. In 1880, the narrow gauge railroad constructed south and established Antonito. The San Juan Extension was built westward from Antonito to Durango, eventually reaching Silverton in 1882. From Antonito, the New Mexico Extension was constructed south to Santa Fe. In 1881, the Denver & Rio Grande entered the San Luis Valley from the north over Poncha Pass to Villa Grove. A branch was constructed to the iron mines at Orient on the eastern edge of the valley. Eventually, the northern portion of the Denver & Rio Grande was connected to the southern portion and created the longest tangent in Colorado by running down the middle of the San Luis Valley. The Denver & Rio Grande also built a line through Monte Vista and Del Norte to Wagon Wheel Gap and South Fork. This line was extended to Creede in 1891. The Denver & Rio Grande converted much of its track to standard gauge. Based on land development schemes, the San Luis Southern built a standard gauge line south from Blanca to Jaroso to serve the southern portion of the valley. Another railroad, the San Luis Central, was constructed between the Denver & Rio Grande to Center near Monte Vista in 1913.

In the late 1870s, deposits of precious metals were discovered on both sides of the northern half of the San Luis Valley. During the 1880s, along the eastern flank of the valley, the towns of Crestone, Spanish, Cottonwood, Duncan and Liberty were founded as mining camps. Only Crestone survives today. At the same time on the western side of the valley, Bonanza, Parkville, Kerber City, Sedgwick and Exchequer were founded. Bonanza has a few residents today, and the other sites, for the most part, are abandoned. Most mining was centered around recovery of gold.

After a court decided that title to the mineral rights belonged to owners of the Baca Grant No. 4, its owners forced the miners out and caused the premature abandonment of a number of mining camps south of Crestone. U.S. marshals evicted the miners, and some of them formed the town of Liberty, south of the grant.

The most profitable gold discovery was at Summitville, southwest of Del Norte. Instead of being located at the base of the mountains, it was located almost on top of a mountain. Gold mining continued there for well over a century, and the town of Summitville lasted nearly that long. Other scattered pockets of mineralization were found south of Summitville and spawned the towns of Stunner, Platoro and Jasper. Several other long-abandoned towns on the western side of the valley include Sky City, Spook City, Bonita and Embargo.

The Spanish-speaking towns were based solely on agriculture. Many of them were partially or completely abandoned with the arrival of rail transportation and improved roads. There was no longer a reason for so many towns in the valley, and over the years, businesses closed or moved to the primary economic centers. In addition, the plaza community outlived its usefulness and was abandoned in favor of individual homes.

This shift in demographics was dramatic in the case of the railroad town of Antonito. The much older towns of Conejos and Guadalupe lost population to nearby Antonito. The same thing happened to the older plazas located along the Rio Grande River near the town of Del Norte.

The San Luis Valley is a remarkable geographic area visitors are not likely to forget. Prevailing winds from the west flow across the northern half of the valley and have picked up grains of sand and particles of dirt over millions of years. Wind velocity drops at the eastern outlet to the valley near Medano Pass. The released grains form the Great Sand Dunes, with some rising 700 feet above the valley floor.

Colorado has four intermontane valleys, and the San Luis Valley is the largest. Elliptical in shape, it has elevations of up to 8,000 feet and measures nearly 100 miles from north to south and 70 miles from east to west at its widest point. The other intermontane basins are surrounded by mountains, but in the case of the San Luis Valley, its southern end is not distinct. On the northern end, the San Juan Mountains close in from the west to touch the Sangre de Cristo Mountains on the east at Poncha Pass. The eastern side of the southern end of the valley is defined by the

Culebra Range. The Sangre de Cristo Range, located on the east side of the north end of the valley, has peaks in excess of 14,000 feet. It forms a natural barrier between the San Luis Valley and the Wet Mountain Valley.

The San Luis Valley has a great many abandoned or partially abandoned towns. Nearly 100 town histories are included in this section, and there are more yet to be documented. The history of most Colorado mountain areas is simple; gold and/or silver were discovered, prospectors arrived, mining camps were established. When the mineral riches were exhausted, the towns were abandoned. The San Luis Valley has a far more complex and diverse history than other areas in Colorado with towns that once were supported by agriculture, precious metal mining, iron mining and the railroads.

AGUA RAMON

Early Settlement Near South Fork

- *Rio Grande County, Agua Ramon Creek drainage*
- *Accessible via graded dirt road*
- *Town did not have a post office; one structure remains*

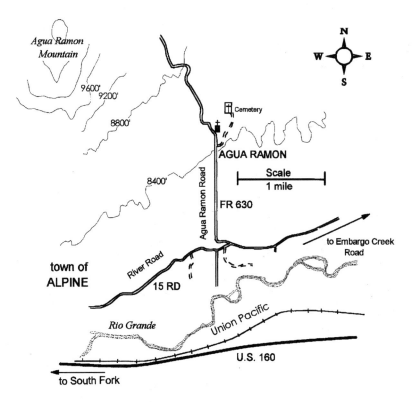

Agua Ramon can be reached by graded dirt roads either from the Embargo Creek Road or from Alpine. Several roads cross over from U.S. 160 in this general area.

A gua Ramon, and its Catholic church and cemetery, is located northeast of South Fork, or more specifically, 3 miles by road from Alpine. Access to the site is off River Road (15 RD) on to Agua Ramon Road, which provides access to microwave and radio towers. It is difficult to say if Agua Ramon was ever a town. More than likely, it was an economic, social and religious center for area ranchers.

The name is a combination of the Spanish word for water and a family surname. Historian Virginia McConnell Simmons relates that it was probably settled by people who moved from Capulin and La Jara in the late 1800s after losing their land to homesteaders.

In addition to a store and school, Agua Ramon had a Penitente morada, or meeting place, for religious ceremonies. A women's auxiliary stood nearby. No post office is listed for the settlement.

The most prominent structure at Agua Ramon is its Catholic church. To the northeast is a small cemetery, but otherwise, there are no other structures dating back to the town's origin. *(Kenneth Jessen SJ122)*

Virginia McConnell Simmons, *The San Luis Valley*, University Press of Colorado, Niwot, Colorado, 1999, p. 274.

ALDER
And The Old Ute Woman

- *Saguache County, San Luis Creek drainage*
- *Accessible via paved road and dirt side road*
- *Town had a post office; several standing structures remain*

A few old buildings remain at Alder east of U.S. 285 near Alder Creek. The town was moved a short distance to the west next to the tracks of the Denver & Rio Grande in 1881. *(Kenneth Jessen 111D7)*

Alder is still shown on some maps, but its days as a town are over. The Alder site is north of Villa Grove on U.S. 285 near the confluence of Alder and San Luis Creeks. Two structures still stand. Alder was among many towns once located along this primary north-south route through the San Luis Valley. The town started with Henry Emmet's blacksmith shop. A roadhouse was constructed on the north bank of Alder Creek opposite his shop. Travelers found lodging and food, and could have their horses or mules shod.

Life changed when the Denver & Rio Grande Railroad constructed its narrow gauge line south from Poncha Springs, over Poncha Pass, through Villa Grove to the Orient iron mines southeast of Alder. The railroad grade passed a quarter of a mile west of the original Alder town site. At first, the railroad construction camp used the name Round Hill Station. Alder then moved next to the railroad. Extra locomotives, called "helpers," were kept at the Round Hill Station to help heavy trains over the pass, and no doubt, the railroad added more buildings.

Alder got its post office coincident with the coming of the railroad in 1881. Except for a brief period in 1911, the Alder post office remained open until 1927.

Associated with the history of Alder is a story recorded by George Harlan in his book, *Postmarks and Places.* John Hice, an early settler in the region, came across an old Ute woman in the scrub brush near his ranch. She was too old to keep up with her tribe and was left behind in their migration across the valley. Hice took pity on her and used his knowledge of the Ute language to communicate. He invited the woman to be his guest at the Hice Ranch. She refused to leave the scrub brush, so Hice brought her food consisting of venison and cornbread. As winter approached, Hice worried that the woman would freeze to death. He remodeled his granary for her, but she would not leave the scrub brush. Eventually, Hice roped the woman and took her to the cabin. He supplied her with food and firewood. One morning, he banged on the door, and there was no response. The old woman had passed away during the night wrapped in buffalo robes. She was buried behind the barn, and her grave was marked by a picket fence. Today, the ranch is known as the Ox Bow and sits on the "new" Alder town site.

George Harlan, *Postmarks and Places*, Golden Bell Press, Denver, 1976, pp. 23-24.

Tiv Wilkins, *Colorado Railroads*, Pruett Publishing Company, Boulder, Colorado, 1974, p. 37.

William H. Bauer, James L. Ozment and John H. Willard, *Colorado Post Offices*, Colorado Railroad Museum, Golden, Colorado, 1990, p. 10.

ANTONITO, CONEJOS, GUADALUPE, LOBATOS and SERVIETA

- *Conejos County, Conejos River drainage*
- *Accessible via paved and graded dirt roads; occupied sites*
- *Some towns had post offices; some original buildings remain*

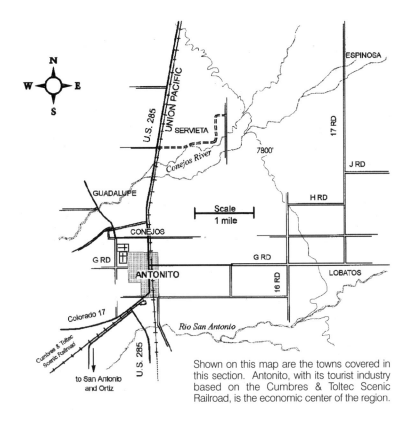

Shown on this map are the towns covered in this section. Antonito, with its tourist industry based on the Cumbres & Toltec Scenic Railroad, is the economic center of the region.

In 1854, the area's first settlers founded Guadalupe on the north side of the Conejos River. The following year, under the leadership of Lafayette Head, some of the people of Guadalupe moved south across the river to higher ground. Here a new plaza was established named Conejos, meaning rabbits. A bridge was placed across the Conejos River in 1858 to connect the two small communities.

The first chapel was constructed in 1857 after a priest arrived. He organized what became the first Catholic parish in Colorado. A church was erected in 1860, but the building burned in 1926. It was replaced by the present-day Our Lady of Guadalupe Catholic Church on the same site. Over the years, two Catholic academies and a public school opened in Conejos.

Colorado Territory was formed in 1861, and Conejos County became one of the state's original counties. Conejos became the county seat. A post office opened in 1862, one of the first in Colorado, and remains open today. A large courthouse was built in 1890, but it burned in 1980 and was replaced by the present-day modern structure.

Although a few people still live in Conejos, it lost most of its population to Antonito when the Denver & Rio Grande arrived in 1880. Today, Conejos is a mixture of abandoned and occupied buildings facing onto the central plaza.

This old store faces onto the plaza at Conejos, site of the oldest Catholic parish in Colorado. *(Kenneth Jessen 121B7)*

Despite the fear of flooding, a few families continued to live in Guadalupe. The name is said to have come from a man who promised to build a church on the spot dedicated to Our Lady of Guadalupe if only his mule would move on. The church was not built, only a small chapel was constructed in 1854. Early settlers included José Maria Jacquez, Vicente Velasquez and Lafayette Head. Jacquez built a flour mill in 1856. The first homes were built around a plaza using upright logs. Guadalupe suffered through several Indian attacks during the mid-1850s. So much livestock was driven off, settlers had to return to New Mexico for more stock. Guadalupe was incorporated in 1869, and records from the following year indicate it had the largest number of tax-payers in Conejos County.

Only a few families live in this historic town today. The plaza vanished generations ago, and the town does not have a defined business center. It is more of an accumulation of homes.

Antonito, unlike Hispanic settlements in the San Luis Valley, was a product of the Denver & Rio Grande. The town was never abandoned, and its history is included here for completeness. In 1880, the narrow gauge line extended south from Alamosa. At the point where the rails of the San Juan Extension headed west and the New Mexico Extension departed south to Santa Fe, the railroad founded Antonito.

Antonito was originally called San Antonio, and its post office opened under that name in 1880. The following year, to eliminate confusion with other towns of the same name, the name was changed to Antonito. The post office remains open today.

The town of Cenicero was located 3 miles due east of Antonito on the road to Mesita. It was settled by people from Cochiti, New Mexico. They brought with them the rules for the Penitente brotherhood, La Hermandad de Nuesto Padre Jesus. The brotherhood constructed the first morada in the San Luis Valley south of Cenicero.

Originally, Cenicero was surrounded by an adobe wall for protection against Indian attack. A plaza was built in the mid-

1850s. The exact date the Catholic Church was organized in Cenicero is unknown, but it was in existence by 1878. In 1860, Presbyterian missionaries arrived and converted some of the Spanish-speaking residents. The missionaries taught the first school in the Presbyterian Church. This structure later became a Catholic church.

A post office opened in 1894, and in 1902, members of the Lobatos family began to serve as postmasters. They changed the name of the town to Lobatos in 1902, and the post office reflected the change. Postal service continued until 1920 with the exception of a year between 1911 and 1912.

The town site is vacant of its business structures today. The newly restored Holy Family Church, with "his" and "hers" outhouses in back, dominate the site. This church was built in 1952.

Although nothing exists today, 2 miles east of Guadalupe was the small community of Servieta. It was in existence by 1852, and a ditch was dug in 1854 on the north side of the Conejos River to provide farmers with irrigation water. The Six Mile Ditch is still indicated on maps. Servieta was on the diagonal road that ran from Fort Garland to Conejos. In 1870, nineteen taxpayers were listed, and the town was listed in Our Lady of Guadalupe Parish records.

Guadalupe and Conejos were founded at about the same time as Servieta and apparently offered better opportunities. The residents abandoned Servieta, although the town remained on the maps until around 1880. The site is east of U.S. 285.

Virginia McConnell Simmons, "Hispanic Place Names of the San Luis Valley," *The San Luis Valley Historian*, Volume XXIII, Number 3, 1991, pp. 7-8, 10-12, 19, 27-28.

Virginia McConnell Simmons, *The San Luis Valley*, University Press of Colorado, Niwot, Colorado, 1999, pp. 278-279, pp. 286-287, 292, 305.

William H. Bauer, James L. Ozment and John H. Willard, *Colorado Post Offices*, Colorado Railroad Museum, Golden, Colorado, 1990, pp. 12, 32, 37, 89, 128.

BISMARK

Named for the Prussian Chancellor

- *Saguache County, San Luis Creek drainage*
- *Site not accessible; private property*
- *Town had a post office; no remaining structures*

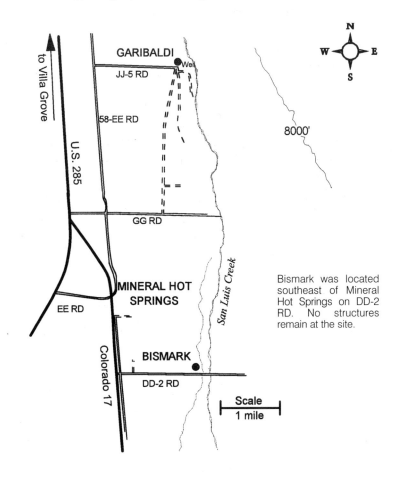

Bismark was located southeast of Mineral Hot Springs on DD-2 RD. No structures remain at the site.

Bismark was composed of a cluster of ranch buildings and was never a town as such. It may have had a school, however. Its post office opened in 1872 and closed seven years later. The place was named after Prince Otto Eduard von Bismarck, the Prussian chancellor, but with a simplified spelling. Bismark's postmaster, Martin Rominger, ran a dairy. His butter was packed into twenty-pound kegs made of aspen. The butter was shipped to various mining camps in the area. Rominger's supply room became a store when others, who lived in the area, needed supplies.

Cabin at Stunner

George Harlan, *Postmarks and Places*, Golden Bell Press, Denver, Colorado 1976, pp. 27-28.

William H. Bauer, James L. Ozment and John H. Willard, *Colorado Post Offices*, Colorado Railroad Museum, Golden, Colorado, 1990, p. 20.

BONANZA

And Secondhand Charley

- *Saguache County, Kerber Creek drainage*
- *Accessible via graded dirt road*
- *Town had a post office; many original structures remain*

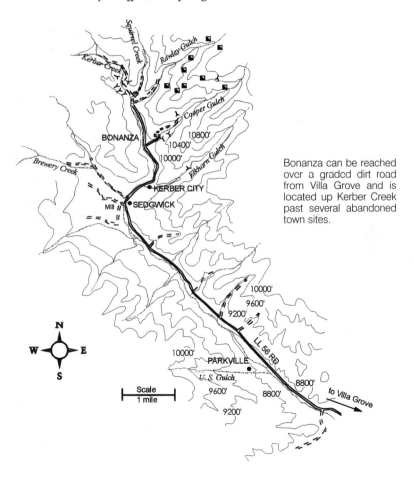

Bonanza can be reached over a graded dirt road from Villa Grove and is located up Kerber Creek past several abandoned town sites.

The Bonanza Mine was located in July 1880 and the town of Bonanza was incorporated in November. The area's best mine, the Rawley, was also staked out the same year. The boom started, and the town grew rapidly. Helen Kemper, who wrote about Bonanza for *The San Luis Valley Historian,* provided a description of it as a camp ringed by aspen trees. She said the town crawled along the intersecting creeks of Kerber and Copper and climbed the surrounding hills along terraced streets and on down the canyon.

For a while, Bonanza was called a second Leadville because of the similarity of the ore. During 1880 and 1881, tents, cabins, false-front stores and shacks made of rough-cut lumber lined the streets of Bonanza. There were forty saloons in the area. A house of ill repute was located high on a hill above the town. Bonanza was quite successful, and over time, it absorbed much of the population from surrounding towns along Kerber Creek. Bonanza reached its peak in 1882 with an estimated population of 1,300.

Bonanza had four smelters and nineteen mills. Concentrates were shipped by wagon to Villa Grove, then to Durango, Leadville, Colorado Springs and Salida for smelting. At one time, the Denver & Rio Grande contemplated constructing a spur over the relatively easy grade to Bonanza.

Bonanza's main street during its prosperous days around 1900. Few, if any, of these structures remain today. *(Denver Public Library x-7331)*

The town had four hotels. The Cañon House Hotel was its best and hosted many prominent visitors. It had a two-room apartment on the first floor. Many women from the surrounding mining camps came there to give birth. The building was torn down in the late 1920s after the town's last boom.

The *Bonanza Bee* was edited in Bonanza and printed in Saguache. The town's second newspaper was the *Bonanza Daily Enterprise.* Other businesses included a shoe repair shop, two barbershops and a number of stores.

The Bonanza Miners was the town's baseball team, and with pride, they accepted a challenge from the Leadville team. The team arrived in Leadville the afternoon before the game and was treated to a parade the length of Harrison Avenue headed by the Leadville City Brass Band. Drinks flowed freely, and a good time was had by both teams. The following day, the Bonanza team was in no condition to play, while the Leadville team was alert and ready. Although the Bonanza Miners fought hard, they never got a man on first base!

In her article, Helen Kemper tells about Secondhand Charley who operated a secondhand store. The poor man was a drunk and didn't have the willpower to quit. Some Bonanza pranksters took advantage of Charley's intoxicated condition by selling back his own articles.

One morning, Helen's grandfather, John Ashley, passed Secondhand Charley's store and was greeted, "Morning, John."

To that, Ashley replied, "Why, good morning Charley. Fine morning isn't it?"

Charley asked Ashley to stop by his place and have some special soup he had cooked up, but Ashley told Charley that people were waiting for him to return home. Charley prevailed, and Ashley concluded that the man would be better off at his cabin than trying to work. After escorting the rubber-legged Charley to his door, Charley opened it. There was the smell of boiling beef, and Ashley saw a pot on the stove. Charley invited him to take the lid off, and as Ashley looked into the pot, staring back at him was the head of a yearling, horns, hair, eyes and all. The tongue hung out of the mouth with a tiny piece of hay still attached. Ashley's senses had been assaulted first by the odor of whiskey, then by the sight of the head in the pot. His stomach rebelled and forced a quick departure, much to the chagrin of the hospitable Secondhand Charley!

Silver prices began to decline because of increased production during the late 1880s and early 1890s. In 1893, the Sherman Silver Purchase Act was repealed. This meant that the U.S. Government was no longer obligated to purchase silver to back the currency. The steady decline in silver prices ended the boom years, and by 1896, only 100 people remained in town. A few years later, there was a resurgence in mining activity with the construction of two concentration mills to treat the area's low grade ore, and several mines reopened.

In 1912, the Rawley Mining Company drilled a tunnel more than a mile long for drainage and development of its silver ore. The tunnel cut into the main vein 1,200 feet below the surface and 600 feet below the lowest level of the mine. Pumping expenses

After most of the town was abandoned, Bonanza's stores began to deteriorate. The date of this photograph is unknown, but a good guess would be during the 1940s. *(Denver Public Library x-7334)*

had forced the mine's closure until it could be drained from below. The ore contained silver, copper, lead and zinc with a small amount of gold.

After its glory days, Bonanza had its ups and downs as mines closed and reopened. In 1917, the Rawley Mine reopened, new families arrived, and new homes were built. One of the mills was put back in operating condition, and a tram was constructed to bring ore down from the mines. The population climbed to 600, and the town got a motion picture theater plus two

Both log and frame abandoned buildings at Bonanza offer many photographic opportunities. *(Kenneth Jessen 100D2)*

schools during the 1920s. The post office, first opened in 1880, remained active until 1938 when the town's population fell below the minimum required. The Empress Josephine Mine was reopened in 1947, and after a few years, it closed for good. During its life, total production reached $7 million.

Today, Bonanza is almost a ghost town, and the many stores that once lined its main street are gone. A few occupied homes sit among Bonanza's many abandoned buildings. The town presents numerous opportunities for interesting photographs.

Helen A. Kemper, "Bonanza and the Kerber Creek District," *The San Luis Valley Historian*, Volume III, No. 2, Spring, 1971, pp. 6, 8-9, 26, 31-32, 36, 44.

Muriel Sibell Wolle, *Stampede to Timberline*, Sage Books, Chicago, Illinois,1949, pp. 298-299.

William H. Bauer, James L. Ozment and John H. Willard, *Colorado Post Offices*, Colorado Railroad Museum, Golden, Colorado, 1990, p. 22.

CAMP COMMODORE
On a Hard-Core Four-Wheel Drive Road

- *Alamosa County, Holbrook Creek drainage*
- *Accessible via difficult four-wheel drive road*
- *Town did not have a post office; no structures remain*

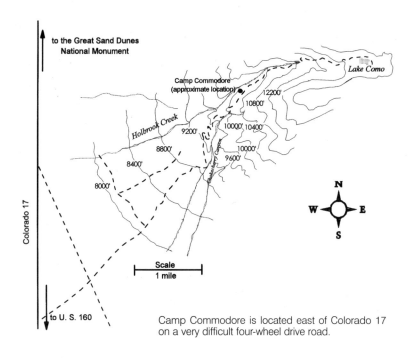

Camp Commodore is located east of Colorado 17 on a very difficult four-wheel drive road.

Camp Commodore was located on the western side of the cirque formed by Ellingwood Point and Blanca Peak. Lake Como is above the site. Gold was located in 1899 in a patch of wild raspberries, and a mining camp developed. It had a store, boardinghouse and two saloons. Several of Camp Commodore's structures remained standing along FR 975 in the 1970s. It is not known if any of these structures remain today. There are several impressive mines above Lake Como.

Driving to the site is a difficult matter. Charles Wells in his book, *Guide to Colorado Backroads & 4-Wheel Drive Trails* says, "This trail is nationally known as perhaps the best hard-core trail in Colorado. The trail has many challenging obstacles that test the most experienced drivers and best equipment!"

Charles A. Wells, *Guide to Colorado Backroads & 4-Wheel Drive Trails*, FunTreks, Colorado Springs, Colorado, pp. 235-237.

Perry Eberhart, *Guide to the Colorado Ghost Towns and Mining Camps*, Sage Books, Chicago, Illinois, 1969, pp. 441-442.

COTTON CREEK
and MIRAGE

- *Saguache County, Cotton Creek drainage*
- *Access to sites via graded dirt roads*
- *Mirage had a post office; one original structure remains*

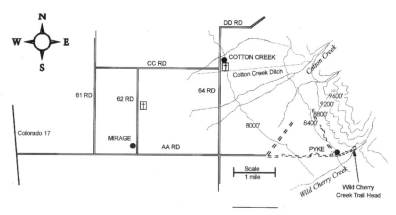

There is little left at Cotton Creek, but it can be identified by its cemetery. At Mirage, the old, log schoolhouse remains standing. There is a log ranch house sitting on the south side of AA RD near the site.

Cotton Creek was originally called Upper Cotton Creek to avoid confusion with Lower Cotton Creek. Lower Cotton Creek was eventually renamed Mirage. Both settlements were located southeast of Mineral Hot Springs. A post office was established at Lower Cotton Creek in 1875, and in 1895, its name was changed to Mirage.

This area was settled by Spanish-speaking people who

moved north from New Mexico. Both communities, located approximately 3 miles apart, shared a store and school.

In 1914, Colorado Fuel & Iron constructed a mile-long steel flume to divert the flow of water in Cotton Creek to its mine at Orient. Without water, this marked the end of agriculture along the creek and death for the settlements.

One of the local stories involved two settlers, Niehardt and Rominger, who fought over the wind used to power their windmills. Rominger complained that Niehardt was stealing the wind and caused his windmill to stop. Windmills were essential to supply water to their cattle. The settlers were commanded to appear in court and to operate their windmills on alternate days. The trial was in jest.

At Mirage stands an old, log schoolhouse. It is in good shape and must have been restored. The site is located where AA RD intersects 62 RD about halfway between Villa Grove and Crestone as the crow flies.

Only a small cemetery marks the site of Cotton Creek on the east side of 64 RD and slightly south of its crossing with Cotton Creek. The town was located along the creek.

This wonderful old schoolhouse stands near the Mirage site. *(Kenneth Jessen 108C10)*

George Harlan, *Postmarks and Places*, Golden Bell Press, Denver, Colorado 1976, pp. 41-42.

William H. Bauer, James L. Ozment and John H. Willard, *Colorado Post Offices*, Colorado Railroad Museum, Golden, Colorado, 1990, p. 39.

COTTONWOOD

Its Post Office Was Lanark

- *Saguache County, Cottonwood Creek drainage*
- *Accessible via graded dirt road*
- *No standing structures remain*

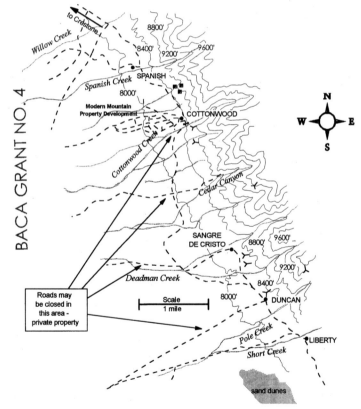

Cottonwood was just one of many mining towns located along the western base of the Sangre de Cristo Mountains. The site can be reached from an access road on the west or along the old railroad grade from Crestone through Spanish. South of Cottonwood, the road is closed and cuts off access to Sangre de Cristo, Duncan and Liberty.

Cottonwood was supported by mines in the nearby side canyons and along the base of the Sangre de Cristo Mountains. Mining began in 1893. Cottonwood's most notable mines were the Irvin, Independent and Bonanza. Ore values ran as high as $50 a ton, and because it was in decomposed quartz ore it could be removed using low cost, simple milling methods. The first mill in Cottonwood was located along Cottonwood Creek and was constructed by Judge Kellogg. Mine owners were constantly complaining that the mill was not efficient and that a great deal of gold was lost. To that, Judge Kellogg moved his mill to the town of Spanish, presumably where he received better treatment.

Daniel Seger selected the name for the Cottonwood post office in memory of his birthplace, Lanark, Illinois. The Lanark post office opened in March 1898 and closed nine months later. Mail arrived six days a week. After it closed, residents of Cottonwood had to travel south to Duncan to collect their mail. The Lanark post office served 175 patrons and was located in the Cottonwood general store.

In 1898, a court ruling gave the owners of Baca Grant No. 4 all mineral rights, and the miners who lived at Cottonwood were evicted. All mining activity ceased in 1900, but a Philadelphia company soon took over, presumably with some of the profits going to the Baca Grant owners. A new mill was constructed, and shipments reached nearly $1 million a month.

In 1901, based on renewed activity at Cottonwood, the Denver & Rio Grande formed a subsidiary called the Rio Grande Sangre de Cristo Railroad Company. A narrow gauge railroad was constructed from Moffat due east to Crestone. At Crestone, the line turned south and ran along the base of the mountains. It passed through Spanish and ended at Cottonwood where the railroad installed a turntable. It served the mines along the way, the largest of which was the Independent. The line was abandoned around 1926, and the rails were removed in 1929.

Gold ore is not a renewable resource and was exhausted by 1907. Interest in the deposits, however, was revived in 1928 when

This interior view of a log cabin at Cottonwood was photographed by Muriel Sibell Wolle in 1942. None of Cottonwood's original structures remain standing today. *(Denver Public Library x-5139)*

several properties were leased. A small flotation mill was constructed along Cottonwood Creek, but nothing of consequence came from this operation. Another company attempted to make money mining in the area in 1935, and another small mill was built. By 1937, all was quiet again in the Cottonwood Creek area. After the town was abandoned, some of its structures were moved to Crestone.

When historian Muriel Sibell Wolle visited the Cottonwood town site in 1942, two or three old cabins were still standing. Today, the concrete foundations of the mill are all that remain at the site. The old railroad grade has been converted into a road and can be used to access the site. A better road comes from below through a mountain property development. Between Cottonwood and Spanish are the remains of the large mill at the Independent Mine.

George Harlan, *Postmarks and Places*, Golden Bell Press, Denver, Colorado, 1976, pp. 116-132.

Muriel Sibell Wolle, *Stampede to Timberline*, Sage Books, Chicago, Illinois, 1949, pp. 308-309.

Tiv Wilkins, *Colorado Railroads*, Pruett Publishing Company, Boulder, Colorado, 1974, pp. 137, 215.

William H. Bauer, James L. Ozment and John H. Willard, *Colorado Post Offices*, Colorado Railroad Museum, Golden, Colorado, 1990, p. 85.

CRESTONE

Survived Where Other Mining Camps Failed

- *Saguache County, North Crestone Creek drainage*
- *Accessible via paved road; occupied town*
- *Town has a post office; several original structures remain*

In 1901, the Denver & Rio Grande constructed a narrow gauge branch from Moffat to Crestone. Some of Crestone's commercial buildings remain standing. *(Denver Public Library x-7575)*

Crestone is not a ghost town and never has been completely abandoned despite some close calls. In fact, since it opened in 1880, its post office has operated continuously.

Crestone began when the Hopkins family constructed a home at the site in 1868. It evolved into a way station with a blacksmith shop to make repairs on wagons bound for new gold mines located to the south in the Baca Grant No. 4. As mining got under way, Crestone became the primary supply point. A boardinghouse opened and a small mill was constructed next to the town site to handle the gold ore. The boom lasted until around 1886, and by 1890, mining activity had slowed. Another boom followed as more veins of gold were discovered.

In 1886, the only legal tenant on the 100,000 acre Baca Grant No. 4 was rancher George H. Adams. All of the others were "squatters" who took what riches they could find. Adams purchased the entire property and won a court battle that recognized his mineral rights to all the land within the grant. In 1900, with the help of U.S. marshals, he had all the squatters on the grant evicted. The occupants of Duncan moved south and established a new camp called Liberty. As the gold ore was exhausted, Liberty was abandoned, and only Crestone, located just outside the Baca Grant's northern boundary, survived.

Mining continued within the Baca Grant No. 4. In 1901, the prospects apparently looked so good for continued operations that the Denver & Rio Grande formed a subsidiary railroad. It was called the Rio Grande Sangre de Cristo Railroad Company, and a narrow gauge line was completed from Moffat to Crestone running due east. At Crestone, the rails turned south along the base of the mountains ending at a turntable in Cottonwood. This line was abandoned in 1926, and the rails were removed in 1929.

By 1972, Crestone's population dropped to fewer than fifty people. Only a few houses were occupied throughout the year, and Crestone was about to

The schoolhouse in Crestone is well maintained and represents an architectural style typical of small country schools. *(Kenneth Jessen 109A5)*

become another Colorado ghost town. At this time, construction began on a major housing development called the Baca Grande. A lake was created, and up against the base of the mountains, luxurious homes began to appear along the old railroad grade, now named Camino Baca Grande. In 1972, the Baca Grande Inn opened, and in 1980, 300 acres were set aside for the Aspen Institute. Today, there are townhouses, a restaurant and conference center. The Baca Grant No. 4 also has become the home for non-traditional religions.

A bridge over Crestone Creek provides access to the back of this privately-owned log home. *(Kenneth Jessen 109A3)*

A new development is underway in the central portion of the old Baca Grant consisting of modest summer homes, some constructed with straw bales as the core material for outer walls. These new developments infused new energy and money into Crestone.

Although many of Crestone's historic structures have been lost over the years to floods, fires and windstorms, quite a few of the original buildings still remain. Many of them have been restored and are in use. Visitors to Crestone are given the feeling of how this old Colorado mining town once appeared.

Gladys Sisemore, *Drillin', Loadin' and Firin'*, self-published, Crestone, Colorado, 1983, pp. 11, 13, 18, 82-83.

Muriel Sibell Wolle, *Stampede to Timberline*, Sage Books, Chicago, Illinois, 1949, p. 300.

Tiv Wilkins, *Colorado Railroads*, Pruett Publishing Company, Boulder, Colorado, 1974, pp. 137, 215.

William H. Bauer, James L. Ozment and John H. Willard, *Colorado Post Offices*, Colorado Railroad Museum, Golden, Colorado, 1990, p. 40.

DUNCAN

Its Residents Evicted

- *Saguache County, Pole Creek drainage*
- *Access limited by private property*
- *Town had a post office; standing structures unknown*

Situated at the mouth of Pole Creek Canyon on the south side of Milwaukee Hill was the mining community of Duncan. The mines that supported the town were a mile or more up Pole Creek. The town was founded and promoted by John Duncan. He followed an old Indian trail into the San Luis Valley over Medano Pass and prospected for days during 1874. He finally discovered gold ore on Milwaukee Hill and constructed a single room cabin at the base of the hill.

Other prospectors, aware of Duncan's find, came into the area. Beginning in 1890, a town grew up around Duncan's cabin. John Duncan surveyed the town and sold lots at $25 each.

Duncan wanted to continue prospecting, and he turned the job of town promotion over to Charles Reed, owner and publisher of the *Duncan Eagle*. This was the camp's weekly newspaper, and it cost $1.50 a year. It presented a full report about activities in Duncan. Editor Charles Reed took sides in national politics and endorsed William Jennings Bryan for president of the United States in 1896. Bryan was quite popular in Colorado and ran on a ticket promoting the free coinage of silver in a fixed ratio to gold. Bryan lost the election.

In 1896, the first of a couple of stamp mills was constructed along Pole Creek to process the gold ore. The simple mills first crushed the ore. It was then treated either with potassium cyanide (to dissolve the gold) or with mercury (to amalgamate the gold).

The ore yielded an average of $30 a ton and cost $8 a ton to process.

The Duncan post office was established in 1892 and operated until 1900. Mail was delivered six days a week, and the population the post office served was listed as 250. The post office offered unique "ride through" service. A person on horseback could get the mail without dismounting. The boxes were at a height so that a rider could open the box from the outside without entering the building.

A variety of businesses once flourished in Duncan, including a dry goods store and two general merchandise stores. There was a freighting business, livery stable and lumberyard. The town also had two saloons. Mrs. P. M. Harper operated a boarding-house and charged 35 cents per meal or $6 a week for all meals. Services in Duncan included a physician, attorney-at-law, assayer and notary public.

A school district was formed in 1893 on behalf of the parents of eighteen students. The building was of log construction, and it served Duncan and Cottonwood. The last classes were held in 1899.

Duncan also established telephone service to Hooper by stretching a single line across the vast expanse of the San Luis Valley. Its installation was a community effort using money donated to purchase the poles and wire. When the telephone line was completed, everyone in Duncan took

The miners at Cottonwood and Duncan were evicted in 1900 based on a U.S. Supreme Court decision giving title to the owner of the Baca Grant where these towns were located. All of Duncan's structures were either razed or moved except John Duncan's cabin. Muriel Sibell Wolle took this photograph in 1942. *(Denver Public Library x-4983)*

turns talking to someone in Hooper.

Unfortunately, Duncan sat within the Baca Grant No. 4, and its occupants were squatters. The owner of the grant contended that he owned not only the grazing rights but also the mineral rights. In 1897, the legal battle ended in the U.S. Supreme Court. The court ruled in favor of the Baca Grant owner. The miners at Cottonwood and Duncan were evicted in 1900 by U.S. marshals. All of Duncan's structures were either razed or moved except John Duncan's cabin. Armed conflicts, minor in nature, resulted. Deputies were temporarily assigned to live in the Duncan area and to carry out court orders. Owners were compensated by the Baca Grant owner $125 per structure and were later allowed to buy back their structures for $10 with the provision that they be moved off the grant.

Duncan is no longer accessible by virtue of road closures and the development of the Baca Grant. The road that runs south to Cottonwood ends at Cottonwood Creek. A gate posted no trespassing blocks further progress. When historian Muriel Sibell Wolle made the trip with a guide in 1942, she remarked that from the south, the road was one of the worst she had ever been over. Only John Duncan's cabin stood at the time, and it was used by the U.S. Forest Service.

It might be noted that most of Pole Creek lay outside the Baca Grant, and a number of structures were built in this small canyon. Gladys Sisemore, in her book *Drillin', Loadin' and Firin',* details the names of the owners of these Pole Creek cabins. It is not known if any of these structures remain today since access to Pole Creek is restricted by private property.

For a map showing the location of Duncan, see "Cottonwood."

Gladys Sisemore, *Drillin', Loadin' and Firin'*, self-published, Crestone, Colorado, 1983, pp. 23-25.

Muriel Sibell Wolle, *Stampede to Timberline*, Sage Books, Chicago, 1949, pp. 304-308.

George Harlan, *Postmarks and Places*, Golden Bell Press, Denver, 1976, p. 56.

William H. Bauer, James L. Ozment and John H. Willard, *Colorado Post Offices*, Colorado Railroad Museum, Golden, Colorado, 1990, p. 117.

EMBARGO and SKY CITY

- *Saguache County, Embargo Creek drainage*
- *No access; private property*
- *Town had a post office; a number of structures remain*

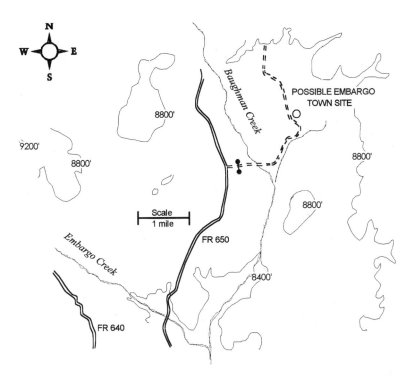

Embargo is probably located on Embargo Creek, however, a local landowner insists that Embargo was located north of the confluence of Embargo and Baughman creeks. A cluster of buildings that look much like a small town is located as indicated on this map.

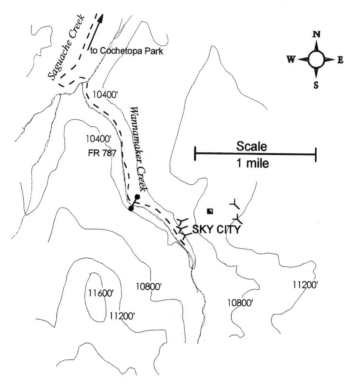

Sky City is so isolated that there aren't any towns anywhere near the site. To the north are Cochetopa Park and Colorado 114. In recent years, Sky City has been fenced off and posted no trespassing.

The Embargo town site is probably located along Embargo Creek near its confluence with Baughman Creek. The site is northwest of Del Norte and was another of the many short-lived mining camps in the area. Its location is in question, however, since historian Muriel Sibell Wolle placed the town site near the headwaters of Embargo Creek. She reported that only one cabin stood at the site. A local landowner, however, places Embargo quite a distance to the southeast near Baughman Creek. More than a half-dozen structures still stand in a shallow valley about a mile inside private property. A county road once served the town and now ends at the fence line.

Wolle's account of the town, however, has a ring of authenticity. It was based on an interview with George Baughman, who lived and worked there. Gold was discovered in Baughman Creek in 1878, but it wasn't until 1882 that any substantial amount of ore was discovered. A chunk of ore the size of a water bucket brought in many prospectors. Houses were placed on either side of the camp's main street. Those that had been constructed previously and were in the middle of the street were moved. Although Embargo didn't have a store, it did have a stable, sawmill and hotel. A post office was established in 1903 and closed in 1905.

The road Wolle traveled ended in Embargo. That being the case, this would have placed the town in Rio Grande County. Postal records, however, indicate it was located in Saguache County. In addition, many mines are in the vicinity of the "lower" Embargo, while up Embargo Creek, very few mines show on contemporary U.S.G.S. maps. Besides, if the town near the confluence of Embargo and Baughman creeks is not Embargo, what is it?

Sky City is one of the most remote ghost towns in Colorado. Sky City is on Wannamaker Creek not far from Embargo Creek, but over a divide. To reach the site requires a 38 mile drive over dirt roads. The trip is through grand country with high ridges,

These buildings are near the confluence of Embargo and Baughman creeks, and the landowner claims this is the ghost town of Embargo. This, however, disagrees with the account of the town's location presented by Muriel Sibell Wolle in *Stampede to Timberline*. (Kenneth Jessen 108D6)

vast open meadows, lava flows and deep canyons. The road also passes along the La Garita Wilderness boundary. Access is via Colorado 114 west of Saguache, then south through Cochetopa Park on FR 804, up FR 597 and over the Continental Divide. The road then descends into the beautiful, open Saguache Park with Chimney Rock off to one side. At the campground at Horse Canyon, the road continues as FR 787 and follows Saguache Creek south. After crossing Saguache Creek, the road follows Wannamaker Creek and ends at a locked gate. This last portion is quite rough and is not suitable for an automobile.

Tom Bowen named the camp, and constructed a road to the camp's mine. The tunnel failed to yield ore of sufficient value to justify continuing, and the small camp was quickly abandoned. The site was purchased and fenced during the mid-1990s. From the gate, two cabins can be seen, one log and the other made of milled lumber, plus a mine building sitting on the mine dump. No other dumps appear in the area. The Sky City Mine was founded on an isolated pocket of ore.

Muriel Sibell Wolle visited this site in 1948 at the upper part of Embargo Creek. This could very well be the ghost town of Embargo, but a local landowner insists it is located near the confluence of Embargo and Baughman creeks. *(Denver Public Library x-3171)*

Muriel Sibell Wolle, *Stampede to Timberline*, Sage Books, Chicago, 1949, pp. 316-317.

William H. Bauer, James L. Ozment and John H. Willard, *Colorado Post Offices*, Colorado Railroad Museum, Golden, Colorado, 1990, p. 51.

GARLAND CITY

It Lasted One Year

- *Costilla County, Sangre de Cristo Creek drainage*
- *Accessible via graded dirt road; site on private property*
- *Town had a post office; no structures remain*

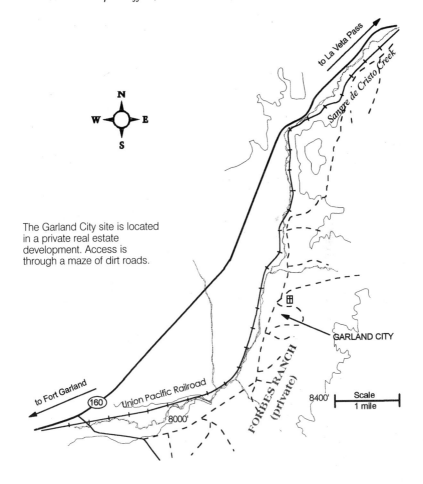

The Garland City site is located in a private real estate development. Access is through a maze of dirt roads.

This was a substantial town with well over 100 buildings and as many as 210 houses. For the Denver & Rio Grande, it was just another end-of-track town. At Garland City, the railroad constructed a substantial depot 110 feet long. The railroad called the place Mortimer.

The tracks reached Garland City in the summer of 1877, and most of its buildings and houses were thrown up in just a matter of weeks. Contemporary historian Virginia McConnell Simmons wrote that, "Hordes of people jostled through the rickety town, and wagons and teams filled the corrals. A dancing bear chained near one of the saloons added to the circus-like atmosphere."

Its most prominent hotel was the Perry House with five bedrooms. The beds, however, were in a long row with each "room" defined by a sheet hanging from the ceiling.

At the age of 30 days, Garland City had added several large warehouses, the McCoy & Haskell Hotel, the Garland Hotel, hardware store, general merchandise store, dry goods store, druggists and billiard hall. J. R. De Remer served as deputy sheriff. A star vocalist from New York City, Miss Julia Palmer, gave a concert, and a telegraph line was installed. The *Independent* moved its newspaper operation from La Veta to Garland City.

During its short life, the town had several murders, a number of knife fights and many shootings. A popular young man by the name of Morgan was one of those killed. A vigilante committee was organized and used masks to hide their faces. They kept the outbound train from leaving town until they could conduct a search of the passenger cars. They found a man they wanted to question and took him to the nearest tree or corral post. They hanged him by the neck four times and revived him between each hanging. They questioned him each time. The outcome is unknown.

By the end of August 1877, fifty businesses were in operation. In just one week, twenty-five houses were built. A banking company opened to handle the bullion from the San Juan mines brought to town by wagon for shipment to Denver. The brother-in-law of Buffalo Bill Cody, A. C. Jester, opened the Bank Exchange

Garland City was a substantial town with hundreds of structures. For the Denver & Rio Grande, it was just another end-of-track town, and the railroad constructed a substantial depot 110 feet long. The railroad called the place Mortimer. Garland City lasted only a year when the end of the track moved west. Some of its structures were moved to Alamosa. Nothing but a sagebrush-covered flat remains at the site today. *(Denver Public Library x-8585)*

Saloon. Dr. Blake was the town's physician. The liveliest and loudest place in town was the Fashion Concert Hall and Saloon. By September, the largest structure in Garland City was Kemp's Dance and Gambling Hall. It had a dozen rooms in the back for its "girls." Later, Kemp built a stage and hosted a troupe from Chicago to celebrate its opening.

Lobbying for women's suffrage was Lucy Stone, who passed through the town. Since there were virtually no women in Garland City, she drew quite a crowd. It was said that every idle man attended! Many of the men in the crowd had not seen a woman for some months, and she could have drawn a crowd by talking on virtually any subject.

W. C. MacLaughlin was wanted in Denver, and when confronted in Garland City, drew his revolver and fired two shots at Deputy Sheriff James Brophy. One bullet passed through the deputy's sleeve and the other nicked him in the neck. Brophy's return fire killed MacLaughlin instantly.

In June 1878, the narrow gauge Denver & Rio Grande reached Alamosa. This spelled the end of Garland City, home to an estimated 1,500 people. The post office closed on June 27. Joe Perry fed his boarders their breakfast at the Perry House and packed them a good lunch. That evening, he boasted he would serve them dinner in Alamosa. The hotel was put onto a flat car during the day and moved to the new town. The Broadwell and Occidental hotels also were moved along with the Gem Saloon. By mid-August, little was left of the once-great Garland City.

Mormon leader John Morgan arrived in Garland City during its last days and wrote, "...Garland begins to move forward, and on every hand we see men tearing down the frail wood structures with which it is built...Soon Garland will be a thing of the past and only battered oyster cans, cast off clothing, old shoes and debris generally will mark the site of where once stood a flourishing city."

Today, sagebrush covers the site. Not even the trace of a foundation or an indentation of where a street once ran can be seen. On the hillside overlooking the town is a small cemetery filled with smallpox victims lost during Garland City's only winter. Garland City is now on part of the Forbes Ranch, a high-end real estate development east of Fort Garland.

Henry A. Clausen, "La Veta Pass and Garland City," *1973 Brand Book Vol. XXIX*, Denver Westerners, Denver, Colorado, 1974, pp. 173-195.

Robert L. Brown, *Colorado Ghost Towns, Past and Present*, Caxton Printers, Caldwell, Idaho, 1977, pp. 105-108.

Virginia McConnell Simmons, *The San Luis Valley*, University Press of Colorado, Niwot, Colorado, 1999, p. 156.

William H. Bauer, James L. Ozment and John H. Willard, *Colorado Post Offices*, Colorado Railroad Museum, Golden, Colorado, 1990, p. 60.

HERARD

And The Skunk

- *Saguache County, Medano Creek drainage*
- *Accessible by four-wheel drive vehicle*
- *Town had a post office; remaining structures unknown*

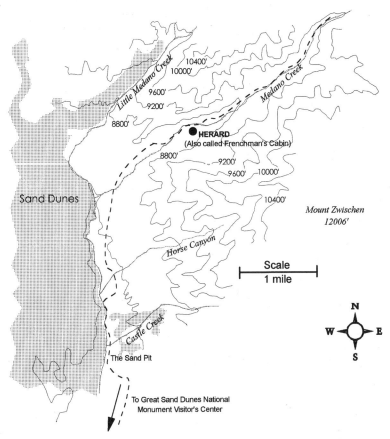

Herard's location was determined by U.S. Forest Service Map MF-22, R-2 published in 1931 combined with information from the National Park Service and a site survey.

Ulysses Herard and his family arrived in the Medano Creek area in 1875. A fish hatchery opened, and by the turn of the century, the Herard Ranch began raising thoroughbred horses in addition to cattle. The post office at Herard opened in 1905 and lasted until 1912. From that point on, the mail was delivered to Liberty.

One time, a skunk got into the Herard cabin. It was after dark and a coal oil lamp provided the only source of light. Herard first tried the gentle approach to remove the skunk by shooing it toward the cabin door. This didn't work so he tried a more direct approach. He got his revolver and fired it. The frightened skunk reacted by running behind the kitchen stove. Herard took aim at the animal and pulled the trigger a second time. The discharge blew out the lamp, and the bullet hit the unfortunate animal. In its dying act, it thoroughly saturated the Herard's kitchen. The girl his wife hired to help with housework couldn't stand the smell and returned to her home in Liberty. The Herards were forced to look for another place to live and ended up moving into their bunkhouse. It is

Between Medano Pass and the Herard site are three old cabins located in a high meadow. *(Kenneth Jessen SJ131)*

not known when the Herard cabin was fit to occupy again.

As Ulysses Herard became older, he lost his hearing. Cruel as it may seem, people called him, "Useless Hear Hard." He could not carry on a conversation without the other party using a pad of paper to write down his or her part of the conversation.

Herard had his problems with the U.S. Forest Service, but in an unusual way. A ranger ran off with Herard's wife, or she ran off with the ranger. Whichever the case, Ulysses Herard carried a Civil War vintage revolver to fend off any other rangers. To ranch in this remote area, however, grazing permits were required. Despite his threats, Herard had to get along with the Forest Service.

The road up Medano Creek starts from the campground entrance in the Great Sand Dunes National Monument. The Herard site requires four-wheel drive to reach, and in the soft sand, a number of vehicles have become stuck. The National Park Service, however, has placed plastic mats in the worst sand holes. In addition, three stream crossings are necessary to reach the site. At 6.2 miles beyond the end of the paved road is a place the Park Service calls Frenchman's Cabin. The ruins of a fireplace sit in a meadow, and this is where Herard was located. Farther up Medano Creek near the pass are the remains of three log cabins, presumably an old homestead.

Arthur H. Carhart, "Passes over the Blood of Christ," *1957 Brand Book*, Denver Westerners, Denver, Colorado, 1958, p. 193.

George Harlan, *Postmarks and Places*, Golden Bell Press, Denver, 1976, pp. 132-134.

William H. Bauer, James L. Ozment and John H. Willard, *Colorado Post Offices*, Colorado Railroad Museum, Golden, Colorado, 1990, p. 71.

HOOPER and MOFFAT
Failed Attempts at Farming

- *Alamosa and Saguache counties; San Luis Creek drainage*
- *Accessible via paved road; occupied sites*
- *Towns have a post office; several original structures remain*

Although there are a number of other abandoned or partially abandoned town sites in the area, Hooper lasted longer than the others. Originally called Garrison, it was founded in 1890 coincident with the arrival of the Denver & Rio Grande. The railroad constructed a depot and siding.

The Garrison post office opened in 1891 and changed its name to Hooper in 1896. The post office remains open today. A mercantile store and a branch of the Bank of Monte Vista formed Hooper's original business center. The town also had a Methodist Church and a newspaper.

Wheat was grown in the area leading to construction of a flour mill in 1892. A second mill followed, but the recession in 1893 caused wheat prices to fall. It was also the beginning of a drought. Soon, the bank failed, and the farmers began to move away.

Economic conditions improved, and the town made a comeback. The name change to Hooper was part of this revival. By the 1920s, irrigation water began to spell the end to farming in the area. Without natural drainage, salts began to work to the surface and sterilized the soil despite construction of drainage ditches.

There remained enough business by 1930 for the Denver & Rio Grande to convert its narrow gauge line to dual gauge using three rails. This allowed standard gauge cars to move north from Alamosa to Hooper. This line was abandoned and dismantled in 1959.

Moffat came close to becoming a town of great importance in the north-central part of the San Luis Valley. Historian Holly Rechel-Felmlee wrote about Moffat in 1980: "A cold wind blows through, swirling dust around old buildings. One can hear the swings on the playground squeaking and a loose door slamming open and shut. At each house, a dog barks, hailing arrivals. Most of the houses are closed tight." Little has changed today.

Only about a dozen homes are occupied. Rechel-Felmlee concluded, "There is so little life that a great horned owl perches daily in a second floor window without fear of harassment."

Moffat was founded in 1890 by the San Luis Town and Improvement Company, a subsidiary of the Denver & Rio Grande.

Moffat is a combination of occupied homes and abandoned buildings. This was probably the Baptist church; however, its cornerstone has been defaced. *(Kenneth Jessen 126B5)*

Operations were managed by David Adams, owner of the Baca Grant No. 4. He named the town for the railroad's president, David H. Moffat.

The year the town was founded, the Denver & Rio Grande completed its valley line from Villa Grove to Alamosa through the town. The last spike was driven on this narrow gauge line 17 miles north of Alamosa. During the early days, cattle supported the economy. Moffat had a brick hotel, a couple of general stores, three restaurants and its own newspaper, the *Moffat Ledger*.

In 1901, based on increased mining activity within the Baca Grant No. 4, a subsidiary of the Denver & Rio Grande constructed a 17-mile branch due east of Moffat to Crestone. At Crestone, the line turned south ending at Cottonwood. Development stagnated until 1908 when the Oklahoma Land and Colonization Company purchased a great deal of land in the area. They also constructed a hotel. The number of town lots in Moffat expanded to nearly 4,000, a figure almost impossible to believe based on a visit to the town.

The land was subdivided and sold off in tracts of up to 160 acres. Prospective buyers could purchase a ticket for a random drawing allowing them to bid on a particular piece of land. A crown estimated at 2,000 showed up for the drawing. People slept in tents, and hundreds of additional beds were brought into the hotel. Promises were made that each tract would have sufficient water. Like so many land promotion schemes, the company never fulfilled its promises.

For a while, Moffat boomed. Rail yards were constructed, and by 1911, the town had a bank, four hotels, lumberyards, livery stables, barbershops, two saloons, a doctor, its own town marshal, a jeweler and a Baptist church. School enrollment climbed, and all twelve grades were taught.

As predicted by newspapers of the day, what ended the dream for many was lack of water. The soil was good and crops grew well, but only with sufficient water. Farfetched plans for an irrigation district, with a large reservoir and many laterals, never materialized. The boom ended, and further attempts at land development failed. Without the water promised by the Oklahoma Land and Colonization Company, farmers sold their land. Much of the land reverted to open range. Salts leached up from the poorly-drained land and poisoned the crops. Moffat dwindled in size to only a few people.

Both Hooper and Moffat are located along Colorado 17.

Holly Rechel-Felmlee, "The Moffat Land Development of 1910," *The San Luis Valley Historian*, Volume XII, No. 1, 1980, pp. 15-21.

Tiv Wilkins, *Colorado Railroads*, Pruett Publishing Company, Boulder, Colorado, 1974, pp. 79, 222, 253, 267.

Virginia McConnell Simmons, *The San Luis Valley*, University Press of Colorado, Niwot, Colorado, 1999, pp. 231-233.

William H. Bauer, James L. Ozment and John H. Willard, *Colorado Post Offices*, Colorado Railroad Museum, Golden, Colorado, 1990, pp. 60, 74, 99.

JASPER
Absorbed the Town of Cornwall

- *Rio Grande County, Alamosa River drainage*
- *Accessible via graded dirt road; occupied site*
- *Town had a post office; several structures remain*

After the mining ended, Jasper became a ranching community as evidenced by this photograph taken after 1900. *(U.S. Geological Survey, J. F. Hunter 406)*

Gold was discovered along the Alamosa River on the west side of Silver Mountain on some undetermined date. In 1879, a small mining camp was formed named Cornwall. It got its own post office the same year. One source indicates that the town was founded by miners from Cornwall, England, who gave it its name. Another historical source indicates that the town was named for its first postmaster, John Cornwall. The Marion Gold Mining Company was organized to work the mines and provided most of the town's employment.

For reasons unknown, a separate community, named Jasper, grew up next to Cornwall. One could speculate that the developers of Cornwall may have asked too much for lots or that a disagreement took place over how Cornwall was managed. Cornwall was platted in 1881, and a year later, the town was merged into Jasper. The Cornwall post office also changed its name to Jasper.

The mines failed to produce enough ore to keep the town going. There was also the high cost of shipping ore to the nearest smelter from this remote region. Jasper lost its population to the point where the post office closed in 1910. Another mining company from Massachusetts opened a mill about 2.5 miles above Jasper, and the town again gained population. The post office reopened in 1913 in response to the operation at the mine and mill.

The mill closed in 1918 coincident with the closure of the Jasper post office. Jasper regained its population in 1920 possibly due to mining activity or an influx of people wanting to make this scenic little town their summer resort.

George Crofutt reported in his 1885 guidebook that Jasper had a population of 200. Crofutt also listed Cornwall, but made no mention of its close proximity to Jasper nor did Crofutt give a population figure. He said that mail was delivered on the back of a bronco and that the old wagon road was impassable beyond Cornwall.

Today, several log buildings stand along the road through Jasper. It is a neat old town and in a scenic location. Few modern structures have been added to disturb the feeling of an authentic Colorado mining town.

George A. Crofutt, *Crofutt's Grip-Sack Guide of Colorado*, 1885 Edition, Johnson Books, Boulder, Colorado, reprint 1981, pp. 84, 109.

Muriel Sibell Wolle, *Stampede to Timberline*, Sage Books, Chicago, 1949, p. 311.

Robert L. Brown, *Ghost Towns of the Colorado Rockies*, Caxton Printers, Caldwell, Idaho, 1977, pp. 189-192.

William H. Bauer, James L. Ozment and John H. Willard, *Colorado Post Offices*, Colorado Railroad Museum, Golden, Colorado, 1990, pp. 38, 80.

KERBER CITY, SEDGWICK, EXCHEQUER, PARKVILLE and CLAYTONIA

- *Saguache County, Kerber and Squirrel creek drainages*
- *Accessible by graded dirt road; some private property*
- *Some towns had post offices; one remaining structure*

One cabin remained at Claytonia in 1947 when ghost town historian Muriel Sibell Wolle took this photograph. The community of Claytonia was located near Kerber Creek west of Villa Grove on the road to Bonanza. *(Denver Public Library x-5144)*

The satellite towns around Bonanza are all gone and left few traces. Sedgwick still has its old Bonanza Mill, and only a U.S. Forest Service sign marks the location of Kerber City. The Forest Service saved and restored a cabin at Exchequer about a mile up the road from Bonanza. Only a mill foundation remains at Parkville. The Claytonia site is on private property limiting exploration.

All of these towns sprang up in 1880 and 1881 during the Bonanza boom years when thousands of prospectors were combing the hills looking for mineral wealth. Sedgwick was settled first and was laid out in July 1880. It grew to a population of 650. The town had the area's only brewery, and it also had a billiard hall, bowling alley, two dance halls and two hotels. Its post office opened in 1880, and in 1885, it was moved to Parkville.

Kerber City sat across from Sedgwick, and was located on the north side of Kerber Creek. Little is known about Kerber City, its size or its population.

Exchequer had a row of a dozen or so frame stores and homes on either side of Squirrel Creek. The town's population was supported by the Exchequer Mine, one of the first mines in the district. Exchequer's only industry was a small mill located near the creek. Prominent among the structures was the false-front Rathvon & Co. hardware, grocery and miner's supply store. Its post office was opened in 1881 and lasted for two years.

The U.S. Forest Service restored this cabin at Exchequer, located just beyond Bonanza. *(Kenneth Jessen 100D1)*

The post office in Parkville opened in 1885 after having been transferred from Sedgwick. It closed a year later. Parkville was a mill town with some mining in U. S. Gulch.

Claytonia was located up against the foothills between the Kerber Creek mining area and Villa Grove. Historian Muriel Sibell Wolle photographed the place showing a lone cabin. Claytonia dates back to 1881, but little else is known about it.

For a map showing the location of Kerber City, Sedgwick and Parkville, see "Bonanza."

Muriel Sibell Wolle, *Stampede to Timberline,* Sage Books, Chicago, 1949, pp. 297-298.

Virginia McConnell Simmons, *The San Luis Valley,* University Press of Colorado, Niwot, Colorado, 1999, pp. 180, 355.

William H. Bauer, James L. Ozment and John H. Willard, *Colorado Post Offices,* Colorado Railroad Museum, Golden, Colorado, 1990, pp. 53, 111, 130.

KLONDIKE, SPOOK CITY and BONITA

Remote Ghost Towns

- *Saguache County, Findley Gulch and Ford Creek drainages*
- *Accessible via dirt roads, Spook City requires four-wheel drive*
- *One camp had a post office; some remaining structures*

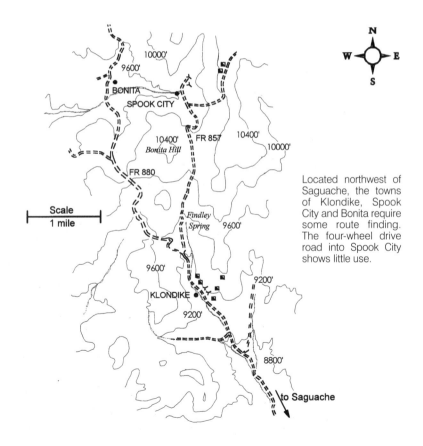

Located northwest of Saguache, the towns of Klondike, Spook City and Bonita require some route finding. The four-wheel drive road into Spook City shows little use.

174

These ghost towns are accessible by heading a short distance west from Saguache on Colorado 114, then turning north on 43 BB. The one remaining cabin at Klondike is on the west side of a small creek running through Findley Gulch at the base of the mountains. A tailing pile sits near the road marking the mine.

Beyond Klondike, the road splits at a wide meadow. FR 857 heads right and leads to Spook City, and FR 880 goes to Bonita.

FR 857 climbs beyond the meadow over a shallow pass at about 10,000 feet with a beautiful interlocking log fence. It then heads down a steep grade and begins to climb again. This road continues past a number of substantial mine tailing piles before coming to a dead end. At the point where FR 857 starts to climb, there is a faint road heading to the left across a small meadow. The road is so faint that hardly a trace of it can be seen in the grass, an indication that Spook City is not often visited. At the end of the meadow, the road drops down a steep, rock-strewn trail that requires four-wheel drive to get back up. Near the bottom of the grade in a dense stand of timber is a well-preserved cabin off to the left. Below it are the collapsed remains of a larger cabin and

Spook City requires some navigation to reach and is visited by few people. Several cabins remain at the site. *(Kenneth Jessen 108D3)*

the foundation of the third cabin. After the road reaches the bottom of the meadow beyond these cabins, it turns to the right. The meadow is "L" shaped and is surrounded by a dense stand of aspen trees. After passing a large tailing pile jutting out into the meadow there is a fourth cabin sitting off in the trees. This is Spook City, and it is about 1.5 miles from the FR 857/FR 880 intersection.

Spook City was founded in 1879-1880 and was still occupied as of 1894, according to an April 1894 article in the Denver *Republican.* The Lost Dickey claim was located by C. J. Hogue and Captain McGuire. They soon sold the claim. Assay results showed the ore to be very rich; 50 ounces of silver and 42 to 100 ounces of gold per ton. Another claim was named Spook and was possibly the origin of the town's name. Despite the excellent assay results, the claims were sold to a Danish syndicate for $5,000. The syndicate took over operations under the name Spook-Dickey Mining Company.

By following FR 880 beyond the Spook City turnoff, the road drops down to Ford Creek. After crossing Ford Creek, a cabin can be seen off to the right. Upon investigation, there are the collapsed remains of a second cabin marking the Bonita site. Unlike Spook City, there is little evidence of mining around Bonita, and the surrounding meadows seem more suitable for ranching.

Under the name "Bonito," Bonita got a post office in 1881, and it closed in 1883. All of these camps were established in the 1880s coincident with increased mining in the nearby Kerber Creek area. It is obvious that Spook City was the largest camp and was surrounded by the most active mines despite the fact that it did not have a post office. Little is known about the population of any of these remote sites or the extent of mining in the area.

Don and Jean Griswold, *Colorado's Century of "Cities,"* self-published, 1958, pp. 292-293.

Virginia McConnell Simmons, *The San Luis Valley,* University Press of Colorado, Niwot, Colorado, 1999, p. 180.

William H. Bauer, James L. Ozment and John H. Willard, *Colorado Post Offices,* Colorado Railroad Museum, Golden, Colorado, 1990, p. 22.

LA GARITA, CARNERO
and BIEDELL

- *Saguache County, Carnero Creek and Biedell Creek drainages*
- *Accessible via paved and graded dirt roads*
- *Each town had a post office; several remaining structures at one site*

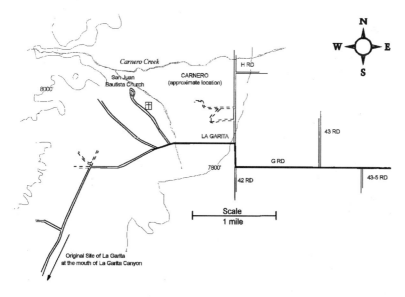

La Garita, its church and the Carnero site are located at the west end of G RD northwest of Center. The original La Garita site is to the south at the mouth of La Garita Canyon. The exact location of Biedell is unknown, but it was to the north of Carnero at or near the mouth of Biedell Creek.

La Garita was originally located at the mouth of La Garita Canyon about 3 miles southwest of the present town site. It was named by Spanish-speaking settlers for an Indian lookout. The settlers had traveled from El Rito, New Mexico, and established a plaza in 1858. At this time, Susano Trujillo and Domacio Espinoza brought in about 3,000 sheep. Crescencio Torres built a trading post at the plaza, and the location was sometimes referred to as Torres. Peace between the Indians and settlers was fragile, and in 1861 or 1862, the services of soldiers from Fort Garland were required. The town gained prominence with its location on the primary wagon road running north from Del Norte to Saguache.

The original church at La Garita burned in 1926 and was replaced by the present-day San Juan Bautista Church. *(Sonje Jessen SJ123)*

In the 1870s, enough Catholics were in the area to merit having the Jesuits at Conejos establish a separate parish with its headquarters at Carnero. The Church of St. John the Baptist was constructed near the site of the Carnero plaza in 1879, north of the original La Garita site. An adobe convent was built east of the church. This church burned and was replaced in 1926 by the present-day San Juan Bautista Church. The convent was abandoned in 1889 in favor of moving the headquarters south to Del Norte, and its ruins can be seen today east of the church near the cemetery. The church was discontinued in the 1960s, but is maintained as a craft studio. Its steeple supports a cross with four horizontal arms.

La Garita got a post office in 1874, but it was closed the following year. It reopened in 1886 only to close again in 1894. La Garita then moved from its original location north to a point east of the San Juan Bautista church. Its post office reopened in 1897 in its new location and remained open until 1972. At some point around the turn of the twentieth century, José Gay became postmaster. For a while, La Garita at its new site was known as Gaytown.

Carnero (meaning sheep or mutton) is an abandoned town site north of La Garita on the south bank of Carnero Creek. After La Garita moved from the mouth of La Garita Creek and was established within a mile of Carnero, La Garita took over as the region's economic center.

Carnero got its start in 1858 or 1859 when the Espinoza brothers and Santiago Manchego brought more sheep into the area. The town got a post office in 1870, and it lasted 6 years. It opened again in 1880 and lasted another four years before being closed. It can be assumed that at this time Carnero's population had moved the short distance to La Garita. It is not known what remains at the Carnero site.

Biedell, founded in 1881 on Crystal Hill, was located north of the Carnero-La Garita area possibly at the mouth of Biedell Creek. A post office was opened at Biedell in June 1883, but it was moved to Carnero in August the following year. Biedell was also referred to as Crystal Hill.

The camp was founded by Mark Biedell, who owned mining property in Silverton and Bonanza. He had owned land in the lower La Garita Creek area in the 1860s and then sold it. Something brought him back, and in 1881, he struck a vein of silver ore. Another account of this discovery was that a sheepherder made the discovery. He worked for Biedell and told him where the lode was located. Biedell rewarded the man by giving him a wagon, a team of horses and about $200 so he could return to his family in New Mexico.

Near Biedell were two mines, the Buckhorn and the Esperanza. The latter went into production in 1883.

Another small camp in the area was called El Carnero. It had two mines, the Spring Chicken and the Humbolt. Historian Virginia McConnell Simmons mentions yet another mining camp in the same region called Bellevue. It apparently lasted only a year, but had a newspaper called the *Crystal Hill Pilot*. The exact location of these camps is uncertain, but it is likely they were in the Biedell Creek area. There are mines shown at the head of Biedell Creek on contemporary maps, and no doubt, the camps were located close by.

Frank White, *La Garita*, self-published, La Jara, Colorado, 1971, p. 22.

Luther E. Bean, *Land of the Blue Sky People*, Sixth Edition, self-published, 1975, p. 55.

Muriel Sibell Wolle, *Stampede to Timberline*, Sage Books, Chicago, 1949, pp. 309-310.

Virginia McConnell Simmons, "Hispanic Place Names of the San Luis Valley," *The San Luis Valley Historian*, Volume XXIII, Number 3, Alamosa, Colorado, 1991, p. 9.

Virginia McConnell Simmons, *The San Luis Valley*, University Press of Colorado, Niwot, Colorado, 1999, pp. 183-184, 257, 259-260, 306.

William H. Bauer, James L. Ozment and John H. Willard, *Colorado Post Offices*, Colorado Railroad Museum, Golden, Colorado, 1990, pp. 19, 30.

LA JARA, CAPULIN
and CENTRO

- *Conejos County, La Jara Creek and Alamosa River drainages*
- *Accessible via paved and graded dirt roads*
- *Towns had post offices; some original structures remain*

The original town of La Jara was located 6 miles west of the present-day town and on the south side of La Jara Creek, not far from Capulin. The site is void of structures. La Jara was founded in 1870. Only nine taxpayers were on the books, but by 1875, the list had grown to forty-one.

La Jara got its own post office in 1875 under the name "Lajara." The post office was moved to the Newcomb ranch in 1884, where it remained for two years. When the Denver & Rio Grande constructed its line south to Antonito in 1880, a station was established under the name El Tanque or "the tank" east of La Jara. Under the name La Jara Station, it got its own post office in 1884. At this time, people in the old town of La Jara began to move to La Jara Station, and the original town was abandoned.

The early settlement of Capulin today is an occupied town with some abandoned structures. It is 8 miles west of the present-day town of La Jara. Farmers diverted water from the Alamosa River in 1862 for their crops. In 1867, a group led by Hipolito Romero moved from Ojo Caliente, New Mexico, and established the town of Capulin.

An adobe church was built in 1878, and the town had a Penitente morada a mile to the north. The small community gained a store in 1881, when a post office was opened. The post office remained in operation until 1922.

The town site of Capulin was platted in 1909. St. Joseph's Church was built in 1912 a mile south of the original Capulin chapel and remains standing today. Benedictine nuns taught at the town school for several years. Capulin also had a workers' protective association called the Sociedad Proteccion Mutura de Tabajodores Unidads.

To the west of Capulin was a small community called El Centro, now simplified on maps as Centro. A two-story school, called the Hot Creek School, was constructed south of Centro on Hot Creek. A junkyard dominates the town site today.

La Jara is located halfway between Alamosa and Antonito on U. S. 285. Capulin and Centro are west of La Jara on Colorado 15.

Virginia McConnell Simmons, "Hispanic Place Names of the San Luis Valley," *The San Luis Valley Historian*, Volume XXIII, Number 3, Alamosa, Colorado, 1991, pp. 8, 23.

Virginia McConnell Simmons, *The San Luis Valley*, University Press of Colorado, Niwot, Colorado, 1999, pp. 255, 258, 263, 277.

William H. Bauer, James L. Ozment and John H. Willard, *Colorado Post Offices*, Colorado Railroad Museum, Golden, Colorado, 1990, pp. 28, 84, 104.

LAS MESITAS, MOGOTE, PAISAJE and CAÑON

- *Conejos County, Conejos River drainage*
- *Accessible by paved and graded dirt roads; partially-occupied sites*
- *Towns had post offices; some original structures remain*

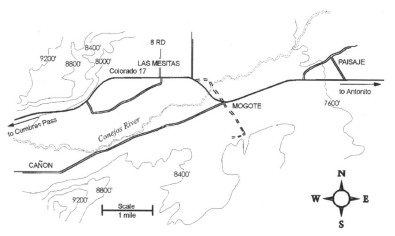

Paisaje, Mogote and Las Mesitas are located along Colorado 17 west of Antonito. Cañon is located along a side road.

A t Las Mesitas, along Colorado 17, is a burned-out church, a few homes, and little else. Las Mesitas is located on the northwest side of the Conejos River about 5 miles west of Antonito. The town's origins go back to 1856 when Juan de Dio Ruybal from Jacoma, New Mexico, came into the area. As the town grew, adobe homes were constructed, and by 1870, twenty-three tax-paying citizens were listed. The original church at Las Mesitas was dedicated to San Ysidro, and in 1919, a more substantial structure replaced the original church. Fire gutted the building in 1975, and it stands as a magnificent ruin on the north side of the highway. According to historian Virginia McConnell Simmons, the church bell was cast of silver and was formerly used at Conejos. The bell was made from jewelry, silverware and coins donated by the parishioners.

Mogote is 1 mile southeast of Las Mesitas and also along Colorado 17. Like Las Mesitas, it was also settled in 1856. Juan Jaramillo from the Chama Valley in New Mexico was among the first in the area. The name of the town came from the mountain peaks to the west that look like stacks of corn.

Mogote had several stores, including a fort-like trading post. It grew into a community of 350 people. In the 1880s, a Presbyterian mission school was constructed, and the school remained in operation until the 1970s. The Presbyterians also constructed a church.

Although Las Mesitas failed to get its own post office, one opened in Mogote in 1897. It remained in operation until 1920 when the population of the area began to decline.

San Rafael was the original name for Paisaje. Located 2 miles west of Antonito, San Rafael was established in 1856. The Velasquez, Chacon, Romero, Gallego and Trujillo families were among its original settlers. By 1870, the tax rolls showed 27 tax-payers. Our Lady of Guadalupe parish was constructed in 1859 and dedicated to San Rafael. The present-day church replaced the original structure in 1929. A Presbyterian mission school was established at the town in 1890.

The San Rafael post office opened in 1890 and in 1895, it closed. In 1906, it reopened under the new name, Paisaje, and remained open until 1920. Unfortunately, San Rafael is noted as the home of the worst serial killers in Colorado history, the Espinosas.

Located along a secondary road parallel to Colorado 17 on the south side of the Conejos River is the town site of Cañon. There are a number of modern homes in the area mixed with abandoned adobe buildings. Today, there is no distinct town center. The settlement predates 1871, and it had a school.

At Las Mesitas along Colorado 17 is this burned out church, a few homes, and little else. Fire gutted the structure in 1975. The origins of Las Mesitas date back to 1856. *(Sonje Jessen SJ100)*

Virginia McConnell Simmons, "Hispanic Place Names of the San Luis Valley," *The San Luis Valley Historian*, Volume XXIII, Number 3, Alamosa, Colorado, 1991, p. 33.

Virginia McConnell Simmons, *The San Luis Valley*, University Press of Colorado, Niwot, Colorado, 1999, pp. 276, 291, 304.

William H. Bauer, James L. Ozment and John H. Willard, *Colorado Post Offices*, Colorado Railroad Museum, Golden, Colorado, 1990, pp. 99, 109, 128.

LASAUSES
Named For The Willows

- *Conejos County, Conejos River drainage*
- *Accessible by graded dirt road*
- *Town had a post office; several structures remain*

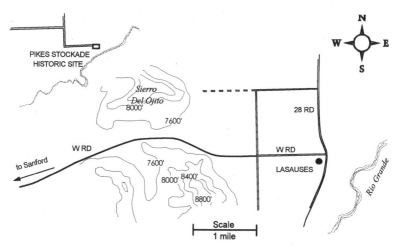

Lasauses is located east of Sanford near the Rio Grande on 28 RD. It is one of the most remote abandoned town sites in the San Luis Valley.

L asauses is located east of Sanford near the Rio Grande where W RD intersects the north-south 28 RD. The abandoned town site is one of the most remote in the San Luis Valley and was originally called La Plaza de Los Sauses, referring to the willows along the Rio Grande. Nearby was Stewart's Crossing, where a ferry across the Rio Grande began operation in 1863. The irrigation ditch in the area dates to 1866. Lasauses grew to include twenty-three taxpayers by 1871. An adobe church was constructed in

1880, dedicated to San Antonio de Padua. It was destroyed by fire and replaced by the structure that remains standing today. An Assembly of God church also was located in this village.

In 1882, the town got its own post office under the name Los Sauses, but it closed the following year. The name was changed to La Sauses when the post office reopened in 1890, and in 1895, the town's name was changed to Lasauses. The post office remained active until 1920, when the town's population began to decline.

One family remains at the site. The picturesque ruin of the Martinez Grocery Store sits on the west side of the road across from the abandoned church.

The Martinez grocery store stands as a reminder of better days in Lasauses. *(Sonje Jessen SJ107)*

Virginia McConnell Simmons, "Hispanic Place Names of the San Luis Valley," *The San Luis Valley Historian*, Volume XXIII, Number 3, Alamosa, Colorado, 1991, p. 29.

Virginia McConnell Simmons, *The San Luis Valley*, University Press of Colorado, Niwot, Colorado, 1999, pp. 226, 293.

William H. Bauer, James L. Ozment and John H. Willard, *Colorado Post Offices*, Colorado Railroad Museum, Golden, Colorado, 1990, pp. 86, 91.

LIBERTY

And Its Tragedy Filled History

- *Saguache County, Short Creek drainage*
- *No access to site; site on private property*
- *Town had a post office; remaining structures unknown*

Liberty's false-front saloon is on the right and Loco Bill's cabin is on the left. Loco Bill was a hermit and possibly Liberty's last occupant. The photograph was taken in 1942 by Muriel Sibell Wolle. *(Denver Public Library x-3690)*

A few settlers began to arrive in the Short Creek area during the 1880s. The real influx of people came in 1900 when those who lived within the Baca Grant No. 4 were evicted under court order by U.S. marshals. Some of the displaced miners at Duncan moved their cabins south just outside the grant and founded the new town of Liberty (also called Short Creek). A post office was established in 1900 in the home of one of the settlers. The post office was eventually moved to the general store and remained open until 1921 when the town was, for the most part, abandoned.

Unfortunately for the miners, the Baca Grant No. 4 included most of the productive gold-bearing ore. After their eviction, it was predicted in the *Saguache Crescent* that the miners would be able to return to their mines and operate on a lease basis. The mineral rights were sold, and the new company would not allow any of the squatters to return to the grant.

A number of claims were filed outside the grant, but most of the lodes contained only low-grade ore. At the mouth of Short Creek Canyon, however, a stamp mill was built. Later, a larger mill was built to process ore from a group of mines called the Liberty Lodes.

Most of the miners worked for the Cripple Creek-Chicago Mining & Milling Company. The company sent a representative one Christmas to distribute the payroll in the form of new paper bills. The representative also brought fancy candied fruits and cheese for the miners and their families. The wives received cologne and chocolates, and the men received cigars and liquor. The children received games. This nice gesture on the part of the mining company brightened the lives of those who toiled under-ground in less than ideal working conditions.

Liberty's newspaper was the *New Distributor.* Besides a grocery store, Liberty also had a hotel, barber shop, bakery, shoe store and livery stable. A school was started in 1906 and remained active until 1919. Church services were held in the schoolhouse. Saturday night dances provided entertainment.

Not only was Liberty short-lived, it was a town filled with tragedy. One December afternoon, Charlie Thompson was forced at gunpoint to crawl down Crestone's main street while barking like a dog. Liberty's town bully, Jim Stewart, held the gun and did this to humiliate Thompson. Stewart was a big man and had an ugly disposition. After Stewart grew tired of tormenting Thompson, he returned to Liberty. His cabin was along Sand Creek above the town.

After the passage of nearly a week, Charlie Thompson's hatred of Stewart grew to the point where he rode up the trail toward Stewart's cabin. Thompson hid behind two large pine trees and waited. Eventually, he heard someone coming down the trail. It was Stewart going down to Liberty to get his mail. As Stewart passed by the trees, Thompson stepped out and used a shotgun to blast Stewart off of his horse. Stewart was badly wounded with a large hole in his side. Thompson rode away quickly. When he reached a ranch in the valley, he stopped to rest his horse. He also confessed his crime to a rancher. The rancher persuaded Thompson to go back to Crestone and surrender.

Later in the day, a teenage boy came up the trail looking for stray cattle when he came across Stewart's saddle horse standing in a thicket. As the boy approached the horse, he heard a voice call out for help. The boy found the wounded man and ran back to Liberty to get help. Stewart was taken to Liberty where he died from his wound. Charlie Thompson was later tried for the murder of Jim Stewart.

Another incident occurred when George Boggs, believed to be mentally unbalanced, knocked on the door of the Charles Boyd home in Liberty a short distance from the cabin occupied by Boggs. Boyd's wife anticipated trouble. After her husband left for work, she nailed the door shut. Boggs broke down the door and fatally wounded her with a .44-caliber revolver. Every effort was made by the local physician to save her, but she and her unborn child died. Boggs returned to his cabin, put the barrel of the gun in his mouth, and blew his brains out.

In a robbery attempt, the cabin of Goldmittcher was ripped apart and set fire. Goldmittcher dug himself out from the burning rubble and headed to his barn. The thief believed that Goldmittcher kept a large sum of cash in his cabin. Instead, the money was in the barn, and Goldmittcher gathered it up. He crawled half a mile down to a neighbor's cabin where his wounds and burns were cared for. He stayed with the family at the cabin for the winter. Goldmittcher returned to his property in the spring to gather up the rest of his things. He paid his neighbors a generous sum, went to a Liberty saloon, and downed a large schooner of beer. He was

never seen again.
When ghost
town historian
Muriel Sibell Wolle
visited Liberty in
1942, she hired a
guide. The road
had deteriorated
to the point where
a great deal of skill
was required to
come within walk-
ing distance of the

The real influx of people came to Liberty in 1900 when those living within the Baca Grant No. 4 were evicted under a U.S. Supreme Court order. Some of the displaced miners in Duncan moved their cabins south just outside the grant and founded the new town. *(Denver Public Library x-4200)*

site. In addition, she had to get permission from the San Luis Valley Land & Cattle Company to cross their property.

At the time of her visit, a number of structures remained at Liberty. In her words, "Hung on the outside of a good-sized cabin was a collection of skulls and bones from horses, steers and sheep. Beyond was a little clearing in the trees, on one side of which was a small, false-fronted cabin which was once the post office and in which, Jim (her guide) told us a harmless lunatic had lived until recently...Across from the cabin ran Short Creek, narrow but clear, and in the midst of the tangle of bushes and trees...stood a large wooden water wheel with a small cabin nearby...A few houses were standing, but their doors and windows were gone and their roofs sagged." According to Wolle, many of Liberty's structures were moved to Crestone after Liberty was abandoned.

Liberty is on private property, and there is no public access to the town site. It is not known if any of its structures remain.

For a map showing its location, see "Cottonwood."

George Harlan, *Postmarks and Places*, Golden Bell Press, Denver, 1976, pp. 141-150.

Muriel Sibell Wolle, *Stampede to Timberline*, Sage Books, Chicago, 1949, pp. 303-304.

William H. Bauer, James L. Ozment and John H. Willard, *Colorado Post Offices*, Colorado Railroad Museum, Golden, Colorado, 1990, p. 89.

LOS CERRITOS, RINECONES, ESPINOSA, LA ISLA, MANASSA and EPHRAIM

- *Conejos County, Conejos River drainage*
- *Accessible via graded dirt roads and paved roads; some private property*
- *Some sites had post offices; a number of original structures remain*

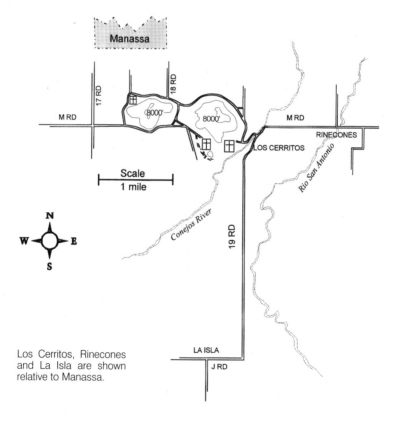

Los Cerritos, Rinecones and La Isla are shown relative to Manassa.

On the east side of two volcanic cones and located on the Conejos River was the town of Los Cerritos. There are two large cemeteries located near the town site on the south side of the two cones. Nothing remains of Los Cerritos except for faint evidence in a small flat area near the river.

Juan Maria Garcia and Pablita Martinez arrived in the area in 1852, but they were soon driven out by Indians. Others came into the area and established a plaza called La Plaza de Los Cerritos meaning the plaza by the small hills. The name was simplified and changed to Los Cerritos. By 1870, the place had 31 tax-paying citizens, and later, Mormon settlers joined the Spanish-speaking settlers. The settlement had both Mormon and Catholic churches and supported a school and store. It also had a dance hall and saloon. A flour mill was constructed between Los Cerritos and Manassa. In 1889, the town got a post office, which lasted until 1914. At this point, the town was slowly abandoned.

Another abandoned town site is east of Los Cerritos and east of the Conejos River near the San Antonio River. Its name was Rinecones (Spanish for the corners). Having traveled from El Rito, New Mexico, Afencio Trujillo trapped in the area in 1847 and noticed the good soil and abundant supply of water for irrigation. He returned the following year to raise crops, and in 1849, he settled at Rinecones. By 1870, twenty-three taxpayers were listed in the county records.

The Salazar family now lives and farms at the site. Most noted among its family members is present-day Colorado Attorney General Ken Salazar.

This abandoned church sits at the Espinosa town site along 17 RD between Manassa and Lobatos. *(Kenneth Jessen 121B8)*

The Salazars were among many settlers who originally came north from Chamita, New Mexico.

Espinosa was originally called Los Fuerticitos de Incarnacion Espinosa or "little fort." The town site is located 2.5 miles south of Manassa. The fortification along a small creek just north of the Conejos River was for protection against the Indians. A chapel was constructed in 1919 dedicated to Santo Nino, and it now stands abandoned at the town site. Also, the town had a school, dance hall and store, all constructed of adobe. Espinosa served a population of about 400 and was still a viable community into the 1940s. Its population moved to other more successful towns, and it slowly died. *For a map showing the location of Espinosa, see "Antonito."*

The abandoned town site of La Isla or "the island" was located south of Los Cerritos in an area between the Rio San Antonio and the Conejos River. It was essentially an island of land between the streams. At the site was a plaza and chapel dedicated to San José. La Isla had thirty-five tax-paying residents listed in 1870. The San José ditch provided water to area farms.

This old farmhouse is located between Los Cerritos and Rinecones. *(Sonje Jessen SJ105)*

Celedonio (also spelled Seledonio) Valdez was one of the primary land owners and petitioned for property within the Conejos Grant. Like other early settlers in this area, he was originally from New Mexico. He settled at La Isla in 1854, and his large land holdings gave him the title of La Isla de Don Seledonio Valdez. One local legend has that $60,000 in gold bars were recovered from the Valdez home when it was razed in the 1930s. At one time, a school near La Isla served the Rinecones-Los Cerritos area. Private property limits exploration of the site.

Although not a ghost town, it is worth noting the history of Manassa, one of the area's most prominent towns. Mormon settlers founded the town in 1879 and named it for a son of Israelite Joseph. The original settlers were headed by church leader John Morgan. The town quickly grew to 400. The Mormons met with opposition from the Spanish-speaking settlers in the area over water rights. The latter dammed the Conejos River upstream to prevent the Mormon farms from becoming successful. Eventually, the issue of water rights was settled.

The most noted resident of Manassa was heavyweight boxing champion Jack Dempsey known as the "Manassa Mauler." Through hard work, the Mormons eventually earned the respect of those in the San Luis Valley.

The Mormons made an unsuccessful attempt northeast at Ephraim. It was established in 1881, but its 150 residents found that the land was poorly drained and not suitable for farming. The town was abandoned between 1886 and 1888.

Virginia McConnell Simmons, "Hispanic Place Names of the San Luis Valley," *The San Luis Valley Historian*, Volume XXIII, Number 3, Alamosa, Colorado, 1991, pp. 16-17, 22-23, 28.

Virginia McConnell Simmons, *The San Luis Valley*, University Press of Colorado, Niwot, Colorado, 1999, pp. 222, 226-227, 298.

William H. Bauer, James L. Ozment and John H. Willard, *Colorado Post Offices*, Colorado Railroad Museum, Golden, Colorado, 1990, p. 91.

MESITA, EASTDALE, JAROSO, GARCIA and COSTILLA

- *Costilla County, Costilla Creek drainage*
  (Costilla, originally in Colorado, is now in New Mexico)
- *Accessible by paved and graded dirt roads; partially occupied*
- *Some towns had post offices; a number of original structures remain*

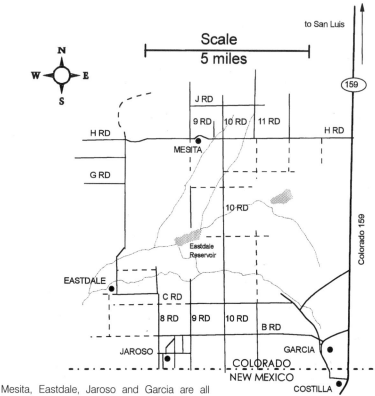

Mesita, Eastdale, Jaroso and Garcia are all located near the New Mexico border and are accessible via graded dirt roads or paved roads.

M esita, sitting alone on a vast flat prairie, seems quite isolated today, but at one time the town was served by a railroad. The San Luis Southern originated in Blanca to the north and terminated at the Colorado-New Mexico line at Jaroso. Mesita got its own post office in 1910. As of 1989, the post office was still open, although the town had been nearly abandoned. There is a well-defined business district with several abandoned stores. A Latter-day Saints church (Mormon) dominates the town, and several homes, constructed of dark volcanic stone, remain occupied. Ruins of other stone structures surround the area.

Mesita was one of the communities developed within the old Sangre de Cristo Grant by the Costilla Estate Development Company. This company also laid out the towns of San Acacio and Jaroso. The town was originally called Hamburg for a town by the same name in Iowa. It grew to several hundred people and had a bank and school. Volcanic scoria is mined near Mesita, but otherwise ranching and farming dominate its economy.

Eastdale, northwest of Jaroso, was one of the last Mormon settlements in the San Luis Valley. Beginning in 1879, Mormon settlers began to move into the valley and took up claims. They established a number of successful communities such as

The tracks are still in place in front of the abandoned depot at Mesita indicating that this photograph was taken around 1957 when the line was abandoned. Mesita was the largest shipping point south of Blanca at one time. *(Denver Public Library x-12320)*

Manassa, Richfield and Sanford. As the best-irrigated land became scarce, settlers attempted to establish settlements elsewhere. Eastdale, on the Costilla Creek, was cut off from the other Mormon communities. Only sporadic ferry service across the Rio Grande east of Antonito allowed families to visit the other Mormon towns. The Eastdale colony constructed a reservoir and canal to irrigate their crops. They purchased two flour mills in San Luis to process their wheat. Self-reliant, they fired their own bricks to build their church and school. Eastdale also had a store and, in 1895, a post office. The post office remained open until 1909 when the town was abandoned. Farmers could not raise enough to pay the debt on the land. Most moved and joined settlers in the more successful Mormon towns. Only a flower-covered meadow, a single cabin and the crumbing walls of an adobe structure remain at the ghost town of Eastdale.

Jaroso is just north of the Colorado-New Mexico line and was the southern terminus for the San Luis Southern in 1910. A year later, Jaroso got its own post office. As of 1989, it was still open, although most of the town is abandoned. The general region was settled by Spanish-speaking people from New Mexico calling it El Bosque de los Caballos (wooded area where horses ranged), and Jaroso grew to become the trade center. In 1910, the Seventh Day Adventist Church had an academy and experimental farm at Jaroso. Its post office opened in 1911. The Great Depression of the 1930s took its toll on Jaroso, and the town was partially abandoned.

Today, the main street is well defined by rows of abandoned buildings. A row of mature evergreens in the center of the street gives Jaroso a unique look in this arid part of the valley. The old Jaroso Hotel is especially interesting with vines growing on one of its walls. A modern grain elevator sits on the south edge of the town, and some of the old sheds along the town's main street are used to store farm machinery.

Garcia is spread out immediately west of Colorado 159 at the Colorado-New Mexico border. It is located on the west side of

Costilla Creek and has a number of abandoned adobe buildings. There are also two fine churches within the town. Garcia has a number of residents, and their private property rights should be respected when investigating the town's old buildings.

Garcia is the oldest settlement in Colorado. It dates back to 1849 when two brothers, Manuel and Pedro Manzanares, brought their families into the area to settle on the Sangre de Cristo Grant. They built La Plaza de Los Manzanares, and a ditch was dug in 1854 to bring water to the farms from Costilla Creek. Mail was delivered to Costilla to the south until 1901 when Garcia got a post office located in a store operated by the Garcia brothers. In 1915, the post office and town took the name Garcia.

Garcia attracted a number of religions. A chapel for Catholic services was constructed early in the town's history. Missionaries from the Presbyterian, Methodist and Pentecostal churches were all represented in Garcia. There also was a Penitente morada (meeting place).

Jaroso's hotel stands as a reminder of the town's better days. It was the southern terminus for the San Luis Southern that was constructed from Blanca in 1910. A year later, Jaroso got its own post office. As of 1989, it was still open although much of the town was abandoned. *(Kenneth Jessen 121B4)*

Costilla, the largest town in the area, is located south of Garcia. It is a historical oddity since Costilla was once within Colorado. In fact, Costilla County is named for this town. When Colorado became a territory in 1861, the 37th parallel was its southern border, and Costilla was within Colorado.

One of two well-maintained churches in Garcia. *(Sonje Jessen SJ104)*

Early surveys often were inaccurate. An official survey in 1869 by the U.S. Government proved that the 37th parallel was north of Costilla.

The first settlers came into the Costilla area in 1848. Those with titles to claims within the Sangre de Cristo Grant arrived the following year. Costilla got its own post office in 1862, one of the earliest in Colorado, although the town is now in New Mexico.

Virginia McConnell Simmons, "Hispanic Place Names of the San Luis Valley," *The San Luis Valley Historian*, Volume XXIII, Number 3, Alamosa, Colorado, 1991, pp. 18, 20, 30.

Virginia McConnell Simmons, *The San Luis Valley*, University Press of Colorado, Niwot, Colorado, 1999, pp. 223-234, 239, 249, 280, 294, 285-286.

William H. Bauer, James L. Ozment and John H. Willard, *Colorado Post Offices*, Colorado Railroad Museum, Golden, Colorado, 1990, pp. 38, 48, 59, 98.

MILTON

Loses Battle for County Seat

- *Saguache County, Saguache Creek drainage*
- *Accessible via graded dirt road; site on private property*
- *Town did not have a post office; several structures remain*

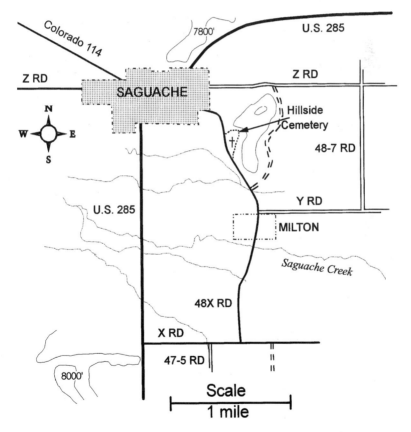

Milton was located just south of the Hillside Cemetery. There are two old buildings sitting on private property at the site, and they can be seen from 48X RD.

A little over a mile southeast of Saguache on 48X RD was the town of Milton. It was abandoned many years ago, and some of its buildings were moved to Saguache. This includes three homes and the Saguache Methodist Church. The site where Milton was located is now part of a ranch, and two of its structures can be seen from 48X RD. One of the buildings is a two-story, false-front hotel.

Milton was started by Absolm Pumphrey who platted the town in 1870 or 1871. He named it for his eldest son. Pumphrey arrived in the Saguache area and built a home on the site around 1867. A hotel and store also were constructed to form the nucleus for a town. A large two-story structure served as the general merchandise store on the ground floor and hotel on the second floor, according to an 1873 account. A visitor to Milton described it as having two small log cabins, some adobe homes and a school.

For a brief time, Milton was a competitor of Saguache. Residents of Milton had high hopes in 1873 when there was a general election for the location of the county seat. Saguache had been the county seat since 1866, but apparently there was renewed interest in the issue.

Otto Mears, Saguache's leading citizen, attempted to bribe John Lawrence into buying the Spanish-speaking people's vote on the county seat issue for $500. Another story relates how one person brought in fifty votes in favor of Saguache. When asked where he got fifty votes, he said that he "voted his oxen." In any event, Saguache retained its title as county seat.

A racetrack south of Milton was the town's most noted feature. Horse racing was the major talk in both Milton and Saguache. Johnny O'Neil arrived in the area in 1873 and became a jockey for John Lawrence and Absolm Pumphrey. On Christmas Day 1877, the black mare Dolly Slane came to race Red Buck, a mahogany gelding owned by Pumphrey. Red Buck was to be ridden by Johnny O'Neil. Red Buck's trainer, however, had laid down some heavy bets on Dolly Slane and asked O'Neil to pull back during the race to assure a win for Dolly Slane. This conversation was overheard and passed on to Pumphrey. Pumphrey's reaction was to draw a gun, point it at O'Neil and threaten that if he did anything to throw the race, his days would be over. Red Buck won by a comfortable margin.

Red Buck won every race entered until 1880 when the

Once located in Milton, this church was moved to Saguache in 1885 to 6th and Christy Avenue and now serves as the Methodist Church. *(Kenneth Jessen 126B6)*

horse was beaten by Little Casino. A lot of money had been bet on Red Buck by Milton and Saguache residents amounting to an estimated $8,000 to $10,000.

Loss of the horse race and the county seat put an end to Milton, and people began to move away. Virginia McConnell Simmons, however, places the blame on marshy soil conditions around Milton. Absolm Pumphrey sold the town site in 1881. After changing hands many times, George Woodard became its owner. It has remained in the Woodard family for some years.

John M. Woodard, "Milton, Colorado," *The San Luis Valley Historian*, Vol. XXIII, No. 4, Alamosa, Colorado, 1991, pp. 5- 24.

Virginia McConnell Simmons, *The San Luis Valley*, University Press of Colorado, Niwot, Colorado, 1999, pp. 201, 204.

MONTVILLE, MEDANO SPRINGS, OREAN, ZAPATA and URRACA

- *Alamosa County, Mosca, Zapata Creek and Big Spring Creek drainages*
- *Accessible via paved and graded dirt roads; private property limits exploration of some sites*
- *All sites had post offices; either there are no structures or remaining structures are unknown*

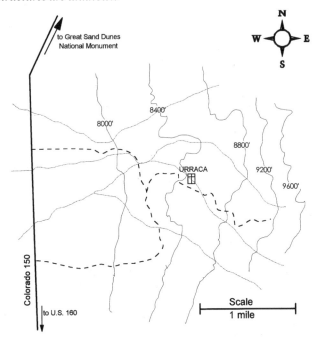

The Urraca site is located above Colorado 150 and south of the Great Sand Dunes National Monument. The road is rough, but with care it can be negotiated by an automobile. There is an occupied home east of the cemetery.

Montville consisted of about twenty houses and was located on the route between Alamosa and Mosca Pass. The town was above the mouth of Mosca Canyon near today's turnoff to the picnic area at Mosca Spring in the Great Sand Dunes National Monument. A short walk of about 100 feet is required to reach the site. The old store has been marked with four white posts by the National Park Service.

The National Park Service marked the store at Montville. It is a short walk to the site from the parking lot on the trail along Mosca Creek. *(Kenneth Jessen 113A1)*

There was an earlier settlement called Mosco (not to be confused with Mosca), and it got its post office in 1880. The office closed 2 years later. Mosco was probably the forerunner of Montville since the Montville post office, which opened in 1887, was located in the old Mosco post office.

To add to the confusion, postal records also indicate that the Montville post office was once called Orean. The Orean post office was open from 1881 to 1887. The settlement of Orean was located about 3.5 miles southwest of Montville at what is today the southern border of the Great Sand Dunes National Monument. Its small cemetery is still marked on topographic maps, but private property limits exploration. A store and campground sit on the site.

Teofilo Trujillo is credited with becoming the first permanent settler at Medano Springs, located directly west of the Great Sand Dunes. His homestead was on Lower Sand Creek. Trujillo's biggest problem was Indians who helped themselves to as many cattle as they wanted. The Indians believed that the resources placed on the earth by the Great Spirit were there for all mankind. Contrary to the western way of thinking, they did not recognize or relate to private property.

Eventually, Trujillo added sheep to his holdings of 800 head of cattle, but his troubles were not over. Other ranchers killed many of his sheep to protest the introduction of this animal to the open range.

The Medano Springs post office got its start in 1874 and lasted only a year before its closure. It was reopened in 1877, based on the demand by local ranchers, but it didn't last more than 2 years. It was housed in a small, log store. This structure was moved to the Medano Ranch and may remain standing today. The ranch is posted no trespassing. The exact location of Medano Springs could not be determined. A good guess would be north of 6N LN on Six Mile

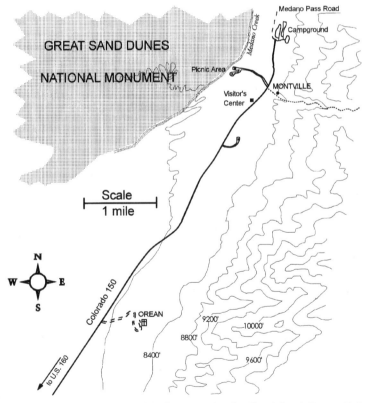

Montville is located near the visitor's center for the Great Sand Dunes National Monument and has been clearly marked with four white posts by the National Park Service. Orean is located at the entrance to the park behind an RV campground.

Lane and south of its intersection with Ten Mile Road.

South of the Great Sand Dunes National Monument was the small community of Zapata, settled in 1864. A church was constructed in 1869, and the area was eventually sold to Anglo investors. In 1879, the town got a post office under the name "Zapato." It also had a school. The post office at Zapata operated intermittently until 1900 when the town was essentially abandoned.

In 1870, a German immigrant named William H. Meyer arrived in the Zapata area. He was followed by other settlers who brought in Texas longhorn cattle. The Spanish-speaking settlers contested the right of the new arrivals and claimed that their land was part of a Mexican land grant. The documents presented were forgeries; consequently, outside investors purchased most of the land in 1876.

The Mormons made an unsuccessful attempt in 1889 at establishing a colony nearby. As more land was added, it became the Blanca Branch of the Manassa Ward. They attempted to dig an irrigation ditch, but this was a failure. Unable to farm, the Mormons turned to harvesting timber and selling it in Alamosa. The effort of the colony ended in bankruptcy, and the land was sold.

The Zapata town site is at or near the present-day Zapata Ranch headquarters. It is not known if any of its original structures remain.

A school was opened in nearby Urraca Canyon south of Zapata Creek in 1887. The Urraca Cemetery sits above Colorado 150 south of the sand dunes and south of its intersection with 6N LN. It is accessible by a graded dirt road. The cemetery is cared for and has a small parking lot. An occupied log home sits near the site and could have been the school. It is not known if any other structures were built at Urraca.

George Harlan, *Postmarks and Places*, Golden Bell Press, Denver, 1976, pp. 46-48, 155-156.

Virginia McConnell Simmons, *The San Luis Valley*, University Press of Colorado, Niwot, Colorado, 1999, pp. 218, 220, 294.

William H. Bauer, James L. Ozment and John H. Willard, *Colorado Post Offices*, Colorado Railroad Museum, Golden, Colorado, 1990, pp. 97, 100-101, 108, 155.

MOSCA
Originally Named Streator

- *Saguache County, no distinct drainage*
- *Access via paved road*
- *Town has a post office; several original structures remain*

The Mosca Mercantile was abandoned more than forty years ago. The town is not abandoned, although it is much smaller than it was a century ago. *(Kenneth Jessen 126B4)*

Few people live in Mosca, and it is far smaller than during its best years. Many of Mosca's original settlers came from Streator, Illinois, in 1887, and Streator was the town's original name. When the Denver & Rio Grande was constructed south through the center of the San Luis Valley, the Mosca Town

Company was formed to develop the land around Streator. Nearly 200 families settled in the area, and the Streator Lateral was dug to bring in irrigation water. For a while it looked like another railroad would be constructed over Mosca Pass, and its residents elected to change the town's name to Mosca.

The town grew to include a general merchandise store, drug store, two hotels and lumberyard. It also supported a furniture store. The Mosca Roller Mills and Elevator provided residents with the greatest job opportunities. An estimate made in 1891 placed wheat under cultivation in the general area at over a million bushels. The town also had two churches and a school.

The post office was established in 1888 under the name of Streator and changed to Mosca in 1890.

George Harlan, *Postmarks and Places*, Golden Bell Press, Denver, 1976, pp. 62-63.

William H. Bauer, James L. Ozment and John H. Willard, *Colorado Post Offices*, Colorado Railroad Museum, Golden, Colorado, 1990, p. 136.

MUSIC CITY
Did It Really Exist?

- *Saguache County, Sand Creek drainage*
- *Exact location unknown*
- *Town did not have a post office; remaining structures unknown*

Some doubt that Music City ever existed. However, historian Muriel Sibell Wolle, a reliable source for ghost town history, includes Music City in her book, *Timberline Tailings*, and also mentions it in passing in *Stampede to Timberline*. The town also shows up in *Colorado's Century of "Cities"* by Don and Jean Griswold, but their belief in Music City is based on Wolle's work.

The Griswolds reasoned that the town must have been near Music Pass and the headwaters of Sand Creek. Wolle's belief in Music City was based on comments by her driver, Sam, who took her to Liberty and Duncan. Her belief was confirmed by a letter from Edgar Dicus of Taos, New Mexico. Dicus refers to an abandoned gold mine where his family stayed in 1910.

Topographic maps fail to shed light on the matter. The only mine in Sand Creek is near Liberty at the mouth of the canyon formed by the creek. No prospects or mines are shown near Music Pass or at the headwaters of Sand Creek.

Don and Jean Griswold, *Colorado's Century of "Cities,"* self-published, 1958, p. 228.
Muriel Sibell Wolle, *Stampede to Timberline,* Sage Books, Chicago, 1949, p. 304.
Muriel Sibell Wolle, *Timberline Tailings*, Sage Books, Chicago, Illinois, 1977, pp. 234-235.

ORIENT
And Its Iron Mines

- *Saguache County, Orient Canyon drainage*
- *Access to site via four-wheel drive road; part of site on private property*
- *Town had a post office; no standing structures remain*

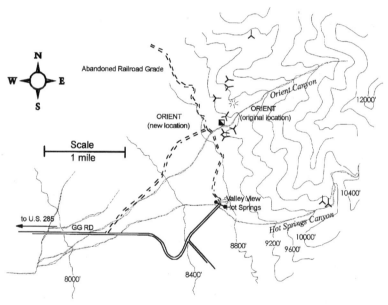

Orient is north of Valley View Hot Springs near the east end of GG RD. The diagonal road that leads directly to the Orient site is quite rough and not suitable for an automobile.

This town had three phases to its history beginning with a settlement called Haumann. East of Villa Grove, iron deposits were discovered, and eventually Frank Haumann recorded a half-dozen claims during the 1870s. The magnetite ore body was in a single large mass within the mountainside. Iron ore is heavy, and any volume production from the mine did not start until the Denver & Rio Grande constructed its narrow gauge railroad from Poncha Springs, over Poncha Pass, to Villa Grove and to the deposit in 1881.

It was at this time that application was made for a post office under the name Haumann. The new post office served a population of about 400 with mail delivery starting in 1882 and continuing until 1885.

The mines and associated iron ore deposits were sold to the Colorado Coal & Iron Company, predecessor of Colorado Fuel & Iron. It was at this time that the settlement became known as Orient or the Orient Mines. The original settlement of Orient was located approximately a mile up Orient Canyon. Its population fluctuated over the years from 200 to 400, according to the demand for iron ore at the C.F.& I. smelter in Pueblo.

In 1885, the lease was not renewed and independent companies tried to continue mining the iron ore. C.F.& I. then renewed its lease and expanded operation to six levels. In 1894, a new post office opened under the Orient name in a corner of the company store.

Orient had a number of structures, including a two-story frame boardinghouse complete with a dining room capable of seating 300. There also was a reading room for the miners and their families. The town had its own barbershop as well. In a 1902 photograph, taken by C.F.& I., twenty-two structures appear, including apartments joined in a long row. Orient also had a schoolhouse.

C.F.& I. lost its lease in 1905, and the post office was closed. Orient was abandoned and soon fell into a state of decay. None of the structures at this location remain today.

The iron mine continued to operate, however, probably under new ownership. It was at this time that a small store opened at Valley View Hot Springs, a mile to the south. Miners could cash their paychecks at the store and purchase supplies. A bathhouse was constructed along with concrete-lined pools.

Valley View also had a dance hall and church.

In 1920, C.F.& I. took over the operation of the Orient Mine again. A new town was developed by the company just below the railroad grade and far removed from the canyon where the original town sat. Generally referred to as New Orient, it consisted of a dozen three-room homes and two eight-room houses. They were all of frame construction and sat on concrete foundations. A large home was constructed for the mine superintendent. One home was designated as the post office, and mail was sorted into individual boxes. Several other structures associated with the mine also were located at the site, including a maintenance shed, blacksmith shop, garage and compressor house.

Mail was delivered to New Orient from Mineral Hot Springs. This arrangement lasted until 1933 when the mines closed and the iron ore was nearly depleted. C.F.& I. developed another more economical source for iron ore in Wyoming. Although mining

Miners pose for the camera in front of the Orient boardinghouse. This photograph was taken in 1901-1902 when Colorado Fuel & Iron operated the mine. *(Kenneth Jessen collection CP023)*

ceased at Orient, the railroad was not abandoned until 1940. C.F.& I. did not officially close its Orient Mine until 1942 when the rails were removed.

The Orient Mine was worked from six levels starting from one drilled near the top of the mountain all the way down to one below the narrow gauge railroad. The ore from upper levels was brought down to the railroad by a cable tram. Today, a dangerous cavity exists on the hillside high above the mine openings. It represents a stope or cavity where ore was removed. The last act by miners, once the ore was depleted, was to blast away the support columns in the stope. With the passage of time, the cavity worked its way to the surface and created a large sinkhole hundreds of feet deep. This area is fenced off.

Unless permission can be obtained to cross the Valley View Hot Springs property, access to a point near Orient requires four-wheel drive. The road to Valley View Hot Springs leaves U.S. 285 at the point where it divides from Colorado 17. The road runs due east, and before reaching the springs, a rough four-wheel drive road angles northeast to the Orient site. The distance is about a mile and three-quarters and could be negotiated on foot. Private property restricts access to the Old Orient site, but the New Orient site is accessible.

At New Orient, rows of concrete foundations can be seen below the railroad grade and piles of tailings. When the mine shut down, all of the buildings were sold and removed.

Camp & Plant, C.F.& I., Pueblo, Colorado, Volume 1, April 19, 1902, pp. 313-323.

George Harlan, *Postmarks and Places*, Golden Bell Press, Denver, 1976, pp. 50-56.

H. Lee Scamehorn, *Pioneer Steel Maker in the West*, Pruett Publishing Company, Boulder, Colorado, 1976, pp. 102-103.

Marjorie Woodward Evans, J. Robert Outerbridge, et. al. "The Orient Mine and the Big Cave-in," *The San Luis Valley Historian*, Volume XX, No. 2., Alamosa, Colorado, 1988, pp. 14-17.

Robert Fisher, "The Orient Mine," *The San Luis Valley Historian*, Volume XIX, No. 3., Alamosa, Colorado, 1987, pp. 11-15.

William H. Bauer, James L. Ozment and John H. Willard, *Colorado Post Offices,* Colorado Railroad Museum, Golden, Colorado, 1990, pp. 69, 108.

ORIENTAL

And "Butcherknife" William Burton

- *Saguache County, Hayden Creek drainage*
- *Access to site via graded dirt road*
- *Town had a post office; no structures remain*

Penciled on the back of this photograph was: "House of a town of 5,000 people in 1880 to 1883. Now nothing left but broken beer bottles, stone foundations, the spring and a few graves on the hillside nearby." This was the last structure in Oriental, which had a population of around 100 or so. *(Denver Public Library x-12575)*

Located at the western tollgate for the toll road over Hayden Pass, the mining camp of Oriental is often confused with Orient. Oriental was apparently named for the Chinese who worked the area mines. Native Americans replaced the Chinese, but didn't stay long.

A post office was established in 1881, but lasted only three years. The population of Oriental was listed in 1900 as 600, a figure that seems high relative to the many other small mining camps along the base of the Sangre de Cristo Mountains. Businesses consisted of a general store, with the post office located inside, a boardinghouse, two saloons and a combination blacksmith shop and livery barn.

If Oriental was known for anything, it was for one of its residents, "Butcherknife" William Burton. The Civil War had turned him against firearms; however, he worked as a gunsmith. When Burton went hunting, he carried only his butcher knife and used a pack of dogs. When game was cornered by the dogs, Burton would use his butcher knife to kill the animal.

During the 1930s, the buildings at Oriental were moved away.

Summitville *(Kenneth Jessen)*

George Harlan, *Postmarks and Places*, Golden Bell Press, Denver, 1976, pp. 49-50.
William H. Bauer, James L. Ozment and John H. Willard, *Colorado Post Offices*, Colorado Railroad Museum, Golden, Colorado, 1990, p. 108.

ORTIZ and SAN ANTONIO

- *Conejos County, Rio de Los Pinos drainage*
- *Accessible via paved road; occupied sites with private property*
- *Towns had post offices; a number of structures remain*

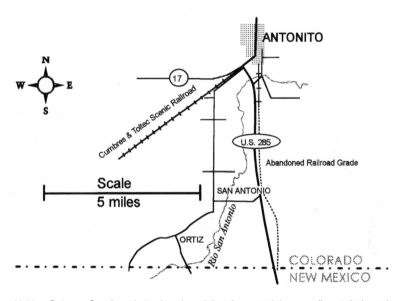

Neither Ortiz nor San Antonio is abandoned, but they certainly are well past their peak. They are easy to reach on paved roads south of Antonito.

Spanish-speaking people visited this area as early as the 1840s, and water rights for a ditch date to 1848. A settlement called Los Pinos began in 1859 on the south side of Rio de Los Pinos. It was located on the main wagon road between the San Luis Valley and Tierra Amarilla, New Mexico. A second trail from El Rito, New

There are several abandoned adobe buildings in Ortiz that stand along its main street. *(Kenneth Jessen 121B6)*

Mexico, also came though this area. A chapel was constructed in 1871, and Los Pinos had a Penitente morada.

José Maria Casias, a Civil War veteran, homesteaded the area north of the river. Nestor Ortiz joined Casias during the early 1870s, and Ortiz opened a store. Ortiz became a wool broker for local ranchers and was noted for his filigree silver pieces. The town was also the home of Pablo Garcia, a well-known weaver.

As the village on the north side expanded, the Ortiz family became prominent. When the town got a post office in 1890, it was given the name Ortiz, possibly to eliminate confusion with other towns within Colorado having the name Los Pinos. The Ortiz post office closed in 1931, but reopened in 1935 and lasted until 1943.

The population of Ortiz reached around 500, and its business district had several stores and saloons. The town had three schools at various times, one public, one run by the Baptists and a third run by the Presbyterians.

Today, Ortiz has a well-defined main street and is southeast of the main paved road and about a mile and a quarter from San

Antonio. Although there are a number of crumbling adobe buildings, Ortiz still has a handful of residents. It is but a fraction of its original size.

A great deal of confusion exists over the name San Antonio since it was used for three distinct places, including Antonito. Today's San Antonio is 3 miles south of Antonito and was originally on the east side of the Rio San Antonio, but the town spread west. A chapel was constructed in 1871 and dedicated to San Antonio. It was part of the widespread mission of Our Lady of Guadalupe Parish. A Penitente morada also was built on the east side of the river. San Antonio had a school, but no post office.

The site today is filled with homes concentrated in a relatively small area along with a few abandoned buildings. Unlike Ortiz, it lacks a defined town center and is located at the base of a cliff.

Seven Mile Plaza *(Kenneth Jessen)*

Virginia McConnell Simmons, "Hispanic Place Names of the San Luis Valley," *The San Luis Valley Historian*, Volume XXIII, Number 3, Alamosa, Colorado, 1991, pp. 28, 32, 37.

Virginia McConnell Simmons, *The San Luis Valley*, University Press of Colorado, Niwot, Colorado, 1999, pp. 254, 293.

William H. Bauer, James L. Ozment and John H. Willard, *Colorado Post Offices*, Colorado Railroad Museum, Golden, Colorado, 1990, p. 108.

PLATORO
Boom to Bust to Boom

* *Conejos County, Conejos River drainage*
* *Accessible via graded dirt road; occupied site*
* *Town had a post office; original structures remain*

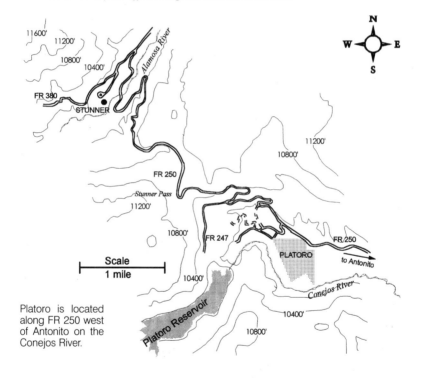

Platoro is located along FR 250 west of Antonito on the Conejos River.

Today, it is difficult to believe that Platoro was once a ghost town. Its old cabins have been converted into summer homes, and the town is alive with activity. There is a general store and an active resort located at the edge of town. It is difficult to find an abandoned building with a ghost town flavor. There are a number of new structures, and most of the older buildings are in excellent shape. This is in contrast to the ghost town historian Muriel Sibell Wolle visited in the late 1940s. She wrote, "There were several well-defined streets and many empty log cabins...two or three cowboys watched us indifferently from the porch of the only newly-painted house in the place."

Platoro was a mining camp formed in the late 1880s in a large, lush meadow surrounded by majestic blue spruce trees. The Conejos River meanders through the north end of town. In 1888, it got its own post office. By the turn of the century, it had a population of around 300. Early businesses included a few saloons, dance hall, barber shop, blacksmith shop and typical livery stables required to house the many animals necessary for transportation.

Its location at 9,900 feet above sea level and isolation at the end of a long, primitive wagon road dictated that only the richest ore could be packed out economically. In 1888, an ore haulage road was constructed from Summitville to connect Platoro with Del Norte, but this was a long, hard trip through the mountains.

Silver ore was discovered at the Merrimac lode on Klondike Mountain. The miners removed a ton and a half of ore and packed it to Del Norte. Although it yielded only $320, word got out and the rush to the Platoro area began. The miners in the area seemed to have a passion for the words "king" or "queen." The major mines included the Forest King, Forest Queen, Valley King and Valley Queen. Others were the Parole, Orekiss, Queen Bess, Glacier and Silver King.

The most important mine was the Mammoth just outside of town. It was eventually developed in three levels with 8,500 feet of tunnels and a concentration mill. Between 1889 and 1906, a quarter of a million dollars in gold and silver was shipped.

During its boom years, Platoro was a typical, nearly all-male mining camp. With few permanent log structures, many lived in tents. As time passed, more log buildings filled in the town's spacious blocks. There were a few saloons and a dance hall. One of

This is one of the few abandoned buildings in Platoro. Most of the town's cabins have been restored for seasonal use. Someone has put a "bus stop" sign on the left-hand corner of this building. *(Kenneth Jessen 095D6)*

Colorado's most colorful characters, Poker Alice, would ride from Creede to Platoro to liven up the place. She would sit at a card table for hours playing poker and smoking cigars.

At the Valley King and Valley Queen mines, a bad accident took the life of Charles Scott. The closest mortuary was over the mountains in Del Norte. When his partner, Charles Barnes, could not find a wagon for rent in Platoro, his only option was to hitch up his own single seat rig. He tied his late friend on the seat beside him. The corpse was propped up in a sitting position. Barnes drove his rig over the long, rough road 40 miles to Del Norte.

By 1906, Platoro was a ghost town. The rich ore that had supported it seemed to play out. The miners moved on. Its remote location and high transportation costs limited further development. Ore that could produce up to $50 a ton, valuable to any of hundreds of other Colorado mines, was discarded on the tailing piles around Platoro. Mine owners could only afford to ship the richest ore.

A second boom occurred with the discovery of gold on Klondike Mountain in 1912 at the Gilmore lode. The gold ore was similar to that found in the Cripple Creek area. With such prospects, hundreds of miners poured into Platoro. Soon, all of the cabins were occupied again. To handle the swelling population, numerous tents were pitched between the cabins. Old businesses reopened along with new saloons, pool halls, stores, restaurants and hotels, many built of canvas. The *Platoro Miner* began

publication. Platoro even had a primitive hospital-drug store run
by Dr. A. P. Heller. Daily mail service arrived from Monte Vista, and
stagecoaches began to serve the town. Improved roads further
reduced the town's isolation.

A mining camp called Gilmore also was formed at this time
on the north slope of Klondike Mountain. It was composed of a
tent and two wooden shacks, and they housed the town's hotel,
store and photographer's studio. The location was not practical,
and Gilmore was soon abandoned.

When the rich ore in Klondike Mountain finally gave out,
Platoro was again a ghost town. There was another small boom in
1916 and 1917, but it didn't amount to much. The post office
closed in 1919 and the town sat empty for many decades.

In 1959, Alfred Hoyle looked over the mine dump at the
Mammoth Mine. He started a project to recover gold from the
tailing pile knowing that only the highest-grade ore had been
shipped. A new mill was constructed, and the concentrate was
hauled to a Pueblo smelter. Eventually, all of the tailings were

Platoro in 1915. Today, the town is very much the same, and few of its original buildings
have vanished over the years. *(U.S. Geological Survey, J. F. Hunter 448)*

processed, and the project was shut down.

Sam Mix and Otto Blake purchased some of the old cabins for back taxes and fixed them up. They rented them to fishermen during the summer. This led to the purchase, repair and rental of more cabins, and soon, Platoro was reborn as a seasonal resort town.

The first permanent residents in the new resort town of Platoro were Mr. and Mrs. Clint Wiley. They constructed the Sky Line Lodge in 1945. The Wileys knew the area from past hunting and fishing trips. With its beautiful location, good fishing, and relaxing atmosphere, the Sky Line Lodge was a success. Not many years passed and all of Platoro's old cabins were purchased and restored.

What solidified summer recreation was the Platoro Dam, constructed above the town. At more than 10,000 feet above sea level, it became the highest reservoir in North America. Work on the dam started in 1947 and lasted until it was completed in 1951. Nearly 100 workers lived in Platoro during the dam's construction. The road along the Conejos River also was improved at this time. To visit Platoro today is like visiting an old mining town from the past, but one that is occupied.

Leland Feitz, *Platoro*, Colorado, self-published, 1969, pp. 3-20.

Muriel Sibell Wolle, *Stampede to Timberline*, Sage Books, Chicago, 1949, pp. 312-314.

William H. Bauer, James L. Ozment and John H. Willard, *Colorado Post Offices*, Colorado Railroad Museum, Golden, Colorado, 1990, p. 115

PYKE

A Lesson in Heating Dynamite

- *Saguache County, Wild Cherry Creek drainage*
- *Accessible via graded dirt road*
- *Town had a post office; standing structures unknown*

L ocated between Cotton Creek and Rito Alto was the small set-tlement of Pyke. It sat near the mouth of Wild Cherry Creek at the base of the Sangre de Cristo Mountains. First called Dickerson, it was started in 1896 when Jim and Elmer Dickerson filed a mining claim establishing the Broken Tree Mine. Financing came from Judge Pyke of Hooper and several other San Luis Valley residents. Pyke got its post office in 1900, and at the time, the population was listed at twenty-one. Postal service lasted only 2 years. The post office was housed in a store with mail delivery six times a week.

Other businesses at Pyke included a transfer company to haul ore to Mineral Hot Springs. The camp also had several cabins and a store that consisted of two cabins joined together.

One winter, Ed Tobler and his son were performing assess-ment work on a prospect near Pyke. It was cold, and the dynamite they carried froze. This created a dangerous situation since droplets of pure nitroglycerin appeared like beads of sweat on the outer wrapper. Nitroglycerin is very unstable and can be set off by a mild shock. A common practice among miners was to heat dynamite in an oven in the hope that the nitroglycerin would be absorbed back into the inert carrier.

The Toblers were doing just this, but the sticks caught on fire. They exploded and blew the iron oven door through the cabin door. The Toblers were uninjured in the accident, although they lost their hearing for weeks.

For years, several log cabins marked the site of this settlement. Today from the public road no structures can be seen, making the town's exact location difficult to find. Recent work in contouring the mine tailings at Pyke makes even their location illusive. Pyke can be reached by taking AA RD east from Colorado 17 past Mirage until it becomes an unimproved, single-lane dirt road. Although this road has been graded, it is quite rough for automobile travel. Just before reaching the end of the road at the Wild Cherry trailhead, an even more primitive road takes off to the left (north) and runs past several mines.

For a map showing Pyke's location, see "Cotton Creek."

George Harlan, *Postmarks and Places*, Golden Bell Press, Denver, 1976, p. 56.

Noel Harlan, "The Cabin in the San Luis Valley," *The San Luis Valley Historian*, Vol. XXVI, No. 3, Alamosa, Colorado, 1994, pp. 43-44.

William H. Bauer, James L. Ozment and John H. Willard, *Colorado Post Offices*, Colorado Railroad Museum, Golden, Colorado, 1990, p. 117.

RITO ALTO
And Its Picturesque Church

- *Saguache County, Rito Alto Creek drainage*
- *Church accessible via graded dirt road; other structures on private property*
- *Town had a post office; at least one original structure remains*

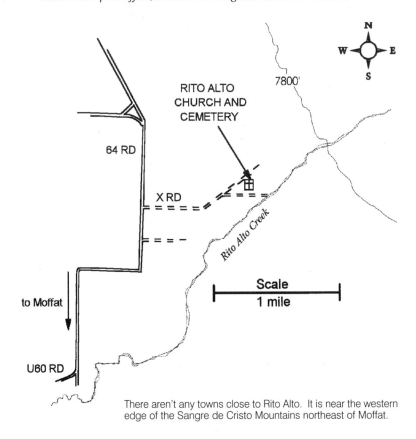

There aren't any towns close to Rito Alto. It is near the western edge of the Sangre de Cristo Mountains northeast of Moffat.

In the late 1860s, several families from Illinois settled along Rito Alto Creek about 3 miles downstream from the mouth of Rito Alto Canyon where the creek emerges from the Sangre de Cristo Mountains. This was the beginning of the settlement of Rito Alto. The first post office was located inside of the log cabin of Harrison Wales and was started in 1872. It remained open for a dozen years. Wales boasted of having the first wooden floor on the east side of the San Luis Valley.

A school was started in 1874, and it began with thirteen students. In 1890, a schoolhouse was built north of the Rito Alto Church. It can be presumed that classes predating the schoolhouse were held in the homes of the settlers.

The primary occupation was ranching. The Wales family produced dairy products and shipped them to mining districts as far away as Fairplay. Some family members worked in nearby mines.

The beautiful Rito Alto Church was constructed in 1889 on 20 acres of land donated by the Wales family. Its ceiling is lined with redwood brought from California or Oregon. Within the church property is a small pioneer cemetery. Large, mature cottonwood trees make this a serene place to visit. The area around the church and cemetery is fenced and is private property.

The church at Rito Alto is one of the most attractive in the San Luis Valley. It sits in a grove of cottonwood trees near Rito Alto Creek. *(Kenneth Jessen 108C12)*

Abigail Wales Shallabarger, "Rito Alto Recollections," *The San Luis Valley Historian*, Vol. XXIX, No. 3, 1997, pp. 5-19.

George Harlan, *Postmarks and Places*, Golden Bell Press, Denver, 1976, pp. 29-33.

William H. Bauer, James L. Ozment and John H. Willard, *Colorado Post Offices*, Colorado Railroad Museum, Golden, Colorado, 1990, p. 122.

RUSSELL

Formerly Called Placer

- *Costilla County, Sangre de Cristo Creek drainage*
- *Accessible via paved road*
- *Town had a post office; several structures remain*

This overview of Russell was taken by O. T. Davis in 1897 and shows many features of the town including buildings associated with the Denver & Rio Grande. The railroad's roundhouse is in the center of this photograph. (Denver Public Library X-13236)

The town of Russell was originally called Placer and was a "helper" station west of La Veta Pass. An extra locomotive was kept under steam ready for use to help push eastbound trains over La Veta Pass. At the pass, the locomotive was turned on a turntable and went back to Russell for use helping another train over the pass.

This gold dredge was located near Russell. The photograph came from the files of the Denver & Rio Grande Railroad. (Denver Public Library X-60128)

A six-stall roundhouse, frame depot and water tank were located in Russell. The depot, incidentally, was unusual for the Denver & Rio Grande in that it had windows with rounded tops. Russell was also the beginning of a 2.1 mile branch line to the Trinchera Mine to the north. The line ended at a tramway that brought iron ore from the mine.

According to an interview conducted by ghost town historian Muriel Sibell Wolle, Russell was named for William Green Russell, who discovered gold near Central City in 1859. Under the name Russell, it got its post office in 1876. Although the post office operated intermittently, it did not close permanently until 1956. To add to the confusion over names, ghost town historian Robert Brown wrote that Russell originally was called Sangre de Cristo. Placer was a short distance to the north. George Crofutt lists Sangre de Cristo as the name of the railroad station for Russell.

Russell began as a placer gold camp with deposits up Grayback Gulch. Hydraulic mining was used to wash the gravel from the riverbank, and a large dredge was brought in to process the gravel in the riverbed. After the arrival of the Denver & Rio Grande in 1877, Russell was all about the railroad. Stores were lined up along its main street running parallel to the tracks. The town had at least two dozen structures including two general stores, saloon, sawmill, schoolhouse, hotel, the post office and several homes. Russell grew to a population of 200 by 1885.

The railroad activity that supported Russell ended in 1899 when the Denver & Rio Grande decided to convert its operations in the San Luis Valley to standard gauge. A new route was selected down Wagon Creek, and 26.5 miles of narrow gauge grade was abandoned. In the process, Russell was bypassed. It became a ranching community and slowly died.

Muriel Sibell Wolle interviewed Charles Guhse, who came to Russell in 1909, well after the town's peak. He told of Margaret Sutton, who ran the hotel. She was known as the Angel of the Sangre de Cristos and got presents from people she knew or who stopped by to see her.

Guhse also remembered a funeral for a 4-year-old girl at the Russell cemetery. An old hunchbacked prospector agreed to give a graveside service and said, "We're all common people. With the sighing of the winds and the whispering of the pines in the shadow of these everlasting hills that she loved, we're laying Little Gladys to rest." Guhse couldn't bear to go to the Russell post office for 2 months after the little girl's death, because Gladys had always run out to greet him.

George A. Crofutt, *Crofutt's Grip-Sack Guide of Colorado*, 1885 Edition, Johnson Books, Boulder, Colorado, reprint 1981, p. 140.

Richard Dorman, *Alamosa/Salida and the Valley* Line, R. C. Publications, Inc, Santa Fe, New Mexico, 1991, pp. 83-86.

Robert L. Brown, *Colorado Ghost Towns, Past and Present,* Caxton Printers, Caldwell, Idaho, 1977, pp. 234-236.

Muriel Sibell Wolle, *Stampede to Timberline,* Sage Books, Chicago, 1949, p. 554.

Muriel Sibell Wolle, *Timberline Tailings,* Sage Books, Chicago, Illinois, 1977, pp. 235-236.

Tiv Wilkins, *Colorado Railroads*, Pruett Publishing Company, Boulder, Colorado, 1974, pp. 19, 39, 123.

William H. Bauer, James L. Ozment and John H. Willard, *Colorado Post Offices*, Colorado Railroad Museum, Golden, Colorado, 1990, p. 125.

SAN ISABEL

Hosts All the Young Girls in the County

- *Saguache County, San Isabel Creek drainage*
- *Access to site limited by private property*
- *Town had a post office; one remaining structure*

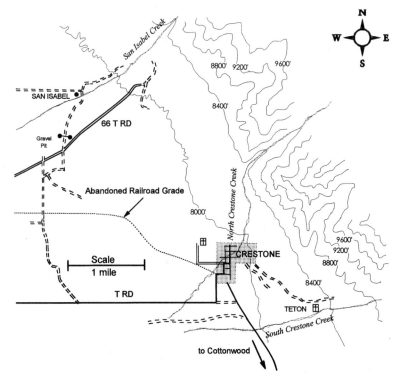

San Isabel is just beyond a gravel pit on 66 T RD. Access to the site is blocked by a gate.

Homesteading along San Isabel Creek began in 1869 by Dewitt Travis and his brother from New York State. There were few people in the valley at that time, and the wife of one of the brothers wrote a friend that she entertained all of the young ladies in Saguache County for dinner. The reply came back suggesting that she must have had her hands full and that she must live in a large house. To that, she replied that there were only four young ladies, including herself, her sister, the local schoolteacher and one other!

San Isabel was never a large community. It consisted of two or three log structures several adobe buildings, and its own post office, which closed in 1912. *(Denver Public Library x-13517)*

The San Isabel post office opened in 1872 and remained in active service until 1912, a lot longer than other offices in the surrounding settlements. San Isabel consisted of two or three log structures and several adobe buildings. The town also had a small school, and classes were held only during the summer months.

Near San Isabel is the site where the first commercial potatoes were grown in the valley. Dewitt Travis harvested 70,000 pounds of potatoes in 1875 and sold them to a Leadville market. An entire industry developed around potatoes, and it remains one of the San Luis Valley's primary crops.

The San Isabel site sits off to the north of 66 T RD. A gate blocks access to the site. It appears that one structure remains.

George Harlan, *Postmarks and Places*, Golden Bell Press, Denver, 1976, pp. 33-34.

William H. Bauer, James L. Ozment and John H. Willard, *Colorado Post Offices*, Colorado Railroad Museum, Golden, Colorado, 1990, p. 128.

SAN PEDRO, SAN PABLO, CHAMA, LOS FUERTES, LA VALLEY and SAN FRANCISCO

- *Costilla County, Ventero, San Francisco, Vallejos and Culebra creek drainages*
- *Accessible via paved and graded dirt roads*
- *Some towns had post offices; many original structures remain*

Southeast of San Luis are a number of small towns in the valley formed by Ventero Creek with the Sangre de Cristo Mountains on the east and San Pedro Mesa on the west. The area has a number of scattered settlements, partially abandoned and only a shadow of what they once were. The land is well watered by

The San Isidro Cemetery sits along the road east of Los Fuertes. *(Sonje Jessen SJ124)*

several creeks that support large, lush meadows.

By driving south from San Luis on P.6 RD then turning onto 21 RD, the road passes through San Pedro and San Pablo. Turning east on L.7 RD is Chama at the mouth of the canyon formed by Culebra Creek. Continuing south from San Pedro and San Pablo along Vallejos Creek is Los Fuertes, La Valley and farther south is

234

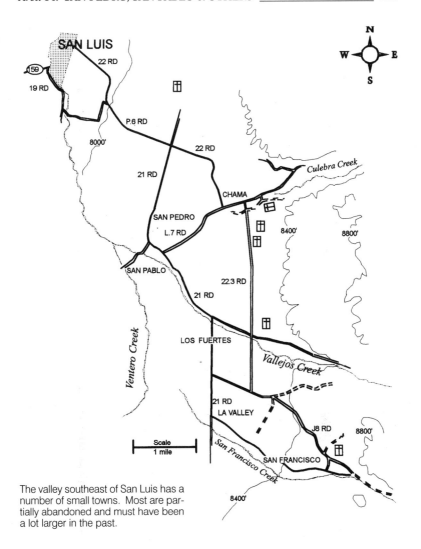

The valley southeast of San Luis has a number of small towns. Most are partially abandoned and must have been a lot larger in the past.

San Francisco on the creek by the same name.

San Pedro was first settled by Spanish-speaking people from Taos in 1851. The buildings in San Pedro were jacales constructed of vertical posts set into the ground adjacent to each other to form a fort.

San Pedro was sometimes called Plaza Arriba or Upper Culebra. The San Pedro ditch dates back to 1852 and is one of the earliest irrigation ditches in Colorado. According to San Luis Valley historian Virginia McConnell Simmons, the area's principal church was constructed at San Pedro. It was built in 1859, and services were initially conducted by priests from Taos. San Pedro got a school in 1890, but until that time, school was conducted in private homes. After a second school was constructed, the building also was used for occasional dances. The building burned in 1936.

Today, San Pedro has a newly restored church, one store and the area's post office. These structures are surrounded by a few abandoned buildings that reflect the town's earlier days.

In contrast, San Pablo lacks a well-defined town center and is an accumulation of both occupied and abandoned buildings. It is located on the south side of Culebra Creek. San Pedro is on the north side a short distance away. The post office has been located in both towns at various times, but it always has been under the San Pablo name. The post office originally opened in 1893 and remains open today.

The original attempt to settle in this area was made by Antonio José Vallejos and others in 1849, but Native Americans drove them away. A second group of settlers returned in 1851. In the late 1880s, the first school was taught in San Pablo by Presbyterian missionaries following the establishment of a Presbyterian church in this predominatly Catholic culture.

To the east of San Pedro and San Pablo is the partially abandoned town of Chama on Culebra Creek. The town site is 4 miles southeast of San Luis and was sometimes called Culebra. It was settled by people from Chamita, New Mexico, and by 1864, Chama had its own chapel. At one time, there were a large number of Penitentes in Chama, and they constructed a morada or meeting place. Both Catholic and Pentecostal cemeteries are located near the town site. A Secidad Proteccion Mutua de Trabajadores Unidas, or workers protective association, was constructed at Chama.

Another jacale, constructed of upright logs set vertically in the dirt, was Fuertecito or "small fort." It also served as protection against Native American raids. Sometimes called Vallejos, it is shown on contemporary maps as Los Fuertes. It was settled around 1853 and was located along Vallejos Creek. Los Fuertes is about 6 miles southeast of San Luis.

The San Isidro Church at Los Fuertes was dedicated to the patron saint of the farmer and remains standing today. Next to the Los Fuertes town site is the San Isidro Cemetery with interesting wooden crosses marking some of the older graves. Private homes are intermixed with abandoned buildings, and there are signs that some of the older homes are being restored.

La Valley was not a town but an area along San Francisco Creek 7 miles southeast of San Luis. To the east end of this area is the town of San Francisco taking its name from the church. To the west end of La Valley was another settlement called Colonias, and the entire group of settlements was called El Rito for the New Mexico town of the same name.

A post office was established in 1903 under the name "Lavalley," and its name was changed to San Francisco in 1918. Also at this location was an active Penitente morada and store.

The owner plans to restore this beautiful adobe home in San Francisco. *(Sonje Jessen SJ103)*

Someone is trying to stabilize this adobe structure in San Pablo. Note the covered well in the background. *(Kenneth Jessen 121A12)*

The original plaza at San Francisco was located at the mouth of the canyon formed by San Francisco Creek and was founded in 1854. The first chapel was constructed in 1856. This town was also the site of a slave-trading industry that brought Pueblo Indian children north from Taos.

With an estimated 6,000 Catholics living on the Sangre de Cristo Grant, new parishes were established in 1869 at Chama and San Francisco.

Today, the restored church at San Francisco and a small store across the road dominate the town. It does have a well-defined main street and several abandoned structures, one made of stone, several of frame construction and a long adobe home the owner plans to restore. It is an occupied site, and private property should be respected.

Virginia McConnell Simmons, "Hispanic Place Names of the San Luis Valley," *The San Luis Valley Historian,* Volume XXIII, Number 3, Alamosa, Colorado, 1991, pp. 10, 18, 27, 37, 40-41, 44.

Virginia McConnell Simmons, *The San Luis Valley,* University Press of Colorado, Niwot, Colorado, 1999, pp. 88, 149, 249, 301.

William H. Bauer, James L. Ozment and John H. Willard, *Colorado Post Offices,* Colorado Railroad Museum, Golden, Colorado, 1990, pp. 86, 128.

SANGRE DE CRISTO
Exact Location Unknown

- *Saguache County, Deadman Creek drainage*
- *No access; private property*
- *Town had a post office; remaining structures unknown*

The Sangre de Cristo post office was one of the last "territorial" offices started prior to Colorado becoming a state in 1876. It was early 1876 that this post office was opened, and it remained in service until 1884. At the time it opened, the next closest post office was a dozen miles away at San Isabel. To the south, there was a post office at Gardner on the other side of Veta Pass. The Sangre de Cristo post office served approximately 100 people. This small mining town had two stamp mills to pulverize the gold-bearing quartz from nearby mines. Little is known about the number of buildings in Sangre de Cristo.

The Golden Phantom Lode was discovered by Thomas Ryan when he was returning to his Davis Gulch cabin one afternoon. He spotted a reflection on the north slope of the gulch, and the following morning, Ryan dug a prospect hole. Here he found rich honeycombed quartz filled with gold flakes. After he began mining, he was called home to care for his father who had taken ill. Unable to return to the San Luis Valley, he tried to sell his claim. Prospective buyers discovered that the ore so highly touted by Ryan was of little value.

The exact location of Sangre de Cristo is not known, but it is likely near mines indicated on topographic maps at the mouth of Deadman Creek. This would place the site halfway between

Duncan and Cottonwood where historian George Harlan located it on his map in his book, *Postmarks and Places.* George Crofutt, however, placed it at the head of Cottonwood Creek with Crestone 6 miles away. The site is on the Baca Grant No. 4, and this part of the grant is closed to the public.

For the most likely location of Sangre de Cristo, see "Cottonwood."

Mill at Summitville. *(Ruth Marie Colville)*

George A. Crofutt, *Crofutt's Grip-Sack Guide of Colorado*, 1885 Edition, Johnson Books, Boulder, Colorado, reprint 1981, p. 104.

George Harlan, *Postmarks and Places*, Golden Bell Press, Denver, 1976, pp. 44-46.

Virginia McConnell Simmons, *The San Luis Valley*, University Press of Colorado, Niwot, Colorado, 1999, p. 304.

William H. Bauer, James L. Ozment and John H. Willard, *Colorado Post Offices*, Colorado Railroad Museum, Golden, Colorado, 1990, p. 128.

SEVEN MILE PLAZA, LOS VALDEZES, LA LOMA DE SAN JOSÉ, LUCERO PLAZA, TORRES and ROCK CREEK

- *Rio Grande County, Rio Grande drainage*
- *Accessible by graded dirt road or paved road; some occupied sites*
- *Only Rock Creek had a post office; some original structures remain*

This collapsed barn sits on the Rock Creek site. Another structure, which could be a home, is located to the west behind the barn. *(Kenneth Jessen 126A20)*

NOTE: Virginia McConnell Simmons provides the only detailed source of information on these relatively obscure San Luis Valley plazas and towns her articles and in her book, The San Luis Valley.

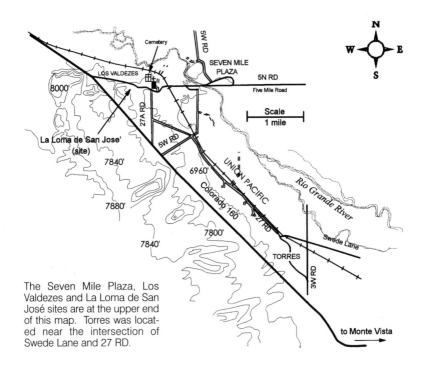

The Seven Mile Plaza, Los Valdezes and La Loma de San José sites are at the upper end of this map. Torres was located near the intersection of Swede Lane and 27 RD.

Southeast of Del Norte and on the north side of the Rio Grande is Seven Mile Plaza. An adobe church was constructed at Seven Mile Plaza. The Anglo name of Seven Mile Plaza most likely was given to the location by settlers during the 1870s. It is indicated on various maps and is an occupied site with several homes. There are also a few abandoned buildings.

This plaza and Los Valdezes, 1 mile west, were established during the 1860s. A church, dedicated to Saint Francis of Assisi, was constructed at Los Valdezes in 1881, and it remains standing. No other structures appear to have survived at Los Valdezes.

West of Los Valdezes at the base of a small hill was La Loma de San José. It was settled on this small rise above the river in 1859 when Juan Bautista Silva led a group of families to this area from Santa Fe and Ojo Caliente in New Mexico. The settlers brought a herd of milk goats and Indian slaves. The families were

joined by others from the Conejos River area. The plaza had a
store and a church dedicated to San José. The Silva ditch was
among the earliest irrigation ditches in the valley. Today, the area
is an open field with no visible foundations.

Another settlement was Lucero Plaza, located 4 miles west
of Monte Vista, where families from New Mexico settled in 1859.
Harsh conditions drove the first group of pioneers away, but a
larger group, led by Manuel Lucero, returned in 1865 to establish a
permanent settlement. The Lucero Ditch provided irrigation
water to the area. The plaza included a dance hall. In the 1870s,
Swedish farmers purchased much of the land in the area. There
are a few abandoned buildings near the site. It is not known if
these were part of the settlement of Lucero Plaza.

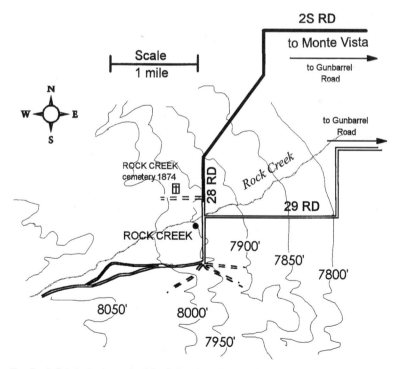

The Rock Creek site is south of Rock Creek and west of 28 RD. Private property limits
exploration; however, the cemetery is on open land.

Torres is .5 mile southeast of Lucero Plaza and was started by Guadalupe Torres from nearby La Loma de San José. Torres operated a store near the tracks of the Denver & Rio Grande. Although there are abandoned buildings near the site, Torres does not appear to have been an organized town with a business district or a street system. None of the settlements covered thus far had post offices.

South of Monte Vista was the isolated town of Rock Creek, no longer indicated on contemporary maps. Settled in 1873, it was located at the mouth of Rock Creek Canyon. In 1879, under the name Piedra, the community got a post office, but it closed the following year. Some of the early settlers were Dunkards from Iowa, and a Presbyterian church was established in 1881. The name Piedra comes from the name of the creek, Piedra Pintada Creek, where Native Americans painted rock pictographs. Today, the site is on private property and is posted no trespassing. From the Rock Creek Cemetery to the north, several log buildings can be seen at Rock Creek.

The only structure remaining at Los Valdezes is this beautifully restored church. *(Kenneth Jessen SJ121)*

Virginia McConnell Simmons, "Hispanic Place Names of the San Luis Valley," *The San Luis Valley Historian*, Volume XXIII, Number 3, Alamosa, Colorado, 1991, pp. 23, 26, 29-30, 42-43.

Virginia McConnell Simmons, *The San Luis Valley*, University Press of Colorado, Niwot, Colorado, 1999, pp. 107-108, 217, 297.

William H. Bauer, James L. Ozment and John H. Willard, *Colorado Post Offices,* Colorado Railroad Museum, Golden, Colorado, 1990, p. 112.

SHIRLEY

A Denver & Rio Grande Construction Camp

- *Chaffee and Saguache counties, Poncha Creek drainage*
- *Accessible via graded dirt road*
- *Town had a post office; no structures remain*

Located right on the line between Chaffee and Saguache counties was the railroad construction camp of Shirley. Initially called Poncha Creek, it was founded in May 1881 by the Denver & Rio Grande. It was the staging site for construction of the narrow gauge line from Salida over Marshall Pass to Gunnison. Located in a long, narrow meadow, Shirley was at the foot of the steep climb over the pass where the 4 percent grade began with a reverse curve. It also served as the terminus for stagecoach travel to Gunnison.

The railroad built bunkhouses, a freight house and a depot. It also had a water tank, coal house and wye for turning locomotives. A short spur track ran south to the Rawley Mill served by a tramway from the Rawley Mine. The railroad allowed eight saloons and dance houses in Shirley. There were also several businesses in tents with false fronts. Historic photographs show two dozen structures in Shirley, many made entirely or partly out of canvas.

After the end of the track had been advanced, Shirley was abandoned and its buildings removed. The town's post office lasted from May 1881 to May 1882. Only empty terraces on the hillside indicate where Shirley's business district was located. Even the depot and freight house were removed.

Russ Collman, "Via Marshall Pass to Gunnison," *Trails Among the Columbine*, Sundance Publications, Denver, 1990, pp. 44-47, 54-55.

Walter R. Borneman, *Marshall Pass*, Century One Press, Colorado Springs, Colorado, 1980, pp. 34, 56.

William H. Bauer, James L. Ozment and John H. Willard, *Colorado Post Offices*, Colorado Railroad Museum, Golden, Colorado, 1990, p. 131.

SPANISH

A Lucky Place To Live

- *Saguache County; Spanish Creek drainage*
- *Accessible via graded dirt road*
- *No standing structures remain*

South of Crestone but north of Cottonwood along the narrow gauge railroad once stood the mining camp of Spanish. It was located on the north side of Spanish Creek. Its residents called their home Lucky, while real estate promoters called it Spanish City. It was quite small with a single street, Harrison Avenue.

The biggest-producing mine in the area was the Independent, which began operation in 1889 with the discovery of gold-bearing quartz. The mine was located halfway between Spanish and Cottonwood. Its ore was treated at a mill in Spanish. The Independent Mine today is marked by its high stone walls and a head frame. Its hoist house remains intact, complete with a steam-powered hoist.

During its early years, the Independent produced a profit of $500 per day. Title to the mine passed to the owner of the Baca Grant No. 4 in 1897 as part of a court settlement. What the Independent was most noted for was the noise from its stamp mill. It had 100 stamps and fifty operated at the same time. Each of the heavy steel rods were raised 2 feet and allowed to fall on a steel die containing the ore. A heavy weight at the end of the rods crushed the ore. It was not unlike taking a sledgehammer and pounding rock to a fine powder on an anvil multiplied by fifty times. The noise was so great that an eyewitness said a person couldn't form a coherent train of thought near the mill. The metallic clanging could be heard in Crestone, a dozen miles north.

Spanish did, despite its small size, have a post office. It was open from May to November 1898. Mail from that point on was delivered to Cottonwood, two miles south.

Businesses along Harrison Avenue included a boarding-house, bottling works, grocery store, barbershop, general merchandise store and dairy. The town also had the Arcade Saloon and a billiard hall. The Miner's Mutual Protective Association raised $150 to construct a schoolhouse.

During a card game at the Arcade Saloon, a feud erupted between Hon Bedford and Frank Tandy. Tandy shouted at Bedford that he was going to kill him. Tandy promptly marched to the merchandise store and purchased a rifle while Bedford ran into the barbershop and got a pistol. In the gunfire that followed, Tandy was mortally wounded. After a funeral in Spanish, Frank Tandy's body was taken to the Cottonwood cemetery for burial. After an hour, Tandy's body was dug up and examined to satisfy some missing detail. Later, Tandy's body was exhumed again and taken to Denver for burial in a family plot.

John Bedford was charged with murder and released on a $8,000 bond. The motion to prosecute for some unknown reason was dropped.

Mining continued well past the turn of the twentieth century to the beginning of World War I. Past this point in time, there was little or no activity, and Spanish was abandoned.

For a map showing the location of Spanish, see "Cottonwood."

George Harlan, *Postmarks and Places*, Golden Bell Press, Denver, 1976, pp. 112-116.

Tiv Wilkins, *Colorado Railroads*, Pruett Publishing Company, Boulder, Colorado, 1974, p. 134.

William H. Bauer, James L. Ozment and John H. Willard, *Colorado Post Offices*, Colorado Railroad Museum, Golden, Colorado, 1990, p. 134.

STUNNER

Now a U.S. Forest Service Campground

- *Conejos County, Alamosa River drainage*
- *Accessible via graded dirt road*
- *Town had a post office; no structures remain*

This photograph was taken by George L. Beam in 1913, when Stunner was repopulated. A sign on the tent reads "Drugs." *(Denver Public Library GB-7964)*

Stunner was first called Conejos Camp, then the name was changed to Loyton. Under the Loyton name, it got its own post office in September 1884. The following month, the post office closed, but in 1886, it was reopened under the name Stunner. The post office lasted until 1894.

When Muriel Sibell Wolle, author of *Stampede to Timberline*, visited Stunner in the 1940s, the site was void of structures. It wasn't until she looked down on the site that she could see faint traces of its streets in the meadow. The first ore was located in the area in 1882, and by 1889, the town had 150 residents. In 1891, only twenty people remained, but between 1892 and 1894, the population increased to around 100.

Stunner was less isolated after 1884 when the Le Duc and Sanchez Toll Road Company constructed a road that followed the Conejos River past Platoro. Above Platoro, a series of switchbacks was cut into the mountainside over Stunner Pass and down into the Alamosa River drainage to reach Stunner.

Florence McCarty lived in Stunner as a little girl and wrote about the time when her father took the family to a deserted cabin in the town in 1912. At the time, there was only one full-time resident, and abandoned cabins sat on both sides of the river. The town was repopulated in 1913 when new veins of silver ore were discovered. A restaurant opened as well as a drug store. The town's only telephone was housed in the drug store. A sawmill kept the town supplied with milled lumber. There was sufficient population to reopen the post office in 1913, but the boom lasted only until the following year when the post office again closed. An old photograph of Stunner reveals that it was never a large town with one false-front store and five cabins.

The site today is difficult to find and sits next to a U.S. Forest Service campground. The dead-end road to the campground passes through the site. There is one cabin on the hillside overlooking the town site that may be of a later vintage.

For a map showing the location of the Stunner site, see "Platoro."

Florence McCarty, "Dad's Mine and a Little Town Called Stunner," *San Luis Valley Historian*, Vol. XXII, No. 4, 1990, pp. 14, 23-25.

Muriel Sibell Wolle, *Stampede to Timberline*, Sage Books, Chicago, 1949, pp. 311-312.

Robert L. Brown, *Ghost Towns of the Colorado Rockies*, Caxton Printers, Caldwell, Idaho, 1977, pp. 344-347.

William H. Bauer, James L. Ozment and John H. Willard, *Colorado Post Offices*, Colorado Railroad Museum, Golden, Colorado, 1990, pp. 92, 136.

SUMMITVILLE

One of Colorado's Largest Gold Camps

* *Rio Grande County, Wightman Creek drainage*
* *Accessible via graded dirt road*
* *Town had a post office; many remaining structures*

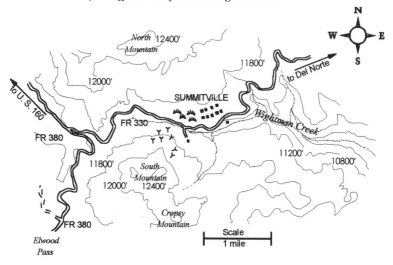

The easiest way to reach Summitville is from U.S. 160 above South Fork on the way to Wolf Creek Pass. FR 380 leads up Park Creek to a turnoff at FR 330 as indicated. There are other routes as well: from the south over Elwood Pass and from Del Norte via Grayback Mountain.

J. L. Wightman, during an exploration into the San Juan Mountains, made the first gold discovery in 1870 at the foot of South Mountain along a small stream. Placer claims were staked out by members of Wightman's group, and a mining district was formed under the name Summit or Summitville. The party panned gold throughout 1870 until winter arrived. A rush of prospectors came into the area the following spring along with

250

the members of Wightman's group. In all, about 150 entered the area, some while the snow still lay deep on the tundra. Many were discouraged by the end of the summer, and all but three left. Among those who stayed were Wightman, P. J. Peterson and J. O. Johnson. The group took their gold dust to Denver and divided it three ways. It was worth only $170.

Very few returned to the area the following summer, but Peterson and Johnson worked their claim as partners. The first lode discovery was made that summer by Dr. R. F. Adams. A mining camp called Summit or Summitville was established on the north side of South Mountain in a wide meadow at an elevation of 11,200 feet. Heavy snow, severe cold and inadequate shelter prevented year-round occupation. Del Norte served as the wintering ground for those working at Summitville.

The year 1873 marked the time the richest mines were discovered, including the Little Annie. It was found based on a piece of gold-bearing float discovered by P. J. Peterson and another man. When one of them showed the piece in a Del Norte saloon, an all-out stampede to Summitville followed.

The old Summitville boardinghouse sits on the opposite side of a shallow valley from the remains of the town. *(Sonje Jessen SJ101)*

An amalgamation mill was constructed in 1875 to remove fine gold particles using mercury. Gold has an affinity to mercury and is relatively easy to separate from the amalgamation using cloth followed by a retort. Substantial cabins were constructed at Summitville to provide adequate shelter for the miners who spent the winter. A post office opened in 1876 under the name "Summit."

The entire South Mountain became covered with 2,500 individual mining claims, but over time, only a dozen or so proved profitable. By 1883, Summitville had grown to become the largest gold producer in Colorado, and no less than nine mills were in operation. The population fluctuated from 300 to 600. Mail was delivered from Del Norte three times a week, and the *Summitville Nugget* began publication. By 1886, Summitville could boast of its fourteen saloons.

Gold ran out in the original deposits, and in 1887, the population began to fall. Just 2 years later, all businesses had closed and only twenty-five people remained. The directors and stockholders of the Golconda Mining Company, owner of most of the claims, decided to sell the company. Thomas Bowen, its president, resigned in 1891, and 2 years later, Summitville was just another

Located in a soggy meadow, the rows of abandoned homes at Summitville are well worth the visit. *(Kenneth Jessen 121C8)*

Colorado ghost town.

In 1907, Jack Pickens was working for the A. C. Reynolds Corporation, owner of the Aztec Mine at Summitville. He found a large piece of gold-bearing float next to an old wagon road that skirted the base of a cliff. Because of its location, it could not have tumbled down from any of the active mines in the region, and it had to have come from the face of the cliff. The following summer, Pickens looked for the source of the gold and saw a piece of rock identical to the float. He chipped away and looked at it; it too was filled with gold. He carefully replaced the rock in its original position to prevent discovery of this new lode.

Pickens set about trying to get a lease on the property where he made his discovery. A. C. Reynolds knew Pickens had found something and accused him of withholding vital information. The cliff, however, was not on the Reynolds property.

After many years, Judge Wiley in Del Norte negotiated a lease on behalf of Pickens, and large-scale mining began in 1934. The following year, the post office reopened. Old mines were reworked and new mines were opened by the Summitville Consolidated Mines, Inc. In the town, seventy new homes were constructed. A water system was developed, and the town got a bathhouse, bunkhouses and large dining hall. Summitville also got its own school as its population climbed to 700. It was Colorado's leading gold producer prior to World War II.

During the war, the U.S. Government ordered all gold mining to stop. Some copper was mined at Summitville, but after the war was over, gold mining resumed.

In 1948, two mills were in operation, and the town now had a couple of stores. Some sixty to seventy of the homes were occupied and a boardinghouse was built to accommodate nearly 300 men. The town grew to an estimated 1,500 with 900 men on the mining company's payroll. The gold ore, however, eventually ran out.

Exploration work was done during the 1950s. In 1956, the town had only thirteen miners, three women and a baby. Since then, Summitville reverted to a ghost town. When mining continued, miners were brought in by bus from Del Norte. Mining ended in the 1990s after a serious potassium cyanide spill. The liner used for heap-leaching leaked this toxic chemical into the Alamosa River.

Today, a good graded road leads from U.S. 160, up a series of switchbacks, to Summitville. From FR 380, a left turn onto FR 330 is necessary to reach the site. From the Alamosa River side, a second road comes in from the south over scenic Elwood Pass. During the spring, this road is muddy and may require four-wheel drive. A third rough, rocky road climbs up Pinos Creek from Del Norte past the radio towers on Grayback Mountain.

Summitville is one of the best-preserved ghost towns in the state. At an elevation of nearly 11,800 feet, it is covered by snow much of the year. The town of ramshackle cabins was built in a poorly-drained meadow at the headwaters of Wightman Creek. Although the cabins can be seen above FR 330, to get to them requires going through a wet area. All but one of the homes constructed in the 1930s was razed and removed, leaving the earlier structures. There are about a dozen abandoned buildings in various stages of collapse sitting in two rows. They have a beautiful backdrop of a lush, green meadow surrounded by a dense forest and high mountains. Across the creek from the town is the old abandoned boardinghouse on private property and fenced off. Beyond the boardinghouse is the open pit mine created during the late 1980s.

Clara Pickens Vickers, "Jack Picken's Secret," *The San Luis Valley Historian,* Volume XXXI, No. 4, Alamosa, Colorado, 1999, pp. 5-8.

Deanna R. Scriver, "History of the Summitville Mining District," *The San Luis Valley Historian,* Volume XXII, No. 1, Alamosa, Colorado, 1990, pp. 7-16.

Mark Coolbaugh, "Summitville Mining and Exploration, 1965-1989," *The San Luis Valley Historian,* Volume XXII, No. 1, Alamosa, Colorado, 1990, pp. 28-32.

Muriel Sibell Wolle, *Stampede to Timberline,* Sage Books, Chicago, 1949, pp. 314-316.

William H. Bauer, James L. Ozment and John H. Willard, *Colorado Post Offices,* Colorado Railroad Museum, Golden, Colorado, 1990, p. 137.

TETON
Named for the High Peaks

- *Saguache County, South Crestone Creek drainage*
- *Access limited by private property*
- *Town had a post office; no structures remain*

Teton was located southeast of Crestone on South Crestone Creek. Its cemetery is still indicated on some topographic maps. The camp was supported by the Pelican Mine discovered in 1877. A stamp mill was constructed on the bank of the creek the following year. Aside from a few cabins, Teton had a boardinghouse and grocery store. Its post office opened in 1881 and lasted less than a year.

The gold ore came in small pockets making mining a risky proposition. Despite this, limited mining activity continued as late as the turn of the twentieth century.

The town was named for the three high jagged peaks north of Music Peak. Early settlers called the creek and the peaks Trios Tetons. English names replaced the Spanish names, and these peaks are now called Crestone Peak, Crestone Needle and Kit Carson Peak. All of them are in excess of 14,000 feet.

Teton is marked by a few scattered headstones at the cemetery. No structures remain at the site. *For a map showing the location of Teton, see "San Isabel."*

George Harlan, *Postmarks and Places*, Golden Bell Press, Denver, 1976, pp. 59-60.

Virginia McConnell Simmons, *The San Luis Valley*, University Press of Colorado, Niwot, Colorado, 1999, p. 185.

William H. Bauer, James L. Ozment and John H. Willard, *Colorado Post Offices,* Colorado Railroad Museum, Golden, Colorado, 1990, p. 140.

TRINCHERA
Home of Tom Tobin

- *Costilla County, Trinchera Creek drainage*
- *Site under Smith Reservoir*
- *Town did not have a post office; no structures remain*

Not a lot is known about the settlement of Trinchera, its size or how long it lasted. It was located south of Fort Garland on Trinchera Creek near its confluence with Sangre de Cristo Creek. Smith Reservoir covers the site today.

Its most famous resident was Tom Tobin. Tom and his wife, Pasquela Bernal, moved from the Taos, New Mexico, area to Costilla County in 1861, and beginning in 1863, spent their summers along Trinchera Creek tending their livestock. They moved to Trinchera permanently in 1872.

The worst serial killers in Colorado history were the Espinosas. All attempts to bring them to justice had failed. When it was learned that the killers were in the San Luis Valley, Colonel Tappin called upon Tobin to track the Espinosas down and to bring back their heads. Although Tobin worked best alone, Tappin forced this former Army scout to take a lieutenant, fifteen soldiers and a Mexican boy. In September 1863, after a relatively brief chase through dense brush along La Veta Creek, Tobin gunned down the Espinosas. He decapitated one of them and the Mexican boy decapitated the other. Tobin then delivered the heads to Tappin in a gunnysack. It took Tobin several years, however, to collect his reward of $1,500.

Kenneth Jessen, *Colorado Gunsmoke*, J. V. Publications, Loveland, Colorado, 1986, pp. 46-47.

Virginia McConnell Simmons, *The San Luis Valley*, University Press of Colorado, Niwot, Colorado, 1999, p. 306.

VIEJO SAN ACACIO and SAN ACACIO

- *Costilla County, Culebra Creek drainage*
- *Accessible via paved and graded dirt roads*
- *One town had a post office; several original structures*

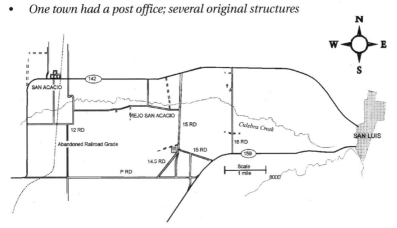

Viejo (Old) San Acacio and San Acacio are located west of San Luis and are easy to find.

Viejo (old) San Acacio was first called Plaza Abajo or Lower Culebra and was settled in 1853 shortly after San Luis. It has the oldest standing church in Colorado, constructed in 1856. Oral tradition holds that settlers came into the area during the 1840s, but that a permanent town was not established until later. According to the information gathered by Virginia McConnell Simmons, a miraculous appearance of Saint James or San Acacio on horseback occurred during a raid by Native Americans. This frightened the Native Americans thus saving the town. The town

257

Viejo San Acacio is the site of the oldest standing church in Colorado. There are several other abandoned buildings in this town, which was settled in 1853. *(Kenneth Jessen 121A6)*

also had a Penitente morada (meeting place). One family hangs on at Viejo San Acacio, otherwise the old town is abandoned. The site is located south of Colorado 142 about three miles east of the "new" San Acacio.

The new town of San Acacio was the most promising town in the region, and the Costilla Estate Development Company and the Sanchez Ditch and Reservoir Company both had offices in the town. San Acacio got its own post office in 1909, and the following year, the San Luis Southern arrived, providing railroad service. The railroad constructed a large two-story depot, which remains standing today. It has been converted into a bed and breakfast. San Acacio also had a vegetable warehouse used until the 1950s. Its businesses included several stores and a hotel.

The San Acacio bank was robbed in 1922 by bandits from a town in northern New Mexico. They hid the $4,000 in loot in an inner tube and a mitten. The Costilla County sheriff used a tip to intercept the thieves and recover nearly all of the money.

After World War II started, many California Japanese were forced into internment camps. Other Japanese-Americans escaped the coastal towns and moved to the San Luis Valley. Some families settled in San Acacio.

Today, there are a number of people living in San Acacio, but the numerous abandoned buildings provide evidence that the town is just a shadow of its former size.

San Acacio has a number of residents, and the old depot is now used as a bed and breakfast. There are, however, a number of abandoned buildings. *(Sonje Jessen SJ102)*

Virginia McConnell Simmons, "Hispanic Place Names of the San Luis Valley," *The San Luis Valley Historian*, Volume XXIII, Number 3, Alamosa, Colorado, 1991, p. 36.

Virginia McConnell Simmons, *The San Luis Valley*, University Press of Colorado, Niwot, Colorado, 1999, pp. 239, 240.

William H. Bauer, James L. Ozment and John H. Willard, *Colorado Post Offices*, Colorado Railroad Museum, Golden, Colorado, 1990, p. 127.

VILLA GROVE, GARIBALDI
Plus a Company Town in Steel Canyon

- *Saguache County, San Luis Creek drainage*
- *Garibaldi site accessible by graded dirt road; Villa Grove located along U.S. 285*
- *Villa Grove is an occupied site; Garibaldi had a post office and is abandoned with no structures remaining*

The valley line of the Denver & Rio Grande connected Alamosa with Salida via Poncha Pass. This train, powered by a narrow gauge steam locomotive, was photographed in 1950 north of Villa Grove by noted railroad photographer Otto Perry. *(Denver Public Library OP-8504)*

Garibaldi was located southeast of Villa Grove near San Luis Creek. At the time it was settled in 1869, Judge de Witt Gravis, a local magistrate, wrote that the settlers were, "... a sturdy band of patriot settlers on the eastern side (of the valley) you could count on your fingers ... Nearly all had worn the blue or the gray. They lived together like a band of brothers."

Until 1870, residents had to travel 75 miles to Fort Garland for their mail. One resident applied for a post office, and its letter distribution desk opened in June in the front room of a home. Mail arrived one day a week for the seven families living in the town. Mail service was transferred to Villa Grove 2 years later. Postal records show that the Garibaldi post office simply changed names.

Villa Grove has changed little over the years. The town is partially abandoned, and as of 1999, these two old stores appear to be up for sale. Its general store remains open and sells homemade pies. *(Kenneth Jessen 111D8)*

Garibaldi was abandoned, but Villa Grove survived. Villa Grove was on the main stage route that ran from Poncha Pass to Alamosa, and in 1881, the Denver & Rio Grande gave the town its all-important railroad connection. Villa Grove remained the terminus for this branch of the Denver & Rio Grande for 9 years. The narrow gauge line was extended to Alamosa and included a 51 miles of perfectly straight track, the longest tangent in the United States. Later, the line was converted to dual-gauge allowing the passage of both standard gauge and narrow gauge cars.

The Villa Grove post office was composed of two boxes, number one and number two. This post office occupied the corner of a card table, and into box number one was placed the incoming mail. The other box was used for the outgoing mail. The outgoing mail was hand stamped and placed in a mail pouch. Other parts of the card table were covered with harnesses and other items associated with the stagecoach business.

At the Garibaldi site is a row of trees marking where its structures once stood. The site can also be recognized by a well. *For a map showing Garibaldi's location, see "Bismark."*

The Colorado Decorative Marble Company constructed a company town 9 miles southeast of Villa Grove in Steel Canyon. This town apparently did not have a name and little information exists on its size. The company constructed a large finishing mill on the hillside above the town and probably began operating in 1890. It is not known what remains since the site is on private property.

The Colorado Decorative Marble Company constructed this company town 9 miles southeast of Villa Grove in Steel Canyon. This photograph was taken between 1890 and 1910. *(Denver Public Library x-13929)*

George Harlan, *Postmarks and Places*, Golden Bell Press, Denver, 1976, pp. 14-16, 19.

Muriel Sibell Wolle, *Stampede to Timberline*, Sage Books, Chicago, 1949, p. 296.

Tiv Wilkins, *Colorado Railroads*, Pruett Publishing Company, Boulder, Colorado, 1974, pp. 37, 79.

William H. Bauer, James L. Ozment and John H. Willard, *Colorado Post Offices*, Colorado Railroad Museum, Golden, Colorado, 1990, p. 59, p. 147.

AREA FIFTEEN 15

Hinsdale and Mineral Counties

AREA 15: Hinsdale and Mineral Counties

Selected Towns

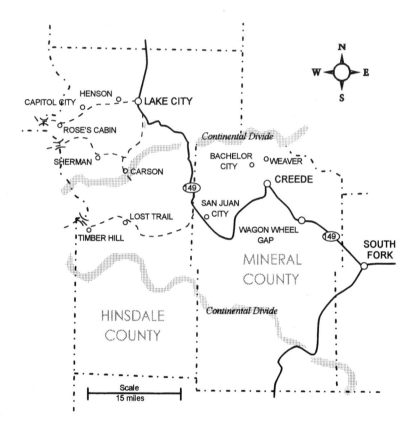

Introduction to Hinsdale and Mineral Counties

A rea 15 consists of Hinsdale and Mineral counties. The earliest settlements were along the primary route to Silverton, up the Rio Grande and over Stony Pass. These settlements date to the early 1870s and include places such as Antelope Springs, San Juan City, Lost Trail and Jennison. No major towns formed in these counties until Lake City was founded in 1874, followed by Creede in 1889. A number of satellite settlements were established around these two principal towns. After the silver ore was exhausted and the mining boom ended, only Lake City survived in Hinsdale County. Creede continues to be the principal town in Mineral County with a small surrounding population in vacation homes and ranches. The ghost towns in Area 15 are scattered over a large area, and some of them are accessible only by four-wheel drive vehicle. Only a few sites are posted no trespassing making this a delightful area to visit.

Alferd Packer, Colorado's Cannibal

One of the most bizarre events in Colorado history took place in Hinsdale County near Lake City. On November 17, 1873, a party of 21 miners left Salt Lake City for the newly discovered silver deposits in the San Juan Mountains. The party and its supply wagons arrived at a Ute Indian encampment at the confluence of the Uncompahgre and Gunnison rivers (near present-day Delta) on January 20, 1874. Chief Ouray was present and advised the prospectors not to continue into the mountains until spring.

Some listened, however Alferd Packer wanted to be among the first to stake a claim. He convinced others that he knew this country and persuaded five men to follow him. They left on February 9 with provisions for only 10 days.

In a blinding snowstorm 65 days later, Packer walked into the Los Pinos Indian Agency alone. The agency was located near Cochetopa Pass south of present-day Gunnison. General Adams welcomed him, but when offered breakfast, Packer turned away at

Looking almost like Charles Manson, Alferd Packer appears in a photograph probably taken prior to his experiences in the San Juan Mountains. He has the distinction of being Colorado's most notorious cannibal. *(Colorado Historical Society F-6433)*

the sight of the food. His strange behavior led to questions. Packer claimed he had been traveling through the mountains subsisting on rose buds and roots. He also said his Winchester rifle did him little good because game was scarce, and after he became ill, his companions abandoned him. General Adams, now even more suspicious, asked Packer about the fate of his companions. Packer deflected this question and provided a vivid description of his suffering, which awakened the sympathy of the people at the agency.

After resting for several days, Packer rode east to Saguache. He went on a drinking binge and spent money freely, although he had claimed he was penniless when he began his trip at the Ute encampment.

A man named Lutzenheiser related that he was also in a party headed into the mountains and ignored Chief Ouray's advice. He managed to escape winter's death grip by killing game to keep from starving. After hearing about Packer's experiences, Lutzenheiser aroused more suspicion about Packer's story. A theory developed that Packer murdered his companions and robbed them of their money and food. Several men were sent from the Los Pinos Indian Agency to Saguache to bring Packer back to act as a guide to find his companions.

Not far from the agency, an Indian discovered what appeared to be a piece of human flesh on the trail used by Packer.

A more sinister theory was put forth that Packer ate his companions to stay alive. When confronted with the evidence, Packer admitted he alone survived and said that the others had been killed, one after the other. He was forced to make a statement under oath and added some details to his story. He said that after running out of food, the party wandered for several days in the mountains. Packer left the group to gather firewood, and upon his return, old man Swan had been killed. The others were sitting around the campfire roasting pieces of Swan's flesh. General Adams was visibly shaken by this vivid account.

After a day, Packer said the remaining members of the party left the camp taking with them chunks of Swan. After 4 or 5 days, Humphreys died and was eaten. After gathering firewood again, Packer returned to the camp and found that Miller had been killed. George Noon and Wilson Bell said they killed Miller accidentally, but Packer knew better. Noon and Bell had agreed previously that Miller would be the next to become a meal. Miller was a stout German, but was sick and held up the party. According to Packer's story, the party remained in camp living off of Miller's

flesh, then Bell shot Noon. This left Packer and Bell, and they lived off of Noon's flesh.

Packer continued his gruesome story and related how he and Bell camped near Lake San Cristobal. Packer admitted killing Bell as an act of self-defense.

General Adams insisted that Packer guide a party to the

The first Alferd Packer trial took place in the Hinsdale County Courthouse in Lake City where Packer was sentenced to die in 1883 for killing his companions. The structure was built in 1877. *(Kenneth Jessen 105B9)*

Gunnison River, then south along the Lake Fork toward the future site of Lake City. Adams promised Packer that if the evidence agreed with his story, he would be released. After retracing his trail for a while, Packer claimed he was lost. Nothing was discovered during this trip to either confirm or deny Packer's story. Packer was, however, placed in irons and sent to the log jail in Saguache.

A second party was dispatched by General Adams to find Packer's companions. They discovered two camps near Lake San Cristobal. The entire party stopped at one camp, while the other camp appeared to have had one occupant. A primitive shelter and neat fireplace indicated that the camp had been occupied for a long time. Had Packer killed his companions, then moved to another camp while he lived off their flesh? No trace could be found of the missing men.

It wasn't until August 1874 that the bodies of Packer's companions were discovered. An artist for *Harper's Weekly* on vacation came across the partially decomposed bodies of five men. They

The five bodies of Packer's victims were buried at this location above Lake San Cristobal on the road over Slumgullion Pass. Benjamin Jessen is shown in this photograph taken in 1983. The bodies were later exhumed to verify that Packer did in fact hack pieces of flesh off his companions. The bodies were then reburied. *(Kenneth Jessen 075A9)*

were together; four were lying side by side with the fifth nearby. Blanket fibers were embedded in open gashes in the heads of four of the victims as if they had been killed while sleeping. One body was missing its head, and chunks of flesh had been hacked off the chest and thighs. At least one other body also was mutilated. By the time word reached Saguache, Packer had escaped.

For 9 years, Alferd Packer lived in freedom under an assumed name. He was finally caught, and on April 13, 1883, he was found guilty of premeditated murder in a trial at the Hinsdale County Courthouse in

At Packer's first trial, Judge Melville Gerry sentenced the cannibal to die. Packer was later granted a stay of execution. *(Colorado Historical Society F-6396)*

Lake City. Packer was sentenced to die by hanging on May 19. This was the first death sentence handed down in Hinsdale County. It was also the first time in Colorado a man had been convicted of murder connected with cannibalism.

Even the worst tragedy can have a humorous twist. Judge Melville B. Gerry allegedly delivered the following stern rebuke at the conclusion of the trial, "Packer, ye man-eatin' son of a bitch, they was seven dimmycrats in Hinsdale County and ye eat five of 'em, God damn ye! I sentins ye to be hanged by the neck until ye're dead, dead, dead as a warnin' ag'in reducing the dimmycratic populashun in the state." Judge Gerry never said anything of the kind, and the statement was an exaggerated version of comments made by an Irish saloon keeper named Larry Dolan.

The story of Alferd Packer did not end, however, and the cannibal was granted a stay of execution because the law under which he was found guilty was unconstitutional. The Gunnison jail, where Packer was held, became a tourist attraction of sorts. The cannibal made trinkets from his hair and bits of wood, which he sold to visitors. His conviction was overturned, but he was found guilty in a second trial in 1886. This time it was on five counts of manslaughter. He was sentenced to five consecutive eight-year terms in prison. In 1901, Packer was paroled by Colorado Gov. Charles S. Thomas. In 1907, the 64-year-old Packer was found unconscious in Deer Creek Canyon suffering from epileptic fits and was taken in by a local resident. He died after repeatedly relating the tragedy of his life.

"A Cannibal's Confession," *Rocky Mountain News*, March 17, 1883.

"A Colorado Tragedy – the Great Trial," Gunnison *Review-Press*, August 4, 1886.

"Change in Venue," Denver *Tribune-Republican*, July 23, 1886.

"Denver Post call for Mercy and Justice," *Denver Post*, January 8, 1900.

Ervan Kushner, *Alferd G. Packer – Cannibal! Victim?* Platte 'N Press, Frederick, Colorado, 1980.

Gladys R. Bueler, *Colorado's Colorful Characters*, Pruett Publishing Company, Boulder, Colorado, 1981, pp. 60-61.

"Governor Thomas tries to clear Myth," *The Silver World*, November 29, 1930.

"Guilty – to be Hanged May 19, 1883," *Rocky Mountain News*, April 14, 1883.

"Human Skull Found One Mile from Scene," *Rocky Mountain News*, August 18, 1875.

Kenneth Jessen, *Eccentric Colorado*, J. V. Publications, Loveland, Colorado, 1985, pp. 51-61.

"Man-eater Packer Captured," *Rocky Mountain News*, March 13, 1883.

Margaret Bates, *Lake City—A Quick History*, Little London Press, Colorado Springs, Colorado, 1973, pp. 14-17.

ANTELOPE SPRINGS
and SAN JUAN CITY
Plus Other Stops Along the Stony Pass Trail

- *Hinsdale, Mineral and San Juan counties, Rio Grande drainage*
- *Sites are accessible via paved, dirt and four-wheel drive roads*
- *Towns had post offices; some original structures remain*

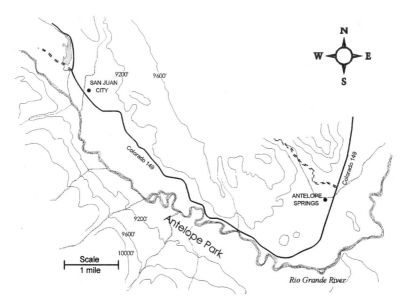

West of Creede along Colorado 149 is the Antelope Springs site, now on private property. At San Juan City, the combination stage stop and store remains standing and is used by the Freemon Guest Ranch.

NOTE: Grassy Hill is in San Juan County and is included in Area 15 because of its economic and physical ties to these other towns.

271

The primary route into the rich mining areas surrounding Silverton was up the Rio Grande and over Stony Pass. The first wagon road to traverse this route was constructed in 1872 by Emery Hamilton. The initial need for this road was to bring heavy machinery to the Little Giant Mill near Silverton. The machinery included a crusher and a 115-horsepower engine.

The road over Stony Pass became increasingly popular. It spawned a number of small communities and stage stops to serve the freighters, teamsters and stagecoach passengers. The end of the Stony Pass route came in 1882 when the Denver & Rio Grande completed its narrow gauge line from Durango to Silverton along the Animas River. Most freight and passenger traffic was then by rail.

The first stage stop along the Stony Pass road was known as Antelope Springs, located in Antelope Park. Today, the site is occupied by the Broken Arrow Ranch. Meals and overnight accommodations were once offered to travelers. During the 1880s, stagecoaches left Antelope Springs on Mondays, Wednesdays and Fridays at 10:30 a.m. and arrived in Silverton at 8:30 p.m. the following day. The schedule from Silverton was for the stagecoach to leave at 5 a.m. on Mondays, Wednesdays and Fridays arriving at Antelope Springs at 2 p.m. the following day.

George Alden came to Antelope Springs in 1875 and started a halfway house on the stage road running between Del Norte and Lake City. The stage line over Stony Pass to Silverton branched off at Antelope Springs. The site was named for a salt lick that attracted antelope and deer. Alden became the Antelope Springs postmaster in 1877, but served only a short time. Mrs. Crowley became the postmaster in 1878. After George Alden's death, Christina Alden sold Antelope Springs.

There was one noteworthy event at Antelope Springs. It occurred in 1878 when a German immigrant, Edward Mennswisch, stopped at Antelope Springs for a noon meal. He was seated inside the stage station's double doors and noticed Montie Moreland, a teenager, standing by the road. Moreland was involved in a heated argument with George Alden. The argument

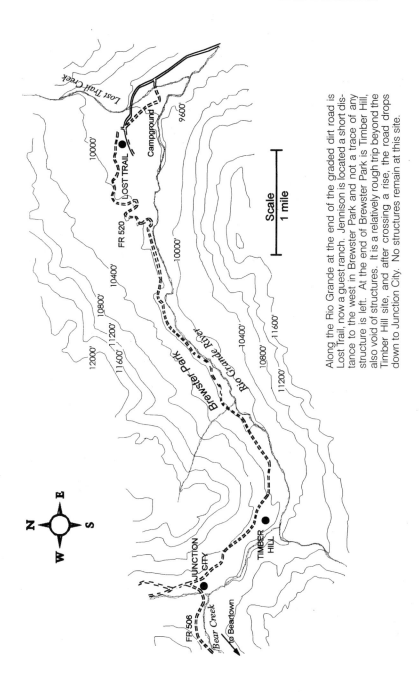

Scale
1 mile

Along the Rio Grande at the end of the graded dirt road is Lost Trail, now a guest ranch. Jennison is located a short distance to the west in Brewster Park and not a trace of any structure is left. At the end of Brewster Park is Timber Hill, also void of structures. It is a relatively rough trip beyond the Timber Hill site, and after crossing a rise, the road drops down to Junction City. No structures remain at this site.

Junction City was located where Bear and Pole creeks join the Rio Grande. The town was laid out in this large irregular meadow in the spring of 1894 as a transportation center and possibly a stage stop. One cabin remained until the 1940s. *(U.S. Geological Survey, C. W. Cross 1003)*

grew more intense, then Moreland pulled a revolver. Alden and Moreland struggled, and a single shot rang out. Alden was mortally wounded in the thigh, but managed to knock Moreland to the ground. Alden then disarmed the teenager. He yelled for someone to help him and collapsed.

Edward Mennswisch and Alden's wife Christina carried Alden into the house. His boots were filled with blood. They laid him on a bed where he soon died from loss of blood.

The dispute between Moreland and Alden began when Alden tried to embarrass Moreland's mother, Mrs. Crowley, into giving up her postmaster's job at the stage station. Christina Alden visited the post office to register several letters on a Sunday. Mrs. Crowley said she couldn't register the letters, but would do so the following day. This angered Christina, and she snatched up her letters and stormed out of the office. Her parting words were, in effect, that Mrs. Crowley's hired girl was there only to entice customers. Mrs. Crowley then accused Christina Alden of being a slut.

The following day, Monday, George Alden returned with the

letters and challenged Mrs. Crowley to repeat the insult she had hurled at his wife. An angry conversation followed, and Alden called Mrs. Crowley a whore.

This prompted Montie Moreland to stick his .44-caliber revolver in his belt and march to the Alden residence. Here he demanded an apology. Alden, upon being confronted, threatened to rip open Moreland's belly if he continued to interfere. The argument ended up on the road. Moreland attempted to hit Alden over the head with the butt of his gun, and Alden was shot. Moreland surrendered to the justice of the peace at Wagon Wheel Gap and pleaded guilty to manslaughter. He was sentenced to 7 years in the state penitentiary at Canon City.

When the Denver & Rio Grande reached Silverton, the station was abandoned, and the stage stop became part of the Soward Ranch. All traces of the original stage station are gone, and the land is privately owned.

Heading north, San Juan City was the next stop on this road. San Juan City was located at the upper end of Antelope Park near the confluence of Crooked Creek and the Rio Grande. It was laid out by an Englishman named Franklin. He envisioned a city of 150 or more blocks. Capt. W. H. Green constructed a cabin at San Juan City, and when the Colorado Territorial Legislature established Hinsdale County in 1874, San Juan City was selected as the temporary county seat. Green's cabin became the courthouse. It was used as such until February 1875, when county residents decided to move the county seat north to Lake City. Businesses in San Juan City included a hotel and store.

James Galloway made San Juan City into a stage stop in 1876 by constructing corrals, shops and storage buildings. Today, the site is part of the Freemon Guest Ranch, and the combination stage stop and store remains the dominant structure. It houses the office for the guest ranch. A small log structure, which once served as the post office, also remains standing.

The original hotel for stagecoach passengers was a long, single-story structure constructed of logs. It had a sod roof and consisted of six or seven rooms, each with their own entrance. Since the days of the stage stop, the structure was used as a stable and storage shed and stood until 1962. Partially collapsed, it had deteriorated to the point where owners of the guest ranch razed the structure.

Contemporary newspaper accounts reported that San Juan City had about a dozen homes, but in a later edition, the newspaper confessed that San Juan City had only one tent and two cabins. In 1874, San Juan City's post office opened. At this location, the post office lasted until 1895, and in 1900, a new post office was established in the same area, but in Mineral County.

The town acted as a transfer point on the Del Norte to Silverton toll road. Freighters heading over Stony Pass would transfer their loads from wagons to pack animals. Eventually, the road was improved so wagons could travel over the pass. James Galloway ran the freight station, and 500,000 to 600,000 pounds of freight were transferred through the station every year until 1882. The arrival of the railroad in Silverton put an end to freight travel over this route. San Juan City became a guest ranch, and cabins were added.

The old barn at Lost Trail is the only remaining original structure and is still in daily use. It is located on the Lost Trail Ranch. The ranch is also the home of contemporary historian Carol Ann Witherill. She can pinpoint the location of the other stage stops along the route over Stony Pass. Visitors are welcome, and a cabin can be rented at this beautiful location. The old stage station once stood near the present-day road to the barn. Depending on rainfall and vegetation, Witherill can point out the ruts of the old wagon road crossing a broad meadow leading to the barn. A small settlement existed at Lost Trail from the 1870s until around 1883. A post office opened in 1878, and A. S. Goodrich opened a store the following year.

Beyond Lost Trail toward Stony Pass, the present-day road requires four-wheel drive. The original stage road climbed up over a knoll, then down the other side to a long meadow called

Brewster Park. Today's road contours around the knoll to enter the park.

The entrance to Brewster Park is marked by a cattle crossing and a sign. It is only three-quarters of a mile beyond Lost Trail. About a quarter of a mile beyond the entrance of Brewster Park, toward Stony Pass, was a stage station called Jennison. Developed by Charles and Irene Jennison, the stage station got a post office in January 1875. After the death of Charles in December, the post office closed. It reopened again in April 1877 after Joel Brewster purchased the stage stop. It closed again in December, then remained open until April 1879. At this time, Joel Brewster decided to move the stage station to the upper end of Brewster Park. The new station was called Timber Hill.

Jennison was located in a broad meadow. Nothing remains of the stage station today, however, metal objects and bits of broken china can be found at the site. Behind the site is a pit where freight wagons could be inspected and repairs made.

The Timber Hill site is at the base of a steep climb. The specific site is on a small side road running around the hillside to a meadow. This road leads a short distance to an informal camping

Now part of the Freemon Guest Ranch, the combination stage stop and store at San Juan City remains standing. *(Kenneth Jessen 122D1)*

area. In this meadow was located the stage station and corral. At one time, the ridgepole and part of the roof for the livery barn could be seen, but today nothing remains at the site. Timber Hill got its post office in April 1879 at the time it was established. The post office remained open until January 1881, a year before the railroad reached Silverton and traffic over Stony Pass declined.

The climb beyond Timber Hill is rough, narrow and steep. Less than 2 miles beyond Timber Hill, the road drops down into the Pole Creek crossing. In the spring, this crossing can be too deep for sport utility vehicles not equipped with a snorkel. Just prior to this crossing, the road to Beartown (FR 506) takes off to the south and immediately crosses the Rio Grande.

Once a substantial log structure, this could have been used as a stage station. It is located just below the east side of Stony Pass. *(Kenneth Jessen 122D7)*

Junction City was in a large irregular meadow where Bear and Pole creeks join the Rio Grande. In the spring of 1894, Junction City was laid out as a transportation center and possibly a stage stop. According to the *Creede Candle*, John Doherty set up a saloon, and a Salida man opened a real estate office. One cabin remained in the meadow at the time ghost town historian Muriel Sibell Wolle visited in the 1940s. Nothing marks the site today.

Beyond this point, the road continues to climb. As it enters a large meadow, the trail up Deep Creek leaves FR 520 for Cunningham Pass. Near this junction was yet another stage stop called Grassy Hill. The stage station once stood a short distance below FR 520 and is hard to locate. Only a few rotting logs mark the site.

Grassy Hill was established in 1878 by William D. Watson. It provided shelter for travelers, and a post office opened in January 1879. The office closed the following summer. A liquor license was issued to D. J. Shaw, who had a cabin that predated Watson's Grassy Hill facility. Since the two locations were close to each other, it can be assumed that Shaw used his cabin as a saloon.

After Grassy Hill, the road makes a switchback on the side of the steep meadow. Beyond Grassy Hill, the road makes a long sustained climb over Stony Pass. At the pass is a large log structure that could have been a shelter of some sort for travelers. There is a small mine near the structure. The road continues down Stony Pass to the Cunningham Gulch Road and on to Howardsville.

Allen Nossaman, *Many More Mountains, Volume 2: Ruts into Silverton*, Sundance Publications Limited, Denver, Colorado, 1993, pp. 98-99, 104-105, 178, 236, 238.

"George Alden Killed by Montie Moreland at Antelope Springs Stage Stop in 1878," *Silver Thread Scenic & Historic Byway*, Lake City, Colorado, Summer 1996, p. 7B

"Hinsdale's First Courthouse Located at San Juan City," *Silver Thread Scenic & Historic Byway*, Lake City, Colorado, Summer 1996, p. 15.

"Thrilling Days of Stage Coach Travel Recalled in Colorful Stony Pass Route," *Silver Thread Scenic & Historic Byway*, Lake City, Colorado, Summer 1996, pp. 1B-3B.

William H. Bauer, James L. Ozment and John H. Willard, *Colorado Post Offices*, Colorado Railroad Museum, Golden, Colorado, 1990, pp. 80, 128, 141.

BACHELOR CITY
High Altitude Town

- *Mineral County, Windy Gulch drainage*
- *Accessible by four-wheel drive road*
- *Town had a post office; no remaining structures*

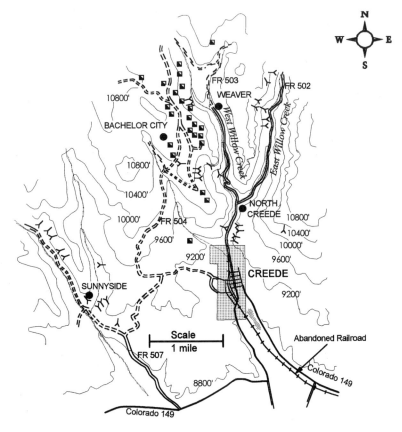

Bachelor City was one of several satellite towns around Creede. The site is accessible over dirt roads and can be approached either from Creede or from West Willow Creek.

A t 10,500 feet, well above Willow Creek, the town of Bachelor City was founded. To the north was the Amethyst Mine, the area's greatest silver mine. Below was the Commodore Mine; southeast of Bachelor City was Creede. John McKenzie located the Bachelor lode, one of the many mines that supported the town.

C. L. Calvin constructed the first home and a boardinghouse at the site in 1891. The town got its name from the absence of women. The Last Chance Mine hit pay dirt to the north, and its owners selected the Bachelor City site for the construction of its bunkhouses and mess hall. Soon, a livery stable was constructed followed by a saloon and other businesses. The town was laid out on an eighty-acre tract and divided into twenty-four blocks. From a meadow surrounded by a dense forest, mountains could be seen for miles from this lofty site. The sloping meadow made one end of the town about 100 feet higher than the other end. By March 1892, Bachelor City had grown to 100 houses, eight stores, assay offices, boardinghouses, hotels, restaurants and a dozen saloons.

As for its social life, one writer described the town saying, "Brawls and pistol-plays were of nightly occurrence in the numerous saloons and gambling dens that infested the place. Knock-down and drag-out fights were mere ordinary modes of recreation..."

What the town needed was religion, at least so thought Father Downey. He sponsored a benefit in Bachelor City's new opera house to raise money to build a Catholic church. The Bachelor City Dramatic Club produced "The Wild Irishman." The play was followed by two recitations and other performances. The evening closed with a dance, and the church building fund received $160.

After fire leveled most of Creede in June 1892, many moved to Bachelor City and its population doubled. The town quickly gained more homes bringing the total to 300. More hotels, grocery stores and hardware stores added to the business district. Bachelor City also had three clothing stores, a couple of barbers, and for the ladies, two milliners and dressmakers. The *Teller Topics* opened for business and solicited subscribers. A schoolhouse was constructed and began the year with 150 students.

A miner's union was active as well as several secret societies. The 1893 *Colorado Business Directory* listed seventy-two business establishments.

Because there was a Bachelor, California, the postal service refused to use the town name and selected Teller. The Teller post office opened in 1892, and at its peak, it served 8,000 people.

A minister, whose wife had died, moved to Bachelor City with his sixteen-year-old daughter. During the winter, she came down with bronchitis. The minister was called away to conduct a funeral and cautioned his daughter about the rough element in the town. He told her to remain in bed and not let anyone in the cabin.

When he returned, a saddle horse was tied outside. He rushed in to find a stranger bending over his daughter. Thinking the worst, the minister drew his revolver and fired. The stranger died on the spot. The daughter explained that the bronchitis had turned into pneumonia and that the stranger was a doctor. The girl soon died, and in remorse, the minister took his own life. The three bodies were discovered the following morning and because of the extreme difficulty in digging into the frozen soil, all three were buried on top of each other near the town site.

Photographs of Bachelor City reveal how large the town became. It spread across the high open plateau, and a row of substantial false-front stores defined its main street. The price of silver began dropping during the late 1880s. In 1893, the Sherman Silver Purchase Act was repealed, and the price of silver leveled off at half of its former value. Most of the silver mines closed, and the population declined to a few hundred. Eventually, all of its residents moved away, and the post office closed in 1912.

Muriel Sibell Wolle, when writing *Stampede to Timberline*, made several efforts during the 1940s to find the town site. She finally ran across the remains of Bachelor City's plank sidewalk stretching across the meadow. A couple of cabins lay half-hidden in a grove of aspen trees. The meadow was littered with debris, including bits of furniture, an old cupboard and a trunk. She also found a few stone foundations and the remains of a picket fence.

In 1952, a *Rocky Mountain News* editor found only the remains of the wooden sidewalk and a couple of rotting cabins. Today, only the corner of one of the town's many log homes remain. All other signs of this substantial town have vanished.

As this 1910 photograph clearly illustrates, Bachelor City was a town of substantial size. None of these structures remain today, in fact, hardly a trace of this street can be found at the site. *(Denver Public Library x-7139)*

Caroline Bancroft, *Unique Ghost Towns and Mountain Spots*, Johnson Publishing Company, Boulder, Colorado, 1961, pp. 75-77.

Don and Jean Griswold, *Colorado's Century of "Cities,"* self-published, 1958, pp. 248-250.

John K. Aldrich, *Ghosts of the Eastern San Juans*, Centennial Graphics, Lakewood, Colorado, 1987, pp. 9-10.

Muriel Sibell Wolle, *Stampede to Timberline*, Sage Books, Chicago, 1949, pp. 328-333.

Nolie Mumey, *Creede*, Artcraft Press, Denver, Colorado, 1949, pp. 154, 156-159.

Russ Collman, "There is no Night in Creede," *Trails Among the Columbine*, 1988, Sundance Publications Ltd., Denver, 1988, pp. 86-89.

William H. Bauer, James L. Ozment and John H. Willard, *Colorado Post Offices*, Colorado Railroad Museum, Golden, Colorado, 1990, p. 140.

BURROWS PARK, TELLURIUM and WHITE CROSS

- *Hinsdale County, Lake Fork of the Gunnison River drainage*
- *Accessible via high ground clearance vehicle*
- *Towns had post offices; several structures remain*

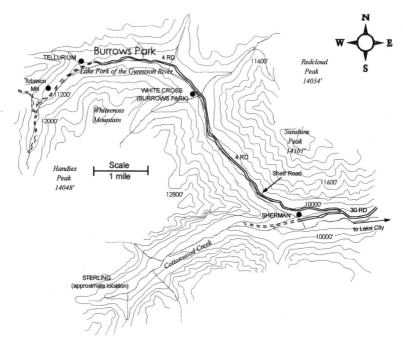

White Cross (Burrows Park) and Tellurium are situated in a high mountain valley. The road from Sherman has been improved in recent years to so that an automobile can reach the area. Beyond Tellurium, a four-wheel drive vehicle is better suited for the trip.

Beginning about 5 miles beyond Sherman and located on the Lake Fork of the Gunnison River were two small mining camps. They were in a long valley called Burrows Park at an elevation well over 10,000 feet. The park was named for Charles Burrows, a prospector whose explorations date to 1873. At the park's upper end was the small mining camp of Tellurium, which got its own post office in 1875. A year later, Burrows Park got a post office. In 1882, the Burrows Park post office changed its name to White Cross. This name came from the nearby mountain with a white quartz cross. By this time, the post office at Tellurium had closed. White Cross continued to receive mail delivery until 1912.

During the winter of 1878-1879, nine families spent the winter in the park. Christmas dinner at Burrows Park in 1881 was covered in a Lake City newspaper. The "Hotel de Clawson" was mentioned and was probably a person's home. From 1890 to 1900, White Cross was listed as having 300 people.

The entire Burrows Park area was dependent on galena ore containing silver, copper and lead. Lack of good roads limited early development, but even after a wagon road was constructed

At Burrows Park, two cabins have been restored by the U.S. Forest Service. They sit at the Burrows Park-White Cross site where Grizzly Gulch and Silver Creek enter Lake Fork. (Kenneth Jessen 105A1)

This was probably the office for the Tobasco Mill. It sits above the road through Burrows Park. *(Kenneth Jessen 105A4)*

from Sherman, the mines in this area produced little relative to other areas.

In 1880, guidebook author George Crofutt passed through the area and listed only Tellurium. He mentioned a mill, but said it was idle most of the time and estimated Tellurium's population at a dozen. To confuse the issue, Crofutt said Burrows Park was sometimes called Argentum and listed its population at 100. And to further add confusion, he wrote, "This place is called by some people Tellurium."

Despite evidence to the contrary, author-historian Robert Brown's research concluded that these towns were seasonally occupied since snow closed the road during the winter. He also stated that the town of Burrows Park was 5 miles long and only one-half mile wide and that its peak population could not have exceeded a few hundred. Historic photographs verify that six cabins once stood along the road at Burrows Park.

The Tobasco Mill was constructed in 1901 above Tellurium and kept the place alive. Using gravity separation, the mill concentrated the ore for shipment to a smelter. The primary area mines were the Tobasco, Little Sarah, Bonhomie, Cracker Jack, Allen Dale, Troy, Providence and Mountain King.

Today, Burrows Park can be reached by vehicles with sufficient ground clearance. Above Sherman, the road is constructed on a shelf. This was an exciting, exposed, single lane road for many years blasted out of a cliff high above Lake Fork. In recent years, the U.S. Forest Service widened and improved the road to allow passage of two-way traffic. At Burrows Park, there are two cabins restored by the U.S. Forest Service. They sit at the Burrows Park-White Cross site where Grizzly Gulch and Silver Creek enter Lake Fork. A parking lot has been established for climbers headed to Redcloud, Sunshine or Handies peaks, all in excess of 14,000 feet. At the upper end of the park, the road continues past the ruins of the Tobasco Mill and over 12,620-foot Cinnamon Pass into the Animas Fork drainage.

Allen Nossaman, *Many More Mountains*, Volume 2: Ruts into Silverton, Sundance Publications Limited, Denver, Colorado, 1993, p. 37.

Don and Jean Griswold, *Colorado's Century of "Cities,"* self-published, 1958, pp. 144-145.

Muriel Sibell Wolle, *Stampede to Timberline*, Sage Books, Chicago, 1949, p. 359.

Robert L. Brown, *Jeep Trails to Colorado Ghost Towns*, Caxton Printers, Caldwell, Idaho, 1963, pp. 64-66, 226-227.

Ron Ruhoff, "Back Country Adventures in Mineral and Hinsdale Counties," *Trails Among the Columbine*, 1988, Sundance Publications Ltd., Denver, 1988, pp. 121-122.

William H. Bauer, James L. Ozment and John H. Willard, *Colorado Post Offices*, Colorado Railroad Museum, Golden, Colorado, 1990, pp. 26, 140, 151.

CAPITOL CITY

And George Lee's Mansion

- *Hinsdale County, Henson Creek drainage*
- *Accessible by graded dirt road*
- *Town had a post office; two original structures remain*

When Muriel Sibell Wolle returned in 1959, only half of the brick Lee Mansion remained. Just a few years later, it was nothing but a pile of bricks. *(Denver Public Library x-5315)*

Established in the spring of 1877 at an elevation of 9,480 feet, where Henson Creek and its north fork join, was a town originally called Galena City. In this broad, flat area surrounded by high mountains, the founders thought that this town had a good chance at becoming Colorado's capital despite its remote location.

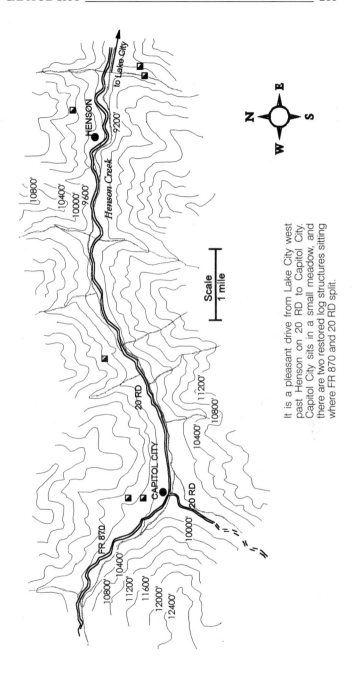

It is a pleasant drive from Lake City west past Henson on 20 RD to Capitol City. Capitol City sits in a small meadow, and there are two restored log structures sitting where FR 870 and 20 RD split.

This was the dream of at least one of its residents, George S. Lee. Lee built a smelter along Henson Creek using 150,000 bricks. In 1879, this smelter produced $3,900 in bullion. Lee purchased a second smelter located above the town site, and its furnaces were fired in 1880. The town also had ample waterpower, and a flume 1,000 feet long was constructed. The name was changed to Capitol City, and it got a post office in 1877. This post office, incidentally, lasted until 1920. The community also constructed a schoolhouse.

Optimistic about the town's prospects, Lee brought his wife to the town and built a remarkable two-story brick mansion in 1879. He hoped this mansion would eventually become the home of the governor of Colorado. Frank Fossett, author of several guidebooks during the 1800s, observed that this was the most elegantly furnished house in all of the southern part of Colorado. Fossett also mentioned the recreation potential of the area.

George Crofutt wrote in his 1885 guidebook that Capitol City had a population of 100. He also observed that the two smelters were idle because of a legal battle between mine owners. Fortunately this was resolved, and Capitol City continued to grow

In 1941, the Capitol City schoolhouse was still standing. Nothing remains of this structure today. *(Denver Public Library x-5312)*

and prosper until the price of silver began to drop during the late 1880s. At the turn of the nineteenth century, the discovery of gold produced a short-lived boom in Capitol City.

The small community never became a city or even a county seat, but it outlasted all other Henson Creek settlements. Long after the town had

Today, two log cabins have been stabilized and restored at Capitol City. Modern homes surround the site. *(Kenneth Jessen 105B5)*

been abandoned, the handsome Lee mansion stood as a reminder of George S. Lee's dream.

When photographer and writer Ron Ruhoff visited Capitol City in 1957, the large brick home of George Lee was partially collapsed. In 1982, Ruhoff was dismayed to note that a new home was under construction where the mansion once stood and that all of the bricks had disappeared. Today, this beautiful location is marked by two restored cabins and several modern homes.

Allen Nossaman, *Many More Mountains, Volume 2: Ruts into Silverton*, Sundance Publications Limited, Denver, Colorado, 1993, pp. 95-97.

Don and Jean Griswold, *Colorado's Century of "Cities,"* self-published, 1958, pp. 143-144.

Ron Ruhoff, "Back Country Adventures in Mineral and Hinsdale Counties," *Trails Among the Columbine*, 1988, Sundance Publications Ltd., Denver, 1988, p. 110.

George A. Crofutt, *Crofutt's Grip-Sack Guide of Colorado*, 1885 Edition, Johnson Books, Boulder, Colorado, reprint 1981, p. 77.

William H. Bauer, James L. Ozment and John H. Willard, *Colorado Post Offices*, Colorado Railroad Museum, Golden, Colorado, 1990, p. 28.

CARSON

On Both Sides of the Divide

- *Hinsdale County, Wager Creek and Lost Trail Creek drainages*
- *Accessible via four-wheel drive road*
- *Lower town had a post office; many structures remain at both sites*

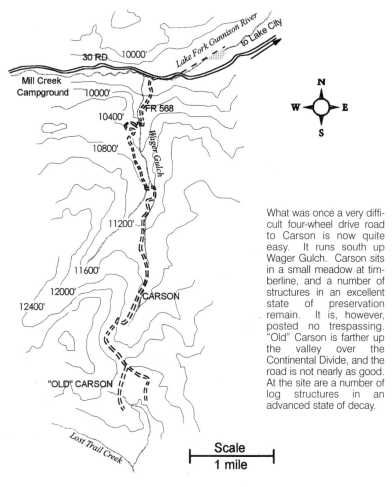

What was once a very difficult four-wheel drive road to Carson is now quite easy. It runs south up Wager Gulch. Carson sits in a small meadow at timberline, and a number of structures in an excellent state of preservation remain. It is, however, posted no trespassing. "Old" Carson is farther up the valley over the Continental Divide, and the road is not nearly as good. At the site are a number of log structures in an advanced state of decay.

The original town of Carson was founded above Lost Trail Creek on the Continental Divide. Many of its structures were above 12,000 feet. Silver ore attracted Christopher Carson to the site when he staked the Bonanza King in 1881. He was instrumental in forming a mining district that straddled both sides of the Continental Divide. A year later, a town of sorts formed near the mines. Its numerous buildings, including a boardinghouse, were spread out across a vast treeless area on the Atlantic side of the divide. Most were of log construction, and the town had no orderly street system.

Prospectors arrived in the area and staked more than 150 claims. These included the Kit Carson, Legal Tender, Iron Mask and Maid of Carson. Later, the St. Jacobs would become the area's largest producer. A road was constructed to Carson up Lost Trail Creek in 1887. In 1892, the *Creede Candle* predicted high revenue from the mines, but a year later, following a steady decline in silver prices, the original town of Carson was abandoned.

Gold was discovered later in Wager Gulch on the Pacific side of the divide, far below the original Carson site and more than a mile away. The second town of Carson was founded in 1889 at 11,600 feet in a small meadow. It got a post office, and a road was constructed up Wager Gulch to provide access from Lake City.

The town of "new" Carson in Wager Gulch has changed little since this 1950 photograph. *(Denver Public Library x-3004)*

Carson is one of the best-preserved ghost towns in Colorado. This photograph, looking down Wager Gulch, shows a barn. This site is now posted no trespassing. *(Kenneth Jessen 104D5)*

The Bachelor Mine was the primary source of income for those living at "new" Carson. Because it was closely associated with the mine, the place was sometimes referred to as Bachelor Cabins. Although the post office closed in 1903 as mining activity tapered off, the Bachelor Mine continued production until around 1910.

The new town had a boardinghouse, store and livery stable as well as a mine office and many other buildings for the mine workers. The Bachelor Mine was directly behind the town and within an easy walk. Other smaller mines can be seen in the valley.

There were at least eighteen buildings constructed at "new" Carson. Many remain standing today, most with new roofs and in relatively good condition. The site, however, recently has been posted "no trespassing". Carson is shown on many maps and is marked by a U.S. Forest Service sign, although the original town has slipped into obscurity.

In 1946, ghost town historian Muriel Sibell Wolle and a friend hired horses to take them up Wager Gulch. The road at the time was so overgrown that it was not passable by motorized vehicle. They came to the partially collapsed log bridge over Wager Creek, and with difficulty, they got their horses across. The bridge later became a major obstacle in reaching Carson and eventually was bypassed by a ford. In the 1960s after Robert Brown drove the road for his book, *Jeep Trails to Colorado Ghost Towns,* he wrote, "The generally hazardous nature of this ore-wagon obstacle course would easily rank it beside the routes to Holy Cross City, or

across Williams Pass, as one of the worst Jeep roads in the state."
A culvert has replaced the ford through Wager Creek making
passage easy. Beyond the stream, the old road became narrow
and was followed by a section of large boulders in the roadway.
All of this has been graded and rebuilt during recent years, and it
is no longer difficult to reach the Carson town site.

When Wolle and her companion reached "new" Carson,
they discovered a large number of frame buildings. A severe
mountain storm prevented them from continuing the trip to the
old town site on the opposite side of the Continental Divide. Wolle
organized another party 2 years later to reach the site. This time,
they used the trail along Pole Creek. She saw the old town with its
many headframes
and cabins scat-
tered well above
timberline and
also could see
"new" Carson far
below.

This contemporary view of the original town of Carson
shows the vast area above timberline where mining took
place. One of the mines was reopened during the 1990s.
(Kenneth Jessen 104D10)

Muriel Sibell Wolle, *Stampede to Timberline,* Sage Books, Chicago, 1949, pp. 361-369.

Muriel Sibell Wolle, *Timberline Tailings,* Sage Books, Chicago, Illinois, 1977, pp. 260, 262.

Robert L. Brown, *Jeep Trails to Colorado Ghost Towns,* Caxton Printers, Caldwell, Idaho, 1963, pp. 77-82.

Ron Ruhoff, "Back Country Adventures in Mineral and Hinsdale Counties," *Trails Among the Columbine,* 1988, Sundance Publications Ltd., Denver, 1988, pp. 117-121.

William H. Bauer, James L. Ozment and John H. Willard, *Colorado Post Offices,* Colorado Railroad Museum, Golden, Colorado, 1990, p. 30.

CREEDE

A Wild Boom Town

- *Mineral County, Willow Creek drainage*
- *Accessible by paved road*
- *Town has a post office; original structures remain*

Lower Creede was originally called Jimtown, and its narrow main street, Creede Avenue, was lined with false-front stores. This part of Creede was totally destroyed by fire on June 5, 1892. *(Denver Public Library x-7913)*

D espite the discovery of silver in the region, Creede didn't take shape until Nicholas C. Creede and George L. Smith located the Holy Moses lode in 1889. The small mining camp developed in the deep canyon formed by Willow Creek. Initially was called Willow, the miners renamed the town Creede.

Nicholas Creede's real name was William Harvey. When the girl he loved married his brother, Harvey changed his name and joined the Union Army. His first discovery in Colorado was at Monarch. While prospecting in the Rio Grande Valley in 1889, he came to the high ridge that separated West and East Willow creeks. He saw an outcropping and struck it with his pick. He pried off a piece and, at least according to legend, exclaimed, "Holy Moses! Chloride of silver, by the Holy Moses." He enjoyed great wealth from his discovery. This, however, did not buy happiness, and in 1893, Creede took an overdose of morphine and ended his life.

The mines supported several towns, and the original town of Creede was located a short distance north of the present-day town. Approximately a mile farther north at the junction of the east and west forks of Willow Creek, North Creede was established. The long line of frame buildings within the narrow canyon between Creede and North Creede was generally referred to as Stringtown. Creede soon outgrew its space, and at the mouth of the canyon, Jimtown formed. Historians speculate that the name came from the corruption of Gintown, a name given by miners for the cheap liquor served in its saloons. Next to Jimtown was South Creede. Early maps generally call the entire place Creede with some making the distinction between Creede proper and North Creede.

Of note is the canyon itself. Willow Creek flows through near vertical volcanic cliffs. Early photographs of Creede are readily identifiable since no other mining town in Colorado had such a scenic backdrop. In places, the canyon was only a block wide and the rows of stores and houses faced each other across the wagon road. After a narrow gauge railroad was constructed, it shared its right of way with the wagon road. The tracks were literally at the doorstep of the buildings. To complicate matters, there was insufficient side track space for all of the box cars used for concentrates, and long strings of cars choked the canyon.

Another unique feature of Creede was its many newspapers, although few lasted more than a year or so. Harry Tabor, with a background in writing for a New York newspaper, started the *Amethyst* in 1891. A weekly, the *Creede Candle,* began publication in January 1892 and lasted until 1930. During the same month, the *Creede News* started, and the following month, the *Creede Daily Herald* hit the streets. *The Chronicle* was published and edited by well-known Colorado journalist Cy Warman. Finally, the *Creede Miner* first rolled off the press in November 1893.

Postal history is most confusing, partially because of the various names used for the towns along Willow Creek. The Willow post office opened in 1891, and its designation soon changed to Creede. In 1908, it was moved to North Creede and lasted until 1919. The Amethyst post office opened in Creede in 1892. In 1909, its name was changed to Creede, and it became the town's surviving post office.

Creede was one of the fastest growing mining camps in Colorado. From July 1890 to the end of 1891, the town expanded from a cabin into a camp of 1,000 or more. Starting in January 1892, 100 structures were completed in four months. The population was estimated at 8,000 by April. The population increased after January 1892 at an estimated rate of 150 to 300 each day. The Denver & Rio Grande pressed as many cars into service as it could, and even at that, there was standing room only. Once a prospector arrived, he found no place to sleep and had to endure long lines to get a meal. The railroad kept five Pullman sleeping cars on a siding for rent to tired travelers willing to pay a high price. J. Z. Adams constructed an enormous restaurant that measured 25 feet by 107 feet and enabled him to feed 1,000 people daily. Its second story had fifty-nine small guest rooms, which were always filled.

Part of the problem was the exaggerated claims made about the ore. A correspondent for the Leadville *Herald Democrat* on March 4, 1892, wrote that, "The impression created in the East is that the streets (of Creede) are paved with silver, and that all one has to do is get a wheel-barrow and a shovel, go out into the suburbs and bring in a load of standard silver dollars."

This July 1892 photograph shows the nature of Creede with the narrow gauge tracks of the Denver & Rio Grande running down the main street. *(Denver Public Library x-7438)*

Stories spread of how men became rich. In August 1891, Theodore Rennica needed his burro for a prospecting trip. He tracked the burro to a grass plateau called Bachelor Hill. The burro was grazing near a rich vein of silver that Rennica named the Last Chance. This discovery made Rennica a rich man.

The Denver & Rio Grande reached Wagon Wheel Gap in 1883, primarily to bring tourists to the hot springs. When the mining boom began around Creede, the narrow gauge line was extended 9.7 miles through Creede to North Creede. The extension was paid for by several Rio Grande officials, and built as the Rio Grande Gunnison Railway Company. Later, the Denver & Rio Grande purchased the extension.

In March 1892, property owners in North Creede, South Creede, Creede and Jimtown discussed incorporation under one name. A motion carried, and Creede, as it is known today, was born. North Creede, however, remained separate.

Creede was famous for its fabulous silver mines, but it was equally famous for acts of violence. It attracted the likes of Bat Masterson as manager of one of its saloons. Bob Ford, the man who assassinated Jesse James, operated a Creede saloon.

One of Creede's most notable characters was con-man Soapy Smith. He became the underworld's dictator. Tall, soft-spoken and always polite, Soapy maintained a certain deceptive air of respectability. While most of Creede dressed in dirty overalls and denim jackets, Soapy wore a black suit. His trim black beard was accented by a black sombrero. A large diamond stick pin set off his black shirt and tie. Soapy's headquarters was the Orleans Club. He rigged an election placing his own men in key positions to protect his illegal activities. Fleecing new arrivals of their grubstake was his specialty. Soapy knew that he had to maintain law and order in Creede for people to flock to the gambling houses and willingly part with their money.

Gunshots rang out early on the morning of March 31, 1892. Bullets shattered windows on both sides of a narrow street as the lives of sleeping residents were endangered. Deputy Marshal

Captain Light was summoned to The Branch Saloon and found faro dealer William "Reddy" McCann intoxicated. Light slapped McCann, knocking the cigar out of his mouth. Light then tried to disarm McCann, but McCann went for his gun. Light and McCann exchanged gunfire when one of Light's bullets found its mark. The mortally wounded McCann uttered his last words, "I'm killed."

Later the same day, Billie Wall and Ella Diamond were on their way home down one of Creede's narrow streets, where the canyon walls closed in on either side. They decided to stop by a saloon for one more drink. Inside was the intoxicated Frank Oliver.

The couple followed Oliver out of the saloon. Wall was ill from too much to drink and began to vomit. Oliver, upon seeing this, taunted Wall. Wall responded with some of his own choice words. Oliver pulled his .38-caliber revolver and fired. Wall fell over, while a couple of witnesses grabbed Oliver and disarmed him. Wall lingered for an hour before passing away. Frank Oliver was placed in jail and later convicted of voluntary manslaughter.

The month of April passed without incident, but on May 4, there was another shooting. The well-educated Jack Pugh came to Creede in the fall of 1891. Always neatly dressed, he was appointed deputy sheriff of North Creede. He was likeable when sober, but mean when drunk. Pugh had been involved in several shootings. According to Creede history expert Dr. Nolie Mumey, Pugh could empty a saloon of its patrons quicker than any man in town.

In January, Pugh "jumped" a lot held by Mr. and Mrs. Osgood. He had some of his thugs haul lumber to the lot owned by the Osgoods and hold it. Mrs. Osgood got word about this matter and returned to Creede with her own force of men. They tossed Pugh's lumber aside, while she stood guard over her property. For this, Pugh always held a grudge against the Osgoods.

In May 1892, Jack Pugh entered the Holy Moses saloon, operated by Mr. Osgood. After drinking the entire day, Pugh became so unruly that Marshal Peter Karg was called to quiet him down. Osgood could see that Pugh was out to settle his old grudge over the lot, and Osgood moved his gun to within easy reach. About 10 p.m., Pugh was making so much noise the patrons asked Karg to act. Karg used a quiet tone of voice to try to talk Pugh into going home, but this enraged Pugh who spun the marshal around. He threatened Karg's life, and Karg dashed for the door at the rear of the saloon. Pugh drew his gun as Karg spun around. Quicker on the draw, Karg dropped Pugh in his tracks. Pugh's body lay where he fell for an hour before being removed.

Later in May, Pugh's live-in girlfriend, Lillie Shields, moved back with her former lover, William Rumidge. The couple went to

The mining camp located at the Amethyst Mine above Creede was referred to as Stumptown on one of the historic photographs at the Denver Public Library. A few rusting structures on a steep hillside mark the site today. *(Kenneth Jessen 084C15)*

the Junction Saloon for a card game. Rumidge teased Lillie about her card playing and so irritated her that she drew her revolver and put a bullet into Rumidge. He was carried back to Pugh's old place where he died.

On June 5, 1892, Creede was almost destroyed by fire. All of its structures were built of rough-cut pine, and the pitch made everything highly flammable. Adding to this was the close proximity of the town's structures. The fire started in a "V" shaped building, Kinneavy's Saloon, and spread quickly. Without a formal, well-equipped fire department, there was little hope of controlling the blaze. Creede's rough element took full advantage of the situation by stealing what liquor had been salvaged. As stated by a *Denver Republican* reporter the following day, "...many cases of wines, bottles of whiskey, boxes of cigars and such goods were seized, and hundreds were drunk before the flames had half burned down."

Creede's boom ended as suddenly as it began. Many were left homeless and drifted to other mining camps. Without the hordes of prospectors, the gamblers and prostitutes left. The final blow came with declining silver prices culminating in July 1893 with the repeal of the Sherman Silver Purchase Act. During the late 1880s and early 1890s, silver fell to almost half of its previous value, and Creede was almost abandoned.

The town weathered decades of stagnation, then after World War II, tourism began to dominate the economy. Creede is well worth visiting and has an active historical society. Many of its historic buildings have been restored. Its setting at the mouth of Willow Creek is among the most spectacular of all Colorado mining towns.

Nolie Mumey, *Creede*, Artcraft Press, Denver, Colorado, 1949.

Tiv Wilkins, *Colorado Railroads*, Pruett Publishing Company, Boulder, Colorado, 1974, pp. 88, 140.

William H. Bauer, James L. Ozment and John H. Willard, *Colorado Post Offices*, Colorado Railroad Museum, Golden, Colorado, 1990, pp. 10, 39, 106.

ENGINEER CITY

A High Altitude Mining Camp

- *Hinsdale County, Palmetto Gulch drainage*
- *Accessible by four-wheel drive vehicle*
- *Town did not have a post office; no structures remain*

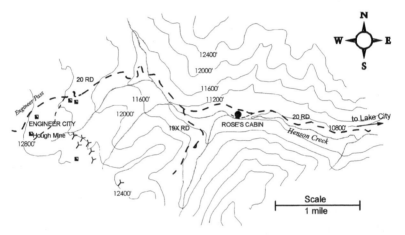

The road over Engineer Pass past Rose's Cabin is exposed in places, but is very scenic. At the pass is a small parking area, and below is the site of Engineer City in a small valley well above timberline. The walls of a stone powder house are all that remain.

Engineer Mountain was referred to as a grand pyramid of rich silver seams. H. A. Woods drove the first location stake for the Annie Woods lode in 1874. A year later, he located the Polar Star near the summit of Engineer Mountain. Woods had a close call, however. The silver lodes on Engineer Mountain were known by other prospectors, but fortunately for Woods, no one had legal title by virtue of working a claim. In March 1875, a Silverton mill owner hired "Sheepskin" Miller to go up the mountain and stake a claim. He was also to bring back ore samples for assessment work.

Woods put together his own party of three men to travel from the Antelope Park side up to Engineer Mountain. Wagons filled with supplies were unloaded and sleds were made for the trip up Stony Pass. On snowshoes, each man pulled 225 pounds on each sled. It must have been a very difficult trip, especially the steep grade up Timber Hill.

The Woods party ran into the Miller party somewhere on the mountain. The two groups apparently camped near each other at Animas Forks. While the Miller party was asleep, the Woods party left quietly in the dark. They arrived at the summit of Engineer Mountain at sunrise, staked out claims and returned to Animas Forks for a long rest. At 11 a.m., they were awakened by the sounds of the Miller party getting ready to assault the mountain. When they saw the fresh snowshoe tracks, "Sheepskin" Miller asked what it meant. With delight, the Woods party was able to tell him that he had been "scooped."

To provide access to the new mining area located at the top of American Flat at 12,860 feet, a trail was constructed over the shoulder of Engineer Mountain and was later widened into a spectacular wagon road. It traversed a long exposed shelf and climbed over a slide area on the south side of Engineer Mountain. Today, the Engineer Pass road has been widened to allow two-way traffic, although it is still a memorable trip.

Following the Woods party, Frank Hough discovered a lode of silver ore and established the Hough Mine. It became the primary producer in the area. In 1882, a tent camp housing 300 prospectors and miners formed near the mine. Jack Davison erected a large tent, which he called the Davison Hotel. By the middle of July, this high-altitude hotel was serving forty to fifty boarders. Food was packed in daily, and Engineer City was the name given to the camp.

In July 1882, a correspondent for the *Silver World* in Lake City said of the place, "It can boast of more inhabitants than

Mineral City, Animas Forks or Capitol City, yet we have no saloon and the boys openly declare that with the grub put up at the Davison Hotel, they can do very well without any. We believe this is the only city in the state that can boast of 300 to 400 inhabitants without a whiskey shop..."

Engineer City was never a town, much less a city, and historic photographs show only a few log cabins, half buried in the snow, located near the mine. It is not known when it was abandoned, but the last newspaper story about Engineer City appeared in 1883. The small parking lot near the summit of Engineer Pass looks down on the Engineer City site. Nothing remains today except the collapsed ruins of a stone powder house near the tailings from the Hough Mine.

Don and Jean Griswold, *Colorado's Century of "Cities,"* self-published, 1958, p. 131.
Lake City Mining Register, Lake City, Colorado, June 13, 1882.
Muriel Sibell Wolle, *Stampede to Timberline*, Sage Books, Chicago, 1949, pp. 414, 416-417.

HENSON

And The Italian Miners' Strike

- *Hinsdale County, Henson Creek drainage*
- *Accessible via graded dirt road*
- *Town had a post office; several original structures remain*

Although on private property, Henson has several occupied cabins. Many of its mill buildings remain standing. Most of these structures can be seen from the road without trespassing. *(Kenneth Jessen 105B7)*

Henson, located 4 miles west of Lake City on Henson Creek, developed around the Ute-Ulay mines. The region was explored in 1871 by Joel Mullen, Albert Mead, Charles Goodwin and Henry Henson. They located the Ute and Ulay lodes that ultimately became the best mines in the Lake City area. Other mines included the Hidden Treasure and the California. The mines, however, could not be developed since they lay within Ute Indian Territory. The Ute Indians gave up the San Juan Mountains with the signing of the Brunot Treaty in 1873. The Henson party returned, and the men officially staked their claims. The Crooke brothers, Lake City mill owners, purchased the mines in 1876 for $125,000.

In 1877, a toll road was completed along Henson Creek over Engineer Pass to Animas Forks. It connected Lake City with Silverton and Ouray. The tollgate was located below the Ute-Ulay mines at the narrow entrance to the canyon.

The Ute-Ulay properties were sold again in 1880 for $1.2 million. As mining operations grew, a town site was laid out and named for Henry Henson, who later became a judge.

A large concentration mill was erected along Henson Creek in 1882. A high concrete dam was constructed, and a flume brought water from the dam to power the mill. The mill employed 300 men.

As the community of Henson grew, a schoolhouse was constructed. The town's post office opened in 1883, but it closed the following year. It reopened in 1892 at the peak of mining activity and remained open until 1913. Historic photographs show that besides numerous mining structures, Henson had fourteen or more homes and a boardinghouse. The homes were located on the side of Crystal Peak. It does not appear Henson had any kind of street system or even a well-defined business district.

The company operating the Ute-Ulay properties ordered all single men to board at the company-owned commissary in 1899. This precipitated a strike by the Italian miners. The eighty or so Italian miners drove off the other miners trying to get to work and posted guards above the road into Henson. When it looked like there might be bloodshed, the Italian consul was called. Dr. Cuneo traveled to Lake City by train, and after he discovered Henson was closed off by his countrymen, he wrote a note to be delivered to the miners. He said that King Humbert of Italy requested his "subjects" at Henson meet with the Lake City militia, county officials and troops sent in by Colorado Governor Charles Thomas. The note was handed to Charles Mairo of Lake City to deliver.

Cuneo looked out of place dressed in a suit, overcoat trimmed in fur and silk hat. Mairo left first, traveling the road leading to Henson followed by Cuneo riding in a buggy. A white flag hung from the buggy displayed so that the guards would not shoot. A half-mile from Henson, a delegation of six miners waited. Salutes and bows were exchanged, and the delegation continued. At Henson, the street was lined with miners and their families. The buggy stopped, and Cuneo got out. He walked over to the crowd, and despite the cold he took off his silk hat and opened his fur-trimmed overcoat displaying his formal suit. He wore a red, white and green ribbon across his chest. The crowd cheered as he addressed them. He told them to salute the state and county officers and to surrender to the Lake City sheriff. Later in the day, Italian miners and their families walked down the road, and apparently, some of the miners were later sent to prison.

After 3 days, the mining company announced a policy that refused work to Italian immigrants and ordered all single Italian miners to leave within 3 days. The families were given 60 days. This dismayed Cuneo, who had settled the miner's strike without bloodshed.

Henson today has several occupied cabins, and many of the mill buildings remain standing. It is all on private property, but it can easily be seen from the road without trespassing.

For a map showing the location of Henson, see Capitol City.

Muriel Sibell Wolle, Stampede to Timberline, Sage Books, Chicago, 1949, pp. 351-353.

Muriel Sibell Wolle, Timberline Tailings, Sage Books, Chicago, Illinois, 1977, p. 255.

Ron Ruhoff, "Back Country Adventures in Mineral and Hinsdale Counties," Trails Among the Columbine, 1988, Sundance Publications Ltd., Denver, 1988, pp. 162-163.

William H. Bauer, James L. Ozment and John H. Willard, Colorado Post Offices, Colorado Railroad Museum, Golden, Colorado, 1990, p. 70.

LAKE CITY
Outlasts All Other Towns

- *Hinsdale County, Lake Fork of the Gunnison River drainage*
- *Accessible via paved road*
- *Town has a post office; occupied site; several original structures remain*

Lake City's business district has changed little since this photograph was taken by Muriel Sibell Wolle in 1959. These stores are located along the west side of Silver Street. *(Denver Public Library x-21)*

L ake City is certainly not a ghost town, but its history is important for an understanding of the region. Although a few people live in some of the outlying town sites, Lake City survives as the only remaining town in Hinsdale County.

The origins of Lake City began with prospectors James Harrison, J. K. Mullen and George Boughton, who camped near the mouth of Henson Creek in 1869 at the future site of Lake City. They remained only a few months, but probably found traces of mineralization. In 1872, another party discovered promising ore southwest of Lake San Cristobal. Neither of these parties could claim land because at the time it was still within Ute Indian Territory. The Brunot Treaty in 1873 changed this, and the Utes were forced to give up all of their land in the San Juan Mountains.

When the area was opened to settlers, Hinsdale County was created. San Juan City, located in Antelope Park, was selected as the county seat.

Lake City got its start in 1874 when Enos Hotchkiss discovered a rich vein of gold and silver ore while surveying a toll road. The discovery was at the north end of Lake San Cristobal and was later developed as the Golden Fleece. Hotchkiss and his partners withdrew up to $50,000 in ore and concluded that the mine was exhausted. After abandoning the mine, it later produced more than $250,000 in ore. Despite his poor judgement, Hotchkiss is regarded as the father of Lake City and later founded the town of Hotchkiss, Colorado.

The discovery started the rush into the area, and in 1875, the Lake City Town Company was formed to survey the site and sell lots. The town quickly grew to sixty-seven buildings with an estimated population of 400. This was also the year the Lake City post office opened. By out-voting other towns for the title, Lake City became the county seat.

The editor of Lake City's *Silver World* noted that during the town's first Fourth of July celebration, no one displayed an American flag. He sent one of his employees on a search for a flag. He quickly found that no flags were displayed in Lake City and failed to locate anyone who owned a flag. The editor had a flag created from a red and blue flannel shirt combined with a white towel. Although lacking stars, it was flown proudly over the newspaper's modest office.

During the following summer, a great number of newcomers arrived. Up Henson Creek, the Ute and Ulay mines were shipping ore. John Crooke arrived in the area in 1877 and constructed the Crooke concentration mill at the waterfall at the south edge of town. This section of Lake City was commonly referred to as

Crookeville. A second and third sawmill tried to keep up with the demand for lumber. A correspondent from the *Rocky Mountain News* estimated that Lake City had grown to 1,000 residents with well over 1,000 more camped in the immediate vicinity.

As many as a dozen wagons arrived daily over the Saguache and San Juan Toll Road bringing in new settlers during the summer of 1874. The Barlow and Sanderson stage line began service the following year over this route. The mail arrived in leather sacks strapped to the top of the coach.

In 1875, Otto Mears completed the Antelope Springs and Lake City Toll Road. It crossed Spring Creek and Slumgullion passes, entering Lake City from the south. In the summer of 1877, the Henson Creek and Uncompahgre Toll Road opened. It ran west up Henson Creek to Capitol City, then over Engineer Pass at 13,190 feet to Mineral Point and on to Ouray. From the San Juan and Saguache Toll Road, north of Lake City, a connecting toll road was built to Gunnison in 1880.

By the end of 1877, an estimated 2,000 people called Lake City home. Houses completed or under construction were estimated at 1,000, a number that seems highly inflated. Regularly scheduled freight service was initiated from Pueblo. The Hinsdale County Courthouse was completed the same year. Because of these roads, Lake City was not as isolated as other mining towns and enjoyed fresh produce, eggs and meat from the farms and ranches to the north along the Lake Fork.

Far too many prospectors came into the area relative to the amount of mineralization. Most ended up disappointed, and by 1878, the better claims had been taken. A number of people began to leave Lake City and its population declined. The remaining residents solidified the town and established permanent homes and businesses.

Outlying camps, such as Sherman, Henson, Capitol City, Carson and those in Burrow Park, took shape. The Ulay and Ute mines on Henson Creek became the area's biggest producers of silver ore. Lake City was the supply center for the entire region.

By the early 1880s the town had seven lawyers, an assayer, four doctors, and a number of wagon makers, blacksmiths and other services. There were three bakers, five druggists, one banker and two engineers. In 1882, Lake City came of age with the installation of a marble soda fountain in Hallard Felders Pharmacy. The town's 135-foot by 50-foot brick opera house opened the following year for live performances. A half-dozen clothing stores, four hardware stores and seven grocery stores made up the business district.

The biggest single event in Lake City's early history was the arrival of the Denver & Rio Grande in 1889. It constructed a branch south 35.8 miles from its main line along the Gunnison River. It was opened for business in August and provided an economic means of delivering supplies and passengers to the town. Ore was hauled from the twenty area mines to distant smelters.

In 1879, Lake City got a telegraph, and 2 years later, its first telephone was installed. A municipal water supply was put into operation in 1890, and the following year, the town got electricity.

Lake City is known for Lake San Cristobal. It is Colorado's second largest natural lake and is located about 4 miles south of Lake City. *(Kenneth Jessen 075A12)*

The telephone was a two-wire system where all subscribers were interconnected. It was sort of an early version of the Internet. This line ran up Henson Creek, passing through Capitol City, Rose's Cabin and over Engineer Pass to Silverton and Ouray. On October 9, 1881, the Lake City operator and Mrs. George Lee at Capitol City started a concert by singing several duets. The audience would gather around the telephone in their town to listen. Performers at Rose's Cabin, Silverton and Ouray joined in, while the listeners continued to enjoy the concert.

This event was covered in the October 20, 1881, *Silver World* as follows:

> Amateur and professional artists gathered in Silverton, Baker's Park, Ouray, Mineral Point, Animas Forks, Rose's Cabin, Capitol City and Lake City. All were connected by the new telephone system, while the residents of the respective towns were invited to listen to the entertainment. A vocal and harmonica solo by Judge R. F. Long of Ouray opened the program.

During this particular event, there was a flute solo performed by a man in Ouray, a violin solo by a man in Rose's Cabin and a piece by the Silverton Choral Group. Yodeling was even included by a man at Mineral Point followed by another solo on a zither, then a banjo selection. Lake City closed the program with a tenor horn solo. Such fun on the telephone system continued through 1882.

Declining silver prices ended the boom. Only the richest mines survived and kept the town alive. After the last ore was shipped, the town was all but abandoned. In 1970, Lake City had only 91 residents and 202 lived in Hinsdale County. As tourists discovered Lake City, it began to grow. It now has a museum and an active historical society.

The Frank-Higgins-Thompson house is among the many historic structures in Lake City. The home was built by pioneer blacksmith Jacob Frank in 1880. An addition was made to the house by Civil War veteran Thomas Higgins in 1882. *(Kenneth Jessen 095D10)*

An Official Guide to Historic Homes, Lake City, Colorado, Hinsdale County Historical Society, (no date)

Silver World, October 20, 1881.

Ron Ruhoff, "Back Country Adventures In Mineral and Hinsdale Counties," *Trails Among the Columbine*, 1988, Sundance Publications Limited, Denver, Colorado 1988, pp. 164-165.

Thomas Gray Thompson, *Lake City*, Colorado, Metro Press, Oklahoma City, Oklahoma, 1974, pp. 1-7, 10, 38.

Tiv Wilkins, *Colorado Railroads*, Pruett Publishing Company, Boulder, Colorado, 1974, p. 73.

William H. Bauer, James L. Ozment and John H. Willard, *Colorado Post Offices*, Colorado Railroad Museum, Golden, Colorado, 1990, p. 84.

ROSE'S CABIN

Founded by Charles Rose

- *Hinsdale County, Henson Creek drainage*
- *Accessible by four-wheel drive road*
- *Location had a post office; remains of one structure*

Unfortunately, little effort was made to preserve the buildings at Rose's Cabin. The combination hotel, saloon and store has long since collapsed, and today only the partial walls of the livery stable remain. *(Kenneth Jessen 105B3)*

In 1876, Charles Rose expanded his cabin into a stage stop, and it grew in popularity on the long haul from Lake City over Engineer Pass to Mineral Point and Animas Forks. Charles Schafer took over Rose's forwarding and stage stop business in 1880. He improved the facility by constructing larger structures. A Mineral Point merchant, William Boot, operated a store at Rose's Cabin.

The hotel at Rose's Cabin consisted of twenty-two small rooms on the second floor and a saloon the entire length of the ground floor. It is a wonder guests could get to sleep with such an arrangement. Schafer was the postmaster for the post office, which opened in 1878 but closed the following year.

The only recorded violence at Rose's Cabin occurred in the fall of 1880 when Andrew MacLauchlan and "Big Joe" Nevis got into an argument over a poker game. Nevis struck MacLauchlan in the forehead with an axe. This didn't kill MacLauchlan, and he defended himself by shooting Nevis in the face. Fatally wounded, Nevis was so disliked that no one at the card game bothered to get up to help. After Nevis died, MacLauchlan turned himself in to authorities at Lake City, the county seat. It can be assumed that this matter was determined to be self-defense.

Ron Ruhoff photographed Rose's Cabin in 1960, when the livery barn was still standing. The combination hotel, saloon and store had long since collapsed. Today, only the partial walls of the livery stable remain. Rose's Cabin was on the primary wagon road through this valley, but now it is on a side road a short distance from a newer road running above the site.

For a map showing the location of Rose's Cabin, see Engineer City.

Allen Nossaman, *Many More Mountains*, Volume 2: Ruts into Silverton, Sundance Publications Limited, Denver, Colorado, 1993, pp. 202-203.

Ron Ruhoff, "Back Country Adventures in Mineral and Hinsdale Counties," *Trails Among the Columbine*, 1988, Sundance Publications Ltd., Denver, 1988, pp. 111, 115.

William H. Bauer, James L. Ozment and John H. Willard, *Colorado Post Offices*, Colorado Railroad Museum, Golden, Colorado, 1990, p. 124.

SHERMAN
Swept Away by Floods

- *Hinsdale County, Lake Fork of the Gunnison River drainage*
- *Accessible via graded dirt road*
- *Town had a post office; one collapsed structure remains*

The Sherman site is located above Lake San Cristobal in the streambed of the Lake Fork of the Gunnison River near its confluence with Cottonwood Creek. It is on a side road 5 miles beyond the Williams Fork campground and immediately beyond where the Cinnamon Pass road begins its climb to Burrows Park. George Crofutt described Sherman's location as, "…a wild and romantic nook, where game and fish abound."

In 1877, A. D. Freeman and others laid out the town of Sherman in blocks with streets 60 feet wide. Storage and forwarding structures were the town's largest buildings. The town also had a butcher shop, slaughterhouse, bakery and a grocery store. The same year Sherman was founded it had fifty voters and got its own post office, but the town grew slowly. In 1881, the Sherman House opened, and a general merchandise store followed. Based on historic photographs, Sherman consisted of ten or more log structures.

Both placer and lode mining kept the town going. Unique to most Colorado mining towns, Sherman's residents held Saturday evening prayer meetings. Its population reached about 100.

The Sherman post office closed in 1886. In response to a second mining boom, the post office reopened in 1895 and remained open for another 3 years.

The area mines included the George Washington, New Hope, Mountain View, Minnie Lee, Irish World, Golden Chance,

318

Clinton, Smile of Fortune, Monster and Black Wonder. The latter
was the principal mine in the region and continued production
until 1897, when it was purchased by a Boston company. Until
this time, the ore was shipped to Lake City. The new owners spent
$200,000 erecting the Black Wonder Mill and improving the mine.
Ore ran as high as $2,000 a ton. Machinery in the mill could be
seen under its collapsed roof until the 1960s. A Wilfley table, used
to concentrate the ore, was plainly visible. The mill sat a short
distance back from the main road through Sherman, and its stone
foundation is still evident today.

Above Sherman, a miner was contracted to construct a high
dam to generate hydroelectric power for the mill. The dam was
located in the narrow gorge and was to be 147 feet high. When
the miner completed the first 64 feet, the mining company went
bankrupt. The dam was later raised to its full height by another
company. A cloudburst caused the dam to fail, washing away
much of the town of Sherman in a wall of water and producing a
new stream channel right through town. What cabins survived

The store at Sherman sat by the main road through the town with the Black Wonder mill
in the background to the left. *(Julia McMillan)*

Mike Arnold stands in front of what is left of one of the cabins at Sherman. *(Kenneth Jessen 104D12)*

were surrounded by river gravel. The last mining done at Sherman was in 1925.

A photograph taken by Muriel Sibell Wolle shows one of Sherman's abandoned cabins sitting out in the coarse river gravel. The riverbed is overgrown with brush, and only the walls of a cabin remain today. The site is posted no trespassing.

Honorable mention goes to a second town in the area located 7 miles up Cottonwood Gulch called Sterling. Little else is known about Sterling, such as when it was founded and how long it lasted. It did not have a post office. The road beyond Sherman is closed to the public limiting exploration of the area around Sterling. *For a map showing the location of Sherman, see Burrows Park.*

Muriel Sibell Wolle, *Stampede to Timberline,* Sage Books, Chicago, 1949, p. 357.

Muriel Sibell Wolle, *Timberline Tailings,* Sage Books, Chicago, Illinois, 1977, p. 263.

Robert L. Brown, *Jeep Trails to Colorado Ghost Towns,* Caxton Printers, Caldwell, Idaho, 1963, pp. 196-197.

William H. Bauer, James L. Ozment and John H. Willard, *Colorado Post Offices,* Colorado Railroad Museum, Golden, Colorado, 1990, p. 131.

SPAR CITY
Converted into a Private Club

- *Mineral County, Lime Creek drainage*
- *Private property, no public access*
- *Town had a post office; presumably there are original structures remaining at site*

This photograph was also taken in 1960 showing what was once a dance hall or hotel. *(Denver Public Library x-13631)*

Spar City was laid out in 1892 coincident with the Creede boom. At first it was called Fisher City after one of the prospectors who first discovered ore in the area. The first claim was made by Tom Maxwell. Rich silver ore was discovered in the gulches to the south with assay values as high as $2,500 a ton. By July, 300 people inhabited the camp, and twenty or so businesses were constructed along its main street. They included a real estate office, four saloons, one tobacco and cigar store, four hotels, a feed store, two meat markets, two livery stables, one assay office and two grocery stores. The town's population jumped by another 200 in February 1893. The *Spar City Spark* was set up as the town's newspaper by the *Creede Candle.*

Spar City grew right at the time silver prices were declining, and with the repeal of the Sherman Silver Purchase Act in 1893, the occupants of Spar City were out of work. The few who remained needed help, and the people of Creede offered them flour and meat. The post office opened the year the town was founded and closed in 1895 after the town's population declined.

The entire town of Spar City was homesteaded by Charles Brandt in 1899. He tried his hand at mining, but the ore was simply not rich enough to make a profit. Brandt was backed financially by Charles King of Kansas. King put together a group to purchase the town site from Brandt in 1906 and turn it into a summer resort. The Spar City Club was incorporated in 1955.

Muriel Sibell Wolle found that Spar City was in a great state of preservation when she visited the caretaker in 1947. The original meat market and grocery store were still standing as well as the jail. The two-story dance hall dominated the buildings along the main street. The bar inside was presumably moved from Creede, where it had been located in Bob Ford's saloon.

The entrance gate into Spar City is posted for members only. The town site is too far from the gate to determine if any of the original structures remain. Spar City is located south of Creede. FR 523 crosses the Rio Grande southwest of Creede and parallels Colorado 149 for several miles. From FR 523, FR 528 heads east along Lime Creek; the entrance to Spar City is off of this road.

Don and Jean Griswold, Colorado's Century of "Cities," self-published, 1958, p. 251.

Joanne Tankersley and Mary Schroder, "Royal Arch Mining District and Spar City," Ribs of Silver, Hearts of Gold, Creede Historical Society, 1992, pp. 37-38.

John K. Aldrich, Ghosts of the Eastern San Juans, Centennial Graphics, Lakewood, Colorado, 1987, pp. 29-30.

Muriel Sibell Wolle, Stampede to Timberline, Sage Books, Chicago, 1949, pp. 332-333.

William H. Bauer, James L. Ozment and John H. Willard, Colorado Post Offices, Colorado Railroad Museum, Golden, Colorado, 1990, p. 134.

SUNNYSIDE, WEAVER and WASON

- *Mineral County, Willow Creek and Rat Creek drainages*
- *Accessible via paved or graded dirt roads*
- *Some towns had post offices; some original structures remain*

Based on physical evidence, Weaver was never a large settlement. This old cabin sits by the graded dirt road into the area. *(Kenneth Jessen 108D11)*

Dick Irwin, for whom the town of Irwin was named, and Charles Nelson discovered several lodes in 1885 in the Sunnyside area. Using California capital, Irwin developed several mines, and the mining camp of Sunnyside began to take shape at the confluence of Rat and Miners creeks. A post office opened in 1886, and closed in 1891. Nothing remains of the original town, and modern homes occupy much of the town site.

Martin Van Buren Wason settled on a ranch near the mouth of Willow Creek long before the Creede mining boom. He constructed a toll road to Antelope Park, thus developing part of the primary route used to Silverton before the arrival of the railroad. Wason, once he saw the rapid growth in Creede, built a toll road along Willow Creek. Since this was the only street in the narrow portion of the canyon, his toll road became exceedingly unpopular. He had to hire bodyguards to enforce the toll. A bitter court battle raged for many years, and finally in 1899, Wason was paid $10,000 by the State of Colorado for his toll road.

The ranch where Wason lived was referred to as Wason, sometimes spelled Wasson. A post office was established at Wason in 1891 and remained open until 1904. In 1893, when Mineral County was formed, Wason was named the county seat. During the first county election, Wason lost its title to Creede. The narrow gauge Denver & Rio Grande also maintained a depot at Wason.

Little information exists on the size of Wason or how many structures it had. Today, the site is on the Wason Ranch and is marked by a row of guest cabins.

Weaver is located below the Amethyst Mine in the West Fork of Willow Creek. Several of its original structures remain standing. The place did not have a post office. It is possible to reach Weaver over a graded dirt road, but the road is very steep.

For a map showing the location of Sunnyside and Weaver, see "Bachelor City."

Muriel Sibell Wolle, *Stampede to Timberline,* Sage Books, Chicago, 1949, pp. 321, 331-332.

Nolie Mumey, *Creede,* Artcraft Press, Denver, Colorado, 1949, pp. 81-82.

William H. Bauer, James L. Ozment and John H. Willard, *Colorado Post Offices,* Colorado Railroad Museum, Golden, Colorado, 1990, pp. 137, 149.

WAGON WHEEL GAP

And the Hot Springs on Goose Creek

- *Mineral County, Rio Grande drainage*
- *Accessible by paved road; hot springs are on private property*
- *Town had a post office; one original structure remains*

Now a private residence, this is the beautiful Denver & Rio Grande railroad station at Wagon Wheel Gap. It was built to serve tourists headed for the nearby hot springs on Goose Creek. *(Kenneth Jessen 084C4)*

A post office was opened at Wagon Wheel Gap in 1875. At the time, it was located in Saguache County. After the formation of Rio Grande County, Wagon Wheel Gap fell within its borders. In 1893, Mineral County was formed and included Wagon Wheel Gap. In 1895, the name of the post office was changed to Thornton, and in 1901, it was changed back to Wagon Wheel Gap. In 1955, the post office became a rural station of Creede.

The sulfur springs, located to the south along Goose Creek, attracted visitors. It was known and used by Native Americans, and like so many other springs, it was thought to have healing properties. The hot springs were first developed as part of a summer resort by J. C. McClellan. He constructed a hotel, bathhouses and cottages. Guests were treated to wild game and fresh trout at dinner. Prices ranged from $2 to $3 a day with weekly rates ranging from $10 to $12. The Denver & Rio Grande extended its track from Del Norte to Wagon Wheel Gap for the tourist trade in 1883. Today the springs are within the 4UR Guest Ranch and are privately owned. Wagon Wheel Gap is located on Colorado 149 about halfway between South Fork and Creede.

George A. Crofutt, *Crofutt's Grip-Sack Guide of Colorado*, 1885 Edition, Johnson Books, Boulder, Colorado, reprint 1981, pp. 154-158.

Muriel Sibell Wolle, *Stampede to Timberline*, Sage Books, Chicago, 1949, p. 319.

Rick Cahill, *Colorado Hot Springs Guide,* Pruett Publishing Company, Boulder, Colorado, 1986, pp. 119-121.

Tiv Wilkins, *Colorado Railroads*, Pruett Publishing Company, Boulder, Colorado, 1974, pp. 49, 88.

William H. Bauer, James L. Ozment and John H. Willard, *Colorado Post Offices*, Colorado Railroad Museum, Golden, Colorado, 1990, p. 141.

AREA SIXTEEN 16

Ouray and San Juan Counties

continued

AREA 16: Ouray and San Juan Counties

Selected Towns

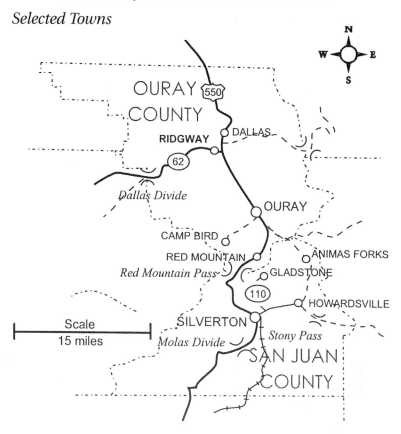

Introduction to Ouray and San Juan Counties

Ouray and San Juan Counties comprise some of the highest and most rugged in Colorado with much of the terrain exceeding 10,000 feet in elevation. Within this two-county area, the only commercial agriculture is at the extreme northern portion of Ouray County, along the Uncompahgre River.

The primary towns are Ouray, Ridgway and Silverton with little population outside of these settlements. At one time, however, many small mining towns existed in this two-county area.

Otto Mears, San Juan Pathfinder

Had it not been for the vision and daring of Otto Mears, development of the San Juan Mountains would have been delayed, possibly for decades. His extensive network of 450 miles of toll roads opened the area to development. Wagon roads were essential to haul men, material, machinery and supplies to the numerous mines. Roads also were necessary to haul the ore to smelters.

Once the Denver & Rio Grande penetrated the San Juan Mountains, Mears turned toward building railroads. Eventually, he owned four lines, all connected to the Denver & Rio Grande. His longest and most famous line was the Rio Grande Southern. Although not trained as such, he was a natural engineer, exhibiting genius for finding routes, solving problems and completing projects where others had failed. Some of these enterprises made money, while others lost money.

Mears charged tolls in proportion to construction costs, but paying for the use of a road was never popular with the public. On several occasions, Mears was forced to sell his toll road to the county where the road was located.

He was part owner of two stores in Saguache and owned a store in Ouray. He also owned the largest freighting company in Colorado. Mears farmed in the Saguache area and sold his wheat to a flourmill in Nathrop. Mears dabbled in politics, learned the Ute language and acted as a mediator during displacement of the Ute Indians from their ancestral land in the San Juan Mountains.

Although Mears was of Jewish heritage, Judaism was more a way of life than a religion as put by Otto Mears biographer Michael Kaplan. Mears was a heavy contributor to Jewish charities and a member of various Jewish honorary associations. He was also known to believe in the principles of Christian Science. At his funeral, an episcopal bishop presided when Otto Mears passed away in 1931. It was fitting that his ashes were taken to Eureka, north of Silverton, where the wind distributed them in the tundra next to the Animas River.

To travel the toll road constructed by Otto Mears between Ouray and Silverton required quite a bit of courage and hope that there would be no oncoming traffic. Otto Mears was able to carve a single-lane shelf hundreds of feet above the Uncompahgre River by using ropes to lower men down the canyon wall. This toll road became the route for U.S. 550, the "Million Dollar Highway." *(Denver Public Library GB-7598)*

Physically, Otto Mears stood only 5 feet tall. He had a dark complexion, and his black eyes matched his black hair and beard. Born in Russia to Jewish parents, Mears found himself alone in the world at the age of 2 when his parents passed away. He came to America at the age of 10 after being passed from one relative to another. He was supposed to meet an uncle in San Francisco, but could not locate the man. The young Mears ended up selling newspapers. He was robbed of his childhood, and his early years were filled with fear and uncertainty. This molded his character into a daring and fearless entrepreneur.

After he was discharged from Company H of the California Volunteers in Las Cruces, New Mexico, Mears started Mears & Company. He moved his store to Conejos to take advantage of the high demand for supplies at Fort Garland. In 1866, seeing even better opportunities in Saguache, Mears purchased over 1,000 acres, part of which he placed under cultivation. In the process, he pioneered crop rotation and scientific farming methods in the San Luis Valley. He moved his store to Saguache and lived in the small community for many years.

The closest flourmill to Saguache was operated by Charles Nachtrieb on the north side of Poncha Pass at Nathrop. Mears soon discovered that there wasn't a road suitable for wagon travel to this location. At the suggestion of Ex-Governor William Gilpin, Mears chartered the Poncha Pass Wagon Road Company in 1870 to descend from Poncha Pass to Poncha Springs and on to Nathrop. The road produced little revenue at first, but it then grew to become the primary route into the San Luis Valley. This got Mears started in toll road construction, and he made even more money when he sold it to the Denver & Rio Grande in 1880 for use as a railroad grade.

After relinquishing their lands in the San Juan Mountains in 1873, the Ute Indians were relocated into the Uncompahgre Valley between Montrose and Ouray, where a government agency was established. Now that the way was clear for development, Mears invested in another toll road. Called the Saguache and San Juan Wagon Toll Road, it ran from Saguache west over Cochetopa Pass to the Lake Fork of the Gunnison River. The project was stalled because of a lack of capital, but after Mears became involved, he quickly raised the necessary funds. The road, finished in August 1874, received good reviews from teamsters. Enos Hotchkiss extended the road south to Lake City.

Mears wanted to publicize the San Luis Valley and in 1873 founded the Saguache *Chronicle*. He employed an experienced newspaperman to run the paper. Always quick to put a favorable spin on the activities of his boss, the editor commented in one issue, "There is no need at saying anything about Mr. Mears, for he is known to almost everybody in Colorado, and Saguache. Without him would be like a play of Hamlet with Hamlet left out." Subsequently, Mears started a printing company to expedite publishing the *Chronicle.*

Another of his many investments was a real estate company that sold lots in Lake City. To promote Lake City and its mines, Mears subsidized Lake City's only newspaper, *Silver World.*

In July 1875, Mears invested in the Antelope Park and Lake City Wagon Toll Road to provide a second route to Lake City. By 1876, Barlow and Sanderson stages were using the Mears road.

His next move was to become a mail contractor by successfully bidding on routes to Ouray and Silverton. For service three

Otto Mears was a hands-on type of person. He is pictured standing in front of locomotive #100 on his Silverton Railroad in this L. C. McClure photograph. Based on the raw look of the ties, this scene most likely was taken soon after completion of the railroad in 1889. *(Denver Public Library MCC-3222)*

times a week, he was paid an annual fee of $4,500. This was not one of his better ideas. The nearest wagon road ended 75 miles away in Lake City and after the enterprise got started, the severe winter of 1875-1876 struck. Acting on the advice of a man from Alaska, Mears attempted to use dog sleds to get through, but the snow was too deep and soft. Mears had to give up on delivering mail to Ouray or Silverton. The U.S. Postal Service threatened Mears with stiff fines and loss of his contract if he didn't resume delivery.

To save on expenses, Mears combined freight and mail on the same sled. His mail carriers had trouble controlling the animals, and the sleds sometimes ended up stuck. Yielding to exhaustion, the driver would flop down on the sled to rest, crushing the freight, including fancy hats for the women in Ouray. The hungry dogs would get into food on the sled, causing the food to intermingle with ladies' apparel. This made the ladies and the merchants in Ouray unhappy.

Mears abandoned the use of the dog sleds in favor of snow-shoes. After a particularly vicious snowstorm, his employees quit, leaving Mears with the task of trudging through the snow alone from the Lake Fork of the Gunnison River to Ouray. Because Mears receives no further mention as a mail carrier, it can be assumed that he got out of this business.

After Ouray became the county seat, Mears looked into building another toll road. In 1876, the Ouray and Lake Fork Wagon Road Company was incorporated. Realizing that this venture was under-financed, Mears purchased the company's stock. He scaled down the project to run from Ouray to Montrose and organized a separate toll road company to make the connection to Lake Fork and to his Saguache and San Juan Toll Road. The new road was completed to Barnum, more than 100 miles from Montrose, in 1878. Barnum, incidentally, was a stage station located a few miles west of present-day Powderhorn.

Taking advantage of his own toll road, Mears bought the contents of a hardware store in Del Norte, moved it by wagon to

Ouray, and opened a new hardware store. Mears also was a partner in two stores in Saguache - a dry goods store and a hardware store.

In the spring of 1879, Mears became aware of the ever-increasing mining activity in the Gunnison River drainage. The closest railhead was at the South Arkansas River, future site of Salida. Using his existing Poncha Pass Toll Road, he constructed a new toll road west over Marshall Pass, under the name Poncha, Marshall and Gunnison Toll Road Company. It issued 1,000 shares of stock at $25 per share. Completed in 1880, the toll road became a lucrative venture for Mears, and he later made even more money selling the right-of-way to the Denver & Rio Grande. Some historians speculate that Mears was able to determine the future route of a railroad, buy the route, build a toll road, and then sell the toll road to the railroad.

Mears incorporated the Dallas and San Miguel Toll Road Company in 1881 to construct a 27-mile-long road from Dallas (located north of Ridgway), over Dallas Divide and down to Placerville. The road continued to Telluride, opening the way for development of that area.

The San Miguel and Rico Toll Road Company also was incorporated in 1881. The mines in Rico were developing, and this small community was one of the most isolated places in the San Juan Mountain region. Financing fell short of the cost required to conquer Lizard Head Pass, and only 6 miles of road was constructed, ending at Ames.

Also in 1881, Mears incorporated the Durango, Parrot City and Ft. Lewis Toll Road Company. He knew at the time that the Denver & Rio Grande planned to reach Durango, a town the railroad founded. Mears purchased an old road and used it as the basis for his new toll road. As soon as it was completed, he sold it to Colonel Peter Swaine, an army officer, who in turn, sold the road to La Plata County. Mears also purchased a toll road running from Gunnison 26 miles to Cebolla, adding to his vast empire.

At the request of mine operators in the Ouray area, Mears

looked over one of the most difficult passages he had encountered up to this time. It was up Canyon Creek to the southwest of Ouray, serving the Camp Bird and Mount Sneffels area only 10 miles away. Following five other unsuccessful attempts at constructing a road over this same route, Mears capitalized the Ouray and Canyon Creek Toll Road Company at $30,000 in August 1883.

This last company was somewhat more successful and had reached Sneffels. The existing road was primitive and not suitable for heavy ore wagons. Mears completed the road, which involved blasting an expensive shelf along a vertical cliff for some distance

It was impossible to avoid paying the toll on Otto Mears's Ouray-to-Silverton toll road at Bear Creek Falls. The tollhouse is next to the log bridge. *(Denver Public Library WHJ-587)*

above Camp Bird. No sooner had the road opened than teamsters complained about the high toll rates. This forced Mears to sell the road to Ouray County and take county bonds as payment.

During this time, Mears became aware of the rapid developments in the Red Mountain area. With the discovery of the Yankee Girl Mine, the demand for a good road connecting Ouray with this district was quite high. A dangerous trail, suitable only for pack animals, followed the Uncompahgre Gorge up to Ironton Park. Several people had lost their lives. Lack of a good wagon road limited production at the mines. To add to the challenge, two previous attempts had been made at constructing a road, and Ouray County had taken over ownership of the last toll road company. Ouray County approached Mears to see if he could complete the job. He probably was their last hope. In 1883, Mears agreed to construct the road provided that he would have controlling interest and could set the toll rates.

One choice of routes was to use the canyon floor. In certain places, however, winter avalanches covered the floor 60 to 100 feet deep with snow-filled debris. The other choice was to blast a shelf out of the cliff on the east side of the near-vertical canyon wall. This route could be kept open year round. By using ropes to lower men down the canyon wall, Mears was able to carve a single-lane shelf hundreds of feet above the Uncompahgre River. Long fuses were used to allow the men to scramble back up to the rim prior to detonation. At Bear Creek Falls, the average height of this exposed section was 580 feet above the canyon floor and cost $1,000 a foot. Mears placed a small hotel and the tollgate here as only a bird could bypass the road without paying the toll. Today, a parking lot along U.S. 550 allows visitors to enjoy this most spectacular place.

This road became the finest achievement in road construction in the United States and proved lucrative for Mears. The cost for a single wagon pulled by a team was $5.00 and $2.50 for a small trail wagon. After 8 years of operation, complaints about the high toll rates forced Mears to sell once again to Ouray County at less than the road's construction cost. Mears made an unsuccessful attempt to have the Colorado State Legislature compensate him for its full cost. Income from the road during his ownership, however, more than compensated Mears for its construction.

Ore flowed from the Red Mountain District down to the smelters in Ouray, and much to the consternation of Silverton smelter owners, Ouray prospered. Silverton's solution was to hire Mears to construct a toll road up Mineral Creek, over Red

Mountain Pass, giving Silverton an equal chance with Ouray.

Mears verbally agreed with San Juan County officials to take on this project in 1883, for $25,000 in bonds. A legal agreement was signed in July of the following year and work began. Using 350 men, Mears completed a two-lane road with modest grades by November. The road connected with his other toll road from Ouray, thereby making wagon travel between the towns possible. The very same route is used by today's "Million Dollar Highway," U.S. 550.

To increase his profits, Mears built a short 6-mile toll road from Barnum to the Denver & Rio Grande station at Sapinero. He completed this project in the summer of 1885.

Mears had hardly a moment to rest and reflect on his accomplishments when San Juan County officials approached him about constructing a toll road north from Silverton along the Animas River, through Howardsville and Eureka, and up the steep grade to Animas Forks ending at Mineral Point. Most of the route was higher than 10,000 feet. The existing road could not support the weight of loaded ore wagons, and they became mired in mud.

The County turned over the old road to Mears along with $15,000 in county warrants, and using the same route, Mears completed a new road to Eureka in the summer of 1885. Above Eureka, the steep grade was exposed to avalanches. It took another year to complete this section. At Animas Forks, the road connected with the road from Lake City over Cinnamon Pass. This was Mears's last toll road project, and now he owned 450 miles of toll roads, costing in today's dollars in excess of $4 million.

Wagons were too slow for Mears, so his next venture was in railroad construction, covering much of the same area as his toll roads. In fact, it was a common practice for Mears to build a railroad on the face of a toll road, thereby greatly reducing grading expenses. Only in cases where the toll road deviated in gradient or curvature from acceptable levels for a railroad was new construction necessary.

The first railroad constructed by Otto Mears started from Silverton and went north up Cement Creek, through Chattanooga,

over Red Mountain Pass, north through Red Mountain Town,
Guston and Ironton, ending at the Saratoga-Albany Mill in
Ironton Park. Organized as the Silverton Railroad Company, it
started construction in 1887 using the toll road that Mears had
constructed earlier over this same route. Not all of the toll road,
however, was suitable for a railroad.

The Silverton Railroad, completed in 1889, made good profits
from the start. Even with the best surveying techniques, performed
by location engineer C. W. Gibbs, the grades were such that a single locomotive could handle only four loaded cars at a time. On
its main line, this railroad included several switchbacks and one
covered turntable.

In 1895, Mears incorporated the Silverton Northern Railroad
with plans to reach from Silverton to Eureka. In 1896, the line was
completed and was extended in 1904 to Animas Forks to serve the
newly constructed Gold Prince Mill. So steep was this section that
a locomotive could handle only one loaded car and one empty car
at a time. In 1905, a branch was constructed from Howardsville
up Cunningham Gulch to the Green Mountain Mill.

The most impressive and extensive railroad project that
Mears constructed was the 172-mile Rio Grande Southern. Again,
Mears called on his talented location engineer, C. W. Gibbs. Built
from 1890 to 1891, this line went through country so rugged and
over trestles so high, that it became one of the greatest feats of
railroad construction in North America. The Denver & Rio
Grande engineers previously had stated that constructing the section from Durango to Rico was not even feasible.

The headquarters for the Rio Grande Southern was in
Ridgway, a town the railroad established. The route from Ridgway
climbed over Dallas Divide, then headed down to Placerville,
where it turned south. At Vance Junction, a branch was constructed to Telluride. Using an amazing series of loops and trestles, the
railroad continued up to "new" Ophir (Ophir Loop) above Ames,
then over Lizard Head Pass after passing around Trout Lake. It
went south through Rico and Dolores, then turned east and ended

in Durango, where it connected with the San Juan Extension of the Denver & Rio Grande.

During the late 1880s, the price of silver fell. Virtually all of the mines along the Rio Grande Southern closed, and not being able to meet its bond payments, the railroad went into receivership. It was sold to the Denver & Rio Grande in 1895, and Otto Mears lost control. The Rio Grande Southern operated until 1951 when it was dismantled.

The Silverton, Gladstone & Northern, constructed in 1899 with money from the owners of the Gold King Mine, was a line Mears had contemplated. In 1910, Mears signed a 10-year lease to operate the railroad, and in 1915, he purchased the line. This was his last railroad investment.

During the latter part of his career, Mears leased and purchased previously abandoned mines and brought them back into production.

Ouray's flamboyant newpaper editor, David Frakes Day, founded the popular *Solid Muldoon.* (drawing by Kenneth Jessen)

D. H. Cummins, "Toll Roads in Southwestern Colorado," *The Colorado Magazine*, Vol. XXIX, No. 2, Colorado Historical Society, Denver, Colorado, April, 1952, p. 101.

Ervan F. Kushner, *Otto Mears: His Life & Times*, Jende-Hagne Bookcorp, Frederick, Colorado, 1979.

LeRoy R. Hafen, "Otto Mears: Pathfinder of the San Juan," *I*, Vol. IX, No. 2, Colorado Historical Society, Denver, Colorado, March, 1932, pp. 71-74.

Michael Kaplan, *Otto Mears, Paradoxical Pathfinder*, San Juan County Book Company, Silverton, Colorado, 1982.

ANIMAS FORKS

Depleted of Its Columbines

- *San Juan County, Animas River drainage*
- *Accessible via graded dirt road*
- *Town had a post office; several original structures remain*

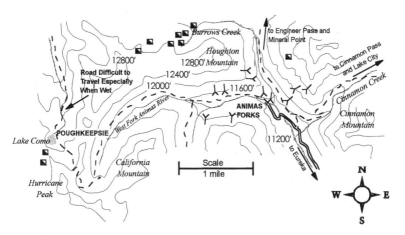

A graded dirt road runs to the Animas Forks site, one of the most popular ghost towns in Colorado. From there, four-wheel drive roads branch off to Engineer and Cinnamon passes and over to Poughkeepsie.

Animas Forks began as the site for the Dakota & San Juan Mining Company's mill. Originally, the mill was to have been erected at Mineral Point. The machinery was ordered, but near the end of 1875, it was apparent that all of the pieces might not arrive for a long time. Some of the lighter parts, including the engine, made it as far as Mineral Point, but the other pieces of machinery were still in Burrows Park, above Lake City. The large flywheel was smashed to pieces in a wagon accident. Other parts were stuck in the winter snow on Slumgullion Pass. Access to Animas Forks was much easier than Mineral Point, so the mining company decided to place the mill at Animas Forks.

In 1876, the mill was constructed on the west bank of the Animas River. It dominated the town site. The mill operated briefly during October 1876 before bad weather forced it to close for the season.

Although not an overwhelming success, the Dakota & San Juan mill spawned the growth of Animas Forks. The town had

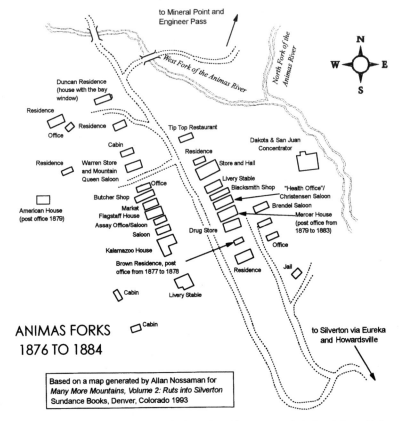

Although only a few of the structures indicated on this map remain today, Animas Forks was a sizable town at one time. The well-known house with the bay window (the Duncan residence) is on the northern end of the site.

None of these false-front stores remain today at Animas Forks. The first store to the left was a general merchandise store, and at the end of the street was the Mercer Hotel. *(Denver Public Library C-158)*

thirty houses and reached its peak in the mid-1880s, supporting a population of 450.

At first, occupation of Animas Forks was seasonal and many of the structures were either tents or primitive log cabins. People could not survive the extreme cold and heavy snow so they left. The Lake City *Silver World* remarked that, during the winter of 1875-1876, the town had dwindled to just two individuals. As the snow melted, many of the residents returned for another season of mining and prospecting. Those who were not successful simply went on to another of the many mining camps located in the San Juans.

During the winter of 1876-1877, an avalanche destroyed the Brown, Epley & Company smelting plant. This left the Dakota & San Juan mill as the only processing plant in Animas Forks.

The first attempt at opening a store in Animas Forks failed, not so much because of the long winters and lack of customers, but because of the erratic behavior of its owners. Other successful stores opened in 1876. The Flagstaff House was the town's first restaurant. A boardinghouse opened in 1876, with twenty-five boarders who paid $8 a week.

Aside from the post office, other businesses included a store, meat market and blacksmith shop. An assayer set up shop at Animas Forks to analyze samples brought in by the hundreds of prospectors working in the area.

When Esther Ekkard opened a boardinghouse at Animas Forks, many miners abandoned their tents in favor of moving to her establishment. As covered by Allen Nossaman in his book, *Many More Mountains, Volume 2*, one of the boarders was John Davie. Davie recalled how one man, who took his meals at the Ekkard boardinghouse, failed to show up one morning. It was assumed that he was sick. Back then, people in these high-altitude towns looked after each other, and a search of the town failed to find the man. Mrs. Ekkard then told the others that the missing man owed her for 3 months room and board and hadn't paid a dime since he arrived.

The most famous building in Animas Forks was constructed by William Duncan in 1879 at the upper part of the town's main street. *(Kenneth Jessen 105A6)*

Upon learning this, a group of men banded together and promised Mrs. Ekkard to recover all the money owed. Now believing that the missing man skipped town, the men rode down to Silverton. There, they soon found the man and strongly suggested that he pay his bill. They gave him given 5 minutes to pay up to avoid being hanged on the spot. Thinking quickly and clearly, the man immediately produced the full amount owed Mrs. Ekkard.

One of the delightful stories to come out of Animas Forks involved Albert Dyer, the town's justice of the peace. A miner was arrested for drunkenness and had to appear before Justice Dyer. He was fined $10 plus court costs, but he refused to pay. The fellow threatened to take the matter to a higher court. Dyer uttered, "There is no such thing. This is the highest court in the United States." At an elevation of 11,584 feet above sea level, Dyer probably was right!

L. M. Gardner opened the town's first saloon but overlooked the required liquor license. After begin fined, he left the area. Things looked brighter when Animas Forks got its first liquor license, and the first "legal" saloon was opened in a primitive l og cabin.

The town's postmaster and assayer, Ed Brown, was performing analysis on some ore from the Dakota & San Juan property when he accidentally got some chemicals mixed in his beard. Near an open flame, the beard caught fire, and he was badly burned.

Employment came from work on a tunnel originating about a mile up the West Fork of the Animas River. This bore ran straight toward Mineral Point and was to have provided access to lodes in that area. The project lasted through 1877 before being abandoned.

By 1877, forty houses stood in Animas Forks, and at the time, businesses included two restaurants and two stores. To survive the cold, residents began to use milled lumber, and this method of construction gradually replaced the drafty log cabins.

That summer, four or five men went on a bender, and Thomas Hughes used his fists to beat Robert Hunter. The following morning, the defeated Hunter armed himself with a revolver and planned to get even. Upon meeting Hughes, Hunter fired at point-blank range, putting a ball through Hughes's face. The round entered under his nose and passed through the opposite side of his face. As serious as the wound was, Hughes recovered. For such an incident, impromptu hangings were normal, and Hunter fled the area, never to be seen again.

In 1878, a 16-foot high dam was constructed across the Animas River to provide power for a sampling mill and a sawmill. A water wheel 18 feet in diameter was used in this project. The sawmill produced 4,000 board feet of lumber per day to satisfy construction needs in the area.

Animas Forks got its first post office in 1875, and by 1877, mail was delivered three times a week. The post office remained open until 1889, then closed for a brief period. The office reopened and lasted until 1891. After 1900, mining activity increased, and the Animas Forks post office opened again in 1904. It closed for good in 1915.

By 1878, businesses included two stores, a boardinghouse, butcher shop, blacksmith shop, three saloons and three hotels—Mercer House, Garrison House and Flagstaff House. The latter was a combination hotel, restaurant and bakery. In addition, this year marked the opening of the town's first drugstore.

In 1882, the town's only doctor and a grocery store shared the same two-story frame building. The town's only Chinaman, Ming Lee, ran a laundry. Ole Christiansen must have had a sense of humor for he named his saloon The Health Office. During the following winter, more residents stayed in Animas Forks than had remained during any previous winter. Some businesses began to operate throughout the year.

In 1879, Ole Christiansen constructed a new place of business, the Mountain Queen Saloon, complete with a billiard hall. William Duncan built the now famous house with a bay window—one of the most recognizable ghost town structures in Colorado. It was built in 1879 at what then was the upper part of the town's main street.

In 1881, Ed and Squire Brown constructed the largest commercial structure in town, the Kalamazoo House. It had a dining room and veranda. It also was the location of the town's only telephone.

The following year saw construction of the Tip Top Restaurant as well as a sturdy jail below the town site. For 4 years, the Animas Forks *Pioneer* brought its readers the latest news. It was the highest newspaper printed in United States.

Animas Forks was abandoned, for the most part, in 1901. The town was revived in 1903 by an extension of the Silverton Northern Railroad, constructed by Otto Mears. The railroad was built on the toll road that Mears owned, running from Eureka. Eureka got rail service in 1896 on a relatively easy 2.5 percent grade from Silverton. From Eureka to Animas Forks, however, the grade was quite steep averaging 5.77 percent, with one stretch approaching 7 percent.

This project required 400 men who stayed in boardinghouses in Eureka and Animas Forks. A big fill had to be constructed above the Sunnyside mill. Today, this is part of the automobile road to Animas Forks. The project was completed in 1904 to serve the newly constructed Gold Prince Mill.

Mears decided to try to keep his railroad open all year by building a snow shed over the most exposed area. Nearly every year, this same point was blocked by an avalanche. After the expenditure of a lot of money, the first slide of the year reduced the massive snow shed to splinters.

Today, the concrete foundations of the Gold Prince Mill are plainly visible below the town site. The Gold Prince Mill operated until 1910 and was dismantled in 1917. The rails of the Silverton Northern remained in place until 1936.

As part of its decorations for a convention in 1911, Denver wanted to solidify its title of "Queen City of the Rockies." What officials needed was a large quantity of lavender columbines, what was to become the Colorado state flower. Mears provided a train to take volunteers up the steep grade to Animas Forks. A dozen galvanized iron tubs were supplied to hold the columbines. In an act that would horrify today's environmentalists, volunteers gathered an estimated 25,000 clumps of columbines, which were

Animas Forks has a number of rundown, abandoned structures, making a visit to the site worthwhile for those interested in ghost towns. *(Kenneth Jessen 105A9)*

shipped to Denver and displayed at the Denver Post Building. Today, the flower is protected by state law, and such a rape of the land would not be tolerated.

Animas Forks is quite easy to reach over a graded road, which was improved during the mid-1990s. There are several exposed stretches above Eureka, however.

Allen Nossaman, *Many More Mountains, Volume 2: Ruts into Silverton*, Sundance Publications Limited, Denver, Colorado, 1993, pp. 186-202.

Allen Nossaman, *Many More Mountains, Volume 3: Rails into Silverton*, Sundance Publications Limited, Denver, Colorado, 1998, p. 114.

Jack Benham, *Silverton*, Bear Creek Publishing Co., Ouray, Colorado, 1977, pp. 17, 20.

Robert E. Sloan and Carl A. Skowronski, *The Rainbow Route*, Sundance Publications Limited, Denver, Colorado, 1975, pp. 260, 265-266.

Robert L. Brown, *Jeep Trails to Colorado Ghost Towns*, Caxton Printers, Caldwell, Idaho, 1963, pp. 46-52.

William H. Bauer, James L. Ozment and John H. Willard, *Colorado Post Offices*, Colorado Railroad Museum, Golden, Colorado, 1990, p. 12.

BANDORA and TITUSVILLE

Obscure San Juan Towns

- *San Juan County, South Mineral Creek and Idaho Gulch drainages*
- *Bandora accessible by four-wheel drive road; Titusville by trail*
- *Neither town had a post office; no structures remain*

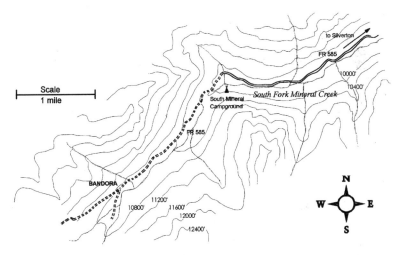

The Bandora site is located up the south fork of Mineral Creek southwest of Silverton. The road is graded to the South Mineral Campground.

Located on South Mineral Creek near the end of a four-wheel drive road and well past the South Mineral Creek campground was a small mining community called Bandora. Ore was discovered in 1882 in this area. In 1940, the Blanco Mining Company bought the claims and continued mining. At this time, ore was brought down South Mineral Creek for processing at the Shenandoah-Dives Mill near Silverton.

This is what was left of Bandora in 1950, when Muriel Sibell Wolle took this photograph. Nothing remains at the site today. *(Denver Public Library x-5251)*

The road to the site is graded to the campground, but it is rough beyond this point and requires four-wheel drive to reach the site. Bandora is located in a small meadow at 10,600 feet.

In 1950, Muriel Sibell Wolle, author of *Stampede to Timberline*, made the trip. At the time of her visit, several cabins were still standing, but only mine dumps mark the site today.

Another obscure mining town, Titusville, sat high on the west shoulder of Kendall Mountain at nearly 11,000 feet, near Idaho Gulch above Silverton. A trail was constructed to the mine, and a tram was used to haul the ore to Silverton. One report listed the population at 500, which seems quite high. A foot trail leads to the site, and no structures remain.

Muriel Sibell Wolle, *Stampede to Timberline*, Sage Books, Chicago, 1949, pp. 433, 531-532.

BEARTOWN

A Remote Mining Camp

- *San Juan County, Bear Creek drainage*
- *Accessible via four-wheel drive road*
- *Town did not have a post office; partially collapsed structures remain*

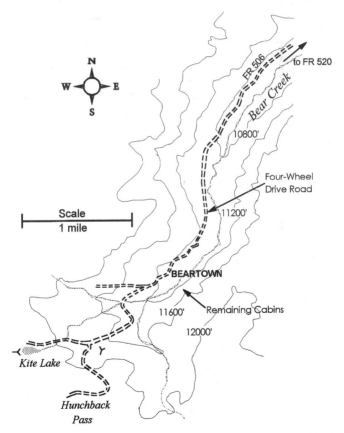

Beartown is in a remote location south of the Rio Grande on Forest Service Road 506. Although nothing remains standing in the meadow at the town site, several cabins can be seen in the trees to the south.

Beartown was constructed as a mining camp 4 miles south of the Rio Grande and its confluence with Pole Creek. It can be reached by taking FR 520 from Lost Trail Station, past the town sites of Jennison and Timber Hill, to where the road comes out of the timber and drops down to the Rio Grande River. FR 506 to Beartown takes off to the left (south) and immediately crosses the Rio Grande River. This turnoff is before the Pole Creek ford. The route to Beartown is an easy four-wheel drive road. Because the site is not marked, it can easily be missed.

Beyond the town site, the road makes a loop to the left, crossing Bear Creek, then to the right, before climbing past a mine to Kite Lake. The only remaining structures at Beartown are half-hidden in the trees off to the southeast across Bear Creek. The original town probably was located in the center of a large meadow, where scattered bits of lumber mark the location of one structure.

The town was supported by the Sylvanite Mine near Kite Lake, about 2 miles beyond Beartown. The mineral sylvanite is a form of tellurium and contains 24.5 percent gold and 13.4 percent silver. This mine was owned by the Syndicate Gold Mining Company. Other mines higher on the mountainside included the Good Hope, Gold Bug and Silver Bug.

Prospectors came into the area in 1893, and by June of that year, hundreds were camped in the valley where Beartown was established. At first, cabins were not constructed, as the prospectors were far too busy exploring the area.

Soon a camp called Gold Run developed. It also went under the name Bear Creek or Silvertip. This same year, a post office opened under the name Sylvanite, but it closed in October of the following year. The place became known as Beartown, but the origin of the name is a mystery.

The town had a grocery store, hardware store, blacksmith shop, boardinghouse, saloon and assayer's office. A weekly newspaper was established by the *Creede Candle* and named the *Gold Run Silvertip.*

Beartown is one of the most remote camps in the San Juans,

and transportation expenses were quite high. Rich hand-sorted ore was packed out and ran as much as $4,000 a ton. Beartown's economy was based on both gold and silver. Mining continued until 1938.

The rich ore from Beartown attracted highwaymen. Muriel Sibell Wolle visited Beartown in 1948 and related a story about road agents hiding behind a large rock on Timber Hill. Full of sacked ore, three loaded wagons were descending from Beartown. Scouts hired to protect the wagons rode ahead and discovered the robbers, but all except one were killed. The surviving scout rode back to warn the teamsters. Quickly the cargo from two of the wagons was dumped in a swamp, but before the last wagon could be unloaded, the robbers appeared. They killed all of the men and the surviving scout. The ore in the loaded wagon was sold to

The Beartown site, located in a large meadow, was photographed in 1948 by Muriel Sibell Wolle. Other structures were built in the forest to the right of the meadow. *(Denver Public Library x-5230)*

a smelter in Silverton, and the rest of the ore remains hidden somewhere in the area.

When Muriel Sibell Wolle reached the Beartown site, only one cabin remained standing in the meadow. She also noted the remains of a mill. She saw a large cabin below the town site with its roof caved in, which might have been a stage station.

One of the cabins is located south of the Beartown site across the creek from the road through the area. *(Kenneth Jessen 123A13)*

Cathy E. Kindquist, *Stony Pass*, San Juan Book Company, Silverton, Colorado, 1987, pp. 79, 81.

Edward S. Dana, *Textbook of Mineralogy*, John Wiley & Sons, London, 1949 (renewed), pp. 441-442.

Muriel Sibell Wolle, *Stampede to Timberline*, Sage Books, Chicago, 1949, pp. 334-338.

William H. Bauer, James L. Ozment and John H. Willard, *Colorado Post Offices*, Colorado Railroad Museum, Golden, Colorado, 1990, p. 138.

CAMP BIRD

Made Thomas Walsh Rich

- *Ouray County, Canyon Creek Drainage*
- *Access limited by private property*
- *Town had a post office; several structures remain*

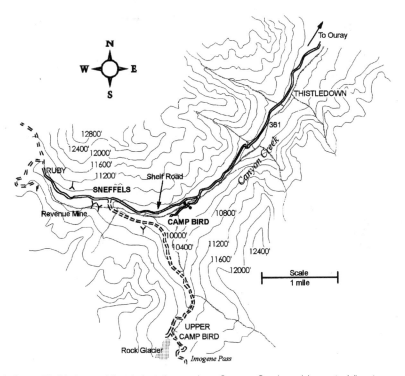

Camp Bird is located just below the road up Canyon Creek and is posted "no trespassing." Upper Camp Bird can be reached over a rough four-wheel drive road. Its location is at the base of a rock glacier just below Imogene Pass.

355

In 1896, Hubbard Reed sold the Gertrude and Una lodes and mill site to Thomas Walsh, a newcomer to the area. Reed was famous for his silver mines and surveyed the Ouray town site. From what Reed thought was worth little, Walsh recovered a fortune. Reed had been looking for silver, but what Walsh discovered was gold.

After Walsh purchased the Gertrude and Una lodes, he wanted to know what he had bought. A snow slide covered the entrance to the Gertrude mine, and Walsh asked one of his men to tunnel through the snow to retrieve some ore samples. The miner brought back ore containing galena, a combination of zinc, lead, copper and a small amount of silver. The ore was of little value and assayed at $8 a ton.

Not satisfied, Walsh went into the mine himself and examined the vein. He spotted the source of the galena ore but also saw a 3-foot-thick section of quartz. Upon close examination, Walsh discovered dark gray tellurium in the form of specks and thread-like circles. His assistant saw him chipping away in an area adjacent to the vein of galena and pointed out Walsh's presumed error. Walsh ignored the comment and took samples of what others had missed. The tellurium was mixed with a great deal of gold and assayed at $3,000 a ton. What the previous owners had discarded in the tailing pile, Walsh sorted and shipped.

By 1898, Walsh was processing his gold ore by first crushing it into a fine powder, then using an amalgamation process. Mercury has a strong affinity for gold. The fine flakes of gold are captured by passing the pulverized ore over copper plates coated with mercury. Periodically the mercury-gold amalgam is scraped off the plates and passed through cheesecloth. Most of the mercury is separated from the gold in this manner, leading to what is called a gold button. To recover the remaining mercury, the gold button is heated in a retort.

A 9,000-foot tramway was constructed to bring ore down to the mill at Camp Bird, located along Canyon Creek. After Walsh got the mine in operation, the only thing the owners of the nearby silver mines could do was watch and wonder at the millions of

To the right is the Camp Bird mine office. In the background is the large mill used to concentrate the ore. This photograph was taken in 1941 by Muriel Sibell Wolle, when the mine was still in operation. *(Denver Public Library x-3054)*

dollars in gold taken down the canyon every year.

Near Walsh's mill, a company town was built and a post office opened in 1898 using the name "Campbird." It remained active until 1918. Wishing to have his miners live in comfort, Walsh constructed a three-story boardinghouse equal in comfort to a good hotel. For example, the lavatories had marble-topped wash basins and porcelain tubs. The beds were made of steel coated with white enamel, with steel springs and good mattresses. The Camp Bird boardinghouse had hardwood floors and was steam-heated and equipped with electric lights. Meals were served on China plates. The workers had access to free subscriptions to leading periodicals including the *New York Sun*, *Cosmopolitan* and *Harper's Weekly*. At the other nearby mines, the miners slept in drafty shacks or bunkhouses. Walsh was proud of the high standards set for his miners.

In 1900, a transmission line was built from the Telluride Power Transmission Company over Imogene Pass to bring ac power to Camp Bird. This was just one example of the latest technology and equipment used at Camp Bird. The tunnels were illuminated with electric lights, the mine locomotives were powered by electricity and the latest in compressed air drills were used to advance the tunnels.

Walsh donated the money for the public library named after him in Ouray. In addition, a general library fund was established to pay the librarian. The library was dedicated in 1901.

Camp Bird was located in the only flat part of the canyon and was exposed to avalanches from above. On March 17, 1906, a large slide destroyed the mill, boardinghouse and associated structures. This slide actually started as two slides, one from U.S. Mountain and the other from Hayden Mountain. Because of a previous power outage, only three men were in the mill at the time, one of whom was killed. Walsh's dog was found packed in the concrete-like snow but still alive. A fire 2 days later finished what was left of the structures, and a new mill was subsequently constructed.

In 1936, at upper Camp Bird, two men and one woman were killed when three separate avalanche gullies all ran at once.

The upper level of the Camp Bird Mine can be seen high on the mountainside to the extreme left. The living quarters for this part of the Camp Bird mining complex were below to the right, near the foot of the prominent rock glacier. *(United States Geological Survey, W. Cross 397)*

The woman, Rose Israel, was the boardinghouse cook, and others killed were the mill superintendent and the blacksmith.

The Camp Bird Mine was developed at different levels. During 1916-1918, a new tunnel was driven from the mill below the ore body. Called the 14th level, it was approximately 500 feet below the lowest level of the Camp Bird Mine. The purpose of

Mike Arnold stands by a corrugated steel building, one of several standing structures at the upper Camp Bird site. A large rock glacier can be seen in the background. *(Kenneth Jessen 122D10)*

the tunnel, which was nearly 2 miles long, was to lower the cost of the mining by eliminating the need to hoist ore to the surface. After reaching the surface, the ore was transported down to the mill. From the new tunnel, gravity could feed ore directly into the mining cars at the 14th level. The new tunnel provided improved ventilation and eliminated costly pumping to drain the mine.

A graded dirt road provides access to lower Camp Bird. To reach upper Camp Bird is an entirely different matter. A rough four-wheel drive road leaves the Canyon Creek Road near Sneffels, high above lower Camp Bird. It runs along the top of the cliff above lower Camp Bird. The view from this cliff is magnificent. Above the cliff, the road crosses several streams, and during wet years these crossings can be quite deep.

At upper Camp Bird, some original structures remain, including what appears to be a bunkhouse. A corrugated steel building may have been used as an office. Some evidence suggests that these buildings had running water. A spring has been capped and water piped to these buildings.

The mine portal at upper Camp Bird is at Level 3 within the mine. Above it is an immense rock glacier coming down from a high cirque. It appears that the rock glacier, in time, will overrun the mine portal. From upper Camp Bird, the road continues over

Imogene Pass, past an even higher opening into the Camp Bird Mine, through the Tomboy site and on to Telluride.

At lower Camp Bird, the area is fenced and posted "no trespassing." In 1999, some of the mine structures were being razed. Still standing, however, was the magnificent home of the mine superintendent, recently painted and restored.

Although some of the structures at Camp Bird have been razed in recent years, the magnificent home of the mine superintendent remains standing. The property, however, is posted "no trespassing." *(Kenneth Jessen 102D9)*

Doris H. Gregory, *The Great Revenue and Surrounding Mines*, Cascade Publications, Ouray, Colorado, 1996, p. 12.

Evalyn Walsh McLean, *Father Struck it Rich*, First Light Publishing, Fort Collins, Colorado, 1996, pp. 32-33.

Jack L. Benham, *Camp Bird and the Revenue*, Bear Creek Publishing Co., Ouray, Colorado, 1980, pp. 39, 42.

P. David Smith, *Images of the San Juans*, Western Reflections Inc., Ouray, Colorado, 1997, pp. 178-179, 184.

William H. Bauer, James L. Ozment and John H. Willard, *Colorado Post Offices*, Colorado Railroad Museum, Golden, Colorado, 1990, p. 27.

CHATTANOOGA
A Logical Place for a Town

- San Juan County, Mineral Creek drainage
- Accessible via paved road
- Town had a post office; no standing structures remain

The steep climb up Red Mountain Pass begins on the Silverton side, where Mill Creek joins Mineral Creek. The grade to the south from Silverton to this point is reasonable. During the mining boom more than a century ago, the climb beyond this point was difficult, especially before a toll road was built. This point became a transfer location, where the ore on pack animals was transferred to wagons for the remainder of the trip to Silverton. It also was the place where supplies destined for the mines at Red Mountain were transferred from wagons to pack animals.

This was a logical location for a town, although it was swampy. In 1882, a small community called Sweetville was established. Soon a second town, called Chattanooga, sprang up next to Sweetville. As both towns grew, they merged under the name Chattanooga.

An early pioneer, Francis Carell, named this place for his Tennessee hometown. Carell was a newspaperman and had been involved in establishing the Animas Forks *Pioneer*. In 1883, Carell constructed one of the town's first substantial buildings and opened the Chattanooga House.

In 1883, a good wagon road was completed by Otto Mears from Silverton to Chattanooga. A toll was charged for its use. The following year, Mears extended this road over Red Mountain Pass to join another of his toll roads originating in Ouray.

The flamboyant editor of Ouray's *Solid Muldoon*, David

Frakes Day, was unimpressed with the road and commented, "The wagon road from Silverton to Chattanooga is dangerous even to pedestrians....The average depth of the mud is three feet. ...The grade is four parts vertical and one part perpendicular." Chattanooga got its own post office in 1883, and it remained open for more than a decade. During its early months, the post office was located in the town's drugstore. One newspaper reported that Chattanooga had twenty-five businesses, but this seems optimistic based on early photographs. Lots sold for $100 to $200 dollars each. The principal streets were Main, First and Second, running east and west, intersected by Water and Silver streets.

During its first 2 years, Chattanooga grew into a fair-sized settlement of sixty people. A livery stable and a forwarding warehouse were constructed. The town had a general store, grocery store and hardware store. A second grocery store opened, with a boot and shoe repair shop within the building. A meat market opened, as did a lumberyard. A tent enclosed a billiard parlor and saloon, which operated briefly. The Chattanooga *Enterprise* survived its first issue on June 1, 1883 and maybe its second, but no more. Chattanooga got a telephone in 1883. The Enterprise Restaurant and The Texas Exchange Saloon rounded out Chattanooga's businesses.

Based on historic photographs, a dozen structures constituted early Chattanooga. Its main street was a corduroy road consisting of logs laid side by side to allow wagons to pass over the soft, waterlogged ground.

In August 1883, work started on the 30-ton per-day concentrator at Mineral Creek Concentrating and Sampling Company. It included crushers, rollers and jig tables. All of the machinery was powered by a 32-inch water wheel. The purpose of the mill wasn't to extract precious metals from ore but rather to remove as much waste rock as possible. In this way, shipping costs were reduced greatly.

The mill operated under a contract with the Silver Ledge Mine above Chattanooga. The process of removing waste rock used gravity and water. After crushing the ore into a fine powder, it was mixed with water to form slurry. The metallic content was separated through a series of vibrating tables. The heavier ore settled to the bottom of shallow ribs and the waste rock was washed away by water. The ore then was dried and placed in sacks for shipment.

The Silver Ledge Mine above Chattanooga was a major factor late in the town's life. Unfortunately, the supports for this headframe are about to buckle, and the structure will collapse. *(Kenneth Jessen 100C9)*

In 1887, Otto Mears constructed the Silverton Railroad from Silverton to Burro Bridge, south of Chattanooga. The following year, the railroad was extended over Red Mountain Pass through Ironton ending at the Saratoga-Albany Mill. This ended the importance of Chattanooga as a transfer point. The rails were removed in 1926, years after the line had been abandoned.

Although cheap rail transportation produced a boom in the Red Mountain District, it spelled the end for Chattanooga. Its population fell to two in 1890 - a saloon operator and a widow who took in washing. After an avalanche leveled a portion of the town, it was not rebuilt.

Above Chattanooga, the Silver Ledge Mine continued to produce and helped boost the area's economy. The shaft house caught fire in 1891, igniting 40 pounds of dynamite and blowing the remainder of the buildings into splinters. After it was rebuilt, the Silver Ledge added magnetic separation equipment to its mill in 1904 to rid the ore of iron. The mine became a profitable producer of zinc combined with some silver. As of 1999, the badly weathered shaft house remained standing.

Although the primary ore found in this region was silver-lead galena, some gold ore was discovered in 1893. It was in quartz and found in the form of pure gold wires. The extent of this lode was limited, and it soon was exhausted.

None of the original structures, which appear in historic photographs, survive today at Chattanooga. The town site can be seen below U.S. 550, where there are a few private homes. *For a map showing the location of Chattanooga, see "Red Mountain City."*

Allen Nossaman, *Many More Mountains, Volume 3: Rails into Silverton*, Sundance Publications Limited, Denver, Colorado, 1998, pp. 278-279, 282-284, 289.

Jack Benham, *Silverton*, Bear Creek Publishing Co., Ouray, Colorado, 1977, p. 29.

Muriel Sibell Wolle, *Stampede to Timberline*, Sage Books, Chicago, 1949, pp. 434, 436.

P. David Smith, *Mountains of Silver*, Pruett Publishing Company, Boulder, Colorado, 1994, p. 48.

The Solid Muldoon, April 13, 1883.

Tiv Wilkins, *Colorado Railroads*, Pruett Publishing Company, Boulder, Colorado, 1974, pp. 72, 209.

William H. Bauer, James L. Ozment and John H. Willard, *Colorado Post Offices*, Colorado Railroad Museum, Golden, Colorado, 1990, p. 32.

DALLAS

Eclipsed by Ridgway

- *Ouray County, Uncompahgre River drainage*
- *Accessible via paved road*
- *Town had a post office; no structures remain*

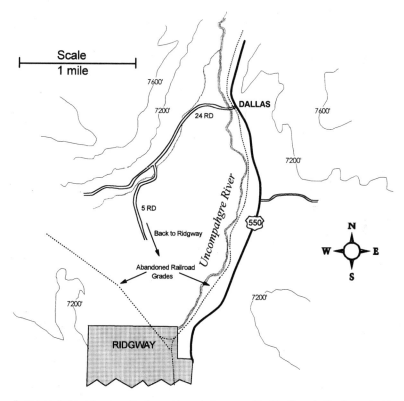

Dallas could have become the largest town in the area. The Rio Grande Southern decided not to use Dallas, but rather construct the new town of Ridgway for its northern terminus. Dallas died, and nothing of the original town remains at the site today.

The town of Dallas was settled during the early 1880s near placer deposits at the confluence of Dallas Creek and the Uncompahgre River. The Dallas Placer Company used high-pressure nozzles to wash the gravel down from old streambeds. Fortunately for the area's ecology, this destructive form of mining lasted only a few years.

In 1884, the Dallas Hotel was constructed in a row of false-front stores as the town began to take shape along its main street.

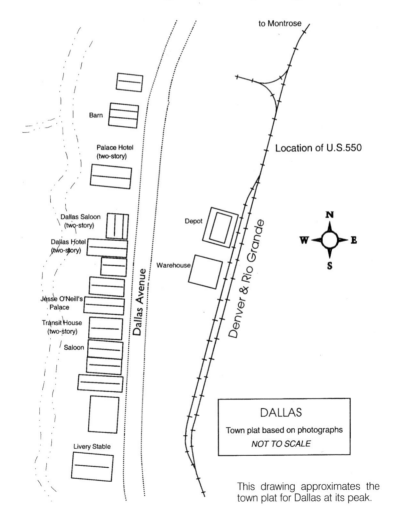

This drawing approximates the town plat for Dallas at its peak.

The substantial town of Dallas, shown in a May 1888 photograph, was located 2 miles north of Ridgway. Nothing remains at the site today. *(Denver Public Library x-11489)*

During this same year, the Dallas post office opened. In 1887, the Denver & Rio Grande Railroad constructed its Ouray branch from Montrose through Dallas. The construction locomotives rolled through the town on August 18, and the town's economy began to boom. Well-known freighter Dave Wood moved his headquarters to Dallas and set up a forwarding business. Freight was delivered to outlying mining areas, and ore was hauled into Dallas for shipment to smelters. David Day's *Solid Muldoon* remarked that Dallas had grown suddenly and could become a dangerous competitor to Ouray and Montrose.

In the fall of 1888, however, Dallas suffered a setback when fire swept through the town. It started around 2 a.m. on a Sunday morning in the Dallas Hotel, and seventeen houses and stores went up in flames. This didn't deter the people of Dallas, and 5 months later incorporation papers were filed. Dallas became an officially recognized town consisting of ten blocks.

The Rio Grande Southern was incorporated to build a railroad from the Uncompahgre River Valley via a route to Placerville, past Telluride, through Rico and Dolores, ending in Durango. The logical place to begin construction was at Dallas. Hundreds of narrow gauge freight cars were packed into the yard at Dallas, loaded with construction supplies. The location engineer for the Rio Grande Southern, Charles Gibbs, established his office in Dallas, but the Rio Grande Southern settled for a site about 2 miles to the south of Dallas. After several name changes, the new town was called Ridgway. Loss of the northern terminus for the railroad spelled the end of Dallas.

In early 1890, businessmen began to move to Ridgway. Editor Ernest Bacon of the Dallas *Western Slope* described the demise of the town's city government. On September 11, 1890, Bacon wrote about how the buildings in Dallas were being dismantled and carted off to Ridgway. Soon the *Western Slope* closed its doors, and Ernest Bacon started the *Ridgway Herald.*

Prior to the fire of 1888, the town of Dallas consisted of a long row of buildings facing east along Dallas Avenue. After the fire, the town was rebuilt along much of the same lines. The railroad tracks paralleled the town's main street to the east. The Denver & Rio Grande constructed a depot and a separate freight house.

Businesses in Dallas included the Placer Hotel, Dallas Saloon, Dallas Hotel, Jesse O'Nells Place, Transit House and a bookstore. In all, a dozen or so structures appear in photographs of the town's business district.

Nothing remains of Dallas. The area now has many expensive homes with an incredible view of the Uncompahgre Range.

Doris H. Gregory, *The Town That Refused to Die; Ridgway, Colorado*, Cascade Publications, Ouray, Colorado, 1991, pp. 11-13.

Russ Collman and Dell McCoy, *The RGS Story, Volume I*, Sundance Books, Denver, 1990, pp. 24-30, 33, 39.

William H. Bauer, James L. Ozment and John H. Willard, *Colorado Post Offices*, Colorado Railroad Museum, Golden, Colorado, 1990, p. 42.

DEL MINO

A Failed Attempt on Cement Creek

- *San Juan County, Cement Creek drainage*
- *Accessible by graded dirt road*
- *Town had a post office; no structures remain*

Del Mino was located north of Silverton along Cement Creek near the mouth of Prospect Gulch. The town was established as a transfer point for wagon and pack animals destined for the Red Mountain Mining District.

A broad meadow marks the spot today along the Cement Creek Road leading to Gladstone. The town originally was laid out in 1883 by a man from Silverton. The *San Juan Herald* reported that the town had ten buildings, but based on a survey of the site, this seems optimistic. A half-dozen structures are known to have been constructed, including a hotel and restaurant. The town also had a general merchandise store.

In 1883, a post office opened in the Del Mino Hotel, but it was closed a year later. The Postal Service called the town "Del Mine" possibly because of a clerical error.

The end came to Del Mino in 1884, when traffic shifted to the road up Mineral Creek and the traffic up Prospect Gulch declined. Its residents had hoped that ore from the Gladstone area and Prospect Basin would keep the town alive. After the abandonment of Del Mino, some of the structures were moved to Gladstone.

About half a mile south of Del Mino, at the mouth of Georgia Gulch, was another town named Vernon. It grew into a group of cabins, but by 1883, only one structure remained standing. *For a map showing Del Mino and Vernon, see "Gladstone."*

Travel to many of the mining towns in the San Juan Mountains required courage. This is among the most rugged areas in the United States outside of Alaska. *(Denver Public Library MCC-1659)*

Allen Nossaman, *Many More Mountains, Volume 3: Rails into Silverton*, Sundance Publications Limited, Denver, Colorado, 1998, pp. 288-290.

William H. Bauer, James L. Ozment and John H. Willard, *Colorado Post Offices*, Colorado Railroad Museum, Golden, Colorado, 1990, p. 43.

EUREKA

Last to Get a Saloon

- *San Juan County, Animas River drainage*
- *Accessible via graded dirt road*
- *Town had a post office; one standing structure*

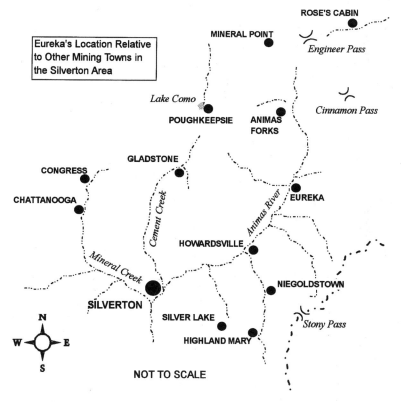

Eureka's Location Relative to Other Mining Towns in the Silverton Area

NOT TO SCALE

For a while, Eureka was the region's second largest town, exceeded only by Silverton. It was located at the base of the steep grade up to Animas Forks and can be reached today by a good, graded dirt road.

371

Eureka was located at the very end of the long, relatively flat floodplain formed by the Animas River. Eureka stood at the base of the steep climb to Animas Forks, 9 miles north of Silverton. The remains of a cabin outside the original town limits and the imposing stair-step foundation of the Sunnyside Mill are all that is left at the site today. A few railroad ties can be seen flush to the ground leading to the mill site.

Alan Nossaman offers the most definitive work on the San Juans, and in his book, *Many More Mountains,* he speculates that pioneer Charles Baker and his party named the place Eureka. Baker was among the first white men to explore the area in 1860-1861. He discovered placer deposits at the mouth of Eureka Gulch. Years later, when Eureka was settled, sluice boxes made of whip-sawed lumber and left by the Baker party were found.

Ruben McNutt is credited with having built the first cabin in 1871-1872, up Eureka Gulch where it joins the South Fork of the Animas River. McNutt, by the way, was the first person to introduce a bill in the Territorial Legislature to create San Juan County. In 1872, three prospectors constructed a cabin well below McNutt's cabin at the future site of Eureka. Many more cabins followed, and in 1874, a town company was formed to develop the site.

A team from the United States Geological and Geographic Survey came through the area in 1874 and took note of the cabins. The name "Eureka" was carved on a sign at the site. As the town grew, it gained its own justice of the peace and constable. A post office opened in Eureka in 1875 based on its increasing population. Unlike the higher camps in the San Juan Mountains, Eureka was occupied through the winter.

Eureka grew relatively slowly and was the last town in the area to have its own saloon. One of Animas Forks' merchants moved his store down to Eureka. Other stores were opened as well, and the Montague combination cabin-store was the polling place for the county's first election in 1876. Montague was named the county judge, and another resident of Eureka was named a county commissioner.

Milton Engleman became one of the most prominent citizens of Eureka. He moved from Cañon City in 1876 to open a store in Eureka and became president of the town company. His relatives acquired the Sunnyside Mine from pioneer Ruben McNutt. Engleman opened a store in 1877, bringing the inventory of goods from his other store in Cañon City. His Eureka store was a log structure with a false front. During the same year, Eureka got its first hotel, a 20-foot by 30-foot log structure called Paradise Regained.

The Lake City *Silver World* described a dance held in one of Eureka's cabins in April 1877. "The damsels" was the term referring to the ladies who arrived on foot and on burros. The men were called the "iron clads." The music was provided by a fiddler and a banjo player. As for the dance, the newspaper called it the "San Juan Polka" and added that it resembled a Sioux War dance. Groundhog was served, along with ox, gravy, bacon, coffee, tea and a variety of pies and cakes. Apparently, the dance lasted until the following morning. What is surprising is that it could draw enough ladies to make it worthwhile, as men vastly outnumbered women.

Eureka grew to become San Juan County's second largest town exceeded only by Silverton. This photograph, taken from the Sunnyside Mill around 1938, shows the town at its peak. All of these structures are gone today. *(Denver Public Library x-8299)*

The primary producing mines supporting growth in Eureka were located to the west in Eureka Gulch. The dominant mine was the Sunnyside, near the head of this gulch at Lake Emma. The mine was discovered in 1873, and an extension of the original ore body was discovered the following year. The Sunnyside, at an elevation of 12,300 feet, had its own boardinghouse and blacksmith shop. The ore produced by the mine was lead-zinc galena containing silver. There were lesser mines in the area such as the Toltec, Golden Fleece and Tom Moore.

Eureka grew slower than other towns in the surrounding area. James Winspear constructed a water-powered sawmill in

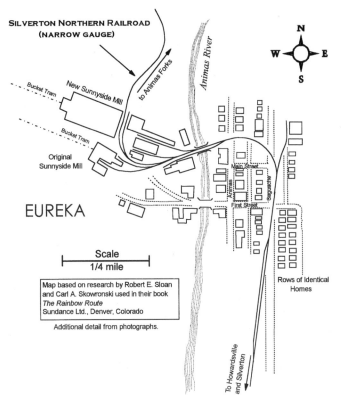

This map of Eureka only approximates the layout of the town. So little is left today that the site is difficult to recognize except for the foundation of the Sunnyside Mill.

1878, and began producing milled lumber for a new reduction works. The mill ran at capacity, producing 10,000 board feet of lumber per day. A shingle mill, operating from the same water wheel, added to Eureka's employment.

Thousands of bricks were ordered for construction of the smokestack at the mill. A retort house and mill building also were erected. A story-and-a-half boardinghouse was built for the mill workers. The Eureka Reduction Works Company was to have provided employment for two dozen men, but mounting debts prevented its opening. The mill structure later was relegated to use as a bar, and the brick smokestack stood for years as a reminder of this failed project.

Among the structures added to Eureka during 1878 were a restaurant and hotel. A liquor license was granted the following year, and the town's first saloon opened. A town plat was filed in 1881 covering 162 acres. Eureka was incorporated 2 years later.

Although Eureka did not have its own newspaper, Theodore Comstock published a monthly pamphlet, the *San Juan Expositor.* Comstock also operated an assay office and managed several mines. In addition, the town's only telephone was kept in his office.

In 1896, the Silverton Northern was extended from Waldheim northeasterly to Eureka. The real challenge was to reach Animas Forks. This portion of the Silverton Northern was completed in 1904 over a distance of 4 miles with grades up to 7 percent. After operations had stopped at the Gold Prince Mill at Animas Forks, the track was removed in 1936. In 1942, the track to Eureka was taken up.

During the late 1880s, the price of silver declined, and in 1893, the United States discontinued the purchase of silver to back its currency. Despite this, the Sunnyside Mill continued to process thousands of tons of ore from its mine. Like other ore in the area, it was a complex combination of lead, zinc, copper and silver. The Sunnyside Mine produced a great deal of low-grade ore, making its operation marginal. A new mill, using the latest technology, was constructed in 1899 to improve efficiency. A

3-mile-long tramway was constructed to connect the mine and the mill, eliminating the expense of hauling ore down a steep wagon road. This breathed new life into Eureka.

Unlike most San Juan towns, Eureka was not abandoned until fairly recently because of the continuous improvements in milling. By 1902, the Sunnyside was ranked among the top-producing mines in the United States. The mill was enlarged in 1918 and used the first commercial selective lead-zinc flotation process. Eventually, however, the cost of mining and milling became too high to continue operations, and the entire operation sat idle for many years. On August 2, 1937, the *Silverton Standard* carried this account of new activity at Eureka:

> Eureka is the center of activity for the past few weeks. Over fifty men are busy preparing the various pieces of equipment for operation of the famous Sunnyside Mine. A steam shovel is building a dam at the mill's tailing pond below Eureka. The Sunnyside Mill is being thoroughly reconditioned. The crew is cleaning out the portal of the mine, and the mine boarding house has been opened to accommodate this crew. Several families have moved to Eureka from Silverton, and several more houses have been allotted to employees for occupancy in the near future.

After sitting abandoned, Eureka recovered to become San Juan County's second largest town, exceeded only by Silverton. In 1939, however, it began to lose population, and in 1942, its post office closed. The demand for base metals during World War II kept the mill operating. In 1948, the Sunnyside Mill closed for good and was sold for its scrap value. It was dismantled, leaving only its stair-step concrete foundation. During its life, it produced about $50 million in metals.

When Robert L. Brown visited Eureka in 1948, quite a few structures were left standing, including a number of cabins on the north end of the site. One of the false-front stores along the main street also stood. Today the site is almost void of structures.

The concrete foundation is all that remains of the large Sunnyside Mill at Eureka. *(Kenneth Jessen 100C5)*

Allen Nossaman, *Many More Mountains, Volume 2: Ruts into Silverton*, Sundance Publications Limited, Denver, Colorado, 1993, pp. 203-211.

Allen Nossaman, *Many More Mountains, Volume 3: Rails into Silverton*, Sundance Publications Limited, Denver, Colorado, 1998, pp. 124-126.

Jack Benham, *Silverton*, Bear Creek Publishing Co., Ouray, Colorado, 1977, p. 20.

Muriel Sibell Wolle, *Stampede to Timberline*, Sage Books, Chicago, 1949, p. 402.

Robert L. Brown, *Jeep Trails to Colorado Ghost Towns*, Caxton Printers, Caldwell, Idaho, 1963, pp. 84-87.

Tiv Wilkins, *Colorado Railroads*, Pruett Publishing Company, Boulder, Colorado, 1974, pp. 113, 151, 232, 241.

William H. Bauer, James L. Ozment and John H. Willard, *Colorado Post Offices*, Colorado Railroad Museum, Golden, Colorado, 1990, p. 52.

GLADSTONE

Located at the Head of Cement Creek

- *San Juan County, Cement Creek drainage*
- *Accessible via graded dirt road*
- *Town had a post office; one original structure remains*

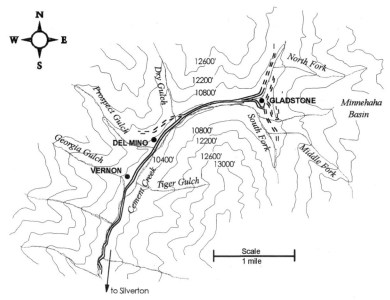

Gladstone is located at the end of the graded dirt road (Colorado 110) running from Silverton up Cement Creek. Of its original structures, only a collapsed mill remains. Nothing is left at the Del Mino or Vernon sites.

Located at the head of Cement Creek, Gladstone was named for a man who would become a future British Prime Minister, William Ewart Gladstone. The level terrain dictated the town's location in a large, flat meadow where the five forks feeding Cement Creek meet. The site also was in proximity to the numerous mines in basins above the area, making it an excellent mill site for processing ore from the area.

In 1879, a wagon road was constructed up Cement Creek, over the shoulder of Hurricane Peak and down Poughkeepsie Gulch. This became one of the preferred routes from Silverton to Ouray. A few cabins were constructed near the Gladstone site, and a small mill was built to handle ore from the area mines. The real boom didn't come to Gladstone for many years.

The Gold King lode was discovered by Olaf Nelson in 1887. At the time, Nelson worked for the Sampson Mine. Several hundred feet into the mountain, the owners hit a vein that was not part of their original claim. Nelson quit the Sampson and estimated the direction of the vein. Using his own muscle power, he sank a shaft 50 feet deep, then ran a 50-foot drift where he intercepted the vein. In 1893, he sold the claim to eastern capitalists for $15,000.

This photograph of Gladstone was taken before 1931, when the tracks of the Silverton, Gladstone & Northerly were removed. *(Denver Public Library x-8674)*

In 1896, a great ore body was discovered at a depth of more than 400 feet, at what became the Gold King Mine. Eventually the Gold King purchased the adjacent

Sampson property. The combined properties eventually were expanded to six levels, and a giant concentration mill 460 feet long was constructed.

Gladstone grew into a small village of about 100 people living around the mills. It had a main street lined with businesses including a meat market, a general store and hotel combination boardinghouse. The latter structure was 20 feet by 30 feet and stood two stories high. In all, the business district had ten other structures. The town also had a row of identical company houses near the Gold King Mill.

Gladstone got a post office in 1878, but it closed in the fall as the town was abandoned temporarily for the winter. The post office reopened in 1883 and operated intermittently until 1912.

The arrival of the Denver & Rio Grande in Silverton in 1882 prompted the influx of new investment capital to revitalize mining operations at Gladstone. The supervisor at the Gold King Mine

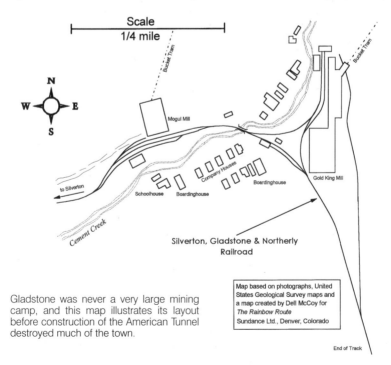

Gladstone was never a very large mining camp, and this map illustrates its layout before construction of the American Tunnel destroyed much of the town.

Map based on photographs, United States Geological Survey maps and a map created by Dell McCoy for *The Rainbow Route* Sundance Ltd., Denver, Colorado

The ruins of this small mill are all that is left of Gladstone's original structures. The town itself was razed to make way for the American Tunnel. *(Kenneth Jessen 113C9)*

approached legendary toll road and railroad builder Otto Mears to construct a line from Silverton up Cement Creek to serve the mill. Mears, however, did not wish to invest any more money in railroads tied to the Colorado mining industry. Stockholders of the Gold King Mine chartered the Silverton, Gladstone & Northerly in April 1899 and built their own railroad, which connected to the Denver & Rio Grande in Silverton. When it was completed, it provided low-cost transportation of the concentrates that the mill produced.

The railroad was narrow gauge and used relatively light 45-pound rail. Operation began in the summer of 1899, using locomotives leased from the Denver & Rio Grande. Eventually the Silverton, Gladstone & Northerly purchased its own locomotives, a combination passenger-baggage car and twenty freight cars.

The railroad also served other mills along Cement Creek, including the McKinley, Yukon, Mammoth, Henrietta and Fisher.

At Gladstone, railroad yards were constructed to handle the traffic at both the Mogul Mill and the Gold King Mill. Both of these mills, incidentally, were at the end of long bucket trams coming down from the mines located in high basins. The railroad remained in operation until 1915, when it was purchased by Otto Mears' Silverton Northern. It remained in operation until 1924 and was dismantled in 1931.

Upon completion of the railroad, a new 100-ton-per-day mill was opened. The mill's capacity was doubled in 1902. By 1918, the ore was almost depleted, and the mill was closed. It reopened on a limited basis in 1924, and operations continued until the 1940s. Later, the American Tunnel was drilled under the mountains from Gladstone to provide access to the Sunnyside and other mines above Eureka. During this time, most of the buildings at Gladstone were razed because much of the business district stood in the way of the new tunnel. Although the American Tunnel is closed at present, a maintenance crew still works there.

In 1962, Robert L. Brown visited Gladstone and found three standing structures. Today, the structures are gone, but the crumbling remains of one of the original mills sits above the road. Contemporary structures associated with the American Tunnel dominate the site. Several four-wheel drive roads radiate in various directions from the end of the graded road up into the high basins.

It is relatively easy to reach the Gladstone site today. The Cement Creek Road leaves from the outskirts of Silverton. It is a good, two-lane graded dirt road suitable for an automobile.

Allen Nossaman, *Many More Mountains, Volume 2: Ruts into Silverton*, Sundance Publications Limited, Denver, Colorado, 1993, pp. 170-173.

Robert E. Sloan and Carl A. Skowronski, *The Rainbow Route*, Sundance Publications Limited, Denver, Colorado, 1975, pp. 132, 134-135.

Robert L. Brown, *An Empire of Silver*, Sundance Publications, Denver, 1984, pp. 71, 73, 219-221.

Tiv Wilkins, *Colorado Railroads*, Pruett Publishing Company, Boulder, Colorado, 1974, p. 233.

William H. Bauer, James L. Ozment and John H. Willard, *Colorado Post Offices*, Colorado Railroad Museum, Golden, Colorado, 1990, p. 62.

GUSTON
Dominated by Mines

- *Ouray County, Red Mountain Creek drainage*
- *Accessible by dirt road; may require four-wheel drive*
- *Town had a post office; several structures remain*

The Yankee Girl Mine at Guston had many employees at its peak. The town of Guston was not organized with a business district or defined street system but rather developed around the area's mines. *(Denver Public Library X-62121)*

The rush to the Red Mountain district started near the Guston site with the discovery of the Yankee Girl. On August 14, 1882, prospector John Robinson was out hunting. In the rarefied air and with the exertion of climbing up the steep slopes of Red Mountain, he had to sit down and rest. He spotted a piece of rock. When he picked it up, he noticed that it was unusually heavy.

This was a sure sign that it was mineralized. When Robinson broke the piece in half, he saw that it was composed of the silver-gray metallic mineral called galena. Galena is typically composed of a mixture of lead, silver and other metals.

Realizing that this was a rich find, Robinson began to search for the source of the galena. He soon found an exposed vein and claimed it in his name and those of his partners, Andrew Meldrum, A. E. "Gus" Lang and August Dietaf.

Robinson returned with his partners to determine the extent of the claim, and the men dug a shallow shaft a dozen feet deep. Much to their delight, they dug through solid metallic ore side to side in the shaft. As a precaution, they staked claims on all four sides, as the ore body seemed to have no limit. Of these claims, the Orphan Boy and the Robinson became major silver producers, but their original discovery, the Yankee Girl, was the mine that drew attention to the Red Mountain area.

It turned out that the men had hit the top of a vertical shaft or chimney of solid ore, a rare occurrence in the mining world.

In 1945, Muriel Sibell Wolle stopped by the little church at Guston and noted that it was leaning to one side, where its foundation had rotted away. On her 1947 visit, the little church had fallen down the hillside and was nothing but a pile of rubble. *(Denver Public Library X-3858)*

The prospectors dug out 4,500 pounds of ore, placed it in sacks and sent a long pack train down to a smelter in Ouray. The mill run produced an average of 88 ounces of silver per ton. More than half of the ore was lead, which was valuable to smelters for use as flux. The Yankee Girl was sold for $125,000 (worth about $1.4 million in today's dollars). This gave the men enough money to finance the development of their other mines.

In 1883, a settlement to be called Missouri City, between the Yankee Girl and the Robinson mines, was proposed. This time, the Yankee Girl, Robinson and Orphan Boy mines were consolidated to improve overall mining efficiency. Approximately seventy-five men lived in a two-story boardinghouse at the Yankee Girl, and establishing a town in the general location made sense.

Missouri City was never built, but nearby Guston survived and grew around the Guston Mine. Guston got its start during the winter of 1886-1887 and became a community with not only stores but also a school and a church. Its post office opened in 1892, late relative to other Red Mountain towns.

Historic photographs of Guston reveal that it was a town of cabins intermingled with mining structures and lacking a well-defined street system. Some structures sat on mine dumps, and others were on the hillside. Many of its structures were head frames, powerhouses and mine office buildings. Some of the houses were log cabins and others were frame homes.

Because of the irregular terrain, the town could not be laid out in the normal sense. In and around the immediate vicinity of Guston were at least fifty buildings. In 1889, the Silverton Railroad was completed from Silverton, over Red Mountain Pass through Guston and down to Ironton. This extended the life of the mines in the area. Low-cost transportation by rail to Silverton smelters allowed the economical extraction of abundant low-grade ore.

Muriel Sibell Wolle visited the Red Mountain district a number of times beginning in 1941. She saw a small frame church with a belfry on a small rise off to one side of the Guston town site. She noticed the badly weathered shingles on the roof. Inside, the roof was beginning to sag and the windows were all missing. She passed by the Guston site two years later and the little church was still standing. In 1945, she again stopped and this time noted that the structure was leaning to one side where its foundation had rotted away. On her 1947 visit, the little church had fallen off the hillside into a pile of rubble.

It is difficult not to become curious about such a place, and Wolle decided to research the church. In the summer of 1891, English-born Rev. William Davis and his family were sent from Denver to the Red Mountain area by the Home Missionary Board of the Congregational Church. As described many years later by Annie Rogers, daughter of Reverend Davis:

> Red Mountain was a thriving mining town, full of saloons, about twenty or more, and plenty of gambling houses, but no room for a church. They didn't want a church, they refused to have one, and were not even polite about it. After father made several attempts to be friendly, they threatened him with violence if he showed up in that town again.

Although Annie Rogers' account is somewhat confusing, she related that her father then approached the people of Ironton. He was welcomed there and its church was dedicated in November 1891. One resident even purchased an organ for the church.

At Guston, $300 was raised to build a church. Rev. Davis had earned a living as a carpenter in his younger years, and the residents brought him donated lumber as he worked on the structure. The towns of Ouray and Silverton also contributed toward building the church. The Cornish miners insisted on a bell to call worshippers to attend services. A belfry was added and a bell installed. Another miner suggested that a whistle be installed since he was used to this sound, and it was done.

The Congregational Church in Guston opened in 1892, and subsequently escaped several fires that destroyed other structures in Guston. The structure outlived most of the mine buildings and all of the homes. It also outlasted its own congregation, but eventually it too slipped away into a pile of rubble.

During the early 1990s, the Guston site was difficult to reach because of contouring of the tailing piles and the concrete channels created to capture mine wastewater. Now that this project is complete, it is possible to drive from U.S. 550 across to the Guston site. A number of structures remain at the site including the covered Yankee Girl Mine head frame. The road requires high ground clearance, and in the spring, four-wheel drive may be necessary. *For a map showing the location of Guston, see "Red Mountain."*

The railroad grade for the Yankee Girl Mine runs past the loading chutes. The boarding-house is on the left. *(Kenneth Jessen 113C3)*

Allen Nossaman, *Many More Mountains, Volume 3: Rails into Silverton,* Sundance Publications Limited, Denver, Colorado, 1998, p. 290-291.

P. David Smith, *Mountains of Silver,* Pruett Publishing Company, Boulder, Colorado, 1994, pp. 35-37.

Muriel Sibell Wolle, *Stampede to Timberline,* Sage Books, Chicago, 1949, pp. 444-448.

Muriel Sibell Wolle, *Timberline Tailings,* Sage Books, Chicago, Illinois, 1977, pp. 271-278.

Robert E. Sloan and Carl A. Skowronski, *The Rainbow Route,* Sundance Publications Limited, Denver, Colorado, 1975, p. 143.

William H. Bauer, James L. Ozment and John H. Willard, *Colorado Post Offices,* Colorado Railroad Museum, Golden, Colorado, 1990, p. 67.

HIGHLAND MARY and SILVER LAKE

- *San Juan County, Cunningham Creek and Arrastra Creek drainages*
- *Highland Mary (lower tram station) accessible by graded dirt road and Silver Lake by four-wheel drive road*
- *Highland Mary had a post office; several collapsed structures remain*

Highland Mary and Silver Lake represent locations where people lived, but they were not really towns. They were mine and mill complexes with boardinghouses, of which there were many in Colorado.

Highland Mary was located at the southern end of Cunningham Gulch. In 1875, the Ennis brothers of New York City paid a spiritualist $50,000 to locate a mine for them. The spiritualist picked a point in the San Juan Mountains, saying that it contained a lake of gold. The brothers spent huge sums of money on the Highland Mary, and it became the first to use steel track for mining cars in the San Juans. Edward Ennis managed the operations and drilled a series of tunnels, but did not release mine production figures, depth or the direction of the tunnels.

As it turned out, the spiritualist directed the operations. The tunnel twisted and turned, went up and down, all without any relationship to the veins of silver ore encountered. Despite this, silver ore from the Highland Mary assayed at $50 to $1,300 a ton.

Miners became nervous when they were told to ignore veins of silver ore and to drill on. It wasn't logical to pass certain riches, and eventually, they refused to enter the mine alone. Enough men lived near the Highland Mary Mine to have a post office, and it opened in 1878. The post office lasted until 1885.

In 1877, Edward Ennis constructed a large, $10,000 white log home next to the trail up Cunningham Gulch. It had a veranda around two sides and latticework covering the foundation supports.

The mine itself was perched at the edge of a cliff. During the mine's later years, an aerial tram brought the ore down in buckets to the lower tram station. A concentrating mill was constructed at Howardsville to process the ore, but it never operated.

After a decade of investing an estimated $1 million in the Highland Mary, the Ennis brothers went bankrupt. Although not nearly as interesting as a spiritualist, the new owners used good old-fashioned geology as their guide. The mine began to turn a profit. During the late 1880s, the price of silver began to fall, and by 1893, the mine stood idle. With renewed interest, the Highland Mary was reopened, and by 1907, it became the second largest producer in the Silverton area. The Highland Mary has continued to operate into modern times.

The narrow gauge Silverton Northern was constructed up

The Silver Lake Mine was located on the shore of Silver Lake, high above the Animas River. An aerial tram carried the ore down to the Silver Lake Mill near the mouth of Arrastra Gulch. *(Denver Public Library X-62274)*

the Animas Valley, and a branch was built to serve several mills in Cunningham Gulch. The railroad ended at the Green Mountain Mill, short of the Highland Mary property. Wagons were used to haul ore from the Highland Mary the short distance to the loading area at the Green Mountain Mill.

The earliest discoveries of silver ore in the area were in Arrastra Gulch, and the Little Giant became the first lode mining operation in the Silverton area. Dempsey Reese constructed the first cabin in Arrastra Gulch. He was a member of the party that made the initial discovery of the Little Giant in 1870.

As time passed, other lodes were discovered in Arrastra Gulch. This resulted in the development of big mines at Silver Lake, a tarn surrounded by high mountains at an elevation of 12,200 feet. Only a steep trail connected the mines to the mills far below. Avalanches, extreme cold and labor problems complicated operations at Silver Lake.

Both the Silver Lake and the Iowa-Tiger mines had large mills and boardinghouses at the edge of the lake, as evidenced by historic photographs. The boardinghouse for the Silver Lake Mine stood four stories high and had an attached four-story outhouse. A post office called "Arastra" was opened at the lake in 1895 and remained open until 1919, when the population at the mines dwindled.

At first, ore was hauled to the Silver Lake Mill located by the Animas River. Only high-grade ore was economical to mine, and low-grade ore was discarded. A concentration mill was constructed at the lake in 1890, allowing the economical processing of the low-grade ore prior to its being taken down to the mill. At its peak, the Silver Lake Mine had 17 miles of tunnels, and aerial trams were constructed to connect the mines with the mills.

Ed Stoiber was the principal mine owner at Silver Lake, and in 1884, he married Helen "Lena" Webster. She immediately became involved in Ed's mining and milling affairs. The couple constructed the largest mansion in the entire San Juans, and it served as both their home and office. The mansion, located along the Animas River at the base of the tramway coming down Arrastra Gulch, was named "Waldheim."

Mrs. Stoiber showed off her husband's wealth by holding lavish parties at the mansion. She also drove into Silverton in a new buggy pulled by a matched pair of horses. Her commanding presence and colorful language earned her the nickname "Captain Jack." At Christmas, she was quite generous and personally delivered gifts to every child in Silverton.

The Stoibers survived the 1893 silver crash and sold out to the Guggenheim brothers in 1903 for $1.3 million (worth about 11 times that amount in today's dollars).

After the Guggenheims purchased the property, the ore appeared to have run out. The mill was closed, but development work continued. A new ore body was discovered, and the mill was placed back in operation. Once again, the bucket tram began hauling concentrate down Arrastra Gulch. In 1907, the original Silver Lake Mill was replaced by one of a modern design. Ultimately, American Smelting & Refining became owners of the property.

The modern steel towers located in Arrastra Gulch were built for the Mayflower Mine. The first portion of the road up Arrastra Gulch is graded and easy to drive. At the end of this road, a narrow shelf road leads up to Silver Lake. At the site are the collapsed remains of several structures and a lot of rubble from the mill. The large boardinghouses are gone. Private property may limit exploration.

For a map showing the location of Highland Mary and Silver Lake, see "Howardsville."

Allen Nossaman, *Many More Mountains, Volume 2: Ruts into Silverton*, Sundance Publications Limited, Denver, Colorado, 1993, pp. 62, 120, 135, 178, 253.

Allen Nossaman, *Many More Mountains, Volume 3: Rails into Silverton*, Sundance Publications Limited, Denver, Colorado, 1998, pp. 101, 104, 307, 317, 325.

Mary C. Ayers, "Howardsville in the San Juan," *The Colorado Magazine*, Vol. XXVIII No. 4, Colorado Historical Society, Denver, October 1951, pp. 242-243.

Muriel Sibell Wolle, *Stampede to Timberline*, Sage Books, Chicago, 1949, pp. 428, 430-431.

Robert E. Sloan and Carl A. Skowronski, *The Rainbow Route*, Sundance Publications Limited, Denver, Colorado, 1975, pp. 29, 133, 172, 177, 190, 192, 205, 260, 338.

William H. Bauer, James L. Ozment and John H. Willard, *Colorado Post Offices*, Colorado Railroad Museum, Golden, Colorado, 1990, p. 72.

HOWARDSVILLE

Site of an Early Brewery

- *San Juan County, Animas River drainage*
- *Accessible by graded dirt road*
- *Town had a post office; several original structures remain*

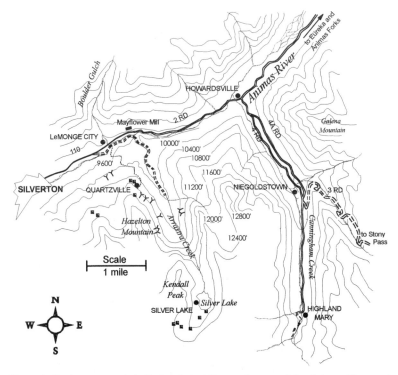

Howardsville is an occupied site located at the confluence of the Animas River and Cunningham Creek northeast of Silverton along a good, graded, dirt road.

Howardsville was second to Silverton as the most stable town in San Juan County. It was founded in 1872 when George Howard constructed his cabin on the site. Today, the town still has a few occupants. Some historical accounts place Howard in the original 1860 Baker party that journeyed into the San Juan Mountains. Howard and his partner, R. J. McNutt, located the Keystone, Ben Franklin, Winnemucca, Sunnyside and other lodes.

Howard's modest cabin was made of heavy logs held together with wooden pins. Long 3-foot slabs of wood were cut with a saw and used as shingles. Howard lived alone and kept the place very neat, scrubbing his floor with lye and sand. He used beautiful animal skins as throw rugs.

Howard constructed his cabin using liquid refreshments to solicit volunteer labor. His cabin was located near the trail over Stony Pass, the main route into the upper Animas Valley. While the cabin was under construction, he set up a primitive bar and purchased a barrel of whiskey. As prospectors passed by, he asked

The first San Juan County courthouse, located in Howardsville, stood for many years after the county seat was moved to Silverton. *(Denver Public Library x-9482)*

them if they would like a free drink for the road. After they became drinking buddies, Howard would ask for a hand with one of the logs. From that moment on, Howard would try to keep his new friend interested in drinking and lifting logs as long as possible. The stranger eventually would become too intoxicated or exhausted to continue. Howard then would wait for his next helper to come along.

Howard made his own buckskin pants and shirts, and they were so well tailored that his clothing was in demand. He kept a number of cats that lived by eating mice and chipmunks. When he left for the winter, he carefully placed his pets in special pockets in his saddlebags for the long journey. When Howard returned the following spring, he brought his cats back with him.

Eventually, Howard and his partner, R. J. McNutt, divided their holdings. McNutt got the Sunnyside and sold it for $10,000. Howard took the Ben Franklin and pocketed $11,000. In today's dollars, these amounts are worth about eleven times as much.

Howard's health deteriorated and he was forced to move to Del Norte, where he constructed a fine residence. He remained a bachelor and passed away in 1920. His pioneer cabin at Howardsville stood on the hillside near Cunningham Gulch into the 1950s.

During its early years, Howardsville had some stable merchants. Its most unusual business, however, was the brewery constructed by Charles Fisher. Built in the 1880s, it was located on the north bank of Cunningham Creek. The first batches of beer were brewed in a washtub, and as demand for his product grew, Fisher purchased regular brewing equipment. The town supported its local product, which could be purchased at a beer hall as well as several saloons. Fisher moved his operation to Silverton in 1889. Other Howardsville businesses included a butcher shop, boardinghouse, reduction plant, and a concentrator.

Another reason for the survival of Howardsville was its strategic location on the major supply route over Stony Pass through Cunningham Gulch. In addition, heavy traffic passed by

Howardsville between Silverton and Animas Forks. These advantages, however, did not prompt its residents to lay out a town formally, and it never was platted or incorporated. Many of its real estate transfers went unrecorded.

When LaPlata County was created in 1874 from a portion of Conejos County, Howardsville became the new county seat. A two-room log courthouse and county office was constructed. Also in 1874, the Howardsville post office opened, and it remained open until 1939.

Judge Hallett presided over an early trial involving a dispute between the owners of two adjacent lodes on Hazelton Mountain. One of the lawyers, N. E. Slaymaker, entered the log courthouse dressed in a flannel shirt and buckskin pants. The pants were held up by a belt, and in the belt was a pair of .45-caliber revolvers. The lawyer for the opposing party objected and asked that Slaymaker be disarmed before the trial started.

Howardsville did not remain the county seat very long, and soon the county clerk, the records and the county seal were moved to Silverton. As the story goes, a group of miners from Silverton went to Howardsville and started buying drinks for everyone. Special attention was paid to consumption by those involved with keeping the county records. After the liberal application of drink and when the Silverton miners were certain that there would be no resistance, they walked off with the records. The county clerk followed.

Historical accounts, however, run contrary to this colorful story and show that Howardsville remained the LaPlata County seat until 1876 when San Juan County was formed. It was then that Silverton emerged as the county seat. For years, the two-room cabin in Howardsville, used as the courthouse, stood by the road.

Although mountain sheep and other game were plentiful, the miners longed for the taste of beef. Beef was in short supply, and a Chattanooga butcher, John Walters, drove steers to Howardsville one winter. He traveled only when conditions were such that a frozen crust on top of the snow could support the weight of his steers. He stopped in Howardsville and butchered a steer, then sold the pieces on skewers to miners who were happy for a change in diet.

William Nichols owned a mill site north of Cunningham Creek, apart from the other scattered buildings that constituted Howardsville. This was supposed to be the site of Bullion City, but it was just another failed attempt at establishing a town in the region. Nichols constructed his home and the Howardsville House, which operated as a hotel and boardinghouse.

Allen Nossaman identified many of Howardsville's early structures in the central portion of the town. The main street, incidentally, was also the road from Silverton to Animas Forks. Looking at a photograph of Howardsville taken in the late 1870s,

The Little Nation tram station at Howardsville is a reminder of the past, when this town once rivaled Silverton and was the San Juan County seat. *(Kenneth Jessen 100C3)*

the Rocky Mountain Brewery, owned by Fischer and Gill, sat parallel to the creek and at an angle to the town's main street. Along each side of the street was a row of structures, many adorned with false fronts. Among the structures were several homes, a saloon, the St. James Restaurant, a second saloon named Jim's Place, a general store and post office, an assay office, a small mill, a log store, a sod-roofed restaurant, a second assay office, the Brewer Saloon and a meat market. The town also had a livery stable and a blacksmith shop.

The Silverton Northern Railroad was incorporated in 1895, and bonds were issued the following year. The toll road between Silverton and Animas Forks was purchased and used for its right-of-way. The mining companies along the route to Animas Forks paid for much of the cost of construction. The railroad ties were laid on the river gravel in the floodplain, with little or no grading. This narrow gauge railroad was completed to Eureka in 1896, and a small depot was constructed at Howardsville.

The Silverton Northern Railroad was asked to construct an extension up Cunningham Gulch to the Highland Mary's lower tram station. In 1905, what became the Green Mountain extension was built partway up Cunningham Gulch to the Green Mountain mill, just above the Old Hundred tram station. The switch for this branch was located in Howardsville.

Several old structures remain today in Howardsville, and it is an easy trip from Silverton over a good, graded road. The lower tram station and mill for the Little Nation Mine dominate the site. This structure was built during the 1920s.

Allen Nossaman, *Many More Mountains, Volume 2: Ruts into Silverton*, Sundance Publications Limited, Denver, Colorado, 1993, pp. 106-107, 110, 214-223.

Mary C. Ayers, "Howardsville in the San Juan," *Colorado Magazine*, Vol. XXVIII No. 4, Colorado Historical Society, Denver, October 1951, pp. 244-247.

Muriel Sibell Wolle, *Stampede to Timberline*, Sage Books, Chicago, 1949, p. 401.

Robert E. Sloan and Carl A. Skowronski, *The Rainbow Route*, Sundance Publications Limited, Denver, Colorado, 1975, pp. 127-150.

William H. Bauer, James L. Ozment and John H. Willard, *Colorado Post Offices*, Colorado Railroad Museum, Golden, Colorado, 1990, p. 74.

IRONTON

And the Remarkable Corkscrew Gulch Turntable

- Ouray County, Red Mountain Creek drainage
- Accessible by dirt road
- Town had a post office; several structures remain

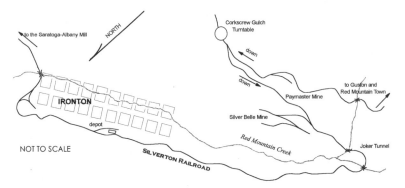

Ironton was located in a relatively flat area, but above the town the steep descent into Ironton Park required a turntable on the main line of the Silverton Railroad.

At the northernmost end of the Red Mountain mining district was the settlement of Copper Glen, near Gray Copper Gulch. The camp was laid out in March 1883, and soon cabins were being constructed. The town's name was changed to Ironton for the region's low-grade iron deposits and the rust color of the surrounding mountains. Its post office opened this same year.

Once the Silverton Railroad was completed in 1889, Ironton got its own railroad depot and railroad yards. Above Ironton in Corkscrew Gulch was the most amazing track alignment ever conceived for the main line of a U.S. railroad. When the narrow gauge Silverton Railroad was constructed, the exceedingly difficult terrain necessitated a turntable to allow the line to drop down to Ironton Park. The turntable avoided the problems associated with a switchback, which would have forced trains to back down to the end of the track. That operation would have placed the cars ahead of the locomotive. To prevent winter snow from curtailing operations, the unique turntable was covered by a circular wooden structure having a conical roof.

The turntable made for an interesting operating procedure, which delighted what few tourists took a trip on the railroad. After leaving Silverton, the train climbed up the Chattanooga Loop and over Red Mountain Pass, in excess of 11,000 feet. From there, the train passed through Red Mountain Town No. 2 and down through Guston. At the Corkscrew Gulch turntable, the train stopped, and the locomotive was uncoupled. The locomotive then coasted down to the turntable and was turned nearly 360 degrees. It then was switched onto the lower level of track leading to Ironton.

The Corkscrew Gulch turntable above Ironton was built by the Silverton Railroad in 1889. The turntable avoided the problems associated with a switchback, which would have forced trains to back down to the end of the track. *(Colorado Railroad Museum)*

Under the brakeman's control, the cars then were allowed to coast down over the turntable and out onto a short piece of track. The locomotive backed up to the cars and coupled on to continue the trip down to Ironton. Civil engineer C. W. Gibbs designed the Silverton Railroad, including its unique turntable.

The railroad continued through Ironton and ended a short distance away at Albany, at the mouth of Albany Gulch, where the Saratoga-Albany Mill was located. A loop was used to turn the entire train for the return trip back up and over Red Mountain Pass. According to historic photographs, no town existed at Albany. The large mill sat on the hillside to facilitate a gravity-fed system for processing ore.

After the steady decline in silver prices during the late 1880s and early 1890s, Ironton was almost abandoned. In 1896, at a time when most Red Mountain mines had closed, the Treasury Tunnel was opened. It was located across the valley from Guston and the Yankee Girl Mine. The idea was to drill under the old mines between Ouray and Telluride in hopes of striking new veins of ore. The Silverton Railroad built a spur across the valley to the tunnel. It was somewhat successful, and the Treasury Tunnel operated for a decade. No doubt, some of the workers resided in Ironton.

The Meldrum Tunnel began operations in 1898. Andrew Meldrum was among the original owners of both the Yankee Girl and the Guston mines. His idea was to drill a railroad tunnel to Telluride, thereby connecting the Silverton Railroad with the Rio Grande Southern. Stock was sold based on a detailed prospectus about how veins of ore would be encountered and would pay for the tunnel. Of the 6 miles necessary to complete this project, only slightly over 2 miles were completed. Meldrum died a pauper and was laid to rest in an unmarked grave in Ouray.

In 1900, Ironton's population stood at seventy-one. This was the last year the Silverton Railroad made a profit. The Barstow Mine ended up being the only employer in the area for a while. Ore containing lead, silver and some gold kept this mine going. An aerial tramway brought the ore down from the portal to

Taken in 1900, this distant view of Ironton shows that it was a sizeable settlement. Although the stores along its main street are gone, several of Ironton's homes are still standing. *(U.S. Geological Survey, W. Cross 472)*

the Barstow Mill for concentrating. It closed in 1917 after producing nearly $750,000 dollars.

The Joker Tunnel was the idea of George Crawford, former director of the Silverton Railroad. His syndicate either owned or used leases to work the Guston, Yankee Girl, Robinson and Genesse-Vanderbilt mines. The Joker was to undercut these mines and use gravity to feed the ore from the upper workings down into ore cars in the Joker Tunnel. A 2-foot by 4-foot channel was dug in the center of the tunnel to drain water from these mines.

The portal was located next to the tracks of the Silverton Railroad, where it looped around from Guston and headed down to Ironton. Crawford purchased the railroad and put in heavier rail.

By 1907, the Joker was nearly a mile long and intersected the Genesse-Vanderbilt shaft 600 feet below the surface. Lateral tunnels were drilled to the Yankee Girl and Guston.

About two dozen men worked at the Joker. The company constructed a boardinghouse, but some of the miners might have lived in Ironton. Employment rose to eighty or so as more men were required to open the old mines. A restaurant and boarding-house opened at Red Mountain Town.

As the mines got deeper, the ore diminished, and the tunnel was closed in 1914. Although people continued to live in Ironton, its population had fallen in 1920 below that required for a post office.

The Saratoga-Albany Mill, at the north end of Ironton Park, was torn down during the 1930s. Its bricks and lumber were used to construct a ski lodge along U.S. 550. A ski tow was installed, but the operation failed. The St. Germain Foundation purchased the lodge. A caretaker accidentally set the lodge on fire, and only its basement survives.

Milton Larson became Ironton's last resident. He and his brother had worked for years on two mines near the town. After his brother passed away, Milton was left alone and was referred to as Ironton's mayor. He died in the mid-1960s, and Ironton became a ghost town.

In recent years, some of Ironton's houses were renovated for workers at the Idarado Mine along U.S. 550. In 1939, the Idarado took over the

Ironton is rich in abandoned buildings, sitting below U.S. 550 and obscured by the trees. This home is in good shape, retaining its bay window and clapboard siding. *(Kenneth Jessen 113B7)*

Treasury Tunnel and consolidated the vast majority of mines in the area. Demand for lead and zinc during World War II financed improvements to the mine. Today, the Idarado operates the mill at Pandora and uses more than 80 miles of tunnels to access lodes below the Ajax-Smuggler, Tomboy, Liberty Bell, Virginius, Barstow and Black Bear.

In *Stampede to Timberline*, which Muriel Sibell Wolle wrote during the 1940s, she remarked how she saw Ironton slowly vanish as the years passed, "...house by house and store by store, as the false-fronted shells crushed to the ground during a high windstorm or after an unusually heavy load of wet snow."

Ironton, now overgrown and completely abandoned, was at one time the region's most substantial town. Its business district had more than twenty buildings, and many homes occupied the side streets. The town was spread out across the width of the valley, where today only small clusters of structures remain. A church shows up plainly in historic photographs.

The site, east of and below U.S. 550, can be reached by a short dirt road. Another road comes into Ironton along the base of a tailing pond from the north. Within the abandoned town site are at least five buildings, but it is difficult to imagine its original size based on what remains today. One old home sits in a dense stand of timber and has a forlorn, ghostly appearance.

For a map showing the location of Ironton relative to other towns in the area, see "Red Mountain."

Allen Nossaman, *Many More Mountains, Volume 3: Rails into Silverton*, Sundance Publications Limited, Denver, Colorado, 1998, p. 278-279.

Muriel Sibell Wolle, *Stampede to Timberline*, Sage Books, Chicago, 1949, p. 444.

Robert L. Brown, *Jeep Trails to Colorado Ghost Towns*, Caxton Printers, Caldwell, Idaho, 1963, pp. 120-121.

Robert E. Sloan and Carl A. Skowronski, *The Rainbow Route*, Sundance Publications Limited, Denver, Colorado, 1975, pp. 62-67.

William H. Bauer, James L. Ozment and John H. Willard, *Colorado Post Offices*, Colorado Railroad Museum, Golden, Colorado, 1990, p. 78.

MIDDLETON, QUARTZVILLE, LaPLATA CITY and LeMOGNE CITY

- *San Juan County, Animas River drainage*
- *Some sites accessible by graded dirt road, others only by foot*
- *Some had a post office; few structures remain*

Middleton, located between Howardsville and Eureka along the Animas River, never was a sizeable town. It was supported by area mines and mines up Maggie Gulch. Among the handful of cabins, the earliest was constructed by Dr. T. M. Crawford, who arrived during the early 1870s to prospect. He constructed a cabin for himself and his two daughters in 1876. Upon the discovery of new lodes, a small smelter was constructed at the site. Originally called Crawfordville, the name was changed to Middleton in 1880, for Middle Mountain, located to the southeast.

A two-story log building was added to Middleton's structures in 1881 to serve as the town's store. Although its residents petitioned for a post office, none was granted. Several sources indicate that Middleton had a schoolhouse. Today, Middleton's structures are gone, some having been moved to Silverton during the 1950s to form the basis for Old Town Square on Blair Street.

Quartzville is one of those obscure ghost towns covered by contemporary historian Allen Nossaman in his multi-volume work, *Many More Mountains*. Its location was high on the side of

Hazelton Mountain above Arrastra Gulch at an elevation of about 10,800 feet. The Aspen Mine and the Susquehanna Tunnel supported this cabin settlement. Its beginning dates back to 1877, and a child was born in the town that year. San Juan County improved the road up to Quartzville, but the town never did gain enough population to support a post office.

The only dramatic event recorded for Quartzville was the death of James Briggs. After having walked from Wagon Wheel Gap, through Creede and over Stony Pass, he was killed in a snow slide in 1878. If any structures remain today in Quartzville, they are unknown to the author.

LaPlata City was founded on paper, and a town was never constructed. It was to have been located where Cinnamon Creek enters the Animas River below Animas Forks. A smelter was constructed at the site, but in 1877, it was leveled by an avalanche. With steep barren slopes and a prodigious amount of snow, LaPlata City was located in a geologically hazardous place.

Another obscure settlement was LeMogne City, at the mouth of Boulder Gulch northeast of Silverton and below the Mayflower Mill. Started in 1875 and platted in 1883, LeMogne City consisted of both frame and log structures. Also called Boulder Gulch, the Reed and Day families occupied the site. A pair of handsome, story-and-a-half frame homes faced out onto the Silverton to Animas Forks road. The town was supported by mines up Boulder and Arrastra gulches. Today, the site is buried under the tailings from the Mayflower Mill.

For a map showing the location of LeMogne City and Quartzville, see "Howardsville."

Allen Nossaman, *Many More Mountains, Volume 2: Ruts into Silverton*, Sundance Publications Limited, Denver, Colorado, 1993, pp. 38, 42-43, 57, 113-114, 127.

Allen Nossaman, *Many More Mountains, Volume 3: Rails into Silverton*, Sundance Publications Limited, Denver, Colorado, 1998, pp. 110-111, 262, 325.

Jack Benham, *Silverton*, Bear Creek Publishing Co., Ouray, Colorado, 1977, pp. 29-30.

William H. Bauer, James L. Ozment and John H. Willard, *Colorado Post Offices*, Colorado Railroad Museum, Golden, Colorado, 1990, p. 117.

MINERAL POINT
Located in a High-Altitude Bog

- *San Juan County, between the Mineral Creek and Animas River drainages*
- *Accessible by four-wheel drive vehicle*
- *Town had a post office; no structures remain*

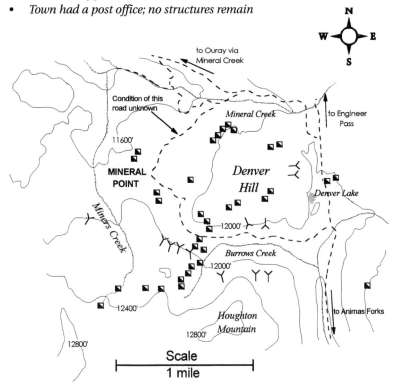

Mineral Point is located to the west of the main four-wheel drive road from Animas Forks to Engineer Pass or Ouray. It sits in a high-altitude saddle, and because none of its structures remain, it is easy to miss. The half-dark squares indicate mine shafts.

Originally, Mineral Point was called Burrows Camp, then it became Mineral City. It was located on the divide at about 11,800 feet between the headwaters of the Animas River and Mineral Creek. Albert Burrows and several prospectors discovered rich veins of silver ore in 1873 and founded the town. Manpower and money to develop mines came from Yankton, South Dakota.

Today, the site can be reached by driving up the four-wheel drive road from Animas Forks toward Engineer Pass. Well above timberline, where Burrows Creek flows into the North Fork of the Animas River, a narrow rough road leads west from the main road. The road goes around Denver Hill to a broad saddle. At the top of the saddle, situated in a bog, was the town of Mineral Point. All of its structures collapsed many years ago, and because of the heavy winter snow, all traces of Mineral Point will probably disappear during the next few decades.

A side road leads from Mineral Point up the steep mountainside to many mines above the town site. The road running

The San Juan Chief Mine is situated about a mile below Mineral Point. Mike Arnold peers out of one of the windows of what probably was the mine's office or boarding-house. *(Kenneth Jessen 105A11)*

through Mineral Point continues around Denver Hill and drops down to the Mineral Creek Road.

When Muriel Sibell Wolle was doing her research on ghost towns in the Mineral Point area, pack trains were still in use. Ore trucks made traffic difficult on the narrow wagon roads. When she asked about the condition of the road to Mineral Point, a miner pointed out that there were two sections of shelf road, each about 1 mile long with no turnouts. He then said, "Go on and try it. All you have to do if you meet a truck is back up a mile." Wolle and her companions elected to walk the 4 miles from Animas Forks to Mineral Point via the San Juan Chief Mine. When she reached the site where most of the buildings once stood, she could not find a way across the bog to the remains of a small mill. Today, a four-wheel drive road skirts the edge of this bog.

In 1876, H.B. Perry constructed the Forest House, the town's first hotel. A log structure, it was replaced in 1880 by a more substantial 40-foot by 60-foot frame building. This became the town's

The stamps, the cams used to lift the stamps and the drive wheel have fallen over at the mill for the San Juan Chief Mine. *(Kenneth Jessen 105A10)*

restaurant and saloon. The town's post office was established in 1875. It closed in 1878, but reopened the following spring. As mining activity died at Mineral Point, the post office closed for good in 1897. Mineral Point had numerous postmasters during its short existence, as that position was rotated among the occupants.

The new 24-foot by 70-foot Mineral Point Hotel opened in July 1882, and people came from Animas Forks and Rose's Cabin to celebrate. The owners held a grand ball. Situated on a north-facing slope, the hotel sat on a knob south of the main portion of the town. It had a porch running its entire length. About fifty men stayed at the Mineral Point Hotel during the summer season. Altitude, poor weather and the condition of the land made the hotel difficult to operate, so it saw only seasonal use.

William Boot was the first to open a store in Mineral Point. Several other merchants followed, but the town never grew to more than a handful of structures.

During the summers the town had an estimated 200 residents. Mineral Point also acted as a supply point for nearby Poughkeepsie (Lake Como).

In 1897, the Silverton *Weekly Miner* described Mineral Point this way:

Long before the famous Yankee Girl or Guston were discovered...Mineral Point was a busy, bustling village of 600 to 700 population, and round it was heard the hum of industry, the music of the saw mill, the diamond and the hand drills, and the echo of the blast as it sounded through the hills.

Another account by the *Ouray Times*, February 7, 1880, added some exaggerated humor to its description of life in Mineral Point:

Mineral City (Point) is held and carefully watched over by Ed Tonkyn, who is mayor of the city, street supervisor, postmaster, proprietor of the Forrest [sic] House, and deacon of all the churches. Monday morning he takes up a collection of the poker chips and sweeps out cigar stubs.

In his Volume 3 of *Many More Mountains*, Allen Nossaman provided a map of Mineral Point showing the store, several cabins and the Forest House. These were located at the north end of the meadow, while the Mineral Point Hotel and one other cabin were at the south end. All in all, the town had only nine structures. The center of the town site was so swampy that a corduroy road made of logs laid side-by-side had to be constructed to span this area.

Typical of much of the exaggerated reporting by newspapers of this era, the *San Juan Prospector* in Del Norte printed that, in August 1875, Mineral Point had its own bank. Also, the town was said to have had about twenty log buildings plus a store. David William Burton set the record straight, reporting in 1875 that the "alleged city" of Mineral Point was a motley assortment of tents and a few poorly constructed cabins. Burton knew firsthand and helped to construct one of the cabins to act as his mining office and residence.

Another visitor in 1875, Alfred Camp, found fifty to seventy-five men and only two women living in Mineral Point. Yet, another visitor described the structures as picturesque and made of hand-hewn logs selected with a disregard for proportions and cabins constructed with neglect for a level or a plumb line. The roofs had shingles made of bark peeled from green trees he wrote.

After 1877, when a sawmill opened near Mineral Point, milled lumber was available for cabins and other buildings. Mineral Point was occupied seasonally with only a couple of people willing to endure the winters at this high elevation.

Throughout 1882, more development work was done on the mines in the surrounding area. One mine yielded an astounding 600 pounds of pure silver. Mines in the area included the San Juan Chief, about a mile below Mineral Point, the Polar Star on Engineer Mountain, the Red Cloud, the Grand Trunk, the Mastodon, the Bill Young, the Dakota (also spelled Dacotch), the Yankton and the Old Lout.

Allen Nossaman related some rather unusual gatherings at Mineral Point. One evening in September 1877, three meetings

Not much remains at Mineral Point except bits of wood and the outline of foundations. *(Kenneth Jessen 122D8)*

were held in the same cabin. The first was a miners' meeting, followed by a meeting of Republicans and ending with a gathering of Democrats. The three meetings took place in the space of just 1½ hours and provided some needed entertainment. The town's final meeting of the season was held in October to advocate the separation of San Juan County from the remainder of the new state of Colorado.

As expected at such a remote location with a brief snow-free season, mail delivery at Mineral Point was uncertain. The post office was on a dead-end route, and the U.S. Postal Service put little effort into reliable mail delivery. Much of the money to keep mail delivery came from private donations. Residents lobbied for better service, but this backfired, as mail delivery was reduced from three times a week to once a week. Residents then demanded one delivery per week by the Postal Service plus one by a private carrier. The result was that no mail was delivered during October 1877, and after that, mail delivery became private.

A high-altitude political debate took place at Mineral Point in 1878 between James Belford, Republican and Thomas Patterson, Democrat. Miners from all over the area came to hear this open-air discussion, which lasted over 4 hours. As the chill of the night set in, all adjourned to nearby saloons.

The local justice of the peace invited many of the visiting miners to sleep on his cabin floor. He even was gracious enough to furnish blankets. He got up early to fix the men breakfast and then went around and woke his visitors. Politics and poor whiskey had had their effect, and one fellow appeared to be asleep. After the rest of the men had eaten, it was discovered that the poor fellow had passed away during the night.

The justice of the peace impaneled a coroner's jury to render some kind of decision as to the cause of death. The verdict was "whiskey," and this outcome was not pleasing to the justice of the peace. He demanded that the jury reconvene, but the outcome was the same. He then asked the men how their families would feel if they were told that their loved one had died of whiskey. Heeding the advice, the jury's final and third decision was "heart failure," a verdict the justice found acceptable.

Allen Nossaman, *Many More Mountains, Volume 2: Ruts into Silverton*, Sundance Publications Limited, Denver, Colorado, 1993, pp. 174, 176-184.

Allen Nossaman, *Many More Mountains, Volume 3: Rails into Silverton*, Sundance Publications Limited, Denver, Colorado, 1998, pp. 116-123.

Muriel Sibell Wolle, *Stampede to Timberline*, Sage Books, Chicago, 1949, pp. 410-414.

William H. Bauer, James L. Ozment and John H. Willard, *Colorado Post Offices*, Colorado Railroad Museum, Golden, Colorado, 1990, p. 98.

NIEGOLDSTOWN
The Dream of a Saxon Castle

- *San Juan County, Cunningham Creek drainage*
- *Accessible by graded dirt road; site itself on private property*
- *Town had a post office: no structures remain*

Reinhart Niegold emigrated to the United States from Germany and is believed to have come to the San Juan Mountains in 1872, as his presence was mentioned at a Fourth of July celebration. His brother, Gustav, soon joined him, and the two located several promising lodes. Other family members arrived, including a half brother, Oscar Roedel.

Most of the Niegold mines were on Green Mountain, south of Stony Gulch near the Pride of the West. Their most famous claim was the Old Hundred, up Cunningham Gulch. In addition, their Philadelphia claim proved rich in silver with assays of over $1,000 per ton. During 1875-1876, the Niegolds sold silver ore to a smelter in Silverton, receiving $200 to $800 per ton in return. They also shipped some of the ore back to their homeland in Germany for refining.

The Niegold's success in mining prompted them to purchase machinery for their own mill, and they had 15 tons of machinery packed over Stony Pass. After being placed in operation, the mill was only partially successful in treating the complex silver ore. (Ore in this area was a complex mixture of lead, zinc, copper and silver.)

The Niegold brothers founded the small community of Niegoldstown along Cunningham Creek near its confluence with Stony Creek. Here they continued the lavish lifestyle they had cultivated in their homeland. They purchased the best food and drinks, including imported wine. They smoked Turkish tobacco, and their food was prepared using European cookbooks. They even contemplated construction of a Saxon Castle.

A Weber grand piano was hauled in over Stony Pass at great expense. Gustav had performed professionally in New York City, and the Niegolds staged what may have been the only opera performed in San Juan County. For the opera, they dressed in knickerbockers and buckled shoes, and they wore powdered wigs.

The silver ore should have supported the Niegolds, but it didn't. Much of their money came from a rich uncle living in Philadelphia. The grand piano, incidentally, was sold later to pay their debts incurred from living this lifestyle.

Despite the lofty dreams, Niegoldstown remained a small cabin community with a store and a hotel. A post office opened in January 1878 and closed in 1881. In March 1884, after Niegoldstown had reached its peak, an avalanche destroyed the mill and three buildings.

The Niegolds sold their claims in 1904. Reinhart moved to Denver, and Gustav moved back to New York City. Oscar Roedel spent his life in Silverton. They all apparently died in poverty.

The town site was located a short distance east of Cunningham Creek and somewhat south of the mouth of Stony Gulch. A smooth, graded road runs south from Howardsville up Cunningham Gulch by the site. Hardly a trace remains today of Niegoldstown, and the land is posted "no trespassing." Near the site, however, is the lower tram station for the Buffalo Boy Mine.

For a map showing the location of Niegoldstown see "Howardsville."

Allen Nossaman, *Many More Mountains, Volume 2: Ruts into Silverton*, Sundance Publications Limited, Denver, Colorado, 1993, pp. 222, 224-225.

Allen Nossaman, *Many More Mountains, Volume 3: Rails into Silverton*, Sundance Publications Limited, Denver, Colorado, 1998, pp. 104-105.

Mary C. Ayers, "Howardsville in the San Juans," *The Colorado Magazine*, Colorado Historical Society, Denver, Vol. XXVIII, No. 4 (October 1951), pp. 248-249.

William H. Bauer, James L. Ozment and John H. Willard, *Colorado Post Offices*, Colorado Railroad Museum, Golden, Colorado, 1990, p. 105.

OURAY, RAMONA, ASH and PORTLAND

- *Ouray County, Uncompahgre River drainage*
- *Accessible via paved road*
- *Town has a post office; many original structures remain*

William Henry Jackson took this view of burros loaded with supplies on Ouray's main street, a common sight during the town's boom years. *(Denver Public Library WHJ-691)*

NOTE: Ouray has never been a ghost town, although its population has fluctuated over the years. Today, its abundant scenic resources attract many tourists. The history of Ouray is included here because its economy is linked closely to that of the surrounding area.

Ouray is situated in a magnificent box canyon surrounded by high cliffs on three sides. So spectacular is Ouray's setting that the normally terse George Crofutt provided the following description:

> The little park in which it is situated is nearly round, and only about one-fourth of a mile in diameter. On all sides, the canyon walls and mountains rise, range upon range, peak overshadowing peak, all grooved and furrowed by the hand of the Great Maker, from the tiniest wrinkle to a chasm of most gigantic proportions, from the smallest depression and most rugged ravine to one of the grandest canyons in the world.

In July 1875, A.W. Begole and John Eckles, both prospectors from Silverton, were among the first to enter the Ouray amphitheater. They had made the hazardous journey down Bear Creek from Engineer Mountain. Like so many men, they were out searching for mineral riches. They found outcroppings of promising ore and told several others. Begole and Eckles returned with other prospectors about a month later. They discovered an outcropping of parallel veins of silver ore, whose appearance suggested rows of crops. The claim was located about 1 mile south of Ouray, and they named it the Mineral Farm. During the next few months, other claims were staked. Cabins were constructed by those wishing to stay during the winter.

On August 28, 1875, Begole, Eckles and others laid out the town of Uncompahgre City in the amphitheater. The name Uncompahgre was a Ute word meaning "warm springs." As more prospectors arrived, more exploration took place. Of note was the discovery of the Wheel of Fortune, high up Canyon Creek in Yankee Boy Basin. It contained a great deal of silver plus some gold and led to many other discoveries including the Virginius.

As winter approached, three prospectors were sent out to Saguache for supplies to enable the rest to be able to survive in the cold, hostile climate. After the wagons returned with supplies, they were emptied, then loaded with ore destined for a smelter.

In 1875, Ouray's post office opened, operating under that name from the start. The original name of Uncompahgre City was dropped. Mail was carried as far as the Ute Indian agency near Colona, where it had to be picked up. Otto Mears held the mail contract, and during the winter, he tried to use dog sleds. This didn't work, and Mears resorted to personally carrying the mail on his back using snowshoes.

The residents of Ouray ran out of food before spring and resorted to killing Ute cattle, which they called "slow elk." This was no laughing matter for the Ute Indians, who had been deprived of their ancestral hunting grounds and were dependent upon their cattle. White settlers began moving north illegally into lush grassland occupied by the Utes as part of their reservation. Agent Wheeler tried to keep them out, and tensions mounted. The Ute Indians, who already had given up the San Juan Mountains, were forced to move again.

Although the Ute Indians posed no threat to the town of Ouray, the town had a militia just in case. Its only duty was marching in parades. The Utes visited Ouray and raced horses, gambled and traded goods. Chief Ouray and his wife, Chipeta, visited the town on occasion to act as a moderator in disputes between Utes and white settlers.

As more prospectors arrived in the spring of 1876, Ouray grew by leaps and bounds. Using a log cabin, Mr. Randall opened the first store. Soon a blacksmith shop opened to sharpen drills and make horseshoes. Another log cabin was converted into Ouray's first hotel. Nate Hart opened a saloon, and Jesse Benton a meat market. Other businesses included two window and door factories, four general stores, several hotels, a sawmill and an ore-sampling mill. A schoolhouse was constructed, and school was started with forty-three students. The number of saloons also grew, and Ouray gained several houses of prostitution. A merchant, operating out of a tent, died and was the first person to be buried in Ouray's cemetery. Frame buildings began to appear, and the

Beautifully maintained, this is the historic Presbyterian church in Ouray. *(Kenneth Jessen 102D11)*

town was officially incorporated. By the end of 1876, the town had a population of 400.

After a sawmill began operation in 1877, the tents and log cabins in Ouray began to be replaced by substantial buildings made of milled lumber. Some of the cabins were given a more sophisticated look with clapboard siding to hide the logs.

Ouray's first election was held in April 1877, and the old town board was ousted by a new group. The old board refused to step down and turn over the town's records. Both groups issued deeds to lots, resulting in confusion. A judge finally ruled that the old board had to step down.

Ouray County was established out of San Juan County in 1877. It encompassed not only what is now Ouray County but Dolores and San Miguel counties as well. Ouray became the county seat, and the second floor of a building was rented to serve as county offices. Typical of the contrast so abundant in early Colorado mining towns, the first floor served as a saloon, church and courtroom - but not simultaneously!

The trail beyond Bear Creek Falls above the Uncompahgre Canyon was so dangerous that several men fell to their death just walking along the trail. In 1883, Otto Mears built a toll road through the canyon, 6 miles of which was blasted out of solid rock. It was terrifying to drive and was one lane wide with a drop-off up to 800 feet. So that no one could get by without paying a toll, he positioned the tollgate at Bear Creek Falls, where the road was supported on a single-lane log bridge. This gave Ouray the most direct route into the Red Mountain District.

The route from Silverton was not nearly as good, and the following year, Mears was contracted to construct another toll road up Mineral Creek to Red Mountain Pass. The result was a reasonably good wagon road linking Ouray and Silverton. Today, it is known as the Million Dollar Highway, U.S. 550.

In 1887, the Ouray Branch of the Denver & Rio Grande was constructed 35.8 miles south from Montrose. This gave the town a substantial boost, allowing passengers and freight to flow freely. Ouray became the transfer point for ore from the surrounding mines that was destined for smelters in Denver and Pueblo.

The first church in Ouray was built by Rev. George M. Darley. In the spring of 1877, he began by organizing a building fund for a Presbyterian Church. The church was completed that fall. A fire department was formed consisting of a horse company. The firemen had elaborate, colorful uniforms and were quite an attraction in Fourth of July parades.

By 1878, Ouray had grown close to 800 people, and the Bank of Ouray opened. Telephone service also came this year connecting the town with Lake City, Mineral Point and Silverton. As the mines near Ouray developed, more smelters were constructed, and by 1879, three were in operation.

In 1885, Ouray's population was estimated at 1,800. The major hotels at the time were the Delmonico and the Sanderson. The number of churches had grown to three, but this was offset by a large number of saloons and "female boardinghouses." Much of the town's social life pivoted around various secret societies. As George Crofutt said in his 1885 grip-sack guide, "The secret orders are so numerous and varied that very few of the citizens think of keeping a secret."

By then, Ouray already had become a tourist attraction, with its numerous hot springs that produced clouds of steam on cold day. A.G. Dunbar developed one of these springs, which had a water temperature of 128o F. Baths were built, and the facility opened to the public. Later in the town's history, Box Canyon was developed as another tourist attraction.

The mines in the area were too numerous to mention. Ouray provided direct access via a spectacular shelf road to Mineral Point, Animas Forks and the mines around Engineer Mountain. Some of the richest mines, producing both gold and silver, were up Canyon Creek, and up the Uncompahgre Canyon, past Ironton, was the vast Red Mountain District. A few mines also were located northeast of town.

In June 1877, the *Ouray Times* began publishing a weekly newspaper. It was followed by the *San Juan Sentinel*, which lasted only a few months. The most notable newspaper published in Ouray was the *Solid Muldoon*, under the guidance of the controversial David Day.

Today, Ouray is a delightful town filled with historic structures, a museum, and hot springs. Box Canyon is located just outside of town. With the Telluride ski area not far away, Ouray also has developed some winter tourist business.

As a side note, David Day, Otto Mears and several other investors organized the town of Ramona. Incorporated in 1886, it was to have been located approximately 4 miles north of Ouray near present-day Portland and would have undermined Ouray's future. At the time, the terminus for the Denver & Rio Grande Railroad was in Montrose. The idea was to convince the Denver & Rio Grande to construct a branch line south, making Ramona the terminus. People would move from Ouray to Ramona, purchase lots and make Ramona's investors rich. Ramona had ample water, a hot spring and spectacular scenery. Unlike Ouray, which is located in a narrow canyon, Ramona had plenty of room to expand.

On the board of directors were notable men such at David Moffat, Edward Wolcott and Otto Mears. Ranchland was purchased and lots were sold to investors. Other names used to designate this proposed town were Dayton and Chipeta. Ultimately, the railroad continued construction through the site and terminated at Ouray. The town company was dissolved and the money was returned to those who had purchased lots.

In addition, north of Ouray in the Dexter Creek drainage was the town of Ash, which grew up around the Bachelor Mine. A rich vein of gold ore was discovered in 1892, and it produced as much as $30,000 in ore per month. Total output from the Bachelor Mine topped $3 million.

The name was derived from the three bachelors who owned the mine—Armstrong, Saner and Hurlburt. The Ash post office opened in 1899 and closed 6 years later when the mine ceased production. Across from the Bachelor was the Calliope Mine, and above the small community of Ash was the Wedge Mine. During its life, the Wedge Mine alone produced $2 million in ore. An estimated 200 miners lived in Ash. Nothing remains at the site today.

Portland is located approximately 4 miles north of Ouray

An old livery barn, constructed in 1883, sits along Ouray's main street. *(Kenneth Jessen 113A11)*

along the Uncompahgre River. The Windham smelter was its early source of employment, but the rich farmland in the area sustained the town. Its post office opened in 1878 and remained open until

1896. Today, a few old structures are left in Portland, but most of the site is occupied by modern homes.

A few old cabins remain in Portland, north of Ouray on U.S. 550. *(Kenneth Jessen 102D12)*

George A. Crofutt, *Crofutt's Grip-Sack Guide of Colorado*, 1885 Edition, Johnson Books, Boulder, Colorado, reprint 1981, pp. 126-127.

Jack Benham, *Ouray*, Bear Creek Publishing Co., Ouray, Colorado, 1976, pp. 7-25.

Michael Kaplon, Otto Mears, *Paradoxical Pathfinder*, San Juan Book Company, Silverton, Colorado, 1982, pp. 70-72.

P. David Smith, *Ouray, A Quick History*, First Light Publishing, Fort Collins, Colorado, 1996, pp. 13-29, 65.

Tiv Wilkins, *Colorado Railroads*, Pruett Publishing Company, Boulder, Colorado, 1974, p. 61.

William H. Bauer, James L. Ozment and John H. Willard, *Colorado Post Offices,* Colorado Railroad Museum, Golden, Colorado, 1990, pp. 14, 109.

PEAKE

Also Called Aurora or Dallas Divide

- *Ouray County, Cottonwood Creek drainage*
- *Accessible via paved road*
- *Town had a post office; no structures remain*

Dallas Divide is at the top of the long, scenic climb from Ridgway to Placerville on Colorado 62. Over the years, many calendars have featured photographs taken at the divide looking southeast toward Mount Sneffels, Cirque Mountain, Teakettle Mountain and Potose Peak.

In 1880, a small settlement called Aurora was founded at the divide. A post office operated there from 1880 to 1884. In 1890, the Rio Grande Southern constructed its narrow gauge line up Pleasant Valley, then over Dallas Divide. In 1894, a new post office opened under the name Dallas Divide and remained open until 1909 when it was moved to Noel, a short distance away in San Miguel County.

The railroad renamed Dallas Divide, calling it Peake, probably to eliminate confusion with the town of Dallas north of Ridgway. At Peake, the railroad constructed two sidings, a wye to turn locomotives, section house, bunkhouse, coal shed, inspection car shed and livestock pens. Above these buildings was a ranch house, which may have served as the post office when the place was called Aurora. After the railroad was dismantled in 1952, all that was left at Dallas Divide was a lone cattle car sitting on the ground, livestock pens and the old ranch house.

Russ Collman and Dell McCoy, *The RGS Story, Volume I*, Sundance Books, Denver, 1990, pp. 200-215.

Tiv Wilkins, *Colorado Railroads*, Pruett Publishing Company, Boulder, Colorado, 1974, p. 85.

William H. Bauer, James L. Ozment and John H. Willard, *Colorado Post Offices*, Colorado Railroad Museum, Golden, Colorado, 1990, pp. 15, 42.

POUGHKEEPSIE

One of the Smallest Towns in the San Juans

- *San Juan County, Uncompahgre River drainage*
- *Accessible by a rough, difficult, four-wheel drive road*
- *Town had a post office; no standing structures remain*

Poughkeepsie was next to Lake Como, and these cabins were built above the town site at the head of Poughkeepsie Gulch. The photograph was taken in 1901 by E. Howe of the U.S. Geological Survey. *(Denver Public Library x-13089)*

William Boot constructed a store on the tundra along the eastern shore of Lake Como at an elevation of 12,300 feet. This location was well above timberline and surrounded by high, barren peaks. Everything had to be hauled in, including the milled

424

lumber used in the store's construction. Boot also opened a saloon inside the store, and he called the place Lake Como. An early photograph shows Boot's store and one other structure, making this one of the smallest towns in the San Juan Mountains to get a post office.

The post office, which opened in January 1880, went under the name Poughkeepsie. The highest post office ever established in Colorado, it closed the following summer. Poughkeepsie existed for about 3 years, and the 1880 census listed one family at the town site.

Prospectors first entered the Lake Como area in 1873 and continued to explore the area for a number of years. Despite its small size, enough prospectors lived near Poughkeepsie for it to become a separate voting precinct in 1877. Most of the mining activity was below the town site, near the junction of Poughkeepsie Gulch and Mineral Creek.

Poughkeepsie is relatively difficult to reach. A rough four-wheel drive road runs south up Poughkeepsie Gulch from the Mineral Creek Road. In wet weather, this road can be dangerous and requires driver skill. Poughkeepsie also can be reached by driving from Animas Forks up California Gulch to Hurricane Peak. From there, a primitive road drops down through a series of switchbacks to Lake Como. Remains of Boot's store stood until the 1980s, but only scattered bits of lumber remain at the site today.

For a map showing Poughkeepsie's location, see "Animas Forks."

Allen Nossaman, *Many More Mountains, Volume 2: Ruts into Silverton*, Sundance Publications Limited, Denver, Colorado, 1993, pp. 146-147, 226.

Robert L. Brown, *An Empire of Silver*, Sundance Publications, Denver, 1984, pp. 15, 99-100.

William H. Bauer, James L. Ozment and John H. Willard, *Colorado Post Offices*, Colorado Railroad Museum, Golden, Colorado, 1990, p. 116.

RED MOUNTAIN CITY
Congress Post Office

- *San Juan County, Mineral Creek drainage*
- *Accessible by paved road*
- *Town had a post office; no structures remain*

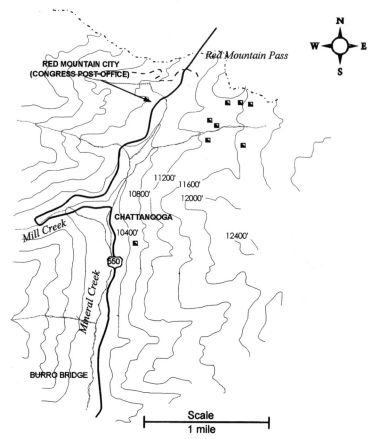

The Red Mountain City site is difficult to locate, and only faint traces of the town remain along U.S. 550 south of Red Mountain Pass.

A great deal of confusion continues to cloud this town's beginnings and its location. On January 6, 1883, the Silverton *La Plata Miner* announced that John Haines had great plans for a new hotel at a new town site called Red Mountain City, to be located immediately south of Red Mountain Pass. Haines had supplies and material shipped to the new site, and John Seymour laid out the town in more than 3 feet of snow. During this same month, ten business lots were sold despite the snow cover. Contracts were let for a half dozen buildings. As the month went on, more lots were sold and more contracts were let for structures along the town's main thoroughfares, Red Mountain Avenue and Congress Street.

Allan Nossaman relates that Red Mountain City started as a single log cabin built by John Lattin during the winter of 1883. The structure was rented to Kutz and Emmerson for use as a meat market. Pattison and Frink soon opened a general mercantile and miners supply store. The *Pilot*, the town's newspaper, was printed in the town's first cabin. An assay office opened, and a small community began to develop.

Confusion surrounding Red Mountain City began when the post office was named Congress. This was not unusual for Colorado mining towns, as the U.S. Postal Service tried to eliminate towns with identical or similar names. Just over the pass, near the Hudson Mine, was another community called Red Mountain Town.

An early photograph of Red Mountain City shows the hand-hewn log, two-story Congress House. At the time, its owner, John Haines, was putting his guests in a large tent next to the structure. Although the exterior of the Congress House was complete, its interior was not. Haines took so long to do the work that by the time the building was ready for business, the town had been abandoned.

Next to the Congress House was the Miners' Exchange Saloon. Across the street was the Patterson and Frink miners' supply store, with a prominent sign in front. In all, approximately eight structures comprised Red Mountain City's business district.

On the same side of the street as the Congress House was the Conley House, the town's other hotel. John Conley opened this establishment in response to the slow progress that Haines was making on the Congress House. Conley brought in two of his sisters to operate the hotel, and they were among the first women to live in Red Mountain City.

Of note is the impractical location where the town was built. The hillside required cribbing to raise the front of the structures on the uphill side of the main street. Structures on the downhill side had entrances at street level and supports in the rear.

The growth of Red Mountain City attracted three prostitutes - Molly Foley, Lizzie Gaylor and "Long Annie." Red Mountain City had only six women, and statistically, half of them were prostitutes!

Because it was on the road between the Red Mountain mining district and the smelters in Silverton, Red Mountain City had a great deal of freight traffic passing through town. The Yankee Girl alone accounted for 10 tons of ore everyday. A livery stable and other facilities necessary to support the freighting business were constructed.

Red Mountain City had a rival in Red Mountain Town, just over the pass. Red Mountain Town was closer to the mines, and sat in the flat meadow rather than on a steep, rocky slope. One visitor commented that both settlements were pathetic excuses for towns, and that the only difference between them was that it took longer for Red Mountain Town to die.

Red Mountain City never reached its first birthday. People began to move away, and most merchants had closed their businesses by the summer of 1883.

After the demise of Red Mountain City, the Congress post office continued to operate. The postmaster, James Edwards, and the publisher of the *Pilot*, Charles Pattison, were the only residents of Red Mountain City. The lucrative mail contract kept Edwards in the town, and Pattison was required to publish legal notices before he could close the newspaper. The newspaper's few subscriptions became the only outgoing mail the post office handled. The two men agreed to leave Red Mountain City at the same time after fulfilling their obligations. When Edwards turned the key in the lock of the post office some time late in the summer of 1883 and walked away with Pattison, the town's population fell to zero. In December, the unfinished Congress House collapsed from the weight of heavy snow.

On the other side of the divide, the first Red Mountain Town, generally referred to as No. 1, did not last long either. During the summer of 1885, it was moved from the meadow below the Hudson Mine to a new location on a terrace occupied previously by Rogersville, next to the National Belle Mine. Its history is covered elsewhere in this book.

Today, the Red Mountain City site is difficult to find. Only faint terraces remain where buildings once stood. The site is located along U.S. 550 six-tenths of a mile south of Red Mountain Pass.

Cabin at Ophir. *(Julia McMillan)*

Allen Nossaman, *Many More Mountains, Volume 3: Rails into Silverton*, Sundance Publications Limited, Denver, Colorado, 1998, pp. 268-272, pp. 277-278.

P. David Smith, *Mountains of Silver*, Pruett Publishing Company, Boulder, Colorado, 1994, pp. 57-58.

William H. Bauer, James L. Ozment and John H. Willard, *Colorado Post Offices*, Colorado Railroad Museum, Golden, Colorado, 1990, p. 37.

RED MOUNTAIN TOWN and ROGERSVILLE

Amid a Mountain of Silver

* *Ouray County, Red Mountain Creek drainage*
* *Accessible via dirt road*
* *Town had a post office; one structure remains*

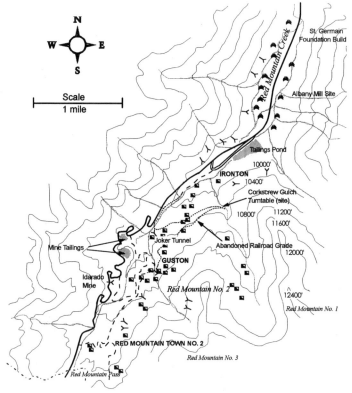

Red Mountain Town was located in the mineral-rich area south of Ouray and north of Silverton in the vicinity of Red Mountain Pass.

The Red Mountain area was so remote that its exploration came late in the history of the San Juan Mountains. The gorge, formed by the Uncompahgre River above Bear Creek Falls, limited access from the north. From the south, reaching Red Mountain Park entailed a long, arduous trip over Red Mountain Pass. During 1881 and 1882, well after the mining industry was established in Silverton and Ouray, silver-galena ore was discovered in the Red Mountain formation at several locations. The vast area between Silverton and Ouray did not have a single town until mines were developed.

At the head of Mineral Creek, north of Silverton, the Congress lode was located in 1881. This was followed by another discovery during the summer of 1882 by John Robinson. His claim was north of Red Mountain Pass, and he called it the Yankee Girl. Other early claims included the Robinson, Orphan Boy and Guston.

The first rich chimney of silver-galena ore was struck at the Yankee Girl in 1882. At other claims, deposits proved to be similar. The ore came in the form of large vertical masses of metallic ore rather than in the form of veins. The ore contained not only

Signs along the main street of Red Mountain Town No. 2 read "City Laundry," "Bath Rooms," "Cosmopolitan," "The Rainbow Restaurant - Meals at all Hours" and "Red Mountain Hotel." During the fire of 1892, all of these structures were destroyed. *(Denver Public Library x-11521)*

lead and silver, but also some gold and copper.

An investor paid a large sum of money for the Yankee Girl based on just 20 feet of exploration work. This prompted the owners of nearby claims to prove that their deposits were just as rich. After a while, the majority of claims were consolidated and were no longer held by their original discoverers.

On a flat meadow, about 500 feet below the Hudson Mine at the south end of Red Mountain Park, a community began to take shape. Initially it was called Hudson, then the town's founders decided on Barilla, the name of an Apache chief. Another town grew 1,500 feet below in a saddle a quarter of a mile closer to the Yankee Girl Mine and east of the knob where the National Belle Mine was located. At first, this town was called Roger City, then it was changed to Rogersville.

Construction started at the two town sites during the winter of 1882-1883. Both Silverton and Ouray claimed that these new towns were within their county. The boundary between San Juan

Only one structure shown in this photograph survives today at Red Mountain Town No. 2. It sits below and slightly to the left of the National Belle Mine. A fire destroyed the main part of the town in 1892. *(Denver Public Library x-62096)*

and Ouray counties was defined by water drainage, and swampy meadows made it difficult to determine in which direction the water flowed. If the water flowed south to Mineral Creek, it was in San Juan County, but if the water flowed to the north into Red Mountain Creek, it placed the location in Ouray County. Both towns, however, turned out to be in Ouray County.

The National Belle Mine sits off in the background, and other than the jail, this is the only structure remaining at the town site. *(Kenneth Jessen 113C8)*

At Rogersville, Daniel Watson erected the first commercial building, a store that he later expanded into a small hotel. Watson also owned a stagecoach line, so it was logical that he would build a livery stable. Watson went about transporting people to and from the area and was successful in getting mail contracts.

After the construction of several cabins, Rogersville began to take shape, covering four or five blocks. A Silverton surveyor made a town plat, and its streets were named Sandstone, Chestnut, Red Mountain and Lake.

Meanwhile a town company was formed at Barilla. The town promoters petitioned for a post office just before Christmas of 1882. At the time, Barilla did not have a single wooden structure. The Postal Service was faced with a problem concerning the name Barilla because Las Animas County had a town called Barela. The Postal Service reasoned that the names were too close in spelling, and residents had to settle for Red Mountain Town. Its post office opened in January 1883 and remained open until 1895.

The Rogersville post office opened in March 1883 but closed just 3 months later. The Postal Service required that any new town submit a map showing its location. The Postal Service might have realized that Rogersville was located close to Red Mountain Town.

San Juan County did not want to lose out to Ouray County. Consequently, Red Mountain City was formed below the Congress Mine, south of Red Mountain Pass. The post office at Red Mountain City was named Congress, and its history is covered elsewhere in this book.

Red Mountain Town got its first newspaper, the *Red Mountain Review*, in 1883. It was printed in a tent. After a cabin was constructed for the *Review*, the post office was moved into the front portion of the structure. A second newspaper, the *Red Mountain Pilot*, was first printed in Silverton, then moved to Red Mountain Town. Pack animals carried a Washington hand press and a Gordon job press to a cabin at the town site.

Many came to the site of Red Mountain Town and promised to build a structure, but few followed through with their plans. The problem with establishing a town was that prospecting was first in the minds of its residents, many of whom were transients and moved from camp to camp. Creature comforts came second. Although heavy timber surrounded the town site and provided an ample supply of raw material, construction was slow .

As the spring of 1883 approached, building activity increased in Red Mountain Town with construction of an 18-foot by 40-foot frame structure using milled lumber shipped by wagon from Silverton. In addition, Frank Schimer opened the Red Mountain Saloon in a tent. A hotel, called the Excelsior House, was constructed by R. H. Rose and Robert Wood. The name was changed to the Hudson House, and soon the Hudson restaurant opened next to the Red Mountain saloon. An impressive two-story saloon, called the Assembly Club, also was built at this time.

A real estate office opened, along with the mining brokerage house. A barbershop was added to the list of businesses along with the Chinese laundry. The first physician in Red Mountain

Town was Dr. J. J. Stoll. A drinking establishment, the Scanida
Saloon, was constructed on Hudson Avenue, and a second hotel
was added to the other businesses. The Red Mountain Billiard
Hall opened in a large tent.

"Professor" Theodore A. Metz brought a variety program to
Red Mountain Town. Metz promised that he would construct a
house of entertainment, which was to be called the P. S. Lodging,
but he left town before any work was done. Coincident with the
professor's visit was the arrival of a prostitute named "Deaf Mat."

George Lockwood worked on a plat of Red Mountain Town.

Red Mountain Town No. 2's structures were destroyed by fire in 1892 and never rebuilt.
Only the jail and a structure associated with the National Belle Mine remain today. This
map shows the Silverton Railroad and its loop into town.

The site of Red Mountain Town No. 1 was so swampy that a corduroy road was necessary to exit the town site. *(Denver Public Library C-111)*

Its principal streets ran southwest to northwest and included Main Street, Hudson Street and Park Street. These streets were intersected by Bluff, First, Second, Third and Fourth streets. Because of the marshy conditions, only a few of the streets identified on the town plat were ever occupied. The plat was filed on June 18, 1883.

A photograph of Red Mountain Town taken in the summer of 1883 reveals a small, primitive settlement with stumps and felled trees along its main street. The *Red Mountain Review* was published in a cabin at the end of this street. The Hudson House was a small, two-story building made of milled lumber in the center of the business district.

In July, mud became a major inconvenience in getting to and from the Hudson mine. A corduroy road was constructed at the south end of town to allow travel over the worst part of the swamp.

Red Mountain Town survived its first full year with a modest increase in businesses. However, on the other side of the pass Red

Mountain City (Congress post office) did not survive. Weather, altitude and terrain conspired to close Red Mountain City. Below Red Mountain Town at Rogersville, growth was slow, and soon this town was abandoned.

In 1885, those living in Red Mountain Town decided to give up on the swampy terrain and move the town to the Rogersville site next to the National Belle Mine. To reduce confusion, historians have added numbers, calling the original Red Mountain Town No. 1 and the second town at the Rogersville site No. 2.

The substantial row of two-story frame structures that lined Red Mountain Town No. 2's main street were consumed by fire in 1892. In all, the fire destroyed fifteen structures. The town was not rebuilt. A photograph taken after the fire shows only two structures in the business district. Outside of the business district, the jail and the railroad depot survived the fire.

Both sites are accessible today from U.S. 550 by taking a dirt side road east from Red Mountain Pass. No. 1 sits on the bench near the pass, and No. 2 is located below at the base of a relatively steep hill. At Red Mountain Town No. 2, foundations are marked today by lumber embedded in the soil. The jail is located on the north end of the town site, and off to one side of the site, one mine building remains at the National Belle.

One of the primary factors in the survival of any mining town was inexpensive transportation. The Silverton Railroad was among four railroads built by pioneer Otto Mears. Work started in 1887, using an earlier survey done by the Denver & Rio Grande up Mineral Creek. Many of the mine owners in the Red Mountain district purchased stock, thereby contributing to the railroad's construction. After the railroad's arrival, mines with low-grade ore reopened.

The Silverton Railroad reached Burro Bridge, along Mineral Creek north of Silverton, in October 1887. The line began operating in 1888 as the rails advanced past the abandoned site of Red Mountain City (Congress post office) and topped out over the pass.

The Chattanooga Loop became one of the railroad's most

prominent features. To maintain a grade of 5 percent, the railroad climbed a short distance up Mill Creek, gaining altitude. Much like the modern-day U.S. 550, it made a switchback or loop from west to east, reversing its direction. The radius of the curve was less than 200 feet. The grade then crossed the mountainside and is plainly visible today above U.S. 550.

So difficult was the terrain at Red Mountain Town No. 2, that the railroad was forced to cross the pass and build around an 11,050-foot knob to a wye. Inside the wye was the Red Mountain Depot constructed on piles. The town's main street paralleled the track serving the National Belle Mine. To continue down to Guston, the train had to be turned on the wye to reverse directions. Operations through this section were complex and involved setting as many as four switches.

As an incidental piece of information, the pass was called Sheridan Pass. A small community, called Sheridan Junction, was established, and its activities centered on the railroad. It had a hotel and several cabins. Passengers could get out, stretch and get a meal at the hotel.

A boardinghouse sits near the site of a small community called Sheridan Junction, at the top of Red Mountain Pass. Its activities centered on the railroad. *(Kenneth Jessen 100C11)*

Allen Nossaman, *Many More Mountains, Volume 3: Rails into Silverton*, Sundance Publications Limited, Denver, Colorado, 1998, pp. 263-266, 270-271.

Robert E. Sloan and Carl A. Skowronski, *The Rainbow Route*, Sundance Publications Limited, Denver, Colorado, 1975, pp. 53-55, 58-59, 114-115, 118.

William H. Bauer, James L. Ozment and John H. Willard, *Colorado Post Offices*, Colorado Railroad Museum, Golden, Colorado, 1990, pp. 120, 124.

RIDGWAY and COLONA

- *Ouray County, Uncompahgre River drainage*
- *Accessible by paved road; occupied towns*
- *Ridgway has an active post office; many original structures remain*

Among many historic structures in Ridgway is this old store. *(Sonje Jessen SJ118)*

NOTE: The development of Ridgway is integral to the history of the area, and although it never has been abandoned, its story is included in this work.

Originally, Otto Mears named the place Dallas Junction. Later he thought of renaming it Megantic, but he settled on Ridgway Junction, named for Robert M. Ridgway, superintendent of the Rio Grande Southern Construction Company. Later the name was simplified to Ridgway.

Ridgway was a railroad town. Its articles of incorporation were filed in 1890 and signed by Dewitt Hartwell, Frederick Walsen and Charles Nix. Hartwell established several of Ouray's businesses, while Walsen was well known for founding the town of Walsenburg in Huerfano County. Charles Nix provided financial backing for some of Hartwell's businesses.

Coincident with the founding of Ridgway was the incorporation of the narrow gauge Rio Grande Southern, backed by Otto Mears and others including Fred Walsen. Ridgway's founders named the town's streets for themselves and family members. This same year, the town got its own water supply from Beaver Creek, and electric power was purchased from a plant in Ouray.

After the formation of a town site company, a bank opened in Ridgway. Officers for the Bank of Ridgway were Otto Mears,

A photograph taken by Robert Richardson shows a Rio Grande Southern galloping goose parked in front of the Ridgway depot in 1951. Use of these motorized cars represented an effort to reduce costs and save the railroad from bankruptcy. Shortly after this photograph was taken, the Rio Grande Southern was abandoned. *(Denver Public Library RR-673)*

Frederick Walsen,
D. C. Hartwell and
Charles Nix. Walsen
was an experienced
banker, having
opened a bank in
Walsenburg.

Ridgway was
the northern termi-
nus and headquar-
ters for the Rio
Grande Southern.
Structures built by

The Ridgway depot looked like this just after the rails of the Denver & Rio Grande were removed in the spring of 1977. It has been converted into a spacious home. *(Kenneth Jessen 036C7)*

the railroad included shops, a depot, freight facilities and a round-house. An exchange track allowed cars to be transferred to and from the narrow gauge Denver & Rio Grande.

The route the Rio Grande Southern took was up Pleasant Valley, over Dallas Divide to Placerville, over Lizard Head Pass and south through Rico and Delores, ending in Durango. Telluride was served by a branch originating at Vance Junction.

Robert Ridgway's experience included four decades in rail-road construction, and he was highly regarded in this field. The terrain over which the Rio Grande Southern traversed was some of the most difficult ever encountered on a North American rail-road. The most famous section was the Ophir Loop, where the railroad had to climb across the face of a series of cliffs using high trestles to gain elevation.

Ridgway was an instant town, and during 1890 and 1891, many of its structures were built. Not only were there railroad structures, but the Mears Railroad Building, Menton Hotel and Criswell Building gave the town a substantial appearance. Dr. Crawford built his office and drugstore, and MacDermott & Company opened a grocery store. Leonard Hunter opened a liv-ery stable, and the Reverend Gray began soliciting subscriptions to build a church. Jesse O'Neill constructed a brick business building, and the Ark Hall, a saloon, opened at this time. Other businesses included a warehouse, lumberyard, coalyard, and ice-house. Even the editor/publisher of the *Western Slope* in Dallas abandoned his business and moved to Ridgway. In January 1891, he published the first issue of the *Ridgway Herald.*

One of the most spectacular structures in Ridgway still stands today, the large two-story frame depot built by the railroad. Once it had an adjoining 70-foot freight room.

In 1892, a two-story schoolhouse was constructed on the south side of town, financed by bonds. Before this, school was held in the town's blacksmith shop.

Ridgway's post office opened in 1890, the same year the town was incorporated. Charles Gibbs became the town's first mayor, with his office located in a brick home. Gibbs worked for Otto Mears as chief engineer and did the design work on the Silverton Railroad into the Red Mountain district. Gibbs also located the northernmost two-thirds of the Rio Grande Southern.

The railroad attracted other businesses, and in 1893, a flour-mill began operation. Brands included "Ouray" and "Chipeta." The demand for flour was so high that the mill purchased all of the wheat grown in the area and had to import additional wheat from the San Luis Valley. In 1906, the Ridgway Creamery Company began operating. Rounding out Ridgway's industries was the Western Slope Box Company.

The Rio Grande Southern operated for over six decades before being abandoned. Mining, which once supported the rail-road, diminished while lumber and agricultural products took over. The railroad also developed tourism. As the roads were improved, trucks and cars took away business. Efforts to save the railroad were made using motorized vehicles, which ran on flanged wheels. These contraptions, a combination of a car or bus body with a sheet metal boxcar, were called "galloping geese." Cost-saving measures delayed the inevitable, and in 1952, service on the Rio Grande Southern ended.

After the railroad was abandoned, only 200 people remained

in Ridgway. For many years, its business district was lined with abandoned stores. The town made the transition from railroads to tourism and much of its economy now is based on a recreational industry. New businesses have opened, and most of its once-abandoned stores are in use. Ridgway is well worth visiting and has retained much of its historic character. The only unfortunate thing is that the depot is the only remaining structure linked to its railroad heritage.

The town of Colona, located along U. S. 550 just inside Ouray County, was founded well before Ridgway. It began as a settlement supporting the Uncompahgre Ute Indian Agency. A post office opened in 1891 and remained active until 1943. After the agency closed, Colona became an agricultural community. Several abandoned buildings, including a home, remain along the highway. The town of Colona is not dead, however, and still has several residents.

The abandoned school is a testimony to Colona's more prosperous days. *(Sonje Jessen SJ115)*

Doris H. Gregory, *The Great Revenue and Surrounding Mines*, Cascade Publications, Ouray, Colorado, 1996, p. 58.

Doris H. Gregory, *The Town That Refused to Die; Ridgway, Colorado*, Cascade Publications, Ouray, Colorado, 1991, pp. 1-7.

Ernest Bacon, *The Western Slope*, August 24, 1890.

Jack Benham, *Ouray*, Bear Creek Publishing Company, Ouray, Colorado, 1976, p. 7.

Russ Collman and Dell McCoy, *The RGS Story, Volume I*, Sundance Books, Denver, 1990, pp. 39, 147.

William H. Bauer, James L. Ozment and John H. Willard, *Colorado Post Offices*, Colorado Railroad Museum, Golden, Colorado, 1990, p. 122.

SILVERTON
County Seat and Sole Survivor

- *San Juan County, Animas River drainage*
- *Accessible via paved road*
- *Town has a post office; a number of original structures survive*

Silverton was just one of many mining towns in the Animas River Valley during the 1800s. Its location, development of businesses and arrival of the Denver & Rio Grande solidified its economic position. *(Denver Public Library X-1772)*

Many books have been written about Silverton. In fact, Allen Nossaman has written three volumes, called *Many More Mountains*, about Silverton and the surrounding area. Although Silverton's population has fluctuated, it has never been a ghost town. It is included in this book, along with the early exploration of the area, because of its strong tie to the area's history.

Of all the many towns founded near the headwaters of the Animas River, only Silverton survives. A few people live in Howardsville, but it no longer can be considered a town. Animas

Forks, Mineral Point, Highland Mary, Niegoldstown, Middleton, Gladstone, Eureka, Congress, Chattanooga and other town sites are void of people.

Charles Baker was one of thousands of prospectors to arrive at California Gulch south of Leadville in 1860. Historical accounts vary as to their numbers, but Baker put together a party of men in July to explore the San Juan Mountains. They traveled up the Lake Fork of the Gunnison River to its headwaters, where they dropped over the divide at or near Cinnamon Pass into the Animas River drainage. They entered the broad floodplain formed by the river, later called Baker's Park, where they panned for gold and explored as far down as the future site of Silverton.

In all likelihood, the party split up to explore the side canyons of the Animas River. Despite the meager amount of gold accumulated during the trip, Baker later bragged about "gold mines" and rich "bar diggings," predicting that 25,000 Americans soon would occupy the area.

Although Baker's reports of mineral riches were highly exaggerated, a great deal of courage was required to venture into the San Juan Mountains. There weren't any accurate maps, and the weather conditions, even in the summer, are harsh. So severe is the climate that San Juan County is one of the few counties in the United States with no land under commercial cultivation. The Baker party also risked attack by Ute Indians.

Based on Baker's optimistic reports upon his return to civilization, the Baker Expedition was organized in Denver later that year. This group of several hundred included women and children. They planned to leave in mid-December, and the *Rocky Mountain News* warned that this was a bad time to venture into the high mountains.

A correspondent at Abiquiu, New Mexico, the closest supply point, visited Baker's Park. He found a number of prospect holes and brought back some of the river gravel for assay. Its value was estimated to be only 35¢ to $2 a ton, not worth mining.

The Baker Expedition traveled south from Denver and

crossed into the San Luis Valley over Sangre de Cristo Pass to Fort Garland. They forded the Rio Grande near Lasauses and followed the Conejos River to Conejos. The route took them through Pagosa Springs, and by the middle of March 1861, they reached the Animas River. Above Hermosa, members of the Baker Expedition constructed a stout bridge, which later became known as Baker's Bridge. At Cascade Creek, fatigue and weather caused many of the party to turn around and head back to the bridge.

Stronger members of the party continued along the Animas River drainage to Baker's Park, where they found Charles Baker and his men. They were panning for gold at the future site of Eureka using whipsawed lumber to construct sluice boxes. As the assays indicated, the panning never paid more than 50¢ a day versus the $10 to $20 a day that prospectors could make in gold-rich parts of Colorado.

Members of the Baker Expedition returned to the bridge and joined other members of the party. Here they constructed as many as twenty cabins to survive the winter. They named this place Animas City, not to be confused with the second Animas City settled during the 1870s 2 miles north of Durango. As a side note, Charles Baker returned to the San Juans with several others in 1868 to continue placer mining. Baker was killed on the return trip, and historical accounts vary as to the exact circumstances.

Baker's Park lay still and void of prospectors until 1870 when gold was discovered in Arrastra Gulch north of the future site of Silverton. George Howard, possibly a member of Baker's original party, returned the following year. He constructed a cabin at the mouth of Cunningham Gulch, which grew into the town of Howardsville. Samples of gold ore from Arrastra Gulch were shown to New Mexico Governor William Pile, and an expedition was financed leading into the area. This led to the discovery of the Little Giant lode.

The United States entered a treaty with the Ute Indians in 1868, giving them the western fourth of Colorado including the San Juan Mountains. After gold and silver were discovered, the

U.S. Army made a token effort to keep white settlers out of the San Juans and off Indian lands. Obviously, the U.S. Army wasn't going to wage war on its own citizens to protect the rights of Native Americans.

Chief Ouray did not want to give up his land to the United States, but he had witnessed how the U.S. Army could crush Indian tribes. Cooperation seemed to be the best way, so Ouray signed the Brunot Agreement in 1873. In the process, the Utes gave up title to 6,000 square miles of high alpine meadows and beautiful mountains, all for the recovery of precious metals.

With the discovery of silver ore, many prospectors entered Baker's Park, and cabins were constructed at various locations in the floodplain along the Animas River. Mining was first on the mind of these early settlers, with little thought given to forming towns. Silverton was an exception. It was designed as a town from its early beginnings, and this, in part, may account for its survival today. It was platted from two 160-acre homesteads at the southern end of Baker's Park where Mineral and Cement creeks join the Animas River. The homesteads belonged to Thomas Blair and William Kearns. A township company took over their property with Demsey Reese serving as president. The first three cabins were constructed by township members Thomas Blair, Nathaniel Slaymaker and Francis Snowden.

Allan G. Bird, *Silverton Then & Now*, Access Publishing, Englewood, Colorado, 1990, p. 1.

Allen Nossaman, *Many More Mountains, Volume 1: Silverton's Roots*, Sundance Publications Limited, Denver, Colorado, 1989, pp. 37-38.

Allen Nossaman, *Many More Mountains, Volume 2: Ruts into Silverton*, Sundance Publications Limited, Denver, Colorado, 1993, pp. 11-17.

Duane A. Smith, *Silverton – A Quick History*, First Light, Fort Collins, Colorado, 1997, pp. 12, 16, 22.

J. Donald Hughes, *American Indians in Colorado*, Pruett Publishing Company, Boulder, Colorado, 1987, pp. 64-66.

Jack Benham, *Silverton*, Bear Creek Publishing Co., Ouray, Colorado, 1977, pp. 7-16, 36.

Thomas Noel, Paul Mahoney and Richard Stevens, *Historical Atlas of Colorado*, University of Oklahoma Press, Norman, Oklahoma, 1994, Section 17.

Virginia McConnell, "Captain Baker and the San Juan Humbug," *The Colorado Magazine*, Vol. XLVIII No. 1, State Historical Society, Denver, Winter 1971, pp. 59-75.

William H. Bauer, James L. Ozment and John H. Willard, *Colorado Post Offices*, Colorado Railroad Museum, Golden, Colorado, 1990, p. 132.

SNEFFELS, RUBY CITY and THISTLEDOWN

- *Ouray County, Sneffels Creek drainage*
- *Accessible via graded dirt road; mine requires four-wheel drive*
- *Each location had a post office; several structures remain at Sneffels*

The original structures in Sneffels itself are gone, but the buildings at the Torpedo-Eclipse Mine nearby remain standing. *(Kenneth Jessen 113B2)*

A lbert Eugene Reynolds and John H. Maugham purchased the Virginius claim in 1880. They developed the Virginius Mine, located between Mendota Peak and United States Mountain on a steep hillside at 12,300 feet. The mining company constructed numerous buildings and a substantial four-story boardinghouse at the mine portal, as commuting to this high, remote location was not practical. More than one hundred men lived in the bunkhouse, and its population was sufficient to merit a post office, which opened in 1887 and closed in 1894.

At first, ore was hauled down on the backs of burros. It required ten of these animals for each ton. Only the highest-grade ore was economical to mine, so low-grade ore was cast off. A tramway replaced the burros, and ore was brought down to a mill near Sneffels Creek for processing. This not only lowered mining costs, but it also allowed all of the ore to be treated.

The Virginius Mine was thought not to be vulnerable to avalanches, given its elevation. There wasn't much terrain above the portal. The buildings were constructed with steep roofs so snow would slide off and not accumulate.

In December 1883, snow fell for 3 days and nights. Avalanches sped down either side of the Virginius, and then one struck the boardinghouse. At the time, a dozen men were in the building and four were killed.

A rescue party was dispatched to help the survivors and bring down the bodies of the men who had perished. On the return trip from the mine, all but two of the thirty-two men in the party were swept away by another avalanche. Some were carried 1,000 feet over a 70-foot cliff. All survived, but the sleds carrying the dead were buried. Any further effort to rescue the others was cancelled until the weather and snow conditions improved.

A constant hazard on the road to Sneffels was the Waterhole Slide, which often covered the road so deep that a tunnel was required through the slide. In 1909, a dozen men were caught in the Waterhole Slide, killing four. That same slide took the lives of twenty-six mules and horses.

The Revenue Tunnel was started in 1889 to undercut other mines including the Virginius, Terrible, Monarch and Sidney. The tunnel reduced the cost of hoisting ore to the surface and eliminated the need for the tramway from the original mine openings. The biggest expense, however, was the cost of pumping water. The Revenue Tunnel was constructed with a water channel parallel to its mine tracks. Because it undercut the existing lodes, all of the water flowed out by gravity. The tunnel opened in 1896.

Well before work on the Revenue Tunnel began, a town had formed at the base of the mountain where the tramway terminal was located. It originally was called Porter, named for store owner George Porter. The post office at Porter opened in 1879 under the name of Mount Sneffels. In 1895, the name was simplified to Sneffels, and the post office remained active until 1930.

When the price of silver began to fall during the late 1880s, the immense Revenue Mill was constructed to process low-grade ore. Just as other silver mines in Colorado were closing, mining at the Revenue increased. The mill could handle larger quantities of ore efficiently, thus extending the life of the mine despite the depressed price of silver. This substantially increased Sneffel's population.

The Revenue Mill was enormous in size, standing six stories high, 180-feet long and 80-feet wide. Other large structures built near the mill included a power plant, car shop, machine shop, sawmill, office, coal shed, transformer house and a large, three-story boardinghouse. The area took on the look of a small city.

The mining company owned most of the buildings, but the two false-front stores, the post office and the Ashenfelter livery barns were privately owned. The site also had several frame homes. The town of Sneffels grew to an estimated population of 600 mill and mine workers.

In August 1915, a fire broke out in the Revenue Mill complex, destroying the mill plus many of the outlying buildings. The mill and mine were not operational at the time, and the structures were considered to be at the end of their useful life. The buildings

next to the portal survived. At the time, the St. John Mining
Company Ltd. of London had an option to buy the property, but it
defaulted on its payment. Retired former manager and part
owner A. E. Reynolds took possession of the property. After the
discovery of a pocket of high-grade ore, mining and milling operations resumed, but on a limited scale.

The tunnel and mill were sold in 1919 to the Tomboy Gold
Mines Company. From 1881 to this point in time, the Revenue
produced $27 million in ore. The Revenue has operated intermit-
tently as late as 1978 under lease agreements, and descendants of
A. E. Reynolds still hold title to this property.

In the 1940s, when Muriel Sibell Wolle visited Sneffels, men
were still working at the mine. Referring to photographs beginning at the time of her visit, the slow but steady deterioration of
the buildings at Sneffels is evident. The Bradley house sat abandoned for many years by the main road, and by 1994, it had collapsed. Today, only the office and one smaller structure remain
near the mill site. Several mining buildings across Sneffels Creek
at the Torpedo-Eclipse Mine are still standing. The stamps at the
collapsed Atlas mill near the portal of the Revenue can be seen on

Sneffels was a small town located along the road up Canyon Creek near the Revenue
mining and milling complex. This photograph shows the Porter store and post office in
a winter scene taken by store owner George Porter. *(Denver Public Library x-11205)*

top of the mine's tailing pile.

From Camp Bird, the drive to Sneffels is quite an experience. During dry years, it is passable by automobile. There is one blind corner on a narrow ledge high above Camp Bird. Beyond this point, the road is cut into the side of a cliff called Hanging Rock. The cliff drips with water, making the surface of the road slick. Beyond this, the road becomes more reasonable. To the left, the four-wheel drive road to upper Camp Bird and Imogene Pass leaves the graded road. Just beyond this intersection is the Sneffels town site, and high above are the rich mines.

Another town site is located above Sneffels. Called Ruby City, it was located where the road splits to Governor Basin and Yankee Boy Basin and is marked by a U.S. Forest Service sign. Established in 1878, Ruby City was still listed in an 1881 business directory, but it grew to just a few cabins. Ruby City did get a post office in May 1878, but the office was closed the following July. The town was supported by area mines including the Ruby Trust and the Mountain Top Mine. Nothing remains at the site today.

Another obscure town site is Thistledown, located halfway between Ouray and Camp Bird on the Canyon Creek road at the mouth of Thistledown Creek. It did not have a post office, and modern homes now occupy much of the site. The collapsed remains of a large frame structure sit near the road.

For a map showing Sneffels, Ruby City and Thistledown, see "Camp Bird."

Doris H. Gregory, *The Great Revenue and Surrounding Mines*, Cascade Publications, Ouray, Colorado, 1996, pp. 11, 27, 40, 109, 111, 191.

Don and Jean Griswold, *Colorado's Century of "Cities,"* self-published, 1958, p. 233.

Muriel Sibell Wolle, *Stampede to Timberline*, Sage Books, Chicago, 1949, pp. 377-381.

P. David Smith, *Images of the San Juans*, Western Reflections Inc., Ouray, Colorado, 1997, pp. 168-169, 176-177,

William H. Bauer, James L. Ozment and John H. Willard, *Colorado Post Offices*, Colorado Railroad Museum, Golden, Colorado, 1990, pp. 102, 125, 133, 147.

AREA SEVENTEEN 17

Dolores, Montezuma & San Miguel Counties

continued

AREA 17: Dolores, Montezuma and San Miguel Counties

Selected Towns

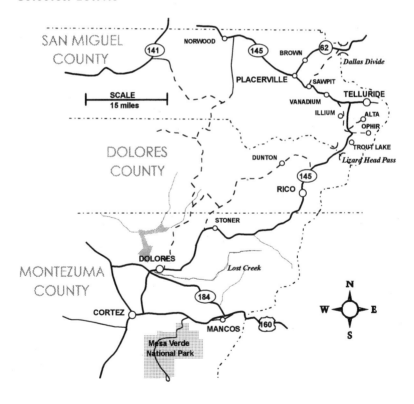

Introduction to Dolores, Montezuma and San Miguel Counties

Butch Cassidy Robs Telluride Bank

Robert LeRoy Parker, going by the name Roy Parker, put together a small band of men consisting of Matt Warner and Tom McCarty. They rode into Telluride during the spring of 1889 and casually blended in with the many other miners and prospectors. They learned the layout of the town and when the payroll would be ready at the San Miguel Valley Bank on Telluride's main street.

At 10 a.m. on June 24, 1889, the men returned to town. While Warner held the reins of the horses immediately outside the door, McCarty and Parker entered the bank. At first, they acted as if they were there to conduct business, but soon they made it known to patrons and employees alike that they were there to rob the bank. They told the assistant cashier not to sound any alarm as they stuffed $20,750 into a bag. Once outside, the three jumped on their horses and galloped out of town, firing their revolvers into the air.

Harry Adsit, a cattleman from the Norwood area, witnessed the men riding west out of town toward San Miguel City. He joined the posse assembled by Sheriff J. A. Beattie, but Adsit had a faster horse and got far ahead of the rest of the men.

On the road between Telluride and Rico, Tom McCarty must have sensed someone was gaining on them and hid behind a rock. As Adsit approached, McCarty jumped out and used his six-gun to relieve Adsit of his pearl-handled revolver. He told Adsit that if he got close again, he would kill him.

In the well-planned style that later would make Parker famous, the gang previously had left fresh horses between Rico and Dolores. After changing horses, they were able to quickly out-distance the posse. When the posse arrived, they found one of the horses used in the robbery. Sheriff Beattie took the animal with him and rode it around Telluride for years to come.

The robbers took refuge in the vast wilderness around the Mancos Mountains before riding to Brown's Park. Brown's Park became a sanctuary for outlaws and part of what became known as the Outlaw Trail. The park is located in a remote valley near where the states of Utah, Colorado and Wyoming join.

Roy Parker left Brown's Park and rode to Rock Springs where he took a job as a butcher under the name George Cassidy. People began to call him "Butch" and the name stuck for the rest of his life. The San Miguel Valley Bank was the first of many bank robberies for Butch Cassidy.

The First Commercial Use of Alternating Current

After many experiments in the theory of transmitting alternating current (ac) over long distances, the world's first practical use was between Ames and the Gold King Mine at Alta. The success at Ames spawned an entire industry of the generation and distribution of ac power.

Lucien L. Nunn arrived in Telluride so broke that he lived on oatmeal and slept in a tent. Ambitious, Nunn worked as a carpenter while he studied law. He was eventually admitted to the bar. Through his law practice and the wise purchase of land, Nunn became wealthy. He purchased the

The original power plant at Ames was a simple frame structure with a pair of high voltage wires that ran to the Gold King Mine at Alta. *(Drawing by Kenneth Jessen)*

This stone structure replaced the original power plant at Ames. There is a small parking lot at Ames and a historical plaque explaining its history. *(Kenneth Jessen 118A28)*

San Miguel Bank in 1888 and soon discovered that the Gold King Mine was about to default on its bank loan. He knew how to analyze cost figures and determined that the Gold King Mine could not make a profit using its existing steam-driven power plant. All of the timber in the area had been depleted. To fuel the boiler, coal had to be packed to the mine on the backs of mules or burros at the cost of $40 per ton. The monthly bill for coal ran as high as $2,500.

Nunn managed to hold off a forced sale of the mine to satisfy its debts. This gave Nunn time to investigate a more economical solution to the cost of generating electric power. Nunn owned water rights on Howard's Fork and thought about using hydroelectric power for the mine. The problem was how to get the electric power from the power plant up to the mine.

Looking back on the history of alternating current, it had a rough beginning. Thomas Edison insisted that direct current was the only practical means of transmitting electric power. Edison installed a dc system for the lights of New York City, and later, a dc system was used to power the subway system.

Opposing Edison was George Westinghouse. He purchased

the patents held by several inventors for an ac distribution system in 1882. Westinghouse saw the many advantages of alternating current. Edison's direct current system was restricted to one voltage. At voltage levels safe for consumers, the wire was large, costly and heavy, thus limiting its practical transmission distance. Alternating current, on the other hand, could be generated at a modest voltage, then transformed to high voltage for transmission over long distances using small, inexpensive wire. At the home or factory, the voltage could then be transformed to a lower voltage.

Westinghouse developed a practical transformer. An experimental ac system generated 500 Volts, which was stepped up to 3,000 Volts for transmission. It was then stepped down to 500 Volts. The big breakthrough came when Nikola Tesla invented the simple ac induction motor, the most common type of motor used in home appliances. Seeing its advantages, George Westinghouse purchased the patent, and Tesla went to work for Westinghouse.

Meanwhile back at Telluride, Nunn was certain that some means of transmitting electrical power could be found, and in 1890, he contacted his brother Paul. Paul told Lucien about the developments made by Westinghouse in ac transmission. Paul was a high school principal in Massachusetts, and Lucien asked him to quit his job, move to Telluride and supervise construction of a power plant. This included a 2.6-mile long transmission line and motor installation at a mine. Lucien contacted Westinghouse with his proposed project to which Westinghouse put up a subsidy of $25,000. Cornell University students were recruited at $30 per month, including room and board, to come to Telluride and do the work. The students were involved in every aspect of the project, including construction of a long flume to carry water from Trout Lake to the head of the 320-foot penstock above the power plant. A matched 100-horse power motor and generator were purchased from Westinghouse.

The generator and Pelton wheel were housed in a simple wooden shack. A copper transmission line, held up by simple cross arms attached to wooden poles, was strung to the mine.

Operation was somewhat complex in that this was a synchronous system. Once the generator came up to speed, driven by the Pelton wheel, a call was made to the mine to bring the motor up to approximately the same speed. It can be assumed that the stationary steam engine at the mine was used for this task. On December 9, 1890, the power was applied, and the generator-motor combination locked together at the same rotational speed. The system eliminated the costly coal-fired plant at the mine.

Nikola Tesla invented the simple ac induction motor, the most common type of motor used in home appliances. He also invented the Tesla coil and devised a means of transmitting electricity through the air. After his patent for the induction motor was purchased by George Westinghouse, Nikola Tesla went to work for Westinghouse. *(Denver Public Library F10289)*

After several name changes, the Telluride Power Company was formed, and a new multi-phase generator was installed at Ames. The transmission line voltage was increased to 10,000 Volts to allow more power to be delivered.

As word spread, other mines wanted ac power. A distribution network was set up, and power lines reached the Smuggler-Union, Liberty Bell and Tomboy mines above Telluride. Power lines were strung over Imogene Pass and down to Camp Bird and the Revenue Mine above Ouray. Nunn constructed a second power plant at Illium using the water from the Ames plant carried by a spectacular flume to its penstock.

Nunn purchased the water rights to Trout Lake and increased the lake's capacity with a dam. In 1909, the dam broke causing a considerable amount of damage and wiping out his Illium power plant. Lawsuits mounted, and Nunn was forced to divest himself of the Telluride Power Company.

The original power plant at Ames was replaced by a stone structure, which remains standing today. There is a small parking lot at Ames, and a sign briefly explains this piece of history.

Colorado's Greatest Ghost Towns

Located in the southern part of Montezuma County, just north of the New Mexico border, are a large number of abandoned villages that predate all other permanent Colorado settlements. The more spectacular villages are located in Mesa Verde National Park. These villages were built by Ancestral Pueblo Indians (also called Anasazi).

These people settled in the Four Corners region about the time of Christ to farm. They also produced fine baskets, pottery, cloth, ornaments and tools. Gradually they developed elaborate villages starting with ones in the Mancos Mesa area and culminating with the apartment-style cliff dwellings. The large numbes of ruins, their age and their location, in natural alcoves on near-perpendicular cliffs, make them the state's greatest ghost towns.

As the Ancestral Pueblo Indians began to move from their individual homes into small clusters, stone masons began to fashion sandstone building blocks. Thick walls allowed some buildings to have several stories. These blocks were laid with mud mortar, and the cracks were filled with smaller shaped stones to provide a draft-free wall. Ceilings were created using logs placed horizontally on top of the walls and held in place by the surrounding wall structure. By 1150 A.D., some of these people began to use this style of building to move into the shelter of natural alcoves in the canyon walls.

Since the alcoves were nearly void of building material, most of the stones and mortar had to be gathered in the canyons and hauled to the sites. The cliff dwellings were not convenient places to live, and for most, water, fuel and food had to be hauled in. Crops were grown on the mesa tops and in the canyon bottoms, sometimes far removed from the dwellings. This meant a daily commute up or down near-perpendicular walls using steps carved in the sandstone or by ladders.

Cliff Palace, a name given by Anglo-Americans, is among the best-known ruin at Mesa Verde. It is the largest with 217 rooms. It could have housed a population of around 250 people. Among the rooms are two towers, one round and the other square. Spruce Tree House had 114 rooms and could house about 150 people. Balcony House, one of the most difficult ruins to reach, had forty-five rooms and a protective wall along its edge to prevent young children from falling to their death. Square Tower House had sixty rooms and a multi-story tower 86-feet high. These are just a few of the many Pueblo Indian ruins in Mesa

The excellent stone masonry with living quarters, storerooms and kivas are all part of Cliff Palace at Mesa Verde National Park. Natural alcoves provided shelter for the Ancestral Pueblo Indians and factored into the high state of preservation of these ruins. *(Denver Public Library MCC-3248)*

Verde National Park. Thousands of other sites dot the southwestern portion of Colorado.

Changes in the climate and depletion of the land may have been among the causes for the abandonment of the cliff dwellings. In any event, they were abandoned in stages around 1300 A.D.

KENNETH JESSEN

Don Watson, *Indians of the Mesa Verde*, Mesa Verde Museum Association, Mesa Verde National Park, Colorado, 1955.

Gilbert R. Wenger, *Mesa Verde National Park*, Mesa Verde Museum Association, Mesa Verde National Park, Colorado, 1980, pp. 38-50.

John Rolfe Burroughs, *Where the Old West Stayed Young*, Bonanza Book, New York, 1962, pp. 119-120.

Richard L. and Suzanne Fetter, *Telluride "From Pick to Powder,"* Caxton Printers Ltd., Caldwell, Idaho, 1979, pp. 52-54.

Russ Collman, Dell McCoy and William Graves, *The RGS Story, Volume IV,* Sundance Books, Denver, 1994, pp. 13-32, covered in "The Founder of the Ames Power Plant, Lucien L. Nunn," by William Graves.

The Ancestral Pueblos (Anasazi), Anasazi Heritage Center, Bureau of Land Management, Colorado, 1999.

Thomas M. Griffiths, *San Juan Country*, Pruett Publishing Company, Boulder, Colorado, 1984, pp. 157-167.

Wilson Rockwell, *Uncompahgre Country*, Sage Books, Denver, 1965, pp. 288-289.

ALTA
Economy Based on Milling and Mining

- *San Miguel County, Gold Creek and Turkey Creek drainage*
- *Accessible via graded dirt road*
- *Town did not have a post office; many structures remain*

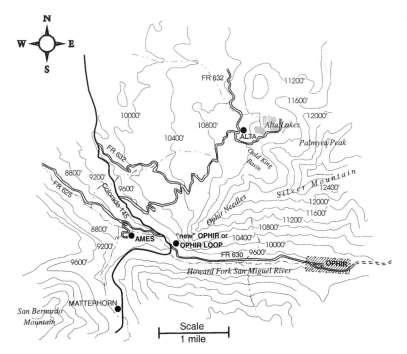

Alta is located at nearly 11,000 feet, high above the towns of Ames and Ophir. The country is rugged, but accessible via a graded dirt road.

A lta, with its numerous buildings, is one of Colorado's best pre-served ghost towns. A rich lode of gold ore was discovered in 1878 by Jack Mann, high in Gold King Basin. He located the Gold

This photograph of the mill at Alta was taken between 1900 and 1920. *(Denver Public Library x-63158)*

King, but litigation delayed the mine's development until 1880. At this time, a stamp mill was constructed at a lower elevation at what was to become the town of Alta. An aerial tramway was constructed from the mine, located at 11,800 feet, down to the mill.

Heavy snow forced the Gold King to operate on a seasonal basis. In addition, lack of water during the winter limited the mill's capacity. The highest of the Alta lakes was created as a reservoir to supply the mill with water. At first, concentrate produced by the mill was hauled north via the Boomerang Road to Telluride. A shorter wagon road was eventually constructed to allow ore to be taken to "new" Ophir (Ophir Loop) and loaded on Rio Grande Southern cars. Eventually, an aerial tramway was constructed to transport concentrate to the railroad.

Lucien L. Nunn, one of the Gold King owners, was responsible for saving the mine from bankruptcy by using hydroelectric power generated far below at Ames. This became the first practical application of alternating current and is covered in the introduction to this area.

The Gold King was not a success. A flood closed the mill in 1902. The mine, however, was worked intermittently until 1910.

Alta's survival came from the Alta Mine, discovered in 1877. In fact, it was the most productive mine in the Ophir area and yielded gold, silver, copper and lead. It was located at nearly 12,000 feet near the Gold King Mine in Gold King Basin.

At first, ore was simply dug out of a surface deposit and placed in sacks. The ore was so profitable that it could be shipped on the backs of pack animals and transported to Silverton for smelting. After the sale of the Alta Mine, differences over how to manage the operation caused it to sit idle for 15 years. A local company purchased the mine and immediately, the mine started shipping ore.

The Blackhawk Tunnel was drilled from Alta under the Bessie Mine. A new mill was built by the owners of the Bessie, but the mill could not process the low-grade ore economically. To provide high-grade ore, the owners of the Bessie purchased the Alta Mine and rebuilt the mill.

The boardinghouse at Alta is one of few standing structures of its type in a Colorado ghost town. *(Kenneth Jessen 036A2)*

New output records were set with peak production in 1906. It was sold to the Wagner Development & Mining Company in 1908. Its owner, John Wagner, operated the Alta Mine for the next 30 years. A 2-mile-long aerial tramway was added to connect the mill with the railroad at "new" Ophir. A larger mill replaced the old mill in 1918. It was never efficient and burned in 1929. A third mill was constructed in 1937, production increased and the following year, over $2 million in ore was removed. The mine and the mill operated through World War II. In 1948, a fire destroyed the entire complex. Apparently, ore reserves were not sufficient to reopen the mine. The road to the Alta site passes by the ruins of the mill and the Blackhawk Tunnel. The abandoned homes at Alta sit on a small hill that overlooks the mill site.

Alta can be reached by FR 632 from Colorado 145 between Society Turn and Ophir. It is a graded dirt road, but in places, the road is rough and steep. Depending on its maintenance, it should be negotiable by automobile. Just beyond the Alta site are the Alta lakes, a popular summer recreation spot. FR 632 continues from Alta north back toward Telluride.

Many of the homes at Alta are clapboard-sided and are more modern than structures in a typical Colorado ghost town. Against the side of the mountain is a large boarding house, constructed in 1939 with its outhouse in back. Many of the buildings are posted "no trespassing."

The location is very scenic. There is the rugged Palmyra Peak above the site and to the south, the spectacular Ophir Needles. Across the valley is Wilson Peak, 14,017 feet in height.

Robert L. Brown, Jeep Trails to Colorado Ghost Towns, Caxton Printers, Caldwell, Idaho, 1963, pp. 31-35.

Russ Collman, Dell McCoy and William Graves, The RGS Story, Sundance Publications Ltd. Denver, 1993, pp. 340-382.

AMES, ILLIUM, MATTERHORN and VANCE JUNCTION

- *San Miguel County, San Miguel River Drainage*
- *Accessible via paved and graded dirt roads*
- *Some towns had post offices; some structures remain*

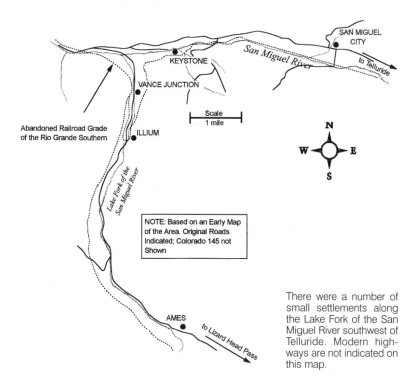

There were a number of small settlements along the Lake Fork of the San Miguel River southwest of Telluride. Modern highways are not indicated on this map.

The world's first commercial ac power plant was built at Ames in 1890. The purpose of the plant was to generate ac power for the Gold King Mine. A long flume carried water across the headwall above Ames from Trout Lake to a penstock for the hydroelectric generator. At first, only the Gold King Mine was served, but eventually, power lines were extended to Telluride and on to Savage Basin to serve the Tomboy Mine. The power lines were taken over Imogene Pass to Camp Bird. For more information on this subject, see "The First Commercial Use of Alternating Current" in the introduction to this area.

Before Ames became famous, the town got its start when Otto Mears constructed a toll road connecting Ouray and Telluride. It acted as a stage stop, and a post office was opened in 1880. In 1900, the Ames post office was moved up to "new" Ophir (Ophir Loop). The town had a business district and a mill. In his 1885 grip-sack guide, George Crofutt reported that about 200 people lived in Ames.

Among the businesses in Ames was the Ames Hotel. This busy town acted as a supply point for the mines in the area. The man in front of the hotel is wearing a white apron, and the woman next to him holds a baby. *(Denver Public Library x-6590)*

The small community of Ames was located at the base of the Ophir Loop. Pack burrows are gathered in front of the Sample Room and the Cabinet Saloon in this photograph taken by noted Colorado photographer Joseph Collier. *(Denver Public Library C-133)*

Ames failed to develop like other mining towns in this area. It was handicapped by its location. It was below the Rio Grande Southern and too far from the area's better mines.

Ames can be reached via FR 625, a graded dirt road. This road descends into the valley a hundred feet or so north of "new" Ophir (Ophir Loop) on Colorado 145 and heads back toward Illium. A short side road drops down to Ames. There is a parking lot at the power plant and a sign summarizing its history.

Not far from Ames is the town of Illium. This was the name assigned by the post office, but its correct spelling is "Ilium." Prior to construction of the Rio Grande Southern in 1891, homesteaders took up claims along the San Miguel River. A small settlement developed called Anderson. After the railroad arrived, the name was changed to Illium. A post office was established and lasted until 1894. In 1910, it reopened for 7 more years.

A power plant was built at Illium in 1900. A covered flume took water from Ames to the head of a penstock for its drop down to Illium. Several homes, including that of the caretaker for the

Matterhorn's abandoned stores were photographed by William Fick in the 1940s. These buildings no longer remain standing. *(Denver Public Library x-63100)*

power plant, were constructed at the site. There was also a cookhouse, boardinghouse and two warehouses. In 1909, a devastating flood, caused by a dam failure at Trout Lake, wiped out the power plant and many of the structures. The site was purchased in 1963 by several Episcopal churches, and the remaining buildings were converted into a home for boys.

Matterhorn was located south of the Ophir Loop at the base of San Bernardo Mountain. The small town also was referred to as San Bernardo for the mountain and the San Bernardo Mine, which supported its economy.

Claims were located in 1886, and in 1888, were sold to London investors who formed the San Bernardo Mining & Milling Company. Development work began on the mine, and a mill was constructed on the west bank of the Lake Fork connected to the mine by an aerial tramway. The mill was water powered, and during the winter, it was closed. The best year was 1900 when 100 carloads of concentrate were shipped over the Rio Grande Southern. The following year, the property was sold to investors from Colorado Springs, and after a year, it was returned to the original investors. The mill was badly damaged in 1909 by the Trout Lake flood, but the mine continued to ship hand-sorted ore. In 1920, a new mill was built at the railroad's grade level eliminating the use of wagons to haul ore to the railroad cars. In 1921, output reached over $100,000 encouraging the owners to rebuild the mill and double its output. After sitting idle for many years, the mine and mill were purchased in 1961 by Silver Hat Mining. The mill was renovated, and it operated until 1969.

The town of Matterhorn consisted of the Rio Grande Southern section house, a two-story saloon/dance hall along the main road, plus several homes. Matterhorn's classic false-front saloon was razed in 1960 for the realignment of Colorado 145. Little else is left of the town.

The Trout Lake post office opened in 1882 and operated until 1885. It reopened in 1890. In 1892, it was moved to San Bernardo (Matterhorn) and closed in 1907. Trout Lake was never a town with a well-defined street system, but consisted of a cluster of cabins near the shore of the lake.

At Vance Junction, the Rio Grande Southern's branch to Telluride left the main line. Structures at Vance Junction included a two-story section house with living quarters for the agent and his family on the second floor. A railroad cafe for Rio Grande Southern employees occupied part of the first floor. An old wooden coach body was used as a depot, and this relic has since been moved to the Colorado Railroad Museum in Golden. There was also an old railroad post office car body and a standard gauge boxcar body at the site for use by the railroad. A coal tipple, located

Trout Lake was a scattered group of cabins and not a town with a well-defined business district or main street. This photograph was taken by Colorado's most noted photographer, William Henry Jackson. *(Denver Public Library WHJ-219)*

a short distance to the north along the main line, was used for refueling locomotive tenders. The tipple remains standing, but is in bad condition.

Other than the railroad agent and his family, Vance Junction's only resident was Colonel Vance. He built a small cabin and later abandoned that cabin in favor of a more comfortable cabin a short distance away at Illium.

John Houk in Josie Moore Crum's classic, *The Rio Grande Southern,* tells of a time he was called away temporarily from his normal job with the Rio Grande Southern to take the agent's place at Vance Junction. Colonel Vance was doing assessment work for area mines and was periodically drunk. He went on a binge every payday and walked to Vance Junction about a half mile from his cabin. At the time, he was suffering from alcoholic withdrawal and was on the hillside catching big, green grasshoppers.

An old cabin sits near the Matterhorn site along Colorado 145. *(Kenneth Jessen 117C8)*

There was a snake charmer named Bosco, who had already put on a show in Telluride and was on his way south to Rico. He traveled with a suitcase full of live snakes. At Vance Junction, he was about to board the train when the conductor stopped him from entering the passenger car. His only choice was to leave the suitcase in the office at Vance Junction for Houk to forward to Rico on the next freight train.

Houk made the mistake of interrupting Vance from his grasshopper catching duties to show him the suitcase. In he came, and in his state of intoxication, Vance feared nothing. He grabbed an armful of the serpents and scattered them all over the office before Houk could react. There were rattlers, water snakes and many other kinds. Houk spent the rest of the day sweeping out the snakes.

In the meantime, when Bosco found out about the incident he expressed his anger to the railroad. He returned to Vance Junction and salvaged what snakes he could find. The rest disappeared in the mountains.

George A. Crofutt, *Crofutt's Grip-Sack Guide of Colorado,* 1885 Edition, Johnson Books, Boulder, Colorado, reprint 1981, p. 67.

Josie Moore Crum, *The Rio Grande Southern,* San Juan History, Inc., Durango, Colorado, 1961, p. 288 (story by John Houk, "Snakes in the Depot").

Muriel Sibell Wolle, *Stampede to Timberline,* Sage Books, Chicago, 1949, p. 390.

Robert L. Brown, *Colorado Ghost Towns, Past and Present,* Caxton Printers, Caldwell, Idaho, 1977, pp. 1-4.

Russ Collman and Dell McCoy, *The RGS Story, Volume I,* Sundance Books, Denver, 1990, pp. 336-359.

Russ Collman, Dell McCoy and William Graves, *The RGS Story, Volume III,* Sundance Books, Denver, 1993, pp. 13-41, pp. 64-73 under "Stations, Siding and Major Buildings" by William Graves and Russ Collman. Also pp. 474-482 under "The Mines in the Ophir Loop Area" by William Graves.

Russ Collman, Dell McCoy and William Graves, *The RGS Story, Volume IV,* Sundance Books, Denver, 1994, pp. 34-37.

William H. Bauer, James L. Ozment and John H. Willard, *Colorado Post Offices,* Colorado Railroad Museum, Golden, Colorado, 1990, pp. 11, 77, 128, 143.

ARLOA, MCPHEE and RUST
Lumber Camps

- *Montezuma County, Dolores River and Lost Canyon Creek drainages*
- *Access unknown*
- *Two towns had post offices; no structures remain*

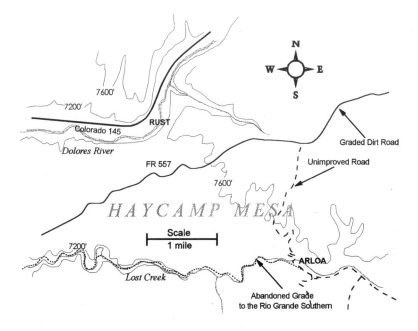

The logging camps of Rust and Arloa took advantage of vast stands of virgin timber on top of several mesas in the Dolores River and Lost Creek region.

Robert L. Brown in his book, *Colorado Ghost Towns, Past and Present*, focused attention to some of the state's abandoned lumber camps, such as Arloa. Arloa was located in remote Lost Canyon and was served by the Rio Grande Southern. The railroad

474

constructed a narrow gauge line through this area in 1891. Attracted by the dense virgin forest and rail service, the Montezuma Lumber Company set up a company town.

Arloa's first sawmill began operating in 1900, and the lumber camp got its own post office 3 years later. Its population fluctuated according to the demand for finished lumber. For example, in 1900, the town had 200 residents, but by 1906, its population fell to 25. Just 2 years later, this figure rose to 125, and by 1913, the town was back to 200.

Teams of horses or mules were used to drag the felled trees along a primitive road to a narrow gauge logging railroad used to haul logs to Arloa. After trees were harvested in one area, the tracks were moved to a new location. The company-owned railroad reached as far as 25 miles from Arloa.

In addition to the mill, Arloa had a box factory and planing mill. The town had a company-owned store, company houses, mill buildings and railroad depot. In 1911, the Rio Grande Southern renamed the settlement Glencoe, and during its declining years, it was known as Millwood. The reasons for the name changes are not known.

Arloa was located in remote Lost Canyon and was served by the Rio Grande Southern. Attracted by the dense virgin forest and rail service, the Montezuma Lumber Company set up a company town. The first sawmill began operating in 1900, and the lumber camp got its own post office three years later. Nothing remains at the site today. *(Denver Public Library x-6680)*

The forests around Arloa were depleted far faster than new trees grew. The last listing for Arloa in the *Colorado Business Directory* was in 1914, the same year its post office and sawmill closed. The town was abandoned and its buildings removed, and all that remains at the site today is scattered slash and a large mound of sawdust.

E.M. Biggs was first to propose a logging business west of Dolores. Since the area encompassed over 200 square miles, work began on the construction of a narrow gauge logging railroad covering much of the southwestern portion of the San Juan National Forest. The railroad system reached a length of over 50 miles and operated as the Colorado & Southwestern Railroad.

The New Mexico Lumber Company took over the operation and established the town of McPhee roughly 4.5 miles northwest of Dolores. Its own post office opened in 1924, and it closed when the town was abandoned in 1948.

The mill was built in 1926, and neat cottages, equipped with electricity, soon were constructed. About twenty of the homes were moved from another lumber camp. A number of Spanish-Speaking Americans were hired, but they were given far less spacious homes than were the Anglo-American workers. The Spanish-Speaking Americans paid $5 per month for their cottages, while the Anglo-American workers paid $10 per month. The two ethnic groups were segregated into their own parts of town.

The three-story mill at McPhee was the town's largest structure and covered a city block. Logs were fed into the mill from a mill pond that could hold 1 million feet of logs. The mill was equipped with both band and circular saws. Attached to the mill was a kiln for drying the milled lumber.

The second largest structure in McPhee was the company office, store and post office. This false-front building sat along the town's main street. Large lettering on its front read, "Office-Store, The New Mexico Lumber Co., McPhee, Colorado."

At the company story, employees were charged wholesale prices plus 10 percent. They received 60 percent of their wages in cash and the remainder in company scrip. The company estimated that 40 percent of a worker's wages went to living expenses. The scrip, unlike the paper used in the coal mining towns, came in the form of thin coins, which could be used to pay rent or buy supplies.

After two mill fires, the McPhee camp was abandoned in 1948. The logging railroad was dismantled, the buildings at McPhee removed and the land turned into farmland. The site is now under McPhee Reservoir.

Unlike Arloa and McPhee, the town of Rust never got a post office. It was named for A. A. Rust, who contracted in the spring of 1902 for finished lumber. Rust was experienced in the business and had logged northwest of Cortez. At a point about 4.5 miles east of Dolores along the Rio Grande Southern, the town of Rust was established. A narrow gauge logging railroad was constructed from Rust up to the top of the forested mesa to the northwest. To reach the top of the mesa, the line used two switchbacks forming a "Z" on the hillside. A secondhand locomotive was purchased in 1902 for use on the line.

The mill at Rust was operated by the Sayre-Newton Lumber Company and sat on the east side of the Dolores River. When the mill was relocated to the top of the mesa, some of the residents at Rust probably moved with the mill. After 4 years, the trees were harvested, the mill closed and the railroad dismantled. Nothing remains at the Rust town site.

Gordon S. Chappell, *Logging Along the Denver & Rio Grande*, Colorado Railroad Museum, Golden, Colorado, 1971, pp. 121-127, 141-166.

Robert L. Brown, *Colorado Ghost Towns, Past and Present*, Caxton Printers, Caldwell, Idaho, 1977, pp. 17-20.

Tiv Wilkins, *Colorado Railroads*, Pruett Publishing Company, Boulder, Colorado, 1974, p. 91.

William H. Bauer, James L. Ozment and John H. Willard, *Colorado Post Offices*, Colorado Railroad Museum, Golden, Colorado, 1990, pp. 14, 97.

BROWN, LEONARD, PLACERVILLE and SAMS

- *San Miguel County, San Miguel River drainage*
- *Accessible via paved road*
- *Some towns had post offices; some original structures remain*

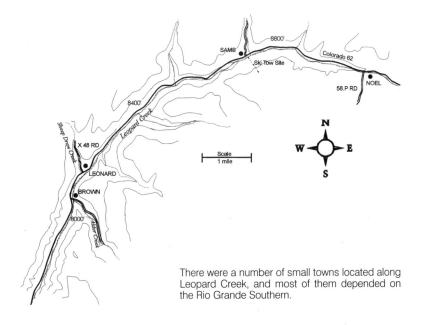

There were a number of small towns located along Leopard Creek, and most of them depended on the Rio Grande Southern.

Brown, located 4.5 miles northeast of Placerville on Alder Creek, is an abandoned site. A number of structures were built by the Rio Grande Southern at Brown, including a bunkhouse and section house. The railroad also had a water tank. In addition to railroad structures, Brown had a grocery store, dance hall, ice

Leonard, also called Haskell's Spur, was the site of a Rio Grande Southern logging spur. One of the Rio Grande Southern's Galloping Goose motor cars is crossing the trestle at Leonard in this 1946 photograph taken by Robert W. Richardson. *(Denver Public Library RR-639)*

house, but lacked a post office. The site is marked by the remains of a stone structure and several other foundations along the dirt road up Alder Creek east of Colorado 62.

Leonard's location is confusing. Early maps indicate it was at the confluence of Sheep Draw and Leopard Creek, while recent U.S. Geological Survey maps indicate it was adjacent to Brown. The Rio Grande Southern's list of stations shows Leonard at Sheep Draw Creek, which is correct. The railroad also called it Haskell's Spur. Leonard was also the location of the Green Mountain Ranch, serving sportsmen. Its post office opened in 1900 and remained open for four decades.

Placerville began as a mining camp near placer deposits along the San Miguel River. Gold was discovered in the river gravel in 1876 by Colonel Baker during his exploration. The area became known as the Lower San Miguel Mining district. In 1877, as prospectors entered the area, a town was laid out, and a post office opened the following year.

The placer gold soon was exhausted, and the town made a transition into a supply point for area mines. The original portion of the town was located at the confluence of Leopard Creek and the San Miguel River and consisted of a half dozen or so cabins. When the Rio Grande Southern entered the canyon in 1891 via Leopard Creek, a new town site was established a short distance to the south. Placerville's original structures have yielded to more modern structures such a bulk oil depot, livestock pens, garage, hotel, warehouse and restaurant. In the new part of town, the railroad constructed a small depot. A general store, hotel, garage and warehouse plus several homes were built near the depot. The handsome stone general store remains in operation today as well as Placerville's post office. Homes also were built along Leopard Creek giving Placerville the shape of a "Y." Today, Placerville can be viewed as either partially abandoned or partially occupied.

Beyond Placerville towards Dallas Divide was Sams. Its post office opened under the name Leopard in 1890 and closed in 1892. In 1903, under the name of Sams, the post office reopened and remained open until 1919. A ski tow was constructed at the site in later years but has since been dismantled. One building remains, but it may have been part of the ski operation.

The Rio Grande Southern's Placerville depot was built south of the original town site. In 1952, the time of this photograph, the railroad was abandoned. (*Denver Public Library x-13045*)

Muriel Sibell Wolle, *Stampede to Timberline*, Sage Books, Chicago, 1949, pp. 381-382.

Russ Collman and Dell McCoy, *The RGS Story, Volume I*, Sundance Books, Denver, 1990, pp. 230, 243, 263, 257, 271

William H. Bauer, James L. Ozment and John H. Willard, *Colorado Post Offices*, Colorado Railroad Museum, Golden, Colorado, 1990, pp. 88, 114

DUNTON

Area's Most Isolated Mining Camp

- *Dolores County, West Dolores River drainage*
- *Accessible near site via graded dirt road*
- *Town had a post office; access limited by private property*

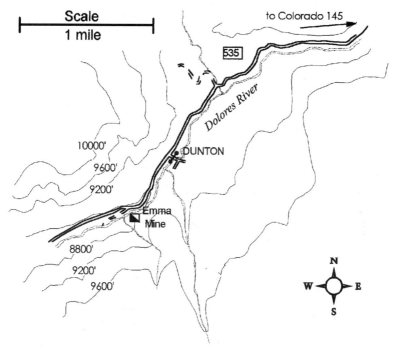

Dunton is an isolated mining area, far from Telluride, Alta, Ophir or the other mineral-rich areas along the San Miguel River. The Emma Mine was Dunton's largest producer. The site is on private property and not open to the public.

Dunton is 10.2 miles over a graded dirt road, FR 535, from U.S. 550. FR 535 leaves U.S. 550 about halfway between Lizard Head Pass and Rico and starts out as a shelf road winding back and forth across a steep aspen-covered hillside. At the top of the climb, it enters a high meadow with the San Juan Mountains in full view. The road drops into the West Dolores River drainage and turns south to Dunton.

At Dunton, FR 535 is on the west side of the river, and the town is on the east side. The bridge to the site is blocked and posted "no trespassing." It is difficult to determine the vintage of the structures remaining on the site.

Dunton was established in 1885 and was supported by several mines about a half-mile downstream. The most successful was the Emma, but the mine's extreme isolation limited its development.

The town's population probably never exceeded 100 until the sale of the Emma in 1897. At that time, a stamp mill was constructed, and Dunton's population increased. The town's best years were around 1905, with a population that may have reached 300. The

Access to Dunton is restricted and posted "no trespassing." There are a number of structures on the site, and some may date to the town's beginnings in the mid-1880s. *(Kenneth Jessen 117B11)*

The Emma Mine was the largest mine near Dunton and supported the town. Its dilapidated buildings were photographed in 1950 by historian Muriel Sibell Wolle. *(Denver Public Library x-17778)*

Dunton post office opened in 1892, and other than a brief closure between 1895 and 1896, it remained open until 1954.

As mining dwindled, people began to leave, and by 1918, Dunton was a ghost town. It was purchased by Joe and Dominica Roscio. They operated the site and the surrounding land as a combination cattle and dude ranch. The Dunton hot springs was the main attraction, and a couple of the town's old saloons were converted into guest cabins. Another saloon was made into a combination bar and restaurant, while the old dance hall became the lodge. The town was sold again in 1980 and again in 1985.

Rick Cahill, author of *Colorado Hot Springs Guide*, was lucky enough to visit Dunton before it was closed to the public. He reported that the town's original structures were converted for use by guests. His impression was that it was a hard place to live. In his interview with the bartender, he learned that Dunton was once a biker hideout. When the bikers were forced to leave in 1977, they set fire to some of the town's historic cabins.

John K. Aldrich, *Ghosts of the Western San Juans*, Centennial Graphics, Lakewood, Colorado, 1988, p. 11.

Russ Collman, Dell McCoy and William Graves, *The RGS Story, Volume V*, Sundance Books, Denver, 1996, pp. 29, 39.

William H. Bauer, James L. Ozment and John H. Willard, *Colorado Post Offices*, Colorado Railroad Museum, Golden, Colorado, 1990, p. 48.

FALL CREEK, SAWPIT
and VANADIUM

- *San Miguel County, San Miguel River drainage*
- *Accessible via paved road*
- *Towns had post offices; some original structures may remain*

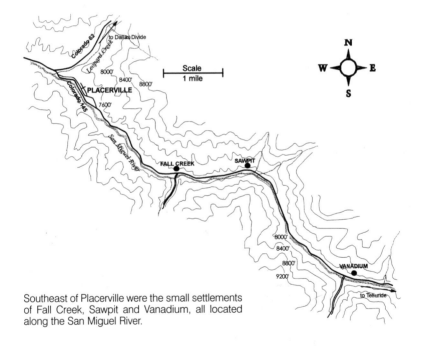

Southeast of Placerville were the small settlements of Fall Creek, Sawpit and Vanadium, all located along the San Miguel River.

A t Fall Creek, carnotite and silver ore were mined. There was also some placer mining along the banks of the San Miguel River. The name of the small community was changed from Fall

Creek to Silver Pick for the principle mine above the site, then changed back to Fall Creek. Its post office opened in 1933 and closed a decade later. It does not appear that any original structures remain at the site, only homes of modern design.

Sawpit (also spelled Saw Pit) was originally called Seymour. It was founded in 1892 as a stop along the Rio Grande Southern. The Champion Belle lode was discovered by James Blake, a blacksmith, in 1895. Blake's first ore shipment of three railroad cars netted him $1,800. The following year the name of the town was changed from Seymour to Sawpit.

Blake's success attracted prospectors, and Sawpit was laid out in generous city blocks. Wheeler and Blake avenues were intersected by Lowe, Hyde and Jackson streets. According to a Sanborn insurance map, only two blocks had structures.

Sawpit had a ball mill to process ore from the Champion Belle Mine brought down by an aerial tram. There was a mine

The Primos Chemical Company mill dominates Vanadium. A company town called Newmire was located nearby. The complex was purchased by the Vanadium Corporation of America in 1922 and continued operation until the end of World War II. This photograph was taken by Joseph Byers between 1914 and 1917. *(Denver Public Library x-62302)*

office, barn and post office. Away from the town center on Jackson Street was a schoolhouse. As the town's population diminished, the post office closed in 1926. Today, there are a few homes on the site, some of modern construction.

Newmire was the original name for Vanadium, and the site is located where Big Bear Creek enters the San Miguel River. Its post office opened in 1895, coincident with the development of the mines in the area. In 1913, the name was changed from Newmire to Vanadium, and the post office remained open until 1942.

In 1898, the Primos Chemical Company constructed a large mill to process vanadium and carnotite ores. It was purchased by the Vanadium Corporation of America in 1922 and continued operation until the end of World War II. Vanadium was shipped to

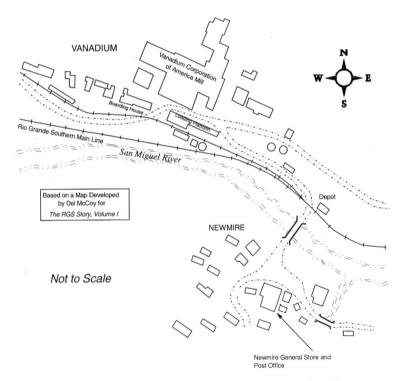

This drawing shows where most structures stood at the Vanadium-Newmire site. Nothing remains today except for foundations.

The tracks of the Rio Grande Southern pass near Fall Creek's only store. This photograph was taken in 1950. *(Denver Public Library x-3220)*

steel mills as a hardening alloy. Later, the mill was used to process uranium. During World War II, the uranium was sent to be purified for use in atomic bomb development.

The mill complex, composed of twenty or more structures, was on the north side of the river, and the residential area was on the south side. The residential area was called by its original name, Newmire. Newmire had a combination general store and post office plus a number of homes. Its peak was around 1900 when 400 men worked at the mill.

A large concrete foundation, which once supported the mill, marks the site along U.S. 550. Nothing remains at the Newmire site.

Russ Collman and Dell McCoy, *The RGS Story, Volume I*, Sundance Books, Denver, 1990, pp. 301, 305, 309.

William H. Bauer, James L. Ozment and John H. Willard, *Colorado Post Offices*, Colorado Railroad Museum, Golden, Colorado, 1990, pp. 53, 105, 130-131.

KEYSTONE, LIBERTY BELL and SAN MIGUEL CITY

- *San Miguel County, San Miguel River drainage*
- *Accessible by paved road*
- *Some of the towns had post offices; few structures remain*

San Miguel City, located west of Telluride, was one of the early mining towns in the area. Today, the site is void of structures. *(Denver Public Library x-13522)*

K eystone was located less than a mile west from present-day Society Turn and was the site of extensive hydraulic mining beginning in 1879 and lasting until 1887. This mining technique was very destructive, causing scars and a great deal of stream erosion. Hydraulic mining uses a powerful jet of water from a nozzle to wash the gold-bearing gravel down to where it can be

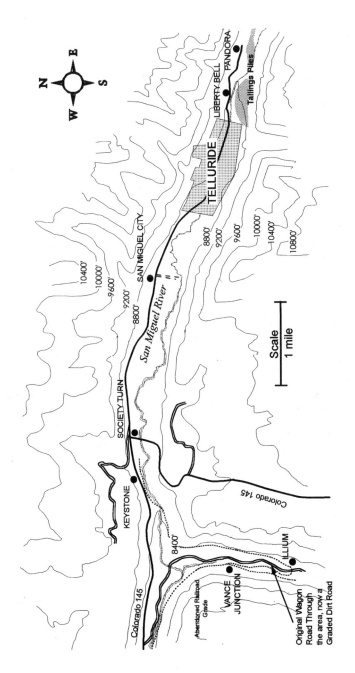

Since Telluride became a ski area, there have been many changes along the San Miguel River. New developments are beginning to take over the old town sites.

run through a sluice. The raw scars from this form of mining are evident around Keystone and will be visible for another century.

What few photographs exist of Keystone show only a mining office with living quarters. The Rio Grande Southern constructed its railroad through the site in 1889 and built a siding for loading gravel.

Liberty Bell was a small company community located between Telluride and Pandora at the Liberty Bell Mill. The Liberty Bell lode was discovered in 1876 by W. L. Cornett. The claim sat idle for years until the Liberty Bell Gold Mining Company took over the operations. They constructed a mill along the San Miguel River and developed the mine, located high above at 10,000 feet. An aerial tram brought the ore down to the mill. The mill was served by the Rio Grande Southern, which built an extension from Telluride to Pandora in 1890.

At the mine, a stand of mature timber provided the false feeling of security from avalanches. On February 28, 1902, after months of heavy snow, a slide started on the 13,000-foot ridge above the mine and raced down Cornet Creek. It crashed directly into the surface structures, splintering one bunkhouse, destroying the boarding house and carrying away the ore crusher and upper tram terminal. The telephone was left intact, and a call for help brought people from Telluride. Steel rods were used to probe the avalanche for bodies.

The high country was not through, and a second slide followed in the tracks of the first. This slide carried away some of the rescuers. A third slide came down the mountain and carried away four others. In this slide, only one survived. The mine foreman called a halt to any further attempts at finding those missing until snow conditions stabilized. The final death toll was sixteen with ten injured making this one of the worst avalanches in Colorado history. Some of the bodies were not recovered until the following spring.

The mining company rebuilt the tram, but placed the bunkhouse and boardinghouse where there was no evidence of

These mine buildings at Liberty Bell have been converted into homes. Liberty Bell is located between Telluride and Pandora. *(Kenneth Jessen 118A34)*

avalanches. As insurance, an enormous timber wall was constructed behind these structures and back-filled with earth and rocks to provide some protection.

Today, the Liberty Bell site is marked on many maps, and its buildings have been converted into homes.

San Miguel City was located between Telluride and Keystone in a beautiful meadow. Only faint traces of where its buildings once stood can be seen today.

San Miguel City was laid out by Thomas Lowthain, F. P. Brown and J. H. Mitchell in August 1876 at the time Colorado became a state. In order to retain its natural beauty, the trees were left standing. As more settlers were attracted to this pleasant location, the town grew to 100. A post office was established in 1877 and continued operation until the town's population began to decline during the mid-1890s. The town had a general store, sawmill, restaurant, two stamp mills and a concentration mill. George Crofutt described San Miguel City in his 1850 guide as having a population of 200. Probably all of those who worked at nearby Keystone lived in San Miguel City. As Telluride grew in importance, San Miguel City was slowly abandoned.

David Lavender, *The Telluride Story*, Wayfinder Press, Ouray, Colorado, 1987, pp. 22, 43.

Don and Jean Griswold, *Colorado's Century of "Cities,"* self-published, 1958, pp. 141-142.

Muriel Sibell Wolle, *Stampede to Timberline*, Sage Books, Chicago, 1949, pp. 382, 384.

William H. Bauer, James L. Ozment and John H. Willard, *Colorado Post Offices*, Colorado Railroad Museum, Golden, Colorado, 1990, p. 128.

OPHIR

Both New and Old

- *San Miguel County, Howard Creek drainage*
- *Accessible via either paved road or graded dirt road*
- *Town has a post office; several original structures remain*

This is how "new" Ophir, also called Ophir Loop, looked during the time it was served by the Rio Grande Southern. The depot is on the left behind the boxcars, and the Quality Store sits on the right by the railroad tracks. None of these structures remain today. *(Denver Public Library x-63115)*

The original town of Ophir is located in the Howard Fork Valley near the base of Ophir Pass, 2 miles east of Colorado 145. The area is exposed to avalanches from the north on Silver Mountain, more than 13,000 feet high, and from the south on Yellow

Mountain. The area was first explored by a group of prospectors under the leadership of Lieutenant Howard, and the first claim was staked by a man named Lindquist. Initially, Spanish-style arrastras were used to grind the gold-bearing quartz ore. During the winter of 1875-1876, seventeen men stayed at what grew

One of the privately owned cottages at "old" Ophir. Note the high mountains in the background, a source of devastating avalanches over the years. *(Kenneth Jessen 098A4)*

to become the small mining community of Ophir.

The primary route from Silverton was over Ophir Pass, and the town played a role as a stopping place for travelers. In 1881, the original trail was improved into a toll road.

The population of Ophir was 200 by 1885, and it had two stores, one hotel, the town hall, two livery stables, a stamp mill and about forty cabins and homes. A school was started with classes held in the town hall; then in 1896, a schoolhouse was constructed. This building burned in 1929, but was replaced by another structure. Ophir also had several saloons. In its red light district, the most unusual structure was "The House of Many Doors," ten in all and no windows.

The *Ophir Mail* began publication in 1897. Published an irregular basis, the paper lasted until 1904.

By 1900, Ophir had grown to 400 people. In 1904, the town got electric lights; then in 1908, it got a telephone. It also developed its own volunteer fire department and a municipal water system. By this time, Ophir contained seventy structures with

Granite Avenue defined as its main street. Its largest grocery store was run by Alex Greig, and its hotels were the Silver Mountain Hotel and Hotel Elliott. The latter was destroyed by an avalanche.

Carrying the mail during the winter over Ophir Pass was difficult and hazardous. Paid mail carriers began using this route in 1879, and during this year, one of the carriers stole all the registered mail. Another carrier took just one trip over the pass and quit. The greatest tragedy associated with Ophir Pass was when Swen Nilson insisted on delivering Christmas letters on December 23, 1883. Because of a heavy snowstorm, he was advised not to attempt the trip by the Silverton postmaster. When Nilson failed to arrive in Ophir, a search party was dispatched, but found no trace of him. The summer passed, and the search continued for Nilson's body. It wasn't until the summer of 1885, his decomposed remains was found in a deep ravine, with his mail sack still strapped to his back.

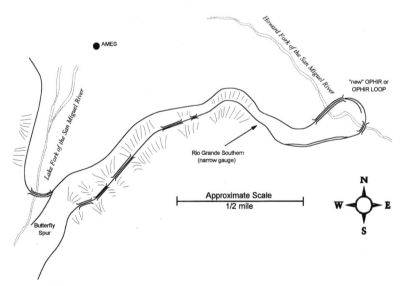

Climbing the headwall above Ames to reach Lizard Head Pass required a remarkable feat of engineering for the Rio Grande Southern. The railroad cut a grade along the base of a cliff, then made a loop back across the cliff using a series of high trestles. The entire section of railroad was known as the Ophir Loop, and the town at the end of the loop took on the same name.

Ophir's post office opened in 1878 and remained an active post office until 1918, when mining in the area decreased and the town's population would no longer support a post office. The post office reopened briefly in 1920. The Ames post office opened in 1880 and in 1900 was moved to "new" Ophir (Ophir Loop). It retained its name until its closure in 1922. At this time, a new post office was opened a quarter of a mile to the east of "new" Ophir.

When ghost town historian Muriel Sibell Wolle visited the original town of Ophir in 1942, she found it abandoned. Water hydrants marked its main street, and a faded sign hung over an abandoned restaurant. The schoolhouse still stood. By 1950, Ophir's population stood at two, Jimmy Noyes and Nellie Tatum. Newspapers joked about the outcome of an election predicting a tie. One was a Democrat and the other a Republican.

The town apparently did not have any year-round residents until 1951, when the Silver Bell Mining Company constructed six cottages for its employees and purchased the entire town site. The company began operating the Silver Bell Mine in 1946, and purchased the Carbonero Mine properties. The primary metal recovered was lead, but in 1954, after the price of this base metal dropped, the mines were closed. Ophir became seasonally occupied with only one full-time resident listed in the 1970 census. In 1972, the Telluride ski area was developed, and the demand for housing within a reasonable distance of Telluride increased. Older homes were rebuilt and restored, and several new homes were constructed. As of the 1990 census, there are ninety permanent residents living in this old mining camp.

To reach Ophir, head south from Telluride on Colorado 145. Turn east just past the dirt road to Ames. The town of Ophir is just over 2 miles on a good graded gravel road.

The "new" Ophir, also called Ophir Loop, was created upon the arrival of the Rio Grande Southern in 1891. The nature of the terrain forced the railroad to construct its roadbed along the base of Sunshine Mountain. After passing along the base of a cliff, the line doubled back on itself, was supported by a series of trestles, and continued its climb to Lizard Head Pass. In a relative short distance, ten trestles were required to span various gulches in this rugged country. As viewed from above, the railroad went up the Howard Fork of the San Miguel River, then back without achieving any horizontal distance. The distance gained, however, was vertical.

At the very end of the loop, the railroad constructed the Ophir depot. This formed the nucleus for the small community of "new" Ophir (Ophir Loop). The town had an irregular shape dictated by the rugged country. The post office was originally located in a store, then moved to the Rio Grande Southern depot. It also had a boardinghouse, barber shop, livery stable and as many as thirty homes. Businesses included the Oilton Club, Mrs. Skillen's Store and the Howard Fork Quality Store.

The community had a unique look. The lower tram station and ore bins for the mining properties at Alta, then owned by the Belmont-Wagner Mining Company, went over the curved track of the Rio Grande Southern. When Colorado 145 was improved, some of the structures were razed. Today, one home remains, and across Howard Fork is the abandoned Silver Bell Mill. *For a map showing Ophir, see "Alta."*

This cabin sits near the Ophir post office, located between "old" and "new" Ophir. (Kenneth Jessen 118A20)

Muriel Sibell Wolle, *Stampede to Timberline*, Sage Books, Chicago, 1949, pp. 390, 392.

Robert L. Brown, *Jeep Trails to Colorado Ghost Towns*, Caxton Printers, Caldwell, Idaho, 1963, pp. 157-158.

Russ Collman, Dell McCoy and William Graves, *The RGS Story, Volume III*, Sundance Books, Denver, 1993, pp. 152-334. (also in this work, "The Little Mining Town of Ophir, Colorado," by William Graves.)

William H. Bauer, James L. Ozment and John H. Willard, *Colorado Post Offices*, Colorado Railroad Museum, Golden, Colorado, 1990, pp. 11, 108.

PANDORA
A Mill Town

- *San Miguel County, San Miguel River drainage*
- *Accessible via paved road*
- *Town had a post office; no structures remain*

The mill at Pandora serviced a vast network of tunnels and recovered a variety of metals including gold, zinc and lead. *(Kenneth Jessen 118A36)*

The town of Pandora, located near the end of the San Miguel River Valley, began as Newport, then became Folsom. Between August and December 1880, it could boast of having Telluride's post office. The details of why Telluride's post office was moved to Folsom, then returned to Telluride, are unclear. In 1881, a post office opened at Folsom under the name Pandora and operated until 1885. Pandora became the accepted name for this mill town. After the construction a large mill in 1902, the post office reopened.

Large quantities of concentrates were brought down to Pandora by aerial tramways from the Smuggler-Union, Sheridan and Tomboy mines. The largest mill at Pandora was the Smuggler-Union. For a number of years, ore from the Sheridan was brought down by a steep surface tramway called the Sheridan Incline. Pandora continued to grow as the Rio Grande Southern was extended through the town to the mills in 1890.

George Crofutt listed Pandora's population at sixty in his 1885 guidebook. Photographic evidence suggests that by 1890, Pandora had approximately twenty structures. By 1904, a Sanborn Insurance map shows that Pandora had grown to thirty-five structures plus sheds and outhouses. The town also had a schoolhouse and several stores.

In 1900, the Smuggler-Union built the big eleven-story "Red Mill" at the end of the railroad tracks. It used a ball mill to pulverize the ore followed by flotation cells to separate the metallic content. As time passed, Pandora was nearly overrun by the sludge pond created by this and other mills.

When Muriel Sibell Wolle visited Pandora in the 1940s, it was much smaller and restricted to the homes of the mill workers and their families. Today, the site is overgrown and difficult to locate. No original structures remain.

David Lavender, *The Telluride Story*, Wayfinder Press, Ouray, Colorado, 1987, pp. 22, 24.

Muriel Sibell Wolle, *Stampede to Timberline*, Sage Books, Chicago, 1949, pp. 389-390.

Russ Collman and Dell McCoy, *The RGS Story, Volume II*, Sundance Books, Denver, 1991, pp. 241-257.

William H. Bauer, James L. Ozment and John H. Willard, Colorado Post Offices, Colorado Railroad Museum, Golden, Colorado, 1990, p. 54, p. 110.

RICO

And The David Swickhimer Story

- *Dolores County, Dolores River drainage*
- *Accessible via paved road; occupied town*
- *Town has a post office; many original structures remain*

The former Dolores County Courthouse now serves as the town's library. *(Kenneth Jessen 117B12)*

Note: Rico is not a ghost town. Its history is presented because of its importance to the area.

Under the leadership of Colonel Nash, a Texan, eighteen men traveled up the Dolores River in 1866 in search of gold. They discovered what they were looking for and began mining. More experienced prospectors followed; however, the Dolores River was within the Ute Indian Reservation established in 1868. One of the prospectors, Joseph Fearheiler, was killed by Ute Indians in 1870.

Greed could not keep prospectors out of the area. Despite fears of attack, R. C. Darling led a large party of prospectors into the area in 1872, financed by U.S. Army officers and other wealthy individuals. The lodes they discovered included the Atlantic Cable, Aztec, Yellow Jacket and Phoenix. This party used a primitive furnace to produce a few bars of metal containing gold and silver.

After the discovery of gold and silver in other parts of the San Juan Mountains, a new treaty was negotiated by Felix Brunot in 1873 with the Utes. In the process, these Native Americans gave up all rights to the San Juan region. After the Brunot Treaty, a flood of prospectors entered the area, including David Swickhimer and his wife, Laura. A mining district was organized in 1878.

A mining camp sprang up near the confluence of Silver Creek and the Dolores River, immediately below the most promising claims. Until 1879, the place was called Carbonate City, but apparently residents were not satisfied with the name. Rico was

Several old narrow gauge railroad cars once sat near the site of the collapsed ruins of the engine house. This photograph was taken in 1977. *(Kenneth Jessen 036A4)*

suggested, and by summer, the town had twenty-nine structures, including seven saloons and four assay offices. The *Rico News* began publication from the office of the *La Plata Miner* in Silverton.

The town site was surveyed in 1880 by J. F. Wannemaker. Streets and avenues were defined in an area a mile long and a half-mile wide. The Grand View Smelter was started this same year. Isolation, however, limited development of both the mines and the town. For fresh meat, cattle were driven as close as possible, slaughtered, butchered and the meat packed into Rico.

Rico has a lot to offer the visitor in terms of historic buildings, including the Enterprise Café & Lounge, a stone structure built in 1892. *(Kenneth Jessen 098A7)*

Outrageous prices were charged by merchants for basic supplies. The *Ouray Times* commented on May 1, 1880, that a long string of pack animals approached the town, and the miners met the pack train carrying baskets, empty syrup cans, sacks and baskets.

Rico was in Ouray County, but a ride of several days was required to reach the county seat in Ouray. In 1881, Dolores County was carved out of Ouray County, and Rico was named the new county seat.

Whenever David Swickhimer could find the time, he went prospecting. He ran a saloon in Rico, and his wife ran a boarding-house. The money they earned was used so Swickhimer could continue prospecting. He purchased the Enterprise claim on Newman Hill above the town and sank a discovery shaft 35 feet deep. Out of money, he abandoned the project. Nearby mines hit silver ore, and this renewed his interest in the Enterprise. Out of money again, he sold his saloon and continued work. The deeper he dug, the deeper Swickhimer got into debt until his creditors refused any more financing. One historical account has Laura climbing up to the mine to give the miners whiskey to keep them on the job.

Their luck changed when Laura purchased a $1 Louisiana lottery ticket and won $5,000. Using his wife's winnings, Swickhimer continued to work, and again, he ran out of money. The couple was about to give up, but they decided to keep their crew of miners working for one final shift. On October 6, 1887, at the depth of 262 feet, his miners uncovered a 15-inch wide vein of high-grade silver ore containing some gold. It assayed at $400 a ton, and the Swickhimers became millionaires. Another account of the discovery has the miners not returning home the next morning and their wives frantic with fear there had been a cave in. Upon investigation, it was discovered that the miners were busy shoveling high-grade ore into sacks for shipment.

The Swickhimers worked the mine, then sold it in 1891 for $1,250,000 (worth approximately eleven times that amount in today's dollars). Laura lost much of her money in bad Denver real estate investments, and David lost his fortune trying to save the Rico State Bank from failing in 1907. Later, the couple divorced.

Rico's transportation problems were solved with the arrival of the Rio Grande Southern in 1891. Ore and concentrates could be shipped directly to Durango for processing, and coal could be brought in from the deposits near Durango. In 1892, the Rio Grande Southern constructed a steep 4.8-mile branch directly to the Enterprise Mine portal using switchbacks and a climb across the face of Newman Hill. The line operated until 1900.

Rico began to die as the price of silver fell beginning in the late 1880s. The repeal of the Sherman Silver Purchase Act in 1893 was the final blow. Although many of the mines lay dormant, the town was never fully abandoned. During the 1920s, metal prices

The Van Winkle Mine has been stabilized and preserved as a reminder of Rico's past. *(Kenneth Jessen 117C2)*

went up, and Rico came back to life. Large outside companies purchased the better mines, and the mills began to work around the clock. During World War II, the demand for base metals, such as lead and zinc, was high, and Rico experienced yet another boom.

Today, Rico is a quiet place with a number of retired people constructing new homes. So many of the town's original structures are preserved that Rico offers a unique opportunity to enjoy a true Colorado mining town.

"Home History," *Dolores News*, January 2, 1886, Volume 7, Number 332, p. 1.

Muriel Sibell Wolle, *Stampede to Timberline*, Sage Books, Chicago, 1949, pp. 393-396.

Muriel Sibell Wolle, *Timberline Tailings*, Sage Books, Chicago, Illinois, 1977, pp. 313-315.

Russ Collman, Dell McCoy and William Graves, *The RGS Story, Volume V*, Sundance Books, Denver, 1996, pp. 69-71, 219-223 including "David Swickhimer and the Enterprise Mine" by William Graves.

Tiv Wilkins, *Colorado Railroads*, Pruett Publishing Company, Boulder, Colorado, 1974, pp. 91, 95, 131.

TELLURIDE
Survived Where Other Towns Failed

- *San Miguel County, San Miguel River drainage*
- *Accessible via paved roads; occupied town*
- *Town has a post office; many original structures*

The historic San Miguel County courthouse was constructed in 1887. *(Kenneth Jessen 098A1)*

NOTE: Telluride has never been abandoned. Its history is presented here to round out the history of the area.

Very much like Ouray and Silverton, Telluride was one of the few towns within its county to survive. Ophir could have developed into a major town, but its mines were not nearly as rich as those were above Telluride. Pandora, located at the far end of San Miguel Park, was limited by the width of the canyon, avalanches and mill tailings. On the west end of the park, Keystone was too far from lode mining, and San Miguel City simply failed to develop. Telluride, due to leadership and location, not only survived but also is growing.

Spanish explorers entered the San Miguel River drainage in 1765 under the leadership of Juan Rivera. They were looking for precious metals. Almost a century passed, and a detachment from the Baker Expedition entered the drainage in 1860-1861, but staked no claims.

John Fallon was in Baker Park when he heard of placer deposits along the San Miguel River. He wasn't especially interested in placer mining, but wondered where the gold found in the stream originated. He and a friend named White left Baker Park in 1874 and headed up the San Miguel River. The first placer claim was filed in 1875, and in October, John Fallon recorded a long list of lode claims in Marshall Basin, including the Sheridan and Fallon.

The law on mining claims limits their size to 1,500 feet by 300 feet. The claimant also had to sink a discovery shaft as part of the assessment work. Fallon spent most of his time on the Sheridan with its exposed vein of lead-silver ore. Next to the Sheridan was the Union.

J. F. Gundaker, John Summa and J. B. Ingram entered Marshall Basin to see if any new veins of silver ore could be found. When they looked over the location staked for the Sheridan and the Union, both were on the same vein. They also discovered that the claims were generous in size. They determined where these claims legally ended and staked out the Smuggler between the two of them.

Historian David Lavender, author of *The Telluride Story*, covers another version of this story. Fallon's partner, White, made

During its last years, these rail buses were used to maintain service along the Rio Grande Southern. They were called "galloping geese" and were a favorite among railfans. This "goose" sits by the San Miguel County courthouse. *(Kenneth Jessen 098A2)*

claims on the extensions of the Sheridan and Union, but failed to do the assessment work. Ingram and his companions simply jumped White's claim and concocted the excess size story. Whatever the case, these lodes were eventually combined under one ownership and became the greatest producers in the region recovering ore worth millions of dollars. Charles Savage also discovered rich silver ore in the basin that bears his name. These rich mines formed the basis of Telluride's economic future.

Telluride was originally named Columbia. Its location was 2.5 miles from the end of the San Miguel Valley in a broad, flat meadow with plenty of room to grow. An election was held to incorporate Columbia in 1878, but when the application was made for a post office, it was denied. Presumably, the denial came because there was a Columbia, California and "Cal." could easily be confused with "Col." This argument hardly held water since Placerville, Colorado, was granted a post office well after the town of Placerville, California, was established.

Some unsung hero suggested the name Telluride. The Telluride post office opened in July 1880, but in August, was moved to Folsom, originally called Newport. Folsom later became Pandora. In December 1880, the Telluride post office bounced back to its original location.

The name Telluride came into common use, and Columbia was dropped. Telluride began to grow with the construction of twenty-six buildings. By the spring of 1881, the *Solid Muldoon* in Ouray reported that every lot had been sold and that among the town's businesses were seven saloons and a dance hall.

Several attempts had been made to construct a good wagon road to Ouray over Dallas Divide. To finish the job, Otto Mears was called upon, and Mears took over with plans not only for a toll road to Telluride, but also to extend the road to Ophir. The job was completed in 1881 and was critical to the town's growth.

After Dolores County was split from Ouray County in 1881, those in Telluride had to travel to Rico over Lizard Head Pass to register claims and conduct other county business. The road was poor, and it was a long ride. State officials were made aware of the situation, and in 1883, San Miguel County was formed with Telluride named as its county seat.

Telluride has a large number of restored Victorian homes making it well worth the visit. *(Kenneth Jessen 098A3)*

Overlooking Telluride is this restored powerhouse, now a home. Bridal Veil Falls drops straight down below this structure. *(Kenneth Jessen 117B6)*

As the mining industry declined, many of the surrounding towns were abandoned. Telluride hung on, and today, it is a year round destination resort town.

David Lavender, *The Telluride Story*, Wayfinder Press, Ouray, Colorado, 1987, pp. 16, 22, 24.

Richard L. and Suzanne Fetter, *Telluride "From Pick to Powder,"* Caxton Printers Ltd., Caldwell, Idaho, 1979.

William H. Bauer, James L. Ozment and John H. Willard, *Colorado Post Offices*, Colorado Railroad Museum, Golden, Colorado, 1990, p. 140.

TOMBOY and SMUGGLER-UNION

High Altitude Mining Towns

- *San Miguel County, Savage Creek drainage*
- *Accessible by four-wheel drive road*
- *Towns had post offices; several structures remain*

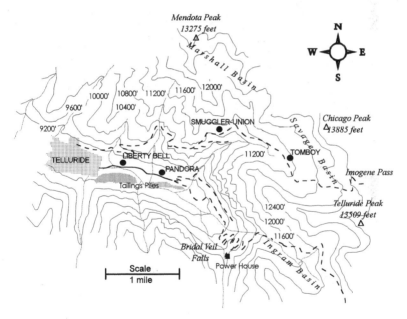

East of Telluride is a series of high basins. This was where the mining camps of Smuggler-Union and Tomboy were located. Ore was brought down from these areas by bucket trams to the large mills at Pandora and Liberty Bell.

Company mining towns developed at both the Smuggler-Union Mine, located high on the side of a cliff above Pandora and at the Tomboy Mine in Savage Basin. Both of these locations, incidentally, are on the same road that runs over Imogene Pass to Camp Bird.

There are a number of structures at Tomboy, such as this double-hip roof house with corrugated steel siding. *(Kenneth Jessen 124A4)*

This road is quite impressive. It leaves from Telluride and is cut across a series of cliffs. It is exposed in places, and in one place, the log cribbing was replaced by steel "I" beams. The beams are nothing but a jumble of metal, which does not inspire confidence as to the integrity of the road.

Although rich silver ore was discovered in Savage Basin in 1880, the Tomboy didn't begin production until the 1890s. In 1894, it was purchased for $100,000 and sold 3 years later to the Rothchilds of London for $2 million. The Tomboy Gold Mines Company took over operation in 1899.

In Savage Basin, the Tomboy mining complex grew to enormous proportions with several concentration mills and a town of several hundred people. The town also was known as Savage Basin Camp. The town had a schoolhouse, livery barn and several small company-run stores. It also had a tennis court at 11,500 feet where the air resistance was quite a bit less. Tomboy had a YMCA with a bowling alley and pool tables.

Dominating the basin was the large Tomboy Mill and flotation plant. Within this complex of thirty-two structures was a

four-story boardinghouse and dining hall. To the east was the
Japan Mine and concentration mill. On the southern edge were
the Iona Gold Mining Company's concentration mill and the
Argentine shaft. Spread out along the access road across the
basin were rows of cottages, thirty or more, including an interconnected cluster of four. Amid the dwelling area was the public

The Smuggler-Union mine and mill complex, boarding house and upper tramway terminal are shown here on the steep hillside between Telluride and Tomboy above Pandora.
(Denver Public Library x-62308)

school. The cottages were little more than shacks and so poorly constructed that snow would drift inside. Nearly every building included a covered walkway to an outhouse. In the case of the school, there were parallel "his" and "hers" covered walkways to the outhouses. The complex did not have a post office.

The Tomboy complex closed in 1927 and was sold to Telluride Mines in 1941. In 1953, the Idarado Mining Company purchased all of the claims and worked the property through miles of tunnels until 1978. Recent activity in both Marshall Basin and in Savage Basin has included environmental restoration work to channel surface water around the vast mine dumps.

When ghost town historians visited Savage Basin during the

Savage Basin where Tomboy was located is littered with metal, mining equipment and the remains of a number of buildings. *(Kenneth Jessen 124A2)*

1940s, almost all of the structures were still standing. Today, only a few buildings survive. Large concrete foundations mark the mill sites, and most of the company homes are gone. The area is littered with nails, rusting pipes, metal siding, boards and other junk.

Unlike the cirque where Tomboy was located, the Smuggler-Union complex sat on a steep hillside. The original mine opening was high above the road. To reduce transportation costs and to provide drainage, the Bullion Tunnel was drilled to undercut the ore deposit. The tunnel and the milling complex were located at the level of the road between Telluride and Savage Basin. At the Bullion Tunnel, the company built a large boardinghouse, clinging to the steep hillside. A post office and company store opened in 1895. The post office went under the name "Smuggler" and didn't close until 1928. A traveling minister came up from Telluride twice a month to hold services at the Smuggler-Union. Along with the minister came a traveling organist with a portable organ. This delighted the Cornish miners, who loved to sing hymns.

A fire broke out in a load of hay at the portal to the Bullion adit in November 1901, and the draft created by ventilation shafts sucked the smoke into the tunnel. Among those working in the adit were two trammers using mules to pull loaded ore cars. Upon seeing the smoke, they cut the animals free from the cars and hung on to their tails. Both trammers exploded through the smoke out into the fresh air, but one of the mules died. Farther inside, twenty-eight men were not so lucky and suffocated. Most were interred at a single service in Telluride, and as the townspeople filed by the open graves, they dropped sprigs of evergreen branches. This was the worst mining disaster in the town's history.

After the complex was abandoned in 1928, the buildings slowly yielded to weather and gravity. Most of them have plummeted down the side of the mountain including the boarding house and the upper tram terminal. Only part of the crusher house remains today, and it is one of Colorado's most spectacular ruins.

Little remains of the crusher house at the Bullion Tunnel along the road to Savage Basin. Soon, this structure will follow the other structures down the mountainside. *(Kenneth Jessen 124A7)*

David Lavender, *The Telluride Story*, Wayfinder Press, Ouray, Colorado, 1987, pp. 42-43.

Muriel Sibell Wolle, *Stampede to Timberline*, Sage Books, Chicago, 1949, pp. 384-385.

Russ Collman and Dell McCoy, *The RGS Story, Volume II*, Sundance Books, Denver, 1991, pp. 398-407.

William H. Bauer, James L. Ozment and John H. Willard, *Colorado Post Offices*, Colorado Railroad Museum, Golden, Colorado, 1990, p. 133.

AREA EIGHTEEN

La Plata County

18

AREA 18: La Plata County

Selected Towns

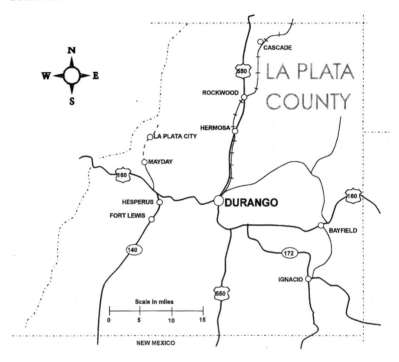

Introduction to La Plata County

L a Plata County was created in 1874 before Colorado became a state. It took the form of a rectangle extending to the Utah-Colorado border. In 1889, Montezuma County was created from the western half of La Plata County. The southern third of La Plata County became the Southern Ute Indian Reservation.

Early in La Plata County's history, several mining towns were established along the La Plata River, but most of the county's economy was based on agriculture. This changed with the arrival of the Denver & Rio Grande. Durango was founded by the railroad and overshadowed its older neighbor, Animas City. Several towns associated with the railroad or with the stagecoach line to Rico came into being north of Durango during the 1880s. With an increase in demand for coal, several coal-mining camps were established south of town.

Durango dominates the region as the principal town, and its economy has shifted from smelting and transportation to tourism and education.

Unlike most areas in *Ghost Towns, Colorado Style,* where precious metal mining or coal mining dominated the formation of towns, La Plata County towns were based on a variety of activities.

KENNETH JESSEN

ANIMAS CITY

Oldest Settlement on the Lower Animas River

- *La Plata County, Animas River drainage*
- *Accessible via paved road*
- *Town had a post office; remaining original structures unknown*

This 1932 view of Animas City was taken when the town was still separate from nearby Durango. The area has since been absorbed into Durango. *(U.S. Geological Survey, C.W. Cross 313)*

The name Animas City has been used twice for settlements on the lower portion of the Animas River. The first Animas City was a product of the Baker Expedition and was located on the east side of the river north of Hermosa. Based on optimistic reports by Charles Baker about the prospects of gold in the upper Animas River drainage, the Baker Expedition was organized in December 1860. This group of several hundred, including women and children, left Denver and traveled south, crossing into the San Luis Valley over Sangre de Cristo Pass to Fort Garland. After fording the Rio Grande, they followed the Conejos River. The route took them through Pagosa Springs, and by the middle of March 1861, they reached the Animas River. Above Hermosa, they constructed a stout bridge that later became known as Baker's Bridge. At Cascade Creek, fatigue and weather caused many to turn around and head back to the camp they made by the bridge.

The stronger members of the party continued along the Animas River drainage to Baker's Park. The group found little gold in the sandbars of the Animas River and returned to the bridge to join the rest of the party. They constructed as many as twenty cabins to survive the winter and named this place Animas City. When spring arrived, members of the Baker Expedition abandoned Animas City and went their separate ways.

Nothing remains at the site of the original Animas City. It is located near the confluence of Elbert Creek and the Animas River. A county road now crosses the stream at the site of Baker's Bridge.

The second Animas City was founded around 1874 as an agricultural center for the lower Animas River valley. It was platted in 1876 and incorporated 2 years later. In 1877, a Presbyterian minister, George Darley, established a church. Animas City got a post office in 1877, and in 1887, its name was simplified to Animas. The post office remained open until 1900. The town also had its

A drug and variety store, post office, Peacock Coal Company office and general outfitting store were all located in Animas City's business center. This photograph was taken between 1880 and 1890. *(Denver Public Library x-6608)*

own school and a newspaper, *The Southwest.* It grew slowly, and the 1880 census reported 286 residents.

George Crofutt covered Animas City in his 1885 edition of his grip-sack guide. At this time, he reported that the town had a population of 200 and several stores. Crofutt mentioned the rich agricultural land along the Animas River, which stretched many miles to the north. Early photographs of Animas City show more than fifty structures, including a small business district.

Farmers and ranchers found a ready market for their goods at the mining camps in the upper Animas River drainage. None of the upper Animas supported agriculture in contrast to the lower Animas where hay, fruit trees and other crops could be grown. It also had abundant grazing land. Nearby were several coal seams that added to the town's economy.

When the Denver & Rio Grande was in the process of constructing its line along the Colorado-New Mexico border, Animas City was a logical destination. The railroad could have converted Animas City into the largest town in southwestern Colorado. The railroad, however, demanded land, money and other concessions from Animas City, and when the town failed to meet these demands, the railroad established its own town. This strategy, in part, was fueled by money made on land speculation by those associated with the railroad. When the rails reached the Animas River in 1881, Durango was founded just 2 miles south of Animas City. This was a fatal blow to Animas City, but it remained a distinct town for some time with over 700 residents. Eventually it was absorbed into Durango.

Allen Nossaman, *Many More Mountains*, Volume 3: Rails into Silverton, Sundance Publications Limited, Denver, Colorado, 1998, pp. 144-147.

Duane A. Smith, *Rocky Mountain Boom Town,* Pruett Publishing Company, Boulder, Colorado, 1980, pp. 6-7.

George A. Crofutt, *Crofutt's Grip-Sack Guide of Colorado*, 1885 Edition, Johnson Books, Boulder, Colorado, reprint 1981, p. 67.

Muriel Sibell Wolle, *Timberline Tailings, Sage Books,* Chicago, Illinois, 1977, pp. 321-322.

Virginia McConnell, "Captain Baker and the San Juan Humbug," *The Colorado Magazine*, Vol. XLVIII No. 1 (Winter, 1971), State Historical Society of Colorado, Denver, pp. 59-75.

William H. Bauer, James L. Ozment and John H. Willard, *Colorado Post Offices*, Colorado Railroad Museum, Golden, Colorado, 1990, p. 12.

CASCADE, SAM SMITH'S PLACE, HERMOSA, ROCKWOOD, TRIMBLE SPRINGS and NICCORA

- *La Plata County, Animas River drainage*
- *Accessible via rail, paved roads or restricted by private property*
- *Some towns had post offices; several structures remain*

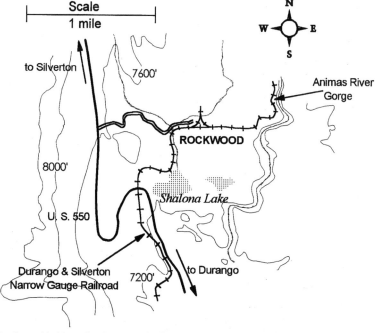

Rockwood is located to the east of U.S. 550 along the tracks of the Durango & Silverton near the beginning of the gorge formed by the Animas River.

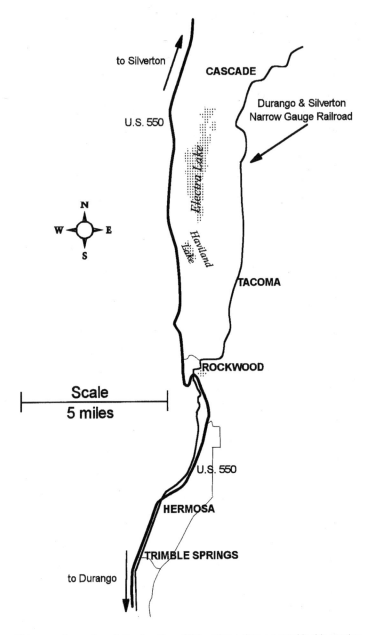

This map shows the relative location of the various sites covered in this section.

Cascade was located at the base of Cascade Hill 9 miles north of Rockwood, where the San Juan Lumber Company operated a sawmill. A stage station was constructed to serve passengers traveling along the route from Durango to Silverton on the Animas Canyon Toll Road. Within the same building was a small hotel and post office. As George Crofutt wrote in his 1885 grip-sack guide, the stage station, post office and hotel were all in "...one little lone cabin." In 1880, grading crews began to arrive to work on the railroad grade along the Animas River. Cascade's population swelled as more laborers arrived. The post office remained open until summer 1882 when the railroad was completed. Nothing of the original settlement remains at the site today.

As a side note, Sam Smith's Place was located near Cascade. It was also on the Animas Canyon Toll Road and by Little Cascade Creek near Aspaas Lake. The site is at the north end of Electra Lake. Sam Smith's Place was not a town, but rather a single, story-and-a-half cabin constructed of hand-hewn logs. Between 1877 and the arrival of the railroad in 1882, Sam Smith's Place was where the stagecoach teams were changed and travelers fed. It also offered overnight accommodations. When the dam was constructed to expand Electra Lake, the cabin was dismantled and floated to the south end of the lake. According to San Juan historian Allen Nossaman, the building still stands near the road to Electra Lake.

Hermosa is located north of Durango along the Denver & Rio Grande narrow gauge line to Silverton. The Hermosa post office opened in 1876 to serve the predominately agricultural area and operated intermittently until 1900. A railroad construction camp was established in 1881. Ernest Ingersoll wrote about this camp in the April 1882 issue of *Harper's Magazine.* He described the buildings as being made "...of logs with dirt roofs, where grasses and sunflowers and purple asters make haste to sprout..." In addition to normal height cabins, there were also little huts about three logs high with flat roofs made with poles, brush and covered with mud. Ingersoll went on to comment, "...in these kennels the laboring men find shelter." A simple depot was completed in January of the following year along with a water tank, section house and siding. The town site is located at the railroad grade crossing along U.S. 550. Remaining structures include the water tank and section house.

During the construction of the Denver & Rio Grande to Silverton, the first camp was established at the mouth of the Animas River gorge in February 1881. The camp was located 19 miles north of Durango and was composed of log cabins and tents. It was situated in a meadow west of the tracks. The place was named Rockwood, and its peak population reached 150. This was where the heaviest grading began with a large cut in the mountainside. Beyond the cut, a shelf was blasted out of solid rock at the edge of a sheer cliff dropping 400 feet into the Animas River. Men had to be lowered by ropes for the initial drilling and blasting. This section of track became known as the High Line, and today it provides passengers on the Durango & Silverton a thrilling view of the gorge below.

A post office was established at Rockwood in 1878, and it remained open until 1940. Rockwood was also where the stage road to Rico began, and a livery barn and blacksmith shop was constructed. The Pioneer Stage Coach Company had its offices in Rockwood. After the grading crews left, the primary industry was freight forwarding. At Rockwood, along with a wye for turning locomotives, the railroad constructed a combination passenger and freight depot.

Rockwood had a dry goods store, grocery store, and hotel able to accommodate fifty guests. Other businesses included a combination restaurant, grocery store and liquor store. Today, Rockwood is easy to visit by taking a side road off of U.S. 550.

Trimble Springs is located in the wide valley formed by the Animas River, approximately halfway between Rockwood and Durango. Frank Trimble and his wife purchased the land, and in the process, they discovered mineral hot springs. Trimble thought the springs were good only for the cure of corns. During the commercial operation of the springs, claims were made that the mineral waters could cure all types of ailments.

Trimble borrowed money from Thomas Burns, a store owner at Tierra Amarilla, New Mexico. When Trimble was unable to make payments, Burns acquired part interest in Trimble's property. In 1882, Burns purchased the land from Trimble, and he and his wife constructed a large hotel called the Hermosa House. The two-story structure was 75 feet long and included a balcony and veranda. Within its 6,500 square feet were fourteen guestrooms, a dining room, parlor and billiard hall. A bath house also was constructed at the site.

In 1883, Trimble Springs got its own post office under the name Trimble, and it operated intermittently until 1900. The Denver & Rio Grande put in a siding and provided passenger service. A small platform was constructed for the convenience of guests. The Hermosa House was destroyed by fire in 1892.

In this early view of Rockwood, the narrow gauge track of the Denver & Rio Grande is in the foreground with a row of false-front buildings in the background. Note the well dressed men and women as well as the burros. Based on the lack of ballast between the ties, a logical guess for this photograph's date would be in the early to mid-1880s. *(Denver Public Library x-13194)*

Apparently, it was rebuilt since Doris Osterwald reported in her book, *Cinders & Smoke,* that the main building was again destroyed by fire in 1963. At this time, the resort was closed. It is not known what remains at the site today since it is on private property.

Niccora was another small settlement along the Animas River. The name was later changed to Tefft Spur for Guy Tefft, a pioneer forest ranger. Niccora got its own post office in July 1877 only to have it close in November. A large sawmill was constructed to cut mine timbers and railroad ties. Douglas fir trees were harvested from the surrounding side canyons. The settlement's existence was tied to construction workers on the Animas Canyon Toll Road. After the trees were harvested, the site was abandoned.

KENNETH JESSEN

Allen Nossaman, *Many More Mountains, Volume 2: Ruts into Silverton*, Sundance Publications Limited, Denver, Colorado, 1993, pp. 88-90.

Allen Nossaman, *Many More Mountains, Volume 3: Rails into Silverton*, Sundance Publications Limited, Denver, Colorado, 1998, pp. 155, 166, 172-179, 195.

Doris B. Osterwald, *Cinders & Smoke*, Western Guideways, Lakewood, Colorado, 1965, 1982 (Fourth Edition), pp. 23, 27, 41.

Duane A. Smith, *Rocky Mountain Boom Town*, Pruett Publishing Company, Boulder, Colorado, 1980, p. 6.

George A. Crofutt, *Crofutt's Grip-Sack Guide of Colorado,* 1885 Edition, Johnson Books, Boulder, Colorado, reprint 1981, p. 78, pp. 151-152.

William H. Bauer, James L. Ozment and John H. Willard, *Colorado Post Offices*, Colorado Railroad Museum, Golden, Colorado, 1990, pp. 31, 71, 105, 123, 142.

DURANGO

Becomes Largest Town in Southwest Colorado

- *La Plata County, Animas River drainage*
- *Accessible via paved road*
- *Occupied town with a post office; many original structures*

NOTE: Durango is not a ghost town nor has it ever been abandoned. It is included because of its impact on the surrounding towns.

Durango's beginning can be traced to the reluctance of Animas City to yield to the demands of the Denver & Rio Grande. Another factor in the founding of Durango was land speculation by those given advance notice of the railroad's planned route. The Denver & Rio Grande founded Durango, and as historian Duane Smith explained in his book, *Rocky Mountain Boom Town*, "Durango built upon Animas City's pioneering; offering no reward and little appreciation." Even the publisher of the Animas City newspaper, *The Southwest*, packed up his press and departed for Durango. Animas City today is part of Durango.

The Durango Trust was organized in 1879 to purchase coal deposits, agricultural land and a town site. In all, 2,300 acres of land was acquired. In September 1880, Durango was surveyed, and the name was suggested by Alexander Hunt, who had been traveling in the Durango, Mexico, area at the time. The sale of lots started immediately. The town was organized by district with the "wholesale" area to be along Main Avenue, and on Second Avenue was Durango's "retail" district. Up on the bench formed by the Animas River, a residential area was defined. This placed the residential area above the dust and noise of the business district.

The initial emphasis was on land sales. What had been a sagebrush-covered flat soon had lots selling for $200, then $300 and even $1,000 for corner lots. Durango grew so fast that a half-dozen sawmills could not keep up with the demand for milled lumber, and brick was manufactured at a frantic pace.

The San Juan Extension of the Denver & Rio Grande from Chama, New Mexico, to Durango was built in 1881. The 68.5-mile route crossed from one drainage after another to reach the Animas River. The route was roundabout keeping the grades low and avoid high mountain passes. On July 27, 1881, a crowd gathered in Durango to witness the driving of a silver spike. The Denver & Rio Grande continued grading and laying track northward along the Animas River reaching Rockwood on November 26. After blasting a shelf across a cliff face above the gorge formed by the Animas River, the railroad reached Silverton the following year.

John Porter, manager of the Greene & Company smelter in Silverton, showed its owners why it would be more economical to move to Durango. The cost of coal and flux hauled up to Silverton was greater than the cost of hauling ore and concentrates down to Durango. Silverton's severe winters hampered operation of the smelter; Durango's mild winter climate was far more favorable. A new smelter was constructed on the west bank of the Animas River south of Durango and was served by the railroad. Coal necessary for the smelter's operation and for the railroad was mined locally.

In Durango, extensive facilities were constructed by the Denver & Rio Grande. A roundhouse, machine shop, car repair shop, large depot and many other structures were built to support Durango as a division point. This further improved the employment picture for the town.

Durango grew quickly. During its first year, Durango had the dubious distinction of gaining nearly a dozen saloons. Other enterprises included seven hotels, several restaurants, two blacksmith shops, two bakeries, various meat markets, general stores and other businesses. Its population soared, and over the years, Durango has continued to dominate as the region's economic center.

Duane A. Smith, *Rocky Mountain Boom Town*, Pruett Publishing Company, Boulder, Colorado, 1980, pp. 9-11, 80-81.

Tiv Wilkins, *Colorado Railroads*, Pruett Publishing Company, Boulder, Colorado, 1974, pp. 35-36, 155.

Robert G. Athearn, *Rebel of the Rockies*, Yale University Press, New Haven, Connecticut, 1962, p. 104.

HESPERUS, MESEROLE and MURNANE

- *La Plata County, La Plata and Hermosa river drainages*
- *Accessible via paved and dirt roads, and by trail*
- *Towns had post offices; some structures remain*

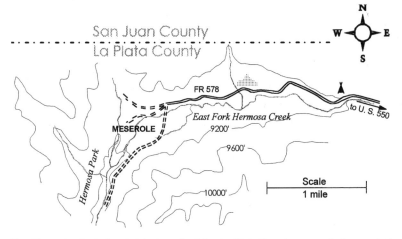

The Meserole site is located just south of the La Plata-San Juan county line west of U.S. 550.

Hesperus is located west of Durango near U.S. 160 along the La Plata River. Agriculture and coal formed the basis for its economy. The town was founded by the Denver & Rio Grande in 1894 under the Hesperus Town and Improvement Company. It was platted by Albert C. Hunt and was served by the narrow gauge Rio Grande Southern. There are several abandoned buildings in Hesperus, but it is an occupied town.

530

An old church sits near the main road through Hesperus. *(Sonje Jessen SJ129)*

Both Meserole and Murnane were located along the stage road between Rockwood and Rico. Both towns had post offices. The post offices were established in 1882, coincident with rail service to Rockwood. The stagecoach route followed Hermosa Creek much of the way. This route was abandoned when the Rio Grande Southern reached Rico in 1891.

Meserole was located at the west end of Hermosa Park where the two major forks of Hermosa Creek meet 18 miles from Rockwood. Meserole was named for pioneer mail carrier George Meserole. There was once log house at the site, and inside this structure was a restaurant and a place for overnight guests. There was also a livery stable. The post office closed in 1884. What remains at the site is unknown.

Murnane was located 9 miles south of Meserole. The place had a restaurant and livery stable run by Daniel and Mary Murnane. The site is on private property and part of a ranch. It is not known if any of its original structures remain.

Allen Nossaman, Many More Mountains, Volume 3: Rails into Silverton, Sundance Publications Limited, Denver, Colorado, 1998, p. 173.

William H. Bauer, James L. Ozment and John H. Willard, Colorado Post Offices, Colorado Railroad Museum, Golden, Colorado, 1990, p. 98, p. 103.

LA PLATA CITY
Founded on Lode Mining

- *La Plata County, La Plata River drainage*
- *Accessible via graded dirt road*
- *Town had a post office; one remaining structure*

At one time, La Plata City had at least a dozen structures as shown in this 1942 photograph. Today, there are a few private homes and a schoolhouse. *(Denver Public Library x-3642)*

The La Plata City site is located near the end of a graded dirt road, 124 RD. There are a few private homes in the area, plus the only remaining original structure, a schoolhouse. At one time, the town had at least a dozen structures including a two-story store.

In 1942, ghost town historian Muriel Sibell Wolle visited La Plata City and noted seven standing structures, many with false fronts, along the town's main street. Robert Brown, also known for his books on Colorado ghost towns, visited the site during the 1960s and noted that only the ruins of several cabins plus the schoolhouse remained. He took a photograph from exactly the same place as one taken when the town was at its prime. In 1972,

Wolle returned and drove through the site without realizing where it was. Only the schoolhouse remained standing.

Based on lode mines, La Plata City got its start in 1875. Prospectors discovered gold in sandbars well below the town site. It was only a matter of time until the source of the gold was discovered. The best mines were the Comstock, La Plata, Lady Eleanor, Cumberland and Snowstorm. Later, the Gold King became the largest producer in the region.

La Plata City's population in 1882 was 200, and by 1889, it was estimated at 500. Until 1882, the town didn't have a post office. The name was simplified to "La Plata" and the post office closed 3 years later. The post office reopened in 1894 under the name "LaPlata" and remained open until 1934.

For a map showing the location of La Plata City, see "Parrott City."

There was a town north of La Plata City called Cumberland. In 1885, a five-stamp mill was built to crush the gold-bearing quartz ore. Little information is known about this mining camp, its size or how long it lasted.

Ghost town historian Muriel Sibell Wolle took this photograph of what appears to have been a store in La Plata City in 1942. Few structures remain at the site today. *(Denver Public Library x-3640)*

Don and Jean Griswold, *Colorado's Century of "Cities,"* self-published, 1958, p. 124.

Muriel Sibell Wolle, *Stampede to Timberline,* Sage Books, Chicago, 1949, pp. 396, 448, 546.

Muriel Sibell Wolle, *Timberline Tailings,* Sage Books, Chicago, Illinois, 1977, pp. 318-320.

Robert L. Brown, *An Empire of Silver,* Sundance Publications, Denver, 1984, pp. 116-117, 121.

William H. Bauer, James L. Ozment and John H. Willard, *Colorado Post Offices,* Colorado Railroad Museum, Golden, Colorado, 1990, p. 85.

PARROTT CITY
The Town Built by John Moss

- *La Plata County, La Plata River drainage*
- *Private property; site not accessible*
- *Town had a post office; no structures remain*

Nothing remains of Parrott City; in fact, the site is on private property and is part of a ranch. This obscure town was once the La Plata County seat and had forty or more structures and its own newspaper.

Although historical accounts vary on the dates, Captain John Moss and C. D. Posten explored the La Plata River area and found placer gold in the gravel. Moss was from San Francisco, and at the time, he was around 45 years old. He had a slender, wiry build with long hair falling over his shoulders. Historians seriously doubt he held the rank of captain and believe the title was honorary.

Moss returned with a group of fellow Californians in 1873. Realizing that he was trespassing on Ute Indian land, he made his own treaty with Chief Ignacio. The Indians granted the prospectors the right to mine and farm on a 36 square-mile section of land. In exchange, the prospectors gave the Indians blankets and 100 ponies. Other accounts relate a darker story; one where Moss gave the Utes whiskey and stolen sheep.

Moss and his party left the area when their food ran short and headed toward the nearest trading post. After one of the men accidentally shot himself, the party divided into two groups. One group continued to the trading post, and the other stayed with the wounded man at a place they named Camp Starvation. For three weeks, they lived on nuts, roots, berries and wild game until the

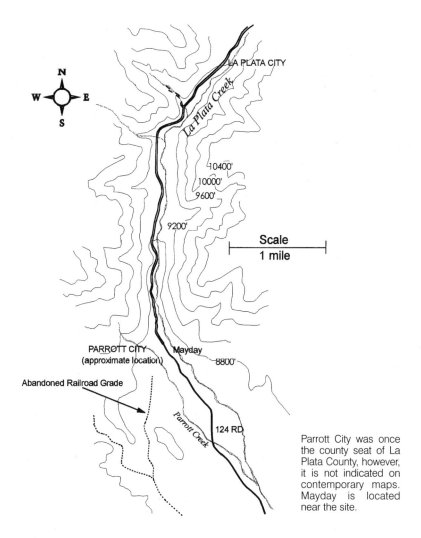

Parrott City was once the county seat of La Plata County, however, it is not indicated on contemporary maps. Mayday is located near the site.

first party returned with provisions.

Moss returned to his San Francisco home with the signed treaty and specimens of gold-bearing quartz. He showed them to a banker, Tibercio (also spelled Tiburcio) Parrott. A mining company was formed, and Parrott provided funds for Moss to continue exploration in the La Plata River area. In exchange, Moss named the small camp Parrott City.

Moss returned to the La Plata area in April 1874, but he only got as far as the Mancos River. Snow prevented farther travel. The party built some cabins and planted crops using seeds they brought with them. They reached the placer deposit the following month only to find a group of Arizona prospectors hard at work. The two groups formed the California Mining District to define the size of each claim and to provide an orderly means of filing new claims.

The nearby stream didn't provide enough water for placer mining, and a ditch was started to bring more water into the area. Prospectors also began to search upstream for the source of the gold nuggets, and one of them discovered the Comstock Lode. Other discoveries followed.

One day, Red Jacket and his band of Ute Indians paid a sudden visit to Parrott City. One of the prospectors, a man named Lewis, used the good neighbor policy to negotiate with the Indians. He gave Red Jacket a dress shirt, then tried to get the Indians to leave. The Indians stayed so Lewis played upon their superstitions by removing his false teeth and waving them in the air for all to see. The Ute Indians found this either disgusting or amazing. In either case, they sprang to their horses and galloped away.

The following day, Red Jacket returned with his squaw and papoose. He was wearing the dress shirt, but he had put it on backwards. He was there for two reasons: to show white men that he knew how to wear a dress shirt and to satisfy his curiosity about an alarm clock he had seen. He believed the ringing to be music and wasn't satisfied until Lewis set off the alarm again and again.

In 1873, the Ute Indians signed a formal treaty with the U.S. Government relinquishing their rights on the San Juan Mountains, including the La Plata River drainage. Moss found out about the treaty the following year.

Word about the area's riches spread, and new visitors arrived. One of the parties was led by Tom Cooper, who told Moss about other settlements farther north, including Howardsville and Silverton.

In 1876, using equipment hauled in by wagon, the first sawmill began operation. At this time, about fifty people lived in Parrott City. As milled lumber became available, two stores, a hotel and a number of shanties were constructed. Parrott City got its own post office in 1876 under the name "Parrott." The post office closed in 1885, then reopened 2 years later and remained active until 1898.

One visitor described Parrott City's residents as engaged in a continuous celebration. Whiskey allegedly was carried around in a water bucket. Everyone in town was invited to take a dip in much the same manner as water is delivered to field hands. John Moss kept a large barrel of whisky in his office. It sat on its side and was tapped with a faucet. Tin dippers hung on the wall behind the barrel, and every visitor was invited to take a dipper full. No restrictions were placed on how many times during the day a visitor might call.

Colorado's most noted photographer, William Henry Jackson, and author-traveler Ernest Ingersoll, paid Moss a visit in

The Mayday schoolhouse and the present-day town of Mayday are located near the Parrott City site. *(Sonje Jessen SJ128)*

1874. Moss had knowledge of the spectacular cliff dwellings south of Parrott City, and after a brief stay, the three traveled to what is now Mesa Verde National Park with Moss acting as guide.

On their return, Jackson and Ingersoll were asked to vote. Moss was running for public office and ignored the fact that Jackson and Ingersoll didn't live anywhere near Parrott City or even in the county. Moss just needed their votes. He also introduced them to all the miners, to all the ranchers and to his infamous barrel of whiskey.

In 1876, the same year Colorado became a state, an election was held to establish a county seat in La Plata County. Moss rounded up his men to cast their votes for Parrott City. Parrott City won and remained the La Plata County seat until 1881 when it was moved to Durango.

John Moss set a record as a state legislator by never attending a single session! Other accounts relate that he arrived at meetings only minutes before they were adjourned and that the total time spent in legislative sessions could be measured in minutes.

By 1885, Parrott City had a population of 250, and more than 500 claims had been filed in the area. Out of these, only twenty were being mined. Some coal was mined nearby, and ranching and farming supported the town's economy.

A mining engineer predicted placer mining at Parrott City would soon end after the removal of the surface gravel. Large boulders, buried deep below the surface, would limit placer mining. In addition, bedrock, where most of the gold was concentrated, was too deep to reach economically. Tibercio Parrott read this report and withdrew his financial support for Moss and Parrott City. The lode mines failed to produce enough rich ore, and further work on the ditch was suspended. Parrott City died, and Moss returned to San Francisco.

An early drawing of Parrott City shows a number of buildings located near the mouth of the La Plata River canyon. The town had two stores and a hotel plus a number of cabins. A weekly newspaper, the *Gazette*, was published from 1876 to 1877.

As Parrott City declined, one old-timer and the postmaster were all that remained. Over the years, the buildings were razed, and the place became a cattle ranch. Ghost town historian Muriel Sibell Wolle states that most of structures were torn down in the 1940s. The Barbee Hotel was the last structure at the site, and it burned to the ground after being struck by lightning in 1963.

Quite a bit of confusion exists as to where Parrott City was located. Some historical accounts contend that Parrott City became La Plata City. This is incorrect. La Plata City is located about 4 miles north in the La Plata River canyon. Parrott City, on the other hand, was located on the alluvial fill near the mouth of the canyon on Parrott Creek. The small town of Mayday is close to the site.

The Mayday Mine came along much later than Parrott City. It produced enough ore for the Rio Grande Southern to construct a 1.87-mile spur to the mine in 1905 starting near Cima Summit at an elevation above 8,000 feet. The spur ran north to a point near 124 RD. This branch remained in operation until 1926 and supported Mayday.

D. B. McGue, "Parrott City, Shortlived Capital of the San Juan County," *The Colorado Magazine*, Vol. XXVI, No. 4 (October, 1949), pp. 291-298.

Don and Jean Griswold, *Colorado's Century of "Cities,"* self-published, 1958, p. 107, pp. 123-124.

Don Watson, *Indians of the Mesa Verde*, Mesa Verde Museum Association, Mesa Verde National Park, Colorado, 1955, pp. 13-14.

George A. Crofutt, *Crofutt's Grip-Sack Guide of Colorado*, 1885 Edition, Johnson Books, Boulder, Colorado, reprint 1981, p. 129.

Muriel Sibell Wolle, *Stampede to Timberline*, Sage Books, Chicago, 1949, pp. 396-398, 546.

Muriel Sibell Wolle, *Timberline Tailings*, Sage Books, Chicago, Illinois, 1977, pp. 316-321.

Robert L. Brown, *An Empire of Silver,* Sundance Publications, Denver, 1984, pp. 117-121.

Robert M. Ormes, *Tracking Ghost Railroads in Colorado*, Century One Press, Colorado Springs, Colorado, 1975, pp. 129-130.

Thomas Noel, Paul Mahoney and Richard Stevens, *Historical Atlas of Colorado,* University of Oklahoma Press, Norman, Oklahoma, 1994, Section 17.

William H. Bauer, James L. Ozment and John H. Willard, *Colorado Post Offices*, Colorado Railroad Museum, Golden, Colorado, 1990, p. 111.

PERINS and PORTER

Coal Mining Towns

- *La Plata County, Lightner Creek drainage*
- *Porter accessible via paved road; Perins accessible by foot only*
- *Both towns had post offices; no structures remain*

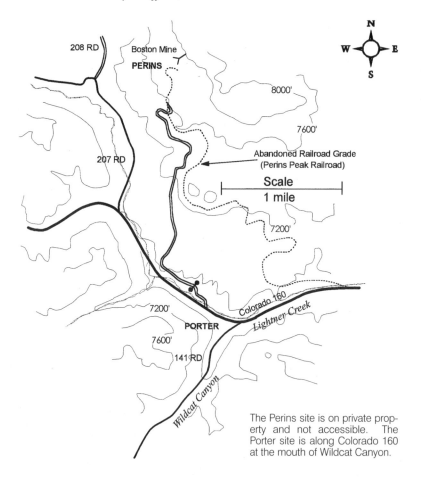

The Perins site is on private property and not accessible. The Porter site is along Colorado 160 at the mouth of Wildcat Canyon.

Coal was discovered in the Durango region during the 1870s, but it wasn't until 1901 that the coal seam near Perins Peak was developed. Originally owned by the Boston Coal and Fuel Company, the Calumet Fuel Company took over ownership in 1906. A steep, twisting narrow gauge railroad was constructed by the Boston Coal and Fuel Company from the Rio Grande Southern's main line at Franklin Junction to serve the mine. It was 4.7 miles long and gained 800 feet in elevation using several reverse loops. The line was leased by the Rio Grande Southern in 1906.

The Perins Peak Mine was developed by George Franklin. He got started in the coal business after he rescued his landlady from her burning home. She knew of the coal deposit on the peak and tried to get her son to develop it commercially. Her son showed no interest, so she told Franklin of its location.

In a shallow valley near the mine, a company town was constructed. The town had a store and boarding house for the single miners. Rows of small cottages were built for the married miners. In all, Perins had about two dozen structures. The population varied depending on the mine's output, and census figures show it varied from 80 to 200 people.

Under the name "Perin," a post office opened in 1902 and closed the following year. It reopened in 1907 under the correct spelling "Perins" and remained open until the mine was closed in 1926.

The road to the mine is closed, and the site is on private property. During the 1960s, author-historian Robert Ormes, in his search for abandoned railroad grades, ventured to the town site and reported that no structures remain.

Another coal deposit just south of Perins Peak along Lightner Creek was developed by the Porter Coal Company in 1890, with John Porter its owner. The small coal mining community near the mine was called Porter. John Porter was vice-president of the Denver & Rio Grande and was instrumental in developing Durango's smelting industry.

The mine portal was located along the tracks of the Rio

Grande Southern and was served by a spur. The specific location was at the mouth of Wildcat Creek about 5 miles west of Durango. A 2,000-foot tunnel reached the seam. The company constructed a boarding house. There was also a general merchandise store and several homes. The population of Porter varied with mine production from 50 to 144.

The Porter Coal Company was sold in 1906 to the Union Pacific Coal Company, a subsidiary of the Union Pacific Railroad. Just 2 years later, the coal seam was exhausted, and the mine closed.

Winter on the Rio Grande Southern. *(Benjamin Jessen)*

Duane A. Smith, *Rocky Mountain Boom Town*, Pruett Publishing Company, Boulder, Colorado, 1980, pp. 26-30, 77, 106, 131, 133, 194.

Robert M. Ormes, *Tracking Ghost Railroads in Colorado*, Century One Press, Colorado Springs, Colorado, 1975, pp. 129, 133, 136.

Tiv Wilkins, *Colorado Railroads*, Pruett Publishing Company, Boulder, Colorado, 1974, pp. 131, 214.

William H. Bauer, James L. Ozment and John H. Willard, *Colorado Post Offices*, Colorado Railroad Museum, Golden, Colorado, 1990, pp. 112, 116.

AREA NINETEEN 19

Las Animas and Huerfano Counties

continued

AREA 19: Las Animas and Huerfano Counties
Selected Towns

Introduction to Las Animas and Huerfano Counties

The vast area encompassing Las Animas and Huerfano Counties contains many abandoned coal-mining towns. Most of these sites have no structures as the practice of the coal companies was to sell structures in place, to be either moved or razed. Coal deposits extend northwest from Walsenburg along the base of the Wet Mountains. Other deposits follow a north-to-south line from Walsenburg through Trinidad south to Raton Pass. From Trinidad, coal deposits also extend west to the base of the Sangre de Cristo Mountains and the Culebra Range.

The dominant coal company in the area was Colorado Fuel & Iron (C.F.& I.), and the company built many of the towns on its land. Other coal companies included the Victor-American Coal Company, the Rocky Mountain Fuel Company and the Alamo Coal Company.

Colorado Fuel & Iron Company

Heavy industry came to Colorado during the late 1800s, when coal mining, steel production and railroads combined to form Colorado Fuel & Iron. Although Colorado's vast coal deposits had been known for some time, the arrival of General

William Palmer's Denver & Rio Grande Railroad into the southern part of the state started the age of coal mining in 1871. In that year the railroad constructed 75.5 miles of light narrow gauge track from Denver to Colorado Springs, and during the following year, continued laying track south to Pueblo. The railroad built a branch 35 miles west to Florence to tap the coal seams at Coal Creek. In 1873, 13,000 tons of coal were

Colorado, Fuel & Iron operated an enormous steel mill south of Pueblo at Minnequa. Nearly all of the coal and coke produced at its many mines was shipped here. Work was dirty and hard. Air quality around the mill was poor. Note the man on the right missing a leg. *(Kenneth Jessen collection CP092)*

The type of dwelling in the background C.F.& I. used as an example of unsanitary conditions. The company desired to have all of its employees in its coal camps or quarry towns live in neat rows of company-built cottages. *(U.S.G.S. W.T. Lee 618)*

removed from the Coal Creek area, and the railroad used much of it to fuel its fleet of steam locomotives. In 1876, the rails reached the coalfields at El Moro, 5 miles north of Trinidad.

The heavy demand for steel rail, combined with the cost of shipping rail from distant steel mills, prompted Palmer to construct a steel mill on the south side of Pueblo. The mill opened in 1879 and operated under the name Colorado Coal & Iron Company. From its very start, the company owned well over 10,000 acres of coal-bearing deposits in Las Animas, Huerfano and Fremont counties. By 1880, Colorado Coal & Iron accounted for half of the coal removed in Colorado.

A similar company, called the Colorado Fuel Company, had been founded by John C. Osgood. It owned 5,500 acres of coal deposits in Las Animas County, with its largest mine at Sopris, west of Trinidad. The two companies merged in 1892 to form the Colorado Fuel & Iron Company (C.F.& I.) with Osgood the chairman of the board of directors and J. A. Kebler president. This company would dominate Colorado industry for decades and become the state's largest employer.

Raw materials for making steel, including iron ore from Calumet and Orient, were available within the Rocky Mountain states. An additional deposit was located at Sunrise, Wyoming. Calcite, used for flux, came from a deposit south of Howard, and limestone was readily available near Pueblo and Cañon City as well as Monarch, west of Salida. Coal mines were spread throughout the southern part of Colorado and northern New Mexico. Much of the coal was converted into coke for use in blast furnaces. Coal also was needed to fuel the boilers at the steel mill.

Under Osgood's leadership, C.F.& I. expanded rapidly, using 3.75 million tons of coal a year. Its steel mill south of Pueblo was named Minnequa Works. By the early 1900s, C.F.& I. grew to employ 15,000 people in four western states. It was by far the largest industry in Colorado, but it grew faster than its financial resources. In 1903, C.F.& I.'s original managers relinquished control to John D. Rockefeller, Jr. and a group of his investors.

Because many of C.F.& I.'s resources were in remote locations far from population centers, the company had to establish towns near its coal mines, limestone deposits, calcite quarries and iron ore mines. In 1900, it embarked on an aggressive task of constructing towns and enhancing other towns that predated the company. In all, C.F.& I. either owned or controlled thirty-eight towns, of which thirty-two were located in Colorado.

Labor problems in the form of strikes slowed the company's progress in the years prior to World War I, notably in 1903-1904 and again in 1913-1914. As the unions began to take hold, wages rose and hours worked per miner declined. This drove up the cost of making steel. When the coal deposits were nearly exhausted or the cost of pumping water out of the mines made further production uneconomical, the company lost its dominant position. After World War II, C.F.& I. started to decline, and by the 1950s, most of its towns were no more than rows of empty foundations.

Colorado & Wyoming Railway

To be able to transport coal and coke from the many mines that C.F.& I. owned, the company had to construct several railroads, all operating under the Colorado & Wyoming Railway name. Where use of existing rail lines was possible, the company did so, but much of the region was without rail transportation.

The Colorado & Wyoming was divided into three divisions. The Northern Division, completed in 1900, was standard gauge, constructed to iron mines at Sunrise, Wyoming.

The Middle Division handled all of the switching at the Minnequa plant south of Pueblo on both standard and narrow gauge tracks. The track in and around the mill totaled more than 100 miles. During the mill's peak years, this division employed 200 men and moved 12,000 cars every month.

The Southern Division was standard gauge and was constructed in stages, beginning in 1902 from Jansen, 2 miles west of Trinidad, up the Purgatoire River 31 miles to Tercio. It was later extended another 2 miles to Cuatro. Another 3-mile branch ran from Segundo to Primero. Passenger service was provided daily,

A Colorado & Wyoming passenger train is readied for departure from Jansen for the coal camps along the Purgatoire River. *(Kenneth Jessen collection CP083)*

serving the coal mining towns en route. This branch had exchange tracks in Jansen with the Atchison, Topeka & Santa Fe and in Trinidad with the Denver & Rio Grande. The Southern Division moved 10,000 cars each month and employed 260 men.

The Colorado & Wyoming also had a detached branch, 1.76 miles long, to the mine at Hezron with a connection to the Denver & Rio Grande. At first, the Colorado & Wyoming operated this branch, but later, operations were turned over to the Denver & Rio Grande.

The railroad owned twenty-nine standard gauge locomotives plus eighteen narrow gauge locomotives. In addition, it had 470 cars, 300 of which were Ingoldsby dump cars for coal and iron ore.

The Colorado & Wyoming maintained its shops at Jansen, and C.F.& I. constructed nice cottages for railroad employees. Jansen got its own post office in 1902. Today the town is not abandoned, and many of the original cottages remain in use.

The Colorado & Wyoming located its shops and car repair facilities at Jansen, just west of Trinidad. *(Kenneth Jessen collection CP085)*

Social Betterment

Colorado Fuel & Iron recognized early on that it could obtain higher productivity if its workers and their families were happy. For this reason, it placed employee welfare under the Sociological Department. Some historians have viewed the activities of the Sociological Department as social manipulation rather than placing the needs of its employees first.

The coal miner lived a difficult life consisting of long hours underground in a dangerous, wet environment. Injuries were frequent leaving many miners crippled for life. No matter how much they bathed, a miner was never able to remove all of the coal dust from a day's work. Worst yet, the coal dust dramatically reduced their life span, and many died from black lung disease. Miners dressed in coveralls, carried a lunch pail and wore a cap or hardhat with lantern clip on the front. Due to explosive methane gas, miners used electric headlamps and were not allowed to smoke.

The hundreds of coke ovens released sulfur smoke into the air day and night. On an overcast winter day, air quality was extremely poor. All of the residents of these coal-mining towns were exposed to the smell of the smoldering slack dumps combined with smoke from the coke ovens.

The company recognized the desirability of improving living conditions. As stated by the company, "...the home the miner is able to construct is often inferior." In these older settlements, miners lived in dugouts, sod-covered log cabins, shacks or adobe buildings, and many towns lacked any defined street system, sewers or running water. C.F.& I. made it a point to contrast the privately owned homes to its neat rows of company-built cottages. It made every effort to clean up the older towns through incentives to move into a company cottage.

The company prohibited individuals from constructing their own dwellings on company property. By way of explanation, C.F.& I. said that miners had built on company ground in these older camps to their "old-world ideas of sanitation and beauty."

Beginning with El Moro, C.F.& I. systematically cleaned up the early camps justified by improvements in the general health of its workers.

C.F.& I. designed several standard cottages, with three, four, five and six rooms. Unlike the boxes that other coal companies constructed, these homes had projecting eaves, porches and some ornamentation. Rather than always being painted white, houses were painted a variety of colors. Architectural style also varied. Some houses had full double-hip roofs, others had partial hip roofs and still others had regular sloped roofs. To avoid monotony, houses of contrasting styles were alternated along a street. Most cottages were single-story; however, Spring Gulch had two-story company houses. Many houses were surrounded by picket fences. Domestic water was supplied to each home, and most towns had a sewage system. The 15,000 company employees accounted for a total-family population of about 60,000, many of whom lived in company houses.

The company also maintained branch health-care facilities, and most towns had their own physician. In 1902, the Minnequa Hospital opened in Pueblo to treat serious injuries and provide long-term care. Camp physicians not only treated diseases and injuries, but also were in charge of the town's sanitation.

C.F.& I. developed an extensive circulating library system for the camps in which a case of new books was sent from one camp to the next. This was complemented by a permanent library at many locations. The notion of a circulating library led to a circulating art show. C.F.& I. added traveling teachers to cover training in sewing and cooking and opened a trade school in Pueblo for C.F.& I. employees.

The Sociological Department developed a complete school system, covering kindergarten and grade school. The company hired teachers and constructed schoolhouses. Under the uniform course of studies, if a coal miner had to transfer to another town, his children could pick up immediately with their lessons.

To provide a forum for its policies, the company had a

C.F.& I. constructed this neat row of cottages at Jansen for its Colorado & Wyoming employees. *(Kenneth Jessen collection CP084)*

weekly magazine called *Camp and Plant,* which covered the history of many of the towns as well as items of local interest. Some of the articles were reproduced in Spanish, Italian and German to reach the company's ethnic groups.

John C. Osgood, chairman of the board of directors, knew of the propensity of many coal miners to find recreation in the form of drinking in local saloons. "Closed" company towns (where the company owned all of the land), allowed no saloons. Instead, the company constructed clubhouses where alcohol was restricted and other activities were emphasized. The most elaborate clubhouse was the two-story stone Redstone Club in Redstone. Other clubhouses included Harmony Hall in Starkville, the Primero Club in Primero, the Floresta Club in Floresta and the Sociological Hall in Sunrise, Wyoming.

Miners were paid in scrip rather than cash, and the chain of thirty Colorado Supply Company stores located in most camps took the scrip for groceries. If an independent store took scrip, when the store cashed the scrip, the company would discount it. Some of the Colorado Supply Company stores were quite elaborate, and each one was quite different. This business employed 322 people.

There isn't any doubt that miners had far better living conditions in a C.F.& I. town than in towns run by competing coal companies.

Jansen is an occupied town today, but does have a number of abandoned structures including this old adobe two-story building. *(Kenneth Jessen 125B5)*

Camp and Plant, Colorado Fuel & Iron, Pueblo, Colorado, Volume I, No. 12, March 1, 1902, pp. 177-182.

Camp and Plant, Colorado Fuel & Iron, Pueblo, Colorado, Volume III, No. 7, February 18, 1903, pp. 145-149.

Camp and Plant, Colorado Fuel & Iron, Pueblo, Colorado, Volume III, No. 23, June 13, 1903, pp. 575-578.

Camp and Plant, Colorado Fuel & Iron, Pueblo, Colorado, Volume IV, No. 19, November 21, 1903, pp. 437-447

H. Lee Scamehorn, *Pioneer Steel Maker in the West,* Pruett Publishing Company, Boulder, Colorado, 1976.

Interview with Al Vigil, Loveland, Colorado, December 15, 2000.

Rick J. Clyne, *Coal People, Colorado History No. 3,* Colorado Historical Society, Denver, 1999, pp. 4-7.

Tiv Wilkins, *Colorado Railroads,* Pruett Publishing Company, Boulder, Colorado, 1974, pp. 7, 14.

William H. Bauer, James L. Ozment and John H. Willard, *Colorado Post Offices,* Colorado Railroad Museum, Golden, Colorado, 1990, p. 79.

ALAMO, TIOGA, STRONG, DELCARBON, CALUMET, GORDON and MORNING GLORY

- *Huerfano County, Ojo de Alamo Arroyo drainage and others*
- *Accessible via paved and graded dirt roads*
- *Most towns had a post office; some structures remain*

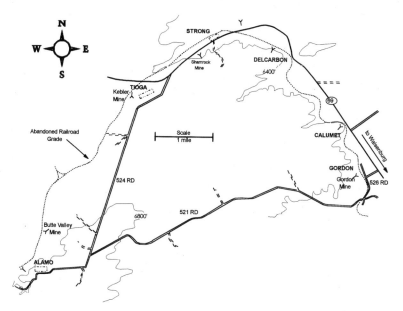

Small mining communities were spread out northwest of Walsenburg along the region's coal deposits. Although some of the sites are accessible, most are on private property.

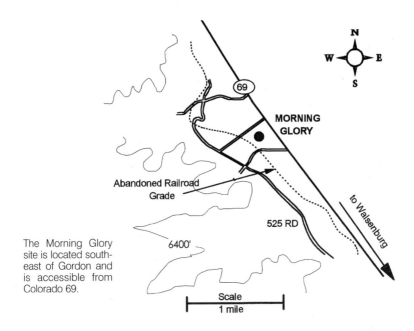

The Morning Glory site is located southeast of Gordon and is accessible from Colorado 69.

The Loma Branch of the Denver & Rio Grande served a number of coal mines and coal mining communities northwest of Walsenburg. The deposits were roughly in the pattern of an inverted "J." Today, Colorado 69 parallels part of the route to these towns.

Starting 10 miles west of Walsenburg, the Alamo Coal Company established the most isolated of these towns, Alamo. Founded in 1923, Alamo got a post office that same year. The site overlooks the entrance to the Wet Mountain Valley and the Sangre de Cristo Mountains. A modern home sits among the ruins of a two-story building, which was possibly a school or a store. The mine and the railroad grade are to the west of the town site at the base of a small hill.

Nearly two-dozen concrete foundations are arranged in neat rows at Alamo. Unfortunately, little history can be found on the town's size or facilities. In 1938, the name of the town was changed to Butte Valley, and its post office continued to operate for eleven more years. Eventually the site was abandoned.

North of Alamo and just south of Colorado 69 is Tioga. The town was founded in 1907, the same year it got its own post office. All of its buildings are gone and only foundations remain, but its main east-west street is defined by a row of trees. Tioga had probably twenty or more structures, and private property limits exploration today. Behind the town is the large coal dump from the Kebler Mine, where a mobile home sits today. The town was abandoned in 1954.

A mile to the east along Colorado 69 is the site of Strong, founded in 1905. Rows of foundations remain, but it is difficult to determine the town's original size. Again, private property limits exploration. Strong's post office lasted until 1929 when the town was abandoned.

A mile and a half to the east was Delcarbon, founded in 1915. This town, too, had its own post office. Today the site is marked by a row of concrete foundations. Its post office closed in

Rows of concrete foundations is all that remains of Alamo. It was the most recent of the towns in this area and was founded in 1923. *(Kenneth Jessen 108B7)*

This is the only remaining structure at Calumet, northwest of Walsenburg along Colorado 69. Founded in 1904, Calumet was one of the few towns in this area that did not have a post office. *(Kenneth Jessen 108B9)*

1953 when the town was abandoned.

One structure remains along Colorado 69 at Calumet, southeast of Delcarbon. Calumet was founded in 1904 and did not have a post office. Nearby is the Calumet Mine.

At Gordon, the mine office building remains standing. The Denver & Rio Grande had several sidings for loading coal cars from the Gordon Mine.

A town called McGuire was established near Gordon in 1905. In 1911, the name of the town was changed to Camp Shumway. In 1924, the post office at Camp Shumway was moved to Gordon. When the mine closed at Gordon in 1937, the town was abandoned. The rails of the Loma Branch of the Denver & Rio Grande were not removed until 1968, well after the coal mines had closed.

A small community called Morning Glory developed near Walsenburg. Its children went to school in Walsenburg, but other details are unknown.

Robert Ormes, *Tracking Ghost Railroads in Colorado*, Century One Press, Colorado Springs, 1975, pp. 34, 36.

William H. Bauer, James L. Ozment and John H. Willard, *Colorado Post Offices,* Colorado Railroad Museum, Golden, Colorado, 1990, pp. 28, 43, 46, 64, 141.

BADITO

Once Huerfano County Seat

- *Huerfano County, Huerfano River drainage*
- *Accessible via paved road*
- *Town had a post office; several structures remain*

This old barn is one of the ruins at Badito. The small community was once the Huerfano County seat and had a post office. *(Kenneth Jessen 108B11)*

Based on the physical evidence at this abandoned site, it is hard to believe that is once was home to ninety people. Badito began as a trading post along the trail leading into the San Luis Valley. The trail crossed the Huerfano River at Badito and ran southwest along Oak Creek then over the Sangre de Cristo Mountains near North La Veta Pass. Badito also supported a tavern and blacksmith shop.

Under the name Little Orphan, a post office opened in 1865. Just months later, the name was changed to Badito, and the post office remained in operation until 1910.

Huerfano County is one of Colorado's seventeen original counties. In 1868 prior to Colorado statehood, Badito was made the Huerfano County seat. The county seat was then moved to Walsenburg in 1874, coincident with the development of the coal mining industry.

As the region's economic center shifted and the trade route changed, Badito was abandoned. Unfortunately, little else is known about life in this small community.

Badito is easy to find. It is located at the southern end of the Wet Mountains along Colorado 69 near its intersection with 520 RD. The site is below the paved road and is accessible via a short side road. A historical marker provides some of the town's history.

George A. Crofutt, *Crofutt's Grip-Sack Guide of Colorado*, 1885 Edition, Johnson Books, Boulder, Colorado, reprint 1981, p. 69.

Lillian Brigham, *Colorado Travelore*, self-published, 1938, p. 57.

Thomas Noel, Paul Mahoney and Richard Stevens, *Historical Atlas of Colorado*, University of Oklahoma Press, Norman, Oklahoma, 1994, Section 17.

William H. Bauer, James L. Ozment and John H. Willard, *Colorado Post Offices*, Colorado Railroad Museum, Golden, Colorado, 1990, pp. 16, 89.

COKEDALE and BONCARBO

One Surviving Town

- *Las Animas County, Reilly Canyon drainage*
- *Accessible via graded dirt road; site occupied*
- *Town has a post office; many original structures remain*

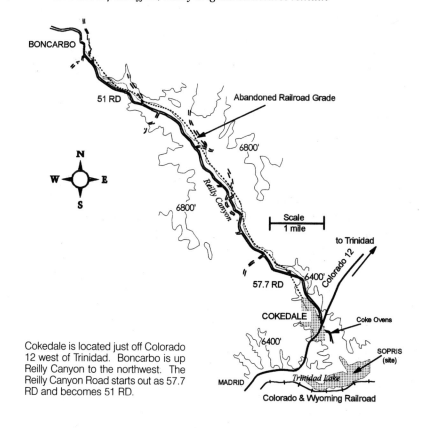

Cokedale is located just off Colorado 12 west of Trinidad. Boncarbo is up Reilly Canyon to the northwest. The Reilly Canyon Road starts out as 57.7 RD and becomes 51 RD.

Colorado Fuel & Iron founded Cokedale in 1906 as a company town, and it got its own post office this same year. To elevate the substandard living conditions so typical of other coal mining towns, C.F.& I. set out to create a model community with comfortable homes and good facilities.

C.F.& I. needed a reliable supply of coke for its steel mill, and the company purchased many coal deposits in Colorado. Reilly Canyon, west of Trinidad, was among the sites.

The company town that developed at the mouth of Reilly Canyon was originally called Reilly Canyon, then the name was changed to Cokedale. The first permanent structure was the mine office. Initially, the residents lived in tents, but soon C.F.& I. invested $1 million to create this substantial town. Buildings consisted of a hotel, shops, houses, a store, a school, a saloon and

The Cokedale coke ovens are just outside of town. *(Kenneth Jessen 107D10)*

bathhouses. The main ethnic groups to move to town were Italians and Germans. In 1907, coke ovens were constructed to the south of town and eventually numbered 350. These long, curved rows of ovens remain today and are some of the best-preserved ovens in the West.

By 1909, the population of Cokedale had reached 1,500. Output of the local mine was 1,500 tons of coal per day, most of which was converted to coke. Output from the coke ovens reached 800 tons per day.

An event on February 9, 1911, attested to the fact that coal mining is a hazardous occupation. An explosion killed seventeen miners, including two men sent in to rescue the others.

World War I increased the demand for copper, lead and zinc, and with it, the demand for coke used in the smelting process. So important was the coke industry that young males of draft age working in the mines or at the coke ovens were granted deferments. After the war, C.F.& I. sold its Cokedale operation to the American Smelting & Refining Company.

In 1917, the mine at Cokedale was running out of coal and the company purchased a second mine from the Thompson-Mitchell Coal Company in Boncarbo (also spelled Bon Carbo). After the American Smelting & Refining Company bought the mine, the company paid the Denver & Rio Grande to build a 7.2-mile-long rail spur up Reilly Canyon. The title to this spur was conveyed to the Denver & Rio Grande in 1929.

This mine produced for another 30 years. Some of the unoccupied homes in Cokedale were moved to Boncarbo for miners who wanted to live near work. Others elected to commute from Cokedale via the railroad.

The best times for Cokedale were probably during the 1920s when business was booming. After the Great Depression beginning in 1929, the demand for coke dipped sharply with an overall decrease in industrial output throughout the United States. Operations at Cokedale were cut, and at one point, the men worked only one day a week. Some families could not afford their

Miners living at Cokedale once used this structure as a dormitory. Among other things, the building now houses a mining museum. *(Kenneth Jessen 125B7)*

rent, and in these cases, the company simply overlooked rent payments. In addition, the company provided for those that ran out of food. The company built a nine-hole golf course for employees to fill their many idle hours and started a community garden to help supply food to those in need. Some families picked pinon nuts to sell and raised chickens or rabbits.

After the start of World War II, recovery followed, but eventually the cost of mining became too high. Operations at Cokedale and at Boncarbo came to a halt in 1947. All of the property, including the homes of miners who lived in Cokedale, was sold to the Florence Machinery Company in Denver.

Faced with the prospect of becoming one of Colorado's many ghost towns, the residents banded together to purchase the town. The company put up seventy-two homes for sale. The cost for a house was $100 per room plus $50 for the lot. These prices were unbeatable, and the typical Cokedale home sold for $450. The only disadvantage was the lack of indoor plumbing, which caused the homes to be dubbed "four rooms with a path," referring to the outhouse out back!

Today, Cokedale stands as one of the best-preserved coal mining communities in the West. Many original buildings are still standing, and the mature trees now provide shade over the town's narrow streets.

Located up Reilly Canyon on 51 RD (which starts out as 57.7 RD), the small mining town of Boncarbo is marked by its large tailing pile. Several families still live in Boncarbo, and it has a small store and post office, the latter of which opened in 1917 when mining operations began. After the Boncarbo Mine closed in 1947, most of its structures were either moved or razed.

Boncarbo, located up Reilly Canyon above Cokedale, has a combination store and post office as well as some homes. *(Kenneth Jessen 107D11)*

"When Perfectly Good Homes Sell..." *Rocky Mountain Empire Magazine*, May 23, 1948, p. 4.

The Chronicle-News (Trinidad), February 10, 1911, p. 1.

Holly Barton, *Cokedale: 1907-1947* (publisher unknown)

Rick J. Clyne, *Coal People*, Colorado History No. 3, Colorado Historical Society, Denver, 1999, p. 100.

Tiv Wilkins, *Colorado Railroads*, Pruett Publishing Company, Boulder, Colorado, 1974, pp. 200, 249.

William H. Bauer, James L. Ozment and John H. Willard, *Colorado Post Offices*, Colorado Railroad Museum, Golden, Colorado, 1990, pp. 22, 35.

EL MORO, ENGLEVILLE and GRAYCREEK

Trinidad Area Coal Towns

- *Las Animas County, Purgatoire River drainage*
- *Accessible via graded dirt road*
- *One site has a post office; no structures remain*

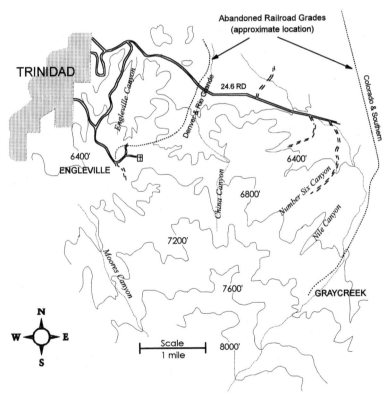

Engleville is located southeast of Trinidad. A number of structures remain, but the site is on private property. Graycreek is in a relatively remote area and also on private property.

In its push south through Colorado, the Denver & Rio Grande reached the El Moro site in 1876. It incorporated the El Moro Railway Company in 1877 to serve new coal deposits in the Trinidad area. The town of El Moro is located about 3.5 miles northeast of Trinidad close to the Purgatoire River and 1.5 miles east of I-25. El Moro began as the terminus for the railroad and was the primary supply point for the southern portion of Colorado and northern New Mexico. It remained the southern terminus for 6 years before the railroad continued its construction south.

About a half-mile south of El Moro, the Colorado Coal & Iron Company constructed six coke ovens, the first ovens in the southern part of the state. They were successful right from the start. In 1879, the company added 200 more ovens, with civil engineer George Engle in charge of construction. Coal to fuel the ovens came from the mines at Engleville. The number of ovens grew to more than 350, and the coke was sent to either the Colorado Fuel & Iron blast furnaces in Pueblo or to smelters in Leadville.

To improve the purity of the coke, a washer was constructed in 1880. A brick laboratory housed a chemist to analyze the quality of the coke.

East of Engleville was Graycreek, served by a branch of the Union Pacific Railroad. Originally called Chapel, Graycreek got its own post office in 1894. The town was abandoned around 1927. *(Denver Public Library MCC-3926)*

The El Moro post office opened in 1876, and in 1880 the town's name was changed to "Elmoro." The post office remained active until 1933. In 1902, the 125 employed men and their families lived in thirty-one company-constructed cottages. Mike Nigro operated the camp's store. A single-story brick public school building was constructed overlooking the camp to educate the town's forty school-age children. El Moro also had a kindergarten.

Located along Colorado 239, El Moro is far from abandoned today. Its homes are scattered over an open rise, and the old railroad grade is evident. A large, stone schoolhouse is now home to one family. A marker at El Moro notes that the Santa Fe Trail passed through the site.

Located 5 miles south of El Moro and southeast of Trinidad was Engleville (also called Engle), one of the oldest coal camps in the area. It lay in a shallow valley where row upon row of company houses was built. Employment grew to more than 400 men. Originally, the Colorado Coal & Iron Company owned the town

The coke ovens at El Moro are shown on the right with men sitting on a Larry car used to deliver coal to an opening in the top of each oven. The large washer and screening plant is in the background, and a cattle car sits on the tracks of the Denver & Rio Grande on the left. *(Denver Public Library Z-221)*

and the mine. In 1892, this company was consolidated into Colorado Fuel & Iron.

The town was named for George Engle, first superintendent of the mines. The mines consisted of the Little Giant, Rope Road, Straight and Riffenburg. Total output was 1,200 tons a day, making it one of C.F.& I.'s highest producing coal mine groups.

Various support buildings near the mines included a compressor house, blacksmith shop and machine shop. The stable, one of the structures moved from "old" Rouse to Engle, could hold twenty-two mules and horses.

A number of abandoned structures at Engleville are on private property. Permission from the property owner is necessary to visit these structures. *(Kenneth Jessen 125B2)*

Camp and Plant tallied the ethnic groups at Engle. The highest percentage was Italian, followed by Mexican. There were also a number of Slavic people and those from Britain. Few were born in the United States. Even though the total population of Engle in 1902 was estimated at 1,000, the town did not have its own post office. Mail was delivered from Trinidad. John Tarabino operated an independent store and a large saloon next to the store. He also acted as a bank, exchanging company scrip for cash.

Fraternal organizations included the Knights of Pythias and the Red Men. Engle also had an active Ladies' Benevolent Society. A library and reading room were located in a company house, which C.F.& I. remodeled for that purpose. The town also had a two-story brick schoolhouse serving thirty-five students.

Engleville is located on private property, and the landowner has to give permission to visit the site. The landowner lives in a

The general merchandise store and saloon in Engleville, owned by John Tarabino. *(Kenneth Jessen collection CP031)*

ranch at the north end of the site. A variety of original homes remain standing in Engleville, making this one of the most interesting of the abandoned coal camps.

East of Engleville was Graycreek (also written as Gray Creek), another coal mining town. A subsidiary of the Union Pacific constructed a branch to the Graycreek Mine in 1888. The town, originally called Chapel, got its own post office in 1894. The name was changed to Graycreek in 1895, and the post office remained in operation for another 26 years. The Victor-American Fuel Company operated the mine. The town was abandoned around 1927, and the railroad dismantled. Private property restricts access to the site, so it is not known if any structures remain.

Camp and Plant, Volume I, Number 23, C.F.& I., Pueblo, Colorado, May 17, 1902, pp. 409-412.

Camp and Plant, Volume I, Number 25, C.F.& I., Pueblo, Colorado, May 31, 1902, pp. 457-461.

M. Beshoar, M.D. *All About Trinidad and Las Animas County,* Colorado, Times Steam Printing, 1882, pp. 60-63.

William H. Bauer, James L. Ozment and John H. Willard, *Colorado Post Offices,* Colorado Railroad Museum, Golden, Colorado, 1990, pp. 32, 51, 65.

FORBES, MAJESTIC, RUGBY, KENNETH, RAPSON and IDEAL

- *Las Animas and Huerfano counties, various drainages*
- *Some sites are accessible; others are on private property*
- *Some towns had a post office; remaining structures unknown*

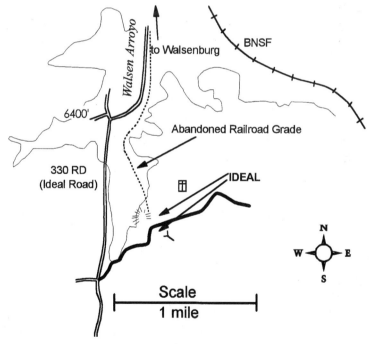

Ideal is south of Walsenburg and east of 330 RD (Ideal Road). A rough paved road runs northeast through the site, which has many old concrete foundations.

Unfortunately, little is known about many of the small, southern Colorado coal-mining towns. Even finding them can be confusing. Forbes, for example, is shown on some maps where 42 RD crosses under the BNSF (Burlington Northern Santa Fe) tracks west of I-25. The town site is actually up Forbes Canyon (also called Tingley Canyon). A railroad was built up to the town and the mine in 1889, and the rails remained in place until 1932. Operated as the Chicosa Canyon Railroad, it eventually became part of the Colorado & Southern (now the BNSF).

Forbes got its own post office in 1889, the year the town was founded. It closed in 1896 as mining activity dropped, but reopened in 1905 and remained open until 1929.

Located north of Forbes was the town of Majestic, in Chicosa Canyon. A branch of the same railroad that ran to Forbes was built to Majestic in 1900. The Majestic Mine was located to the south and high above the town. A cable tram brought the coal down to the tipple. The mine, post office and town lasted from 1900 to 1914.

North of Aguilar, but still within Las Animas County, was a group of coal mining communities including Rugby. Rugby had a post office that operated from 1879 to 1880, and again from 1893 to 1895. Its two-story brick store remains standing on the west

The Rocky Mountain Fuel Company once owned the mines at Forbes. This photograph of the town possibly was taken during the 1913-1914 coal miner's strike. *(Denver Public Library x-61181)*

side of I-25 near the rest area. The store is on private property and is part of a ranch. Immediately to the south of Rugby was Kenneth. A rail spur came in from the east, turned at Rugby and terminated at Kenneth. Nothing remains at the Kenneth site.

The Ideal site has rows of foundations, including this ruin of a relatively large building. *(Kenneth Jessen 126D30)*

On another rail spur and also to the south of Rugby was Rapson. The Rapson post office operated intermittently from 1911 to 1934, in keeping with fluctuations in the town's population. The road into Rapson is closed, and the site is on private property, limiting exploration.

In Huerfano County north of "old" Rouse was the town of Ideal, in Ideal Canyon. The post office opened in 1910 and remained open until 1929, when the Ideal Mine closed. Colorado Fuel & Iron purchased the mine in 1912. Extensive ruins and foundations mark the site, which can be seen to the south of Ideal Road (330 RD). A rough paved road passes directly through the site. The railroad grade leading to Ideal is also evident.

H. Lee Scamehorn, *Pioneer Steel Maker in the West*, Pruett Publishing Company, Boulder, Colorado, 1976, p. 169.

Robert Ormes, *Tracking Ghost Railroads in Colorado*, Century One Press, Colorado Springs, Colorado, 1975, p. 39.

Rick J. Clyne, *Coal People, Colorado History No. 3*, Colorado Historical Society, Denver, 1999, p. 16.

William H. Bauer, James L. Ozment and John H. Willard, *Colorado Post Offices*, Colorado Railroad Museum, Golden, Colorado, 1990, pp. 54, 77, 93, 119, 125.

HASTINGS and DELAGUA

Victor-American Fuel Company Towns

- *Las Animas County, Delagua Creek drainage*
- *Accessible via graded dirt road*
- *Towns had post offices; no standing structures remain*

A 1914 photograph shows the Victor-American Fuel Company's screening plant and trestle at Hastings. The false-front building to the left center foreground is the Charles Niccoli Saloon. Nothing remains of these structures. *(Denver Public Library MCC-4296)*

Hastings first appeared in the *Colorado State Business Directory* in 1890 with a listed population of twenty. Its post office had opened the year before. By 1893, the population of Hastings had grown to fifty and the town had seven businesses, among them the Hastings Hotel, a butcher shop and the grocery store of P. H. Bocco & Company. The Niccoli brothers operated the town's saloon.

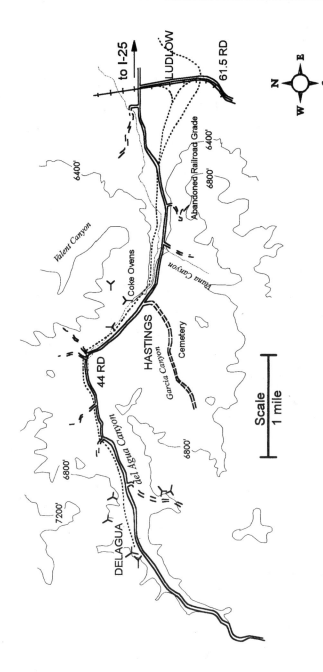

The Hastings and Delagua town sites are located wes t of Ludlow along 44 RD, a graded dirt road.

To serve the Victor-American Fuel Company mines at Hastings, a railroad was constructed up Canyon del Agua in 1888. It was extended to the mines at Delagua in 1903. Built under the name Cañon D'Agua Railroad, the railroad became part of a Union Pacific subsidiary. In 1899, its ownership passed to the Colorado & Southern.

Stimulated by the railroad and increased coal production, the population of Hastings jumped to an incredible 1,500 by 1894. At this time, the town had its own government including a mayor and a city clerk. The railroad had an agent living in town, and the following year Hastings had a physician. Then coal production dropped and so did the town's population. By 1898, Hastings had a population of 1,000, and 2 years later, it had fallen to 600.

Most noted in the history of Hastings was a mine explosion in 1917. A monument at the town site on the south side of 44 RD recalls this tragedy.

On the morning of April 27, the mine had been inspected, including the large fan that circulated fresh air through the passages. At around 9 a.m., a string of empty coal cars was descending the slope into the mine. The cars stopped unexpectedly, and the man riding the cars got off to see what happened. He first smelled smoke, then saw a cloud of black smoke rising toward him from the depths of the mine. He ran as fast as he could up the incline to the surface and sounded the alarm as the smoke poured out of the mine portal.

Rescue efforts had to wait until the smoke cleared. After 30 hours, the first dead miner was brought up. The bodies had been burned, indicating a methane gas explosion. Near the center of the explosion, the miners had been dismembered and one man had been blown in half.

As the days passed, it became clear that all 121 men working in the mine that day had been killed. After 7 months, bodies were still being brought to the surface, and it is likely that not all were recovered. After the explosion, coal production was erratic, and the mine was abandoned and sealed off in 1923. A few individuals continued to live in the town for a number of years.

Hastings is located in Canyon del Agua at the mouth of Garcia Canyon. Although no structures remain at the site, it is immediately recognizable by the long double row of coke ovens in a meadow on the north side of the road. A few ruins are partially standing in the trees on the south side of the road, but this area is fenced off. The Hastings cemetery is up Garcia Canyon.

Delagua, located about 3 miles west of Hastings, was founded in 1903. Its post office opened this same year and remained open until 1954, serving area ranchers, as mining activity had all but ceased by this time. The railroad grade ends at the mines at the Delagua site. Little is left of the town itself, making estimates of its size difficult. A mountain property development limits exploration.

The two-story Longfellow schoolhouse in Delagua was constructed in 1906. *(Denver Public Library MCC-3925)*

Francis B. Rizzari, "When Hastings, Colorado Counted Their Dead," *Brand Book 1968*, Volume 24, The Denver Westerners, Denver, Colorado, 1969, pp. 67-90.

Robert Ormes, *Tracking Ghost Railroads in Colorado*, Century One Press, Colorado Springs, Colorado, 1975, p. 39

William H. Bauer, James L. Ozment and John H. Willard, *Colorado Post Offices*, Colorado Railroad Museum, Golden, Colorado, 1990, pp. 43, 69.

LIME

And Its Limestone Quarry

- *Pueblo County, St. Charles River drainage*
- *Accessible via graded dirt road*
- *Town had a post office; no structures remain*

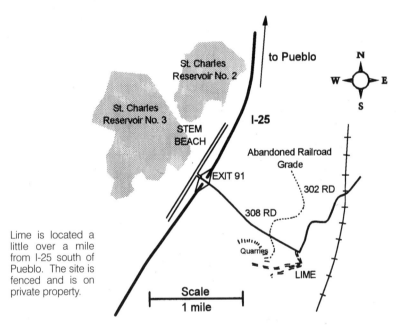

Lime is located a little over a mile from I-25 south of Pueblo. The site is fenced and is on private property.

Contractors Orman and Crook began quarrying limestone at Lime on a lease basis in 1892. Under the ownership of Colorado Coal & Iron Company, the quarries were expanded, and Lime was founded in 1898. The town began with just a boarding-house, stables and a few dwellings. This same year, the town got its own post office, which remained active until 1943 when the quarries were abandoned.

After Colorado Fuel & Iron took ownership, new cottages were added to those originally constructed for the quarry workers. Unlike other C.F.& I. towns, Lime had an independent company store, which was run by Jacketta and Nigro. They also operated the boardinghouse.

The St. Charles River served as the town's source of domestic water. The water was pumped into a storage tank, then distributed by pipes to each cottage. Lime also had a one-room schoolhouse.

The sixty quarry workers at Lime were Italians and Austrians. The work was simple: black powder was used to blast loose the limestone, then the rubble was broken by sledges. The limestone was loaded into pit cars for transportation to the crusher. The rock was reduced to an average size of 2 inches for use in blast furnaces as a flux. The output to feed the C.F.& I. steel mill at Minnequa, just 6 miles to the north, was 600 tons a day. Some uncrushed limestone was sold to the American Smelting and Refining Company's Pueblo plant for use as flux in smelting precious metal ore.

The Lime town site is south of Pueblo and east of I-25. It can be seen from Road 308, but is fenced. Only foundations remain.

These C.F.& I. constructed cottages were built around 1900. Nothing but foundations remain at the site today. *(Kenneth Jessen collection CP201)*

Camp and Plant, Volume II, Number 1, C.F.& I., Pueblo, Colorado, July 5, 1902, pp. 1-3.

William H. Bauer, James L. Ozment and John H. Willard, *Colorado Post Offices,* Colorado Railroad Museum, Golden, Colorado, 1990, p. 89.

LUDLOW

And Its Bloody Massacre

- *Las Animas County, Canyon del Agua drainage*
- *Accessible via graded dirt road*
- *Town had a post office; several structures remain*

A long the dusty main street of Ludlow stand the abandoned remains of several businesses, and to the south are a couple of abandoned frame homes. This is all that is left of Ludlow. Were it not the site of a massacre, it would be just another deserted coal mining town. This event took place on April 20, 1914, during a

The monument to the Ludlow Massacre stands at a "T" intersection in view of I-25. *(Kenneth Jessen 107D12)*

bloody miner's strike. At the north end of the Ludlow site is a fenced-in monument to those killed. If ever a Colorado ghost town could be haunted, it would be Ludlow.

The complex set of events leading up to the Ludlow massacre began when miners tried to improve their working conditions. They initiated an unsuccessful strike in 1903-1904, followed by another attempted strike in 1913. Because of the prolonged exposure to coal dust, the life expectancy of a coal miner was 40 years or so. What miners wanted was better compensation for this hazardous work and a reduction in the workday from 10 to 8 hours. The miners also were being cheated in some cases by the "weighmen," who determined how many tons had been mined. These were employees representing the best interest of the company, and the miners wanted them to be replaced by fellow miners. The miners also wanted the right to trade at any store and not to be paid in scrip, which forced them to use company stores.

During the strike, the coal companies evicted the miners and their families from the company-owned cottages. Homeless, many ended up living in a tent city established at Ludlow. Some were forced to live in the open or under their wagons. Families that had tents put wood slabs part way up to provide a little more shelter. They dug pits under the tent floors for storage. With no sanitation or running water, living conditions were horrid. The tent camp's population swelled to more than 1,000 as more miners and their families were evicted. Louis Tikas became the camp leader of the camp having an estimated 275 tents.

Even though few of the striking miners were union members, about 70 percent of the labor force in Southern Colorado were on strike. This amounted to 9,000 miners in the Trinidad-Walsenburg area.

The mine owners hired guards, who were backed by local deputies. Joining this armed force were undisciplined militiamen. Some of the mine owners also hired thugs to harass the miners and their families. One such thug was Bob Lee, who picked on the wives until he was stopped by a load of buckshot in his neck.

The violence escalated when mine owners brought in scabs to keep the mines operating. The scabs were housed in the very same cottages where the striking had miners once lived.

Officials used a Colorado Fuel & Iron Company automobile to go on a joy ride to view the misery at Ludlow. The strikers found the car a tempting target and opened fire. Although no one was killed, the Colorado National Guard was summoned.

To further intimidate the miners, the company installed search lights on top of the low foothills around the Ludlow camp. An innocent cowboy out tending his livestock was shot to death. Miners then purchased every available gun in Trinidad.

As the situation grew worse, the sheriff tried to disarm the strikers. This led to a gun battle in which 600 or so shots were fired, killing one miner. During another gun battle, three more miners were killed on the streets of Walsenburg.

The railroad tracks ran through Ludlow, and the little town had its own depot. A train loaded with fifty deputies and a dozen militiamen tried to pass through Ludlow to relieve those under attack at Berwind. The train came up from the south, across the shallow valley where Ludlow was located, and several hundred miners fired on it. During this conflict, two more miners were killed, but the deputies were repelled.

The Colorado National Guard established its own tent camp just 500 yards from Ludlow. Above Ludlow, guardsmen patrolled the tops of the surrounding hills.

On the morning of April 20, officers of the Colorado National Guard came into the Ludlow tent camp to question strikers about a missing man of theirs. A large force of strikers used this opportunity to slip into an arroyo where they opened fire on guardsmen stationed on one of the hills. The guardsmen threw dynamite bombs to alert other guardsmen that they were under attack. The strikers had repeating rifles, where as the guardsmen had single-shot, trapdoor breech Springfield carbines. But, the guardsmen also had machine guns.

As bullets cut through the air, women and children took shelter in pits or fled to the railroad's pump house. By 9:30 a.m., gunfire was widespread as the strikers hid in the arroyo and in latrine pits. The guardsmen fired down into the colony from the raised railroad grade, pouring hundreds of rounds into the pump house and the tents until their ammunition ran low. Inside the tents, bullets shredded the canvas, ricocheted off the iron stoves and shattered the furniture. Anyone out in the open was either

killed or wounded. Meanwhile, more guardsmen were summoned from other camps at Hastings, Berwind and Segundo.

One of the captains brought in fifty men, including some of
the most ruthless strike breakers in the county. A train was com-
mandeered, but the train crew refused to haul men to Ludlow. A
railroad superintendent intervened and got the train moving. At
around 4 p.m., this armed force got off south of Ludlow and forced
the driver of a passing automobile to give up his vehicle. The
armed force took a machine gun to the top of one of the hills surrounding the tent camp. Under the cover of machine gun fire, the
officers ordered the guardsmen to advance on the camp. Bursts of
machine gun fire suppressed any return fire by the miners.

William Snyder had no weapon and remained with his wife
and six children in a pit under their tent. While his 11-year-old
son Frank was getting his baby sister a drink of water, a bullet
blew out his brains. Snyder had time only to fold the dead boy's
arms across his chest before diving back into the pit.

One of several abandoned buildings remains standing at the ghost town of Ludlow.
(Kenneth Jessen 108A1)

Around dusk, guardsmen and militiamen used flaming brooms dipped in coal oil to ignite the tents. At the Pedrogone tent, thirteen women and children suffocated from the smoke.

In the ensuing investigation, the National Guard claimed the tent camp to be empty. They also claimed that bullets striking the stoves had caused the stoves to overturn, igniting the tents. After the fire though, photographs showed that the heavy iron stoves remained standing and eyewitness accounts refuted the National Guard claims.

The massacre at Ludlow had few repercussions. A monument was erected listing the eighteen miners and their families killed in this event. The ages ranged from adults to two children who were less than a year old. In all, twenty strikers and thirteen militiamen were killed during the 14-hour struggle.

Ludlow was a supply center, and the site was not located next to any of the mines. Its post office opened in 1896. Immediately prior to the strike, Ludlow had a population of fifty, and its businesses included two meat markets, a dairy, a book and stationery store, a bakery, a brewery, two grocery stores, a livery barn, five saloons, a blacksmith shop and a boardinghouse. The town wasn't abandoned until the mid-1950s coincident with the closure of mines in the area.

For a map showing the Ludlow site, see "Tabasco, Berwind, Tollerburg, Vallorso and Albertson."

George McGovern and Leonard Guttridge, *The Great Coalfield War*, University of Colorado Press, Niwot, Colorado, 1996, pp. 102-224.

Rick J. Clyne, *Coal People*, Colorado History No. 3, Colorado Historical Society, Denver, 1999, pp. 10-13.

Robert L. Brown, *Colorado Ghost Towns, Past and Present*, Caxton Printers, Caldwell, Idaho, 1977, pp. 169-174.

William H. Bauer, James L. Ozment and John H. Willard, *Colorado Post Offices*, Colorado Railroad Museum, Golden, Colorado, 1990, p. 92.

MORLEY

Its Beautiful Church in Ruins

- *Las Animas County, Raton Creek drainage*
- *Site can be viewed from public road; private property limits exploration*
- *Town had a post office; one partially standing structure remains*

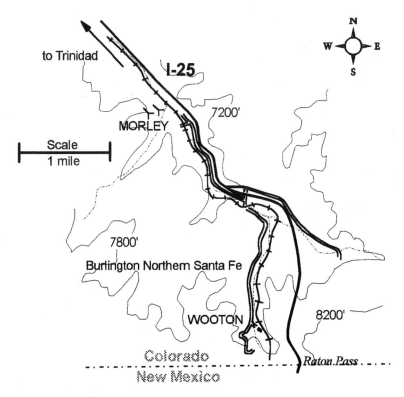

Morley is located just north of the Colorado-New Mexico line along I-25. The ruins of its church can be seen from the interstate.

One of the most picturesque of the ghost town ruins, the St. Aloysius Catholic Church, can be seen from I-25 south of Trinidad at the abandoned coal-mining town of Morley. Morley was a railroad station established in 1878 along the Atchison, Topeka & Santa Fe and had a population of sixty railroad employees. At Morley, heavy trains bound for Raton Pass to the south were divided into two sections for the hard pull. William Raymond Morley, a Santa Fe construction engineer, located the grade over the pass. Although accounts differ as to how the town of Morley got its name, his name is the most likely source.

A post office opened in 1882 and closed later the same year. It opened again in 1884 only to close in 1885. The post office opened for the third time in 1888, and with the exception of two weeks, the Morley post office remained open until 1956.

When Colorado Fuel & Iron shifted from coal suited for conversion to coke to coal for locomotive and domestic use, it opened new mines, including the one at Morley. The Morley Mine began production in 1907, and the east side drift remained in production until 1929. The west side drift continued to produce until 1956. With its closure, the town of Morley died. Capacity of the Morley mine was approximately 1,000 tons a day, with peak production in 1928. At this time, 500 miners were employed at the site, and the town grew on both sides of the railroad tracks.

Morley had more than 100 homes, a clubhouse, a grade school and the St. Aloysius Catholic church overlooking the town. The houses for the miners and their families were identical and were arranged in neat rows sitting on stone foundations, each with its own identical outhouse. The houses were of a C.F.& I. design - square with a window at either side of the front entrance. The back door had a small porch with windows at either side. The chimney came up through the center of the double-hip roof.

Other than the mine buildings, the largest structure in Morley was the Colorado Supply Company store (owned by C.F.& I.), which also included the physician's office. As ghost town historian Bob Brown observed, its appearance suggested that of the Acoma Indian Church in New Mexico. C.F.& I. issued scrip as payment to the miners, which they could exchange for merchandise and groceries at the company store. This was a good arrangement for C.F.& I., whereby the company profited not only through the sale of coal, but also from merchandise sold to its miners. Prices at the company store were generally inflated relative to prices in Trinidad, and many miners traveled there in an effort to save money. Merchants in Trinidad, however, were reluctant to take company scrip in lieu of cash.

Mining at Morley was not highly mechanized because of the danger of methane gas explosions. Most of the operations were done by hand, including extraction of coal from the coal seam, and mules were used to pull coal cars from the working faces within the mine to a collection point. From there, a rope haulage

Only the front and a few feet of the side walls are left of the St. Aloysius Catholic church at the ghost town site of Morley. The church sits on a hill overlooking the town site, and produces curiosity among motorists passing by on I-25. *(Kenneth Jessen 107A8)*

system was used to pull strings of cars out of the mine. No open flames were allowed in this mine. Because of its potential create a spark, all electrical machinery was excluded from the mine.

As time passed, the railroads moved to diesel-electric locomotives and the steel industry purchased less and less coke. The mine was shut down temporarily in 1954 and permanently in 1956. By that time, only twenty families remained. When the mine closed for good, 11 million tons of coal had been removed from the Morley Mine. The few remaining residents moved to either Starkville or Trinidad. C.F.& I. razed or moved the buildings, leaving only foundations. The church was left to deteriorate and eventually collapse.

Morley sits 3 miles north of the New Mexico border and 13 miles south of Trinidad, immediately west of I-25. When headed south on I-25, travelers can use a parking area overlooking the Morley site. Beyond this parking area is an exit and a gravel frontage road. By heading back north, it is possible to get closer to the site. This frontage road parallels I-25 and sits below the interstate. Morley is on private property being developed as mountain ranches. Permission can be obtained to visit the site from the development company.

On the hill overlooking the town is the ruin of the St. Aloysius Catholic Church. Only the front facade remains standing, and what is left of its stucco-covered adobe walls outlines the foundation. Below the church are numerous foundations defining Morley's street system. Some of the eastern portion of the site was covered when I-25 was constructed.

H. Lee Scamehorn, *Pioneer Steel Maker in the West*, Pruett Publishing Company, Boulder, Colorado, 1976, pp. 128-131, p. 169, p. 170.

Interview with Al Vigil, Loveland, Colorado, December 15, 2000.

Rick J. Clyne, *Coal People*, Colorado History No. 3, Colorado Historical Society, Denver, 1999, p. 46.

Robert L. Brown, *Colorado Ghost Towns, Past and Present,* Caxton Printers, Caldwell, Idaho, 1977, pp. 188-192.

Tiv Wilkins, *Colorado Railroads*, Pruett Publishing Company, Boulder, Colorado, 1974, p. 21.

William H. Bauer, James L. Ozment and John H. Willard, *Colorado Post Offices*, Colorado Railroad Museum, Golden, Colorado, 1990, p. 101.

PICTOU

Named for Town in Nova Scotia

- *Huerfano County, Pictou Arroyo drainage*
- *Accessible via graded dirt road; occupied site*
- *Town had a post office; some original structures may remain*

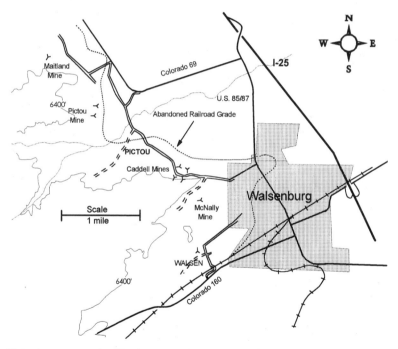

Pictou is easy to reach, either by a secondary road or via Colorado 69 from Walsenburg.

Just 1.5 miles from Walsenburg is another of the many Colorado Fuel & Iron Company towns, Pictou. Founded in 1887, it was supported by several mines including the Caddell, Maintland and Pictou mines. Mine superintendent Thomas Lawther named the place for his hometown of Pictou, in Nova Scotia, Canada. Pictou offers an excellent view of the mountains, and the C.F.& I. publication *Camp and Plant* took advantage of this by giving Pictou the following spin:

> In plain sight of the camp, and even within walking distance, are fine sights and awe-inspiring scenery, with beautiful hills and shady groves, while beyond them, capped by the eternal snow, stand the grandest mountains of Colorado.

The post office opened in 1889 and closed in 1932 when the town's population fell below what was required to maintain a post office. Pictou had seventy cottages, a supervisor's home and two boardinghouses—one for "colored" and the other for "white." Ethnic groups included Italians, Irish, Scottish, Spanish, German, Polish and Russian. Which of these ethnic groups lived in the boardinghouse for "colored" is unclear. Levy opened the first store in Pictou, and in 1890, it was purchased by the Colorado Supply Company to become a company store.

The Pictou Mine had three coal seams up to 6 feet thick. Daily output varied from 500 to 1,000 tons. Some twenty-five mules were used to haul the mine cars to the breaker. For each trip from the mine, a mule pulled nine loaded cars.

In 1890, the Colorado Supply Company purchased what began as an independent store in Pictou. *(Kenneth Jessen collection CP113)*

Pictou was unique in that it was where C.F.& I. had its manufacturing facility for 2-ton mine cars for all of its mines throughout Colorado. This facility could build up to ninety cars a month.

Dr. Baird, the town's doctor, handled the routine health problems of a mining town and monitored the town's sanitary conditions. He designed a schoolhouse that was accepted by C.F.& I. for use in several other company towns. The Pictou schoolhouse was constructed in 1902. The second floor

Deep in the Pictou Mine was this large water pump, driven by an electric motor. Most of the mines in the area required constant pumping to keep them dry. *(Kenneth Jessen collection CP037)*

was divided into two classrooms. Baird's design was flexible in that a partition could be taken down to create one large room for use as an assembly hall.

Although Pictou may have seen its better days, it is not a ghost town. A number of mobile homes plus several frame houses remain on the site. Because private property limits exploration, it is not known if any of Pictou's original structures remain.

Camp and Plant, Colorado Fuel & Iron, Pueblo, Colorado, Volume I, No. 28, June 21, 1902, pp. 529-531.

William H. Bauer, James L. Ozment and John H. Willard, *Colorado Post Offices*, Colorado Railroad Museum, Golden, Colorado, 1990, p. 112.

PRIMERO

One of Colorado Fuel & Iron's Larger Mines

- *Las Animas County, Smith Canyon drainage*
- *No access; private property*
- *Town had a post office; no standing structures*

The lower part of Primero was located in the barren hills west of Trinidad. Note the long trestle in the background, where mine cars could be taken across the valley from the mine opening to the tipple. *(Kenneth Jessen collection CP068)*

North of Segundo was the mining town of Primero. The two towns were connected by a 3.5-mile twisting branch of the Colorado & Wyoming and a wagon road. Primero was 17 miles west of Trinidad.

Founded in 1901, Primero initially was called Smith Canyon, then Purgatoire. In 1902, the town became Primero. Half the output from its coal mine was shipped to the coke ovens at Segundo and the rest to outside markets including railroads. This was a modern mine that used electric locomotives. At its peak, the mine produced 55,000 to 65,000 tons of coal per month making it among C.F.& I.'s largest mines. When the mine at Primero finally closed in 1925, it had yielded 8.2 million tons of coal from its six openings.

The town sat in a shallow valley at the head of Smith Canyon in an arid area void of trees. A creek separated Primero into an upper and a lower town. A reservoir above the town supplied drinking water. The town had at least 100 homes of C.F.& I. design and a handsome two-story railroad depot. Rent was the standard C.F.& I. $2 per room per month. Most of the homes were L-shaped and painted attractive colors - quite different from the uniform white paint applied to dwellings in other coal mining towns.

Primero had a grade school, a high school and even a night school, with highly qualified teachers. The schoolhouse was an imposing two-story structure with four classrooms, a ballroom and a stage. The clubhouse was equipped with billiard and pool tables as well as card tables. The idea was to provide alcohol-free recreation for the miners. The Colorado Supply Company store, owned by C.F.& I., was quite large and took payment in the form

The upper portion of Primero sat at the head of Smith Canyon. After the town was abandoned, all of its buildings were razed or removed. *(Kenneth Jessen collection CP072)*

of scrip issued to the miners for their wages. C.F.& I.'s Sociological Department designated the town as a model community. Of the 600 men who worked at Primero, many were Spanish speaking as well as Italian and Slavic. Primero got its own post office in 1901, which remained open until 1933.

Primero was well connected with the outside world via twice-daily passenger train service to and from Jansen, 15 miles away and just outside of Trinidad. From Jansen, passengers could travel over the Atchison, Topeka & Sante Fe system. Connections also could be made with the Denver & Rio Grande or the Colorado & Southern in Trinidad.

In January 1907, a miner informed his mine supervisor of a dangerous accumulation of coal gas. The miner was ordered back to work and warned not to alarm others. Just as he was collecting his tools, a small explosion took place, leaving the miner permanently injured. Just three days later, a bigger blast killed twenty-four miners. According to safety procedures, the mine was

A dark side of coal mining was the use of children in the mines. These are identified as Italian miners. Note the two small boys in coveralls with faces blackened by coal dust. *(Kenneth Jessen collection CP066)*

The Colorado Supply Company store at Primero was of a Spanish Mission style and measured 44 feet by 135 feet. *(Kenneth Jessen collection CP070)*

supposed to be sprayed periodically to remove coal dust from the air. This was done, however, only when the state mine inspector could be seen coming up the road. In 1910, the Primero Mine exploded again, taking seventy-nine lives. C.F.& I. officials blamed carelessness on the miners' part as the root cause of the problem.

Ghost town historian Bob Brown, who visited Primero during the 1960s, reported that it was difficult to reach. Permission had to be obtained to cross private property. The railroad grade and the old wagon road had long since washed away, forcing Brown to climb down and back up countless gulches for 3 miles one way. Brown discovered that when the mine closed and Primero was abandoned, all of the structures were removed. Nothing but foundations remained at the site.

For a map showing the approximate location of Primero, see "Segundo."

Robert L. Brown, *Colorado Ghost Towns, Past and Present*, Caxton Printers, Caldwell, Idaho, 1977, pp. 211-214.

Camp and Plant, Volume II, No. 17, C.F.& I., Pueblo, Colorado, October 25, 1902, pp. 393-398.

George McGovern and Leonard Guttridge, *The Great Coalfield War*, University Press of Colorado, Niwot, Colorado, 1996, pp. 53-54.

H. Lee Scamehorn, *Pioneer Steel Maker in the West*, Pruett Publishing Company, Boulder, Colorado, 1976, pp. 123-124, 132-135, 154, 170.

William H. Bauer, James L. Ozment and John H. Willard, *Colorado Post Offices*, Colorado Railroad Museum, Golden, Colorado, 1990, p. 116.

ROUSE
Old and New, including HEZRON

- *Huerfano County, Mayne Arroyo, Hezron Gulch and Santa Clara Creek drainages*
- *Accessible by dirt roads; private property*
- *Towns had a post office; no structures remain*

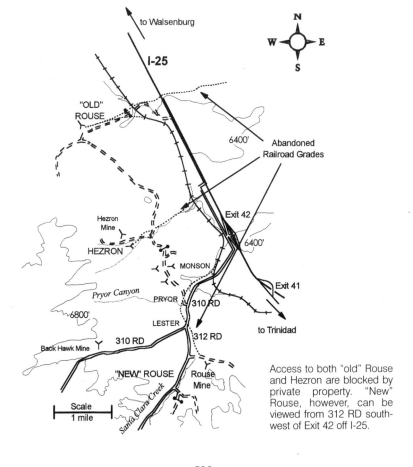

Access to both "old" Rouse and Hezron are blocked by private property. "New" Rouse, however, can be viewed from 312 RD southwest of Exit 42 off I-25.

The mine at "old" Rouse opened in 1888 and coke ovens were constructed this same year. Rouse was located about 7 miles south of Walsenburg. The town was built near the mine among the pinon trees and cedars on the eastern flank of the foothills. It was named for Samuel Rouse, a Colorado Fuel Company official. Colorado Fuel & Iron's Sociological Department encouraged various alcohol-free social activities at Rouse, having discovered that this discouraged miners from spending their leisure time drinking.

The area is arid, with little surface water and no continuously flowing streams. Ironically, too much water was what ended "old" Rouse. When excess water became a problem in the mine, a power plant had to be constructed to run the pumps day and night to keep the mine dry. As the mine got deeper, large pumps had to be installed, and eventually pumping capacity grew to 1,500 gallons a minute. This was enough water to supply a town of several thousand. In 1899, the cost of pumping made mining unprofitable. The superintendent announced that the battle was lost and that the mine had "drowned." Many of Rouse's buildings were jacked up, set on wheels and moved. Most were taken south 4.5 miles to "new" Rouse.

The tunnels at "old" Rouse eventually collapsed, blocking the flow of water. The water broke through the surface in the form of a spring, and settlers dug ditches to use the water for irrigation.

The night prior to moving the buildings from "old" Rouse to

The old town of Rouse was located in an arid area, but excess water flooded the mine and ended the town. The settlement was moved 4 1/2 miles south to Santa Clara Creek and retained the same name. *(Kenneth Jessen collection CP055)*

Structures at the old Rouse town site were jacked up on sets of wheels and pulled by horses south to the new town site. *(Kenneth Jessen collection CP056)*

"new" Rouse, a ball was held to celebrate the occasion. Using a contractor, the slow process of removal began on March 14, 1900. To encourage miners to move to the new town, C.F.& I. offered free lots. Today, private property blocks access to the "old" Rouse site.

At "new" Rouse, the Colorado Coal Company had operated its Santa Clara Mine for several years. The mine was situated on part of the 1871 homestead of A. M. Pryor. In 1899, the company opened a new mine near the Santa Clara Mine, with an output that grew to 900 tons of coal a day. The Denver & Rio Grande had a railroad spur to the mine. The mine was abandoned in 1920 because of excessive water.

Under the direction of C.F.& I., "new" Rouse was very neat and sat in a shallow valley formed by Santa Clara Creek. The miners' homes sat in rows, while the surgeon and supervisor lived in large houses close to the mine. In 1902, the population was 900, with a little over 200 employed at the mine. The town contained 125 homes, many of which the miners owned. The boarding-house at Rouse had a capacity of fifty men, and its food was said to have been very good. A Colorado Supply Company store sat in the middle of the town. The Rouse post office opened at the old

site in 1889, then was moved to "new" Rouse. It continued to
operate until 1929.

The Osgood School in Rouse, named for C.F.& I.'s president,
had well over 100 students. The structure was among those
moved from the old town site. C.F.& I. boasted of having the only
kindergarten in Huerfano County at the time. Adult education,
including a high school, was also available. Probably the most
unusual social activity at any Colorado coal town was the drill in
parliamentary law at Rouse. A resident surgeon served both
Rouse and nearby Hezron.

A good graded road goes from I-25 west along Santa Clara
Creek past the site of "new" Rouse. The road first passes Pryor,
with its piles of waste rock and several occupied homes, then goes
by Lester before reaching Rouse. Concrete foundations remain all
along this route, some of considerable size. A posted gate into the
Black Hawk Ranch prevents entry into the Rouse town site, but
the rows of
foundations can
be seen from the
public road. The
mine is located
south in a shal-
low side canyon.

Between
"old" and "new"
Rouse was
Hezron. The
town was situat-
ed above the
mine among the
pinon-covered

Named for C.F.& I. president John Osgood, the Osgood
School at "new" Rouse was among the structures moved
from the old town site. *(Kenneth Jessen collection CP009)*

hills about 1 mile up from the base of the foothills. From the
Hezron site, the Spanish Peaks dominate the view to the west.
Hezron was served by a Colorado & Wyoming Railroad spur con-
nected to the Denver & Rio Grande's main line to the east. This

spur was completely detached from the rest of the Colorado & Wyoming track system, and the Denver & Rio Grande eventually took over.

By C.F.& I. standards, Hezron was a small town with only 246 men company employees and another seventy-four working for the railroad. The post office opened in 1902, the year the town was built, and closed in 1912, the year the site was abandoned. Access roads into Hezron, both from the south and from the east, are blocked by fences or gates.

North of Pryor is this abandoned schoolhouse, which probably served Rouse and the other small towns in the area. *(Kenneth Jessen 125A5)*

Camp and Plant, Volume I., Number 13, C.F.& I., Pueblo, Colorado, March 8, 1902, pp. 193-198.

Camp and Plant, Volume II., Number 7, C.F.& I., Pueblo, Colorado, August 23, 1902, pp. 181-182.

H. Lee Scamehorn, *Pioneer Steelmaker in the West,* Pruett Publishing Company, Boulder, Colorado, 1976, pp. 87, 122.

Rick J. Clyne, *Coal People, Colorado History No. 3,* Colorado Historical Society, Denver, 1999, p. 16.

Robert L. Brown, *Colorado Ghost Towns, Past and Present,* Caxton Printers, Caldwell, Idaho, 1977, pp. 229-233.

William H. Bauer, James L. Ozment and John H. Willard, *Colorado Post Offices,* Colorado Railroad Museum, Golden, Colorado, 1990, pp. 71, 124.

SEGUNDO

Only Foundations Remain

- *Las Animas County, Purgatoire River drainage*
- *Accessible via graded dirt road; private property*
- *Town had a post office; no structures remain*

An overview of Segundo shows the rows of identical cottages that Colorado Fuel & Iron constructed to rent to its employees. Varros is in the background, left center. *(Kenneth Jessen collection CP079)*

Ghost town historian Bob Brown noticed, when he was taking a before-and-after photograph of Segundo, that the original site was completely void of structures. Where there had once been 145 cottages, today only foundations remain. The old town of Varros, now called Segundo, is located along Colorado 12 on the north side of the Purgatoire River.

Varros was settled by Spanish-speaking people and formed around cabins at the entrance to Smith Canyon. Varros is just a quarter of a mile from the original town of Segundo. The town originally contained a number of unpainted adobe structures, a few yellow frame buildings with false fronts and the St. Ignatius Catholic church. It had its own post office from 1902 to 1903.

Segundo, founded in 1901 by Colorado Fuel & Iron, was originally called Humoso (smokey in Spanish). It was located on the south side of the Purgatoire River across from Varros on higher ground. The town was completed by 1903 and contained 145 homes of common C.F.& I. design with three to five rooms. Most of the houses were square with a double-hip roof and a central chimney. They rented for C.F.& I.'s standard price of $2 per room per month.

The Jerome school was constructed at Segundo in 1902 and had two large classrooms on the second floor. On the first floor was an auditorium with a stage. At the time, the school enrollment was more than 100 students. Segundo also had a doctor's office with a full-time surgeon. The company did not allow any

Children gathered about a horno or beehive-shaped oven in Varros. *(Kenneth Jessen collection CP058)*

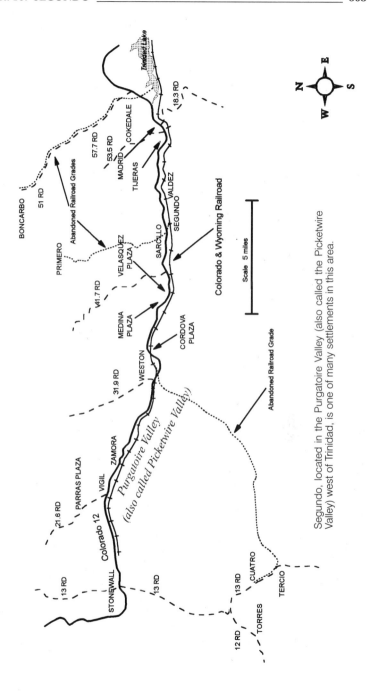

Segundo, located in the Purgatoire Valley (also called the Picketwire Valley) west of Trinidad, is one of many settlements in this area.

saloons or gambling halls. A post office was established at Segundo in 1901.

By the river, the company constructed 800 coke ovens in four double rows. This was the largest coking plant west of Chicago, with a combined capacity of 1,500 tons of coke a day. Most of the coal came from Primero to the north at the head of Smith Canyon and was brought down by rail. The coke was shipped via the Colorado & Wyoming to Jansen to be hauled by rail to the C.F.& I. steel mill in Pueblo.

The coke ovens were charged using a Larry car. The car was loaded with coal at the washer, then lowered by gravity on a gentle 1 percent incline across a track built on top of the coke ovens. A man riding the car could apply the brakes to stop directly over the opening of an oven to be charged with coal. The man would dump the coal, which dropped through the bottom of the car into the oven. Mules hauled the empty Larry cars back to the tipple.

By 1903, 427 men were employed, mainly at the coke ovens and washer. Half were Italian, and making up the rest were Spanish-speaking people, Austrians plus a few Anglos. The population of Segundo was estimated at 1,500.

After World War I, the demand for coke at various smelters dropped off. The coke ovens at Segundo continued to operate

The coal tipple and washer at Segundo are on the left, and the roundhouse for the Colorado & Wyoming is on the right. *(Kenneth Jessen collection CP080)*

At the crossing over the Purgatoire River is a Colorado & Wyoming coal train serving the mines west of Trinidad. It also provided passenger service to towns in the area. *(Kenneth Jessen collection CP076)*

until 1929, when a fire destroyed the washer. It was not rebuilt, and the ovens were never used again.

Around 1933, the town was razed, and some of the structures were moved to the north side of the river at Varros. At that time, Varros took on the name Segundo, probably because that name was better recognized.

To reach the old Segundo town site, cross south over the Purgatoire River from Colorado 12 and cross the railroad tracks, then turn west. The site is immediately west of Valdez. Segundo was located where the road ends at a gate near the restored Colorado & Wyoming depot. This land is posted as private property, but the developer may give permission to enter. After a short hike to the top of the rise, rows of foundations can be seen.

Camp and Plant, Volume III, Number 16, C.F.& I., Pueblo, Colorado, April 25, 1903, pp. 363-371.

H. Lee Scamehorn, *Pioneer Steel Maker in the West*, Pruett Publishing Company, Boulder, Colorado, 1976, pp. 125, 169.

Interview with Al Vigil, Loveland, Colorado, December 15, 2000.

Robert L. Brown, *Colorado Ghost Towns, Past and Present*, Caxton Printers, Caldwell, Idaho, 1977, pp. 237-240.

William H. Bauer, James L. Ozment and John H. Willard, *Colorado Post Offices*, Colorado Railroad Museum, Golden, Colorado, 1990, pp. 130, 146.

SOPRIS

Site Below Trinidad Lake

- *Las Animas County, Purgatoire River drainage*
- *No access; town site below a reservoir*
- *Town had a post office; all structures were removed*

The business district in Sopris can be seen in the center distance. *(Kenneth Jessen collection CP013)*

Elbridge B. Sopris was a Trinidad businessman who initially owned the coal deposits southwest of town. The Denver Fuel Company purchased these deposits in 1887 and named the mining town Sopris. In 1889, Denver Fuel sold the mine to the Colorado Fuel Company, which later became part of C.F.& I. At this point, Sopris became one of thirty-eight company towns run by C.F.& I. in New Mexico, Colorado and Wyoming. It grew to become the largest mining town in the Trinidad area.

Sopris had a handsome schoolhouse. *(Kenneth Jessen collection CP012)*

All of the coal mined at Sopris was converted to coke for use in many Colorado precious metal smelters, as well as the steel mill at Pueblo. The first 100 ovens were constructed in 1888, and another 100 were added in 1892.

R. C. Hills, a Colorado Fuel & Iron geologist, invented a far more efficient oven. The amount of air introduced during the coking process could be precisely controlled. In 1893, C.F.& I. constructed 120 of these new ovens at Sopris, and in 1900, added 50 more ovens. The coke ovens at Sopris could produce 3,000 tons of coke per day.

A washer, to clean the coal prior to coking, was constructed in 1894. A crusher also was added near the tipple structure. Daily coal production from the mine reached 1,000 tons, and more than 300 men worked at the C.F.& I. Sopris facilities.

The town had neat rows of two-story duplexes, a number of single family dwellings and a large clubhouse for social activities. Sopris also had its own public school and a circulating public library. Rent was C.F.& I.'s standard $2 per room per month. Sopris got its own post office in 1888, which remained open until 1969. At its peak, Sopris had a population of about 1,500.

Camp and Plant, published by C.F.& I. to paint a rosy picture of life in its mining towns, reported from Sopris that "Thanksgiving found our bright little camp full of good cheer and happiness... Nature was never sunnier and the dear old flag on school and storehouse carried joy to all..." They added that company cottages were, "...neat and comfortable."

The mine at Sopris had three drifts of bituminous coal. It was ideal for steam, gas or coke. A rope system was used to pull the cars out of the mine.

In 1928, when the mine closed, nearly 9 million tons of coal had been extracted. In 1968, plans were made for a large reservoir at the Sopris site. The following year the town was vacated and all structures removed. The site now is under the Trinidad Reservoir.

The washer and tipple at Sopris were part of C.F.& I.'s facilities. Most of the output from the mine was converted into coke for use at the Minnequa steel mill located south of Pueblo. *(Kenneth Jessen collection CP015)*

Camp and Plant, Volume I, Number 15, C.F.& I., Pueblo, Colorado, pp. 225-230.

H. Lee Scamehorn, *Pioneer Steel Maker in the West,* Pruett Publishing Company, Boulder, Colorado, 1976, pp. 60, 70, 84, 87-88.

George McGovern and Leonard Guttridge, *The Great Coalfield War,* University of Colorado Press, Niwot, Colorado, 1996, p. 11.

William H. Bauer, James L. Ozment and John H. Willard, *Colorado Post Offices,* Colorado Railroad Museum, Golden, Colorado, 1990, p. 133.

STARKVILLE

Survives Today

- *Las Animas County, Raton Creek drainage*
- *Accessible by paved road; occupied site*
- *Town has a post office; a number of original structures remain*

This panoramic view of Starkville was taken around 1900 showing the main road through the town and the two-story schoolhouse in the center. *(Denver Public Library Z-220)*

Starkville, 4 miles south of Trinidad, is not a ghost town, but easily could have been abandoned. Coal mining began there in 1865, and in 1879, a place called San Pedro grew near the mine. That name was changed to Starkville after a local landowner, Albert G. Stark.

The town got its post office in 1879. Most of the town came under the control of the Trinidad Coal and Coking Company, a subsidiary of the Santa Fe Railroad. Starkville was located along the railroad's main line over Raton Pass.

By 1882, Starkville had thirty-five frame and log homes plus a store and mine offices. Employment stood at 300, and the town had its own school with forty-five pupils.

The small coal companies that operated the mines were the Carbon Coal & Mining Company, the Scandinavian Coal & Mining Company and the Trinidad Coal & Mining Company. At the time, seventeen coke ovens were in operation converting slake (coal with impurities) to coke. The pure coal was sold to the Atchison, Topeka & Santa Fe for locomotive fuel.

Colorado Fuel & Iron took over mine operations, and the town became part of the collection of C.F.& I. towns existing all over the southern part of Colorado. C.F.& I. installed washers for the coal and built a power house to supply the mine and town with electric power. Coal production grew to 40,000 tons a month from the largest underground network of tunnels of any C.F.& I. mine. The company employed 650 men at Starkville.

Ed's Tavern in Starkville is a reminder of better times when the mine was operating, and the tavern provided a meeting place for the miners after work. C.F.& I. was against drinking and did everything it could to encourage the use of its clubhouse. *(Kenneth Jessen 107D3)*

In 1897, the Colorado Supply Company opened a large 132-foot by 56-foot store in Starkville and carried a variety of goods. The store contained a bank offering what C.F.& I. termed "liberal interest rates" to encourage saving. C.F.& I. also built Harmony Hall to house the kindergarten and to serve as a recreation center.

By 1900, Starkville had a population of more than 3,000. Fraternal organizations were the Knights of Pythias, Red Men, Odd Fellows, Star of Italy and Tyrolean Hunters. The town had two churches, the Sacred Heart of Jesus Catholic church and a Congregational church. Three public schools opened their doors with 450 "

Starkville church. *(Drawing by Julia McMillan)*

students. The main schoolhouse was a 38-foot by 21-foot stone structure with its own library. The other two schoolhouses were of adobe construction.

The mine closed in 1922, but unlike so many other C.F.& I. towns, Starkville survived because of its location.

Camp and Plant, Volume I, Number 21, C.F.& I., Pueblo, Colorado, May 3, 1902, pp. 361-364.

H. Lee Scamehorn, *Pioneer Steel Maker in the West,* Pruett Publishing Company, Boulder, Colorado, 1976, pp. 32-33, 58, 62, 98, 121-122, 153, 170.

M. Beshoar, M.D. *All About Trinidad and Las Animas County, Colorado,* Times Steam Printing, Trinidad, Colorado, 1882, pp. 64-67.

William H. Bauer, James L. Ozment and John H. Willard, *Colorado Post Offices,* Colorado Railroad Museum, Golden, Colorado, 1990, pp. 128, 135.

TABASCO, BERWIND, TOLLERBURG, VALLORSO and ALBERTSON

- *Las Animas County, Berwind Creek drainage*
- *Accessible via graded dirt road*
- *Town had a post office; one structure remains*

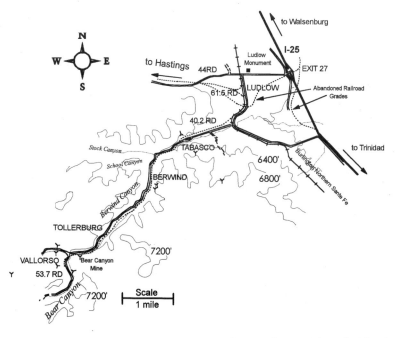

A number of coal mining towns were located up Berwind Canyon (also called Road Canyon). Foundations extend from Tabasco all the way to Tollerburg, and two buildings are still standing at Vallorso. Albertson is a few miles west of Vallorso up 40.2 RD.

Hundreds of foundations line Berwind Canyon (also called Road Canyon) for over 2 miles, illustrating the once sizable population of this area. At the mouth of the canyon is the Tabasco town site. Farther up the canyon are Berwind and Tollerburg. The rail line ended at Vallorso, where Bear Canyon and Berwind Canyon meet. Where once thousands of people lived, today one family occupies the old Colorado Supply Company store in Tabasco and modern homes sit near the Berwind site. The remainder of the canyon is void of population.

Tabasco was founded in 1900 under the control and ownership of Colorado Fuel & Iron. It got its own post office the following year. Tabasco's population reached 1,500, with 485 employed at the mine and at its aboveground facilities. The mine, designated C.F.& I. No. 34, was at the west edge of the town. It operated through a single opening and had a 5-foot coal seam. Most of the coal was converted into coke, 90 percent of which was sent to the steel mill at Minnequa, south of Pueblo. Other facilities included a large coal washer and 302 beehive coke ovens. The smoldering

Larry cars used at Tabasco were designed specifically to haul coal from the washer to the coke ovens. *(Kenneth Jessen collection CP110)*

fires from this many coke ovens must have produced very poor air quality.

Berwind got its start when Colorado Coal & Iron Company purchased the tract of land in Berwind Canyon and opened the El Moro No. 2 coal mine in 1888. The little camp near the mine was originally called El Moro (not to be confused with the El Moro north of Trinidad). Little prospecting was required, as a 6-foot coal vein was exposed at the foot of the mountain. Mining was easy, and the coal was suitable for either coke or for fuel.

By 1902, nearly 400 men worked at the mine. Colorado Coal & Iron Company became part of Colorado Fuel & Iron in 1892, and the latter company took over the mine. The name of the mine and the town was changed from El Moro to Berwind, the name of the C.F.& I. president at the time. The post office at Berwind opened in 1892 and remained active until 1931.

By 1901, the mine employed nearly 400 men, and Berwind had an estimated population of 1,500. The ethnic composition was primarily Italian. To educate the children, a school was

The stone retaining wall is all that remains of Berwind today at this location. The photograph was taken during the 1913-1914 coal miners' strike. *(Denver Public Library x-60377)*

constructed halfway between Tabasco and Berwind, serving both communities. It was built on an elevated knoll and had approximately sixty students. The school included a circulating library. Soon the original building was replaced by a larger structure to house

The Berwind jail is the only remaining structure at this site. *(Kenneth Jessen 108A6)*

kindergarten students and to support a night school. A number of homes were constructed on the same knoll.

In the C.F.& I. publication *Camp and Plant*, its Sociological Department described Berwind as "...situated in Road Canyon, one of the most attractive and delightful spots in Southern Colorado. The scenery about Berwind is unsurpassed." As for its occupants, "The people of Berwind are industrious, sober and thrifty, and show a disposition to provide well for old age."

Much of the coal mined at Berwind was shipped the short distance to Tabasco. There it was converted into coke for use at the C.F.& I. steel mill south of Pueblo.

Berwind had an independent store owned by John Aiello, which predated C.F.& I. control. At Tabasco, the Colorado Supply Company ran the only store. Tabasco shared the company physician with Berwind.

Both towns had company-constructed cottages with either five or six rooms for the miners and their families. The frame houses were supported by concrete foundations and painted in a variety of colors. Based on a visit to the site, some cottages appear to have had walls made of a lime-sand concrete. The cottages

The overview of Berwind shown here was taken around 1901 or 1902 for C.F.& I.'s Camp and Plant. Note the rows of identical company cottages and a store on the right. *(Kenneth Jessen collection CP002)*

were arranged in groups of a half-dozen or so set in neat rows. Long stone retaining walls were constructed to terrace the land for the cottages. The surgeon and mine superintendent had more comfortable quarters than the miners, and their spacious homes had different floor plans.

Tollerburg was located above Berwind, and the construction of its buildings, in terms of material and style, is identical. Little information exists about the population of this coal town. It did, however, get a post office in 1909. The post office remained open until 1931, when the town was abandoned and the mines closed.

The railroad up Berwind Canyon initially was called the Road Canyon Railway. A subsidiary of the Union Pacific Railroad graded it in 1889 and laid track in 1891. The track was extended a half-mile in 1898. The Colorado & Southern took over the railroad in 1899 and extended the track to Vallorso in 1917.

Several structures remain at Vallorso, including what might have been a store and one house. The railroad went a few hundred yards up Bear Canyon and terminated near the store after passing over a small trestle. Although Vallorso is only a short distance from Tollerburg, it also had its own post office, which opened in 1918 and remained open until 1954. Like Tollerburg, little information is available about Vallorso.

After the end of World War I, the demand for coal dropped. Between 1922 and 1930, C.F.& I. closed thirteen mines, including those at Tabasco and Berwind. Although this spelled the end for the towns, the railroad tracks were not removed until 1955.

These ghost towns are located west of I-25 at the Ludlow exit. After heading west from the interstate, a graded dirt road runs south past the abandoned Ludlow business district. This road parallels the railroad tracks. South of Ludlow, a graded dirt road turns west through a narrow tunnel under the tracks of the Burlington Northern Santa Fe Railroad and up Berwind Canyon.

Past the old Colorado Supply Company store and the tailing piles is a rise at the mouth of School Canyon, where once stood the schoolhouse serving both Tabasco and Berwind. A cluster of partially collapsed, concrete-walled homes is located on top of this rise. Continuing up Berwind Canyon are more ruins, and at the west end of Berwind is the town's jail. Stone retaining walls,

Nothing but foundations remain today of the substantial town of Tollerburg. The company store, operated by the Colorado Supply Company, is the building in the center, and the boardinghouse is the square structure in the back center. *(Denver Public Library x-17573)*

Albertson was probably little more than a ranch, but a store might have served the area. *(Kenneth Jessen 125B12)*

used to elevate the homes above creek level, are prominent along the road. Beyond Berwind is Tollerburg, with its long row of foundations and crumbling walls. The tailing piles and railroad grade end at Vallorso.

Farther up Berwind Canyon was Albertson. Its cemetery is marked on topographic maps, and some maps indicate the town site itself. A small, clapboard, frame house sits above the road on the north side, and behind it is a collapsed log cabin. The cemetery is on the south side of the road, but it is difficult to locate. Albertson seems to be nothing more than a homestead and did not have a post office.

Camp and Plant, Colorado Fuel & Iron, Pueblo, Colorado, Volume I, No. 5, January 11, 1902, pp. 57-58.

H. Lee Scamehorn, *Pioneer Steelmaker in the West,* Pruett Publishing Company, Boulder, Colorado, 1976, pp. 20, 58-59, 69, 88, 125, 170.

Robert L. Brown, *Colorado Ghost Towns, Past and Present,* Caxton Printers, Caldwell, Idaho, 1977, pp. 41-44.

Robert Ormes, *Tracking Ghost Railroads in Colorado,* Century One Press, Colorado Springs, Colorado, 1975, pp. 35, 39.

William H. Bauer, James L. Ozment and John H. Willard, *Colorado Post Offices,* Colorado Railroad Museum, Golden, Colorado, 1990, pp. 19, 142, 146.

TERCIO and CUATRO
Isolated Coal Mining Towns

- *Las Animas County, Purgatoire River drainage*
- *Accessible via graded dirt road; town sites on private property*
- *Towns had a post office; one structure remains*

In the center of this interesting photograph of Tercio is a small steam locomotive used to haul mine cars. On the right is the trestle leading from one of the mine openings, and to the left is the framework of the washer under construction. *(Kenneth Jessen collection CP052)*

In an isolated valley at the base of the Sangre de Cristo Mountains is the abandoned coal mining community of Tercio. The site is 32 miles west of Trinidad. Colorado Fuel & Iron opened a large coal mine in 1902, well inside the old Spanish Maxwell Grant. According to C.F.& I. records, Tercio was originally called Torres, then Rincon, and finally it was named Tercio. Contrary to C.F.& I. records, the town of Torres has always been located 4.5 miles to the west of Tercio.

In the eyes of C.F.& I., any coal land not being mined was unproductive. As put by *Camp and Plant,* the area was changed from "a non-producing isolated mountain valley" to a place where "modern energy and science have transformed it into a scene of bustling industrial activity. The bleating of sheep on the hillside has given way to the whistle of the locomotive and the hum of machinery."

The company constructed more than 100 cottages varying from three to six rooms. They were laid out in a grid across the spacious meadow above the washer-tipple area. Because of natural rainfall in this mountain valley, many homes had green lawns. This was not possible for most C.F.& I. coal camps because of their arid surroundings. Garbage was collected every day in Tercio from trash boxes near each cottage. Tercio also had a school with a circulating library.

The ethnic groups dominating Tercio were Spanish-speaking people and Italians. There were also a few Germans, Scots and Swedes. One part of Tercio was occupied primarily by the Italian miners, who lived in some homes of stone and mud. They constructed dome-shaped outdoor bread ovens.

Camp and Plant had this to say about Saturday nights in the Italian Quarter, "All restraint seems to be thrown off, and amusement holds entire sway. Strains of the concertina, chords from the

The Colorado Supply Company store, owned by C.F.& I., is the only structure left standing in Tercio, and it is on private property. *(Kenneth Jessen 108B2)*

Tercio had a nice schoolhouse. Children from nearby Cuatro came here as well. *(Kenneth Jessen collection CP095)*

violin, laughter, shouts and dancing, further carry out the picture."

Tercio was served by the standard gauge Colorado & Wyoming, owned by C.F.& I. The railroad was constructed in 1902-1903 to Tercio along the South Fork of the Purgatoire River. Passenger trains ran twice a day to connect Tercio with Trinidad. In 1951-1952, the track from Tercio to Weston was removed, and new track was laid to the Allen mine at Vigil.

To provide access to the coal seams, which were 4 to 12 feet thick, six openings were made into the hillsides. Output at Tercio climbed to 400 tons a day, about 80 percent of which was converted to coke in ovens near the mine. To the south was the Vega Mine, and a small mining gauge railroad hauled coal cars to the tipple at Tercio.

Tercio had 600 coke ovens arranged in two tiers of 300 units each, stretching three-quarters of a mile. Construction of the ovens was completed in 1902 to process the slack (coal mixed with impurities) from the area mines. C.F.& I. used the coke produced at Tercio at their steel mill south of Pueblo. The operation also included a large washer and tipple.

Mining at Tercio continued until 1915. From that point on, the coke ovens were used only on a limited basis. Production at the mine during its life exceeded 1.5 million tons of coal.

Probably the most attractive of all locations for a coal camp was Cuatro, at 8,300 feet elevation along the upper part of the South Fork of the Purgatoire River. The upper part of the town was located amid tall pine trees, and the lower portion sat out in a small meadow near the tipple. As *Camp and Plant* described the town:

Trim in appearance, and variegated in color, the cottages, half hidden among the trees, with their cozy little porches and projecting eaves, seem ideal dwellings.

Ruins of Tercio's Catholic church are near the gravestones in the town's cemetery. *(Kenneth Jessen 108B3)*

Upper Cuatro and the lower portion of the town were separated by about a mile. A 6,220-foot dual-track railroad connected the mine to the tipple at lower Cuatro. The system was operated using a continuous wire rope similar to that used in a cable car system. The cars were hooked to the moving cable and lowered to the tipple. Empties returned to the mine on the parallel track. The first shipments were made in early 1903, and output from the mine reached 100 tons per day. Lump coal was sold to the railroads as locomotive fuel, and the rest was converted into coke.

Estimated employment at Cuatro was 100 miners. The town got its own post office in 1903, and it closed in 1907. The company constructed fifty dwellings with three to six rooms each. C.F.& I. charged its standard rent of $2 per room per month. The smaller units had simple sloped roofs, and the larger units had a double hip roof. School-age children were taken to the school at Tercio.

To reach Tercio, drive west from Trinidad on Colorado 12 beyond the Allen Mine at Vigil. Near the point where the paved road swings north is a small store at Stonewall. Turn south on 13.0 RD. From this point, Tercio is 9 miles. This graded dirt road leads to a "T" intersection. To the right (west) is the settlement of Torres, and to the left (east) are the Cuatro and Tercio sites. Cuatro does not have any structures. The Tercio Ranch is located where the graded road swings across the valley. The ranch, occupying the entire Tercio town site, is posted "no trespassing." The road passes the small Tercio cemetery including the foundation of a Catholic Church.

Where the Purgatoire River enters the canyon a short distance south of the cemetery, the two-story Colorado Supply Company store can been seen about a quarter of a mile from the public road. The only remaining structure, it is built of native stone. At one time, row upon row of identical houses, built by C.F.& I., sat in the valley to either side of the public road. Large tailing piles are located along the road and off in the distance.

Because the Tercio Ranch owns the entire site, visitors cannot explore the area without permission. Bob Brown reported in his book, *Colorado Ghost Towns Past and Present,* that when the land was open, the foundations for the rows of coke ovens could be found. ***For a map showing the location of Tercio and Cuatro, see "Segundo."***

Cuatro was in an attractive location at the edge of a meadow. *(Kenneth Jessen collection CP100)*

H. Lee Scamehorn, *Pioneer Steel Maker in the West,* Pruett Publishing Company, Boulder, Colorado, 1976, pp. 20, 58-59, 69, 88, 125, 170.

Robert L. Brown, *Colorado Ghost Towns, Past and Present,* Caxton Printers, Caldwell, Idaho, 1977, pp. 41-44.

Camp and Plant, Volume II, Number 6, C.F.& I., Pueblo, Colorado, August 13, 1902, pp. 129-133.

Camp and Plant, Volume VI, Number 20, C.F.& I., Pueblo, Colorado, November 28, 1903, pp. 460-466.

Robert Ormes, *Tracking Ghost Railroads in Colorado,* Century One Press, Colorado Springs, Colorado, 1975, pp. 43-44.

William H. Bauer, James L. Ozment and John H. Willard, *Colorado Post Offices,* Colorado Railroad Museum, Golden, Colorado, 1990, pp. 19, 41.

VALDEZ

Site of Frederick Mine

- *Las Animas County, Purgatoire River drainage*
- *Accessible via dirt road; occupied site*
- *Town had a post office; a number of old structures remain*

Valdez is 13 miles west of Trinidad and a mile east of Segundo. Colorado Fuel & Iron operated the large Frederick Mine at Valdez. By the time it closed in 1960, output from this single mine had reached an astounding 20 million tons. Most of the coal was shipped to the coke ovens at neighboring Segundo to be converted into coke.

A partially occupied town, some of the older structures at Valdez are being restored. This could have been an old hotel or a boardinghouse for the miners working at the Frederick Mine. *(Kenneth Jessen 108A11)*

Valdez sits along the south side of the Purgatoire River. To reach the site from Colorado 12, cross the bridge and go over the tracks of the Colorado & Wyoming Railroad. The railroad depot has been restored and is now a private residence. A few new homes are mixed among occupied and abandoned original structures.

H. Lee Scamehorn, *Pioneer Steel Maker in the West*, Pruett Publishing Company, Boulder, Colorado, 1976, pp. 136, 139, 170.

William H. Bauer, James L. Ozment and John H. Willard, *Colorado Post Offices*, Colorado Railroad Museum, Golden, Colorado, 1990, p. 146.

WALSEN

Built West of Walsenburg

- *Huerfano County, Cucharas River drainage*
- *Accessible via paved road*
- *Town has a post office; no structures remain at original site*

The coal-mining town of Walsen was located about a mile west of the much older community of Walsenburg. The Walsen site is marked by the old power plant, the only remaining structure. Discarded coal is strewn about the site among the foundations.

Fred Walsen came from Fort Garland in the San Luis Valley in 1867 to establish a store and trading post on the Cucharas River. The site was an established ford across the river. The settlement of Walsenburg grew around his trading post and became the Huerfano County seat in 1874. Under its original spelling "Walsenburgh," the town got its own post office in 1870. For some unknown reason, the name of the post office was changed to Tourist in October 1887, and the following month, it was changed back to Walsenburgh. The spelling was changed to Walsenburg in 1892. By 1885, the town had a population of 850.

Coal was discovered in the area, and the first mine was opened in 1876. It was operated by Fred Walsen and Colorado Governor Hunt. Fred Walsen sold his holdings to the Colorado Coal & Iron Company, which later became part of the Colorado Fuel & Iron Company.

In 1902, the Colorado Fuel & Iron Company decided to create a company town called Walsen at the Walsen Mine. Even though the distance to Walsenburg was only a mile, Walsen got its own post office that same year, and it continued to operate until the town was abandoned in 1932.

The coal seam at the Walsen Mine was 8 feet thick, and the mine reached a depth of 3,500 feet. Its output was 500 tons a day. C.F.& I. employed 300 men at the Walsen Mine and nearby Robinson mines.

The older part of Walsen was located near the power plant and tipple. Some of the structures were moved from "old" Rouse. The newer part of Walsen to the west, was composed of twenty-five duplexes constructed by C.F.& I. The town also had a school-house, Colorado Supply Store and a circulating library.

The only remaining structure at Walsen is the powerhouse on the north side of the railroad tracks along U. S. 160. *(Kenneth Jessen 125A6)*

Camp and Plant, Volume I, Number 17, C.F.& I., Pueblo, Colorado, April 5, 1902, pp. 265-267.

George A. Crofutt, *Crofutt's Grip-Sack Guide of Colorado,* 1885 Edition, Johnson Books, Boulder, Colorado, reprint 1981, p. 156.

William H. Bauer, James L. Ozment and John H. Willard, *Colorado Post Offices,* Colorado Railroad Museum, Golden, Colorado, 1990, p. 148.

INDEX

Ironton. *(Sonje Jessen SJ125)*